*Sue Pauley*

# SOURCES
**Notable Selections in** *Marriage and the Family*

## About the Editors

**ROBERT L. DelCAMPO** is a professor of family science at New Mexico State University in Las Cruces, New Mexico. He is a licensed marriage and family therapist, clinical member, and approved supervisor of the American Association for Marriage and Family Therapy. He also holds memberships in the International Family Therapy Association, the National Council on Family Relations, and the New Mexico Association for Marriage and Family Therapy. He received a B.S. from the State University of New York, an M.S. from Virginia Polytechnic Institute and State University, and a Ph.D. in family relations and child development from Florida State University. His work has appeared in such journals as *Family Relations* and *Contemporary Family Therapy*.

**DIANA S. DelCAMPO** is the child development and family life specialist with the New Mexico Cooperative Extension Service at New Mexico State University in Las Cruces, New Mexico, and holds the rank of professor. She is a member of the National Council on Family Relations and the National Extension Family Life Specialists' Association. She received a B.S. from Concord College (West Virginia), an M.S. from Virginia Polytechnic Institute and State University, and a Ph.D. in curriculum and instruction from the University of Michigan. She presently develops educational programs in child and family development, supervises grant projects, and coordinates projects with other state agencies in New Mexico. She has published educational guides, chapters in several books, symposium proceedings, and articles in various journals.

# SOURCES

## Notable Selections in
## *Marriage and the Family*

**Edited by**

**ROBERT L. DELCAMPO**
*New Mexico State University*

**DIANA S. DELCAMPO**
*New Mexico State University*

*Dushkin/McGraw·Hill*
*A Division of The McGraw·Hill Companies*

© 1999 by Dushkin/McGraw-Hill, A Division of The McGraw-Hill Companies, Guilford, Connecticut 06437

Copyright law prohibits the reproduction, storage, or transmission in any form by any means of any portion of this publication without the express written permission of Dushkin/McGraw-Hill and of the copyright holder (if different) of the part of the publication to be reproduced. The Guidelines for Classroom Copying endorsed by Congress explicitly state that unauthorized copying may not be used to create, to replace, or to substitute for anthologies, compilations, or collective works.

Manufactured in the United States of America

First Edition

123456789FGRFGR321098

**Library of Congress Cataloging-in-Publication Data**
  Main entry under title:
    Sources: notable selections in marriage and the family/edited by Robert L. DelCampo and Diana S. DelCampo.—1st ed.
    Includes bibliographical references and index.
    1. Family. 2. Marriage. I. DelCampo, Robert L., comp. II. DelCampo, Diana S., comp.
                                                    306.85
  0-07-303234-4                                      ISSN: 1521-7736

 Printed on Recycled Paper

# Preface

Marriage and the family as a distinct field of study did not truly emerge until the latter half of the twentieth century. Prior to that time, scholars from a variety of fields, including psychology, sociology, biology, anthropology, education, religion, medicine, and home economics, contributed to this body of knowledge. Although scholars from many diverse disciplines continue to contribute to our field, there are perhaps thousands of institutions of higher education worldwide that now offer curricula specifically focused on the study of marriage and the family. Many thousands of undergraduate and graduate degrees have been awarded in North America alone in the latter portion of the twentieth century in the discipline of marriage and the family. There are also numerous scholarly journals, periodicals, books, and textbooks dedicated to publishing information in this field.

All of the selections in *Sources: Notable Selections in Marriage and the Family* are ones that we feel have enduring value and have influenced the corpus of knowledge in the marriage and family discipline. The selections found herein are excerpts from what we believe are classic empirical studies, theoretical papers, books, and speeches written by some of the most distinguished researchers, theorists, and clinicians in the field.

This book includes excerpts from articles written as early as the 1920s through contemporary classics written in the 1990s. The goal of the collection is to portray some of the classic, enduring ideas that are basic to the study of marriage and the family. Although recent empirical studies may have expanded our understanding of various concepts presented within the selections chosen, the selections should be read with a historical context in mind. In many cases these original sources have withstood the test of time and the ideas presented are still most relevant to contemporary marriage and family research, theory, and education.

*Selection procedure.* The selections in this book were chosen because they met three criteria: (1) The work was appropriate for one of the parts of the book (the parts themselves were chosen and sequenced so as to follow a developmental approach to the study of marriage and the family); (2) the selection contributed information that has enduring value to the field; and (3) the selection was written by one or more historically distinguished contributors to the field.

*Plan of the book.* The selections in this book are well suited to courses that move beyond a cursory view of the field of marriage and the family. The selections are organized developmentally around topics usually found in textbooks on marriage and the family. When used in conjunction with a typical textbook, *Sources* can significantly expand the student's exposure to many of the major theories, ideas, and issues in the field. Each selection is preceded by a brief headnote that discusses the relevance of the selection and provides biographical information on the author or authors. Also, each part in this book is preceded by an *On the Internet* page that provides a list of Internet site addresses (URLs) that are relevant to the part.

*A word to the instructor.* An *Instructor's Manual With Test Questions* (multiple-choice and essay) is available through the publisher for instructors using *Sources* in the classroom.

*Sources: Notable Selections in Marriage and the Family* is only one title in the Sources series. If you are interested in seeing the table of contents for any of the other titles, please visit the Sources Web site at `http://www.dushkin.com/sources/`.

*Acknowledgments.* We were most grateful for the support that we received from the Dushkin/McGraw-Hill publishers when we first proposed this book to them. This book had long been in our minds as one "to do" sometime. They afforded us the opportunity to make the book a reality. We also would like to thank Dr. Leland Axelson and Dr. Michael J. Sporakowski for their expertise and feedback of early drafts of the outline of this book. We were also most fortunate to have students at New Mexico State University of the caliber of Heather Brija and Kristin Hughes Wallin. We thank them for their efforts in helping us to amass the scores of articles and related information necessary to complete this project. Perhaps most of all, we are indebted to all our former professors and mentors who were responsible for igniting our excitement about our discipline and who originally exposed us to these scholarly writings years ago, during our graduate training.

Finally, we want to thank our son, Rob DelCampo, for his encouragement and support for endeavors such as this book.

We welcome your feedback and observations about the selections in this volume. Please write to us with suggestions for other selections or changes to be considered in future editions of *Sources*. Send your comments to us either via electronic mail at `rdelcamp@nmsu.edu` or `ddelcamp@nmsu.edu` or in care of *Sources*, Dushkin/McGraw-Hill, Sluice Dock, Guilford, CT 06437.

Robert L. DelCampo
New Mexico State University

Diana S. DelCampo
New Mexico State University

# Contents

*Preface*   i

## PART ONE   *Foundations of Marriage and the Family*   1

### CHAPTER 1   Definitions of the Family   3

**1.1**   **WILLIAM J. LEDERER AND DON D. JACKSON,** from *The Mirages of Marriage*   3

"[M]arriage used to be an institution for the *physical* survival and well-being of two people and their offspring.... Today... we have primarily the struggle for *psychological* and *emotional* survival.... But so far, the changes in the structure, form, and processes of marriage have been too few and too unsystematic to cope with the new psychological and emotional problems."

**1.2**   **ERNEST W. BURGESS,** from "The Family as a Unity of Interacting Personalities," *The Family*   13

"At any rate the actual unity of family life has its existence not in any legal conception, nor in any formal contract, but in the interaction of its members.... The family lives as long as interaction is taking place and only dies when it ceases."

**1.3**   **IRA L. REISS,** from "The Universality of the Family: A Conceptual Analysis," *Journal of Marriage and the Family*   22

"[F]ollowing is the universal definition of the family institution: *The family institution is a small kinship structured group with the key function of nurturant socialization of the newborn.*"

### CHAPTER 2   Theoretical Approaches to the Study of the Family   32

**2.1**   **CARLFRED BRODERICK AND JAMES SMITH,** from "The General Systems Approach to the Family," in Wesley R. Burr et al., eds., *Contemporary Theories About the Family, vol. 2*   32

"'A system is a set of objects together with relationships between the objects and between their attributes.'... Implicit in the... definition is the existence of a boundary that delineates the elements belonging to the system and those belonging to its environment."

**2.2 DAVID H. OLSON, DOUGLAS H. SPRENKLE, AND CANDYCE S. RUSSELL,** from "Circumplex Model of Marital and Family Systems: I. Cohesion and Adaptability Dimensions, Family Types, and Clinical Applications," *Family Process* 42

"At the extreme of high family cohesion, *enmeshment*, there is an overidentification with the family that results in extreme bonding and limited individual autonomy. The low extreme, *disengagement*, is characterized by low bonding and high autonomy from the family."

**2.3 GEORGE C. HOMANS,** from "Social Behavior as Exchange," *The American Journal of Sociology* 52

"If we define profit as reward less cost, and if cost is value foregone, I suggest that we have here some evidence for the proposition that change in behavior is greatest when perceived profit is least."

# PART TWO  Mate Selection and Marriage  63

## CHAPTER 3  Premarital Relationships  65

**3.1 WILLARD WALLER,** from "The Rating and Dating Complex," *American Sociological Review* 65

"Although there are endless variations in courtship customs, they are always functionally related to the total configuration of the culture and the biological needs of the human animal."

**3.2 MARGARET MEAD AND RHODA METRAUX,** from *A Way of Seeing* 73

"I believe that we need two types of marriage, one of which can (though it need not) develop into the other, each with its own possibilities and special forms of responsibility. The first type of marriage may be called an *individual marriage*, binding together two individuals only.... [T]he second type of marriage... *parental marriage*, would be explicitly directed toward the founding of a family."

**3.3 CARL A. RIDLEY, DAN J. PETERMAN, AND ARTHUR W. AVERY,** from "Cohabitation: Does It Make for a Better Marriage?" *The Family Coordinator* 81

"The degree to which cohabiting experiences prepare individuals for marriage depends in part on the needs, goals, motivations, and competence of the persons involved."

## CHAPTER 4    Theories of Mate Selection   90

**4.1**    **ALAN C. KERCKHOFF AND KEITH E. DAVIS,** from "Value Consensus and Need Complementarity in Mate Selection," *American Sociological Review*   90

"[A] series of 'filtering factors' operate in mate selection at different stages of the selection process.... [S]ocial status variables (class, religion, etc.) operate in the early stages, consensus on values somewhat later, and need complementarity still later."

**4.2**    **ROBERT F. WINCH,** from "Another Look at the Theory of Complementary Needs in Mate-Selection," *Journal of Marriage and the Family*   98

"In mate-selection each individual seeks within his or her field of eligibles for that person who gives the greatest promise of providing him or her with maximum need gratification."

**4.3**    **BERNARD I. MURSTEIN,** from "Stimulus—Value—Role: A Theory of Marital Choice," *Journal of Marriage and the Family*   108

"The more 'A' likes 'B,' the more he discloses his private world to 'B.' In a 'dating' situation, such a disclosure is rewarding to 'B' because it marks him as worthy of receiving intimate information and, accordingly, raises his self-esteem."

## CHAPTER 5    Marital Adjustment   122

**5.1**    **HARVEY J. LOCKE AND KARL M. WALLACE,** from "Short Marital-Adjustment and Prediction Tests: Their Reliability and Validity," *Marriage and Family Living*   122

"[M]arital-adjustment and marital-prediction tests, constructed with a relatively small number of basic and fundamental items, achieve results approximately comparable with the longer and more complex adjustment and prediction tests."

**5.2**    **WILLIAM STEPHENS,** from "Predictors of Marital Adjustment," in William Stephens, ed., *Reflections on Marriage*   130

"[T]he data seem to say that conventional people and conventional marriages stand the best chance.... Perhaps it merely happens that conventional people are less willing to seek divorce, and less able to face the truth about their marriages when they take marital adjustment tests. Perhaps, but I think not."

## CHAPTER 6 Marital Role Satisfaction 140

**6.1 ROBERT O. BLOOD, JR., AND DONALD M. WOLFE,** from *Husbands and Wives: The Dynamics of Married Living* 140

"The balance of power between husband and wife is a sensitive reflection of the roles they play in marriage—and, in turn, has many repercussions on other aspects of their relationship."

**6.2 JOHN F. CUBER AND PEGGY B. HARROFF,** from "The More Total View: Relationships Among Men and Women of the Upper Middle Class," *Marriage and Family Living* 146

"[T]he more overriding generalization about man-woman relationships in marriage is that continuity based upon 'alien considerations,' mere tradition, practical convenience, austere social sanctions, appear to be the rule rather than the exception, and that what we have called qualitatively good relationships are the exception rather than the rule."

# PART THREE  *Parenthood*  155

## CHAPTER 7  Maternal Attachment 157

**7.1 MARY D. SALTER AINSWORTH,** from "Infant–Mother Attachment," *American Psychologist* 157

"It is clear that the nature of an infant's attachment to his or her mother as a 1-year-old is related both to earlier interaction with the mother and to various aspects of later development."

**7.2 MARGARET MEAD,** from "Some Theoretical Considerations on the Problem of Mother-Child Separation," *American Journal of Orthopsychiatry* 166

"[F]indings in the field of child care may now be rapidly generalized, affecting medical practice, hospital design, and public health practices all over the world. This new capacity for the rapid dissemination and translation into practice of research findings places an extra burden of responsibility for the very careful examination of the theoretical basis of research on those of us concerned in either the research itself or the experimental translation of the research into practice."

CHAPTER 8    Childrearing    177

8.1    **E. E. LeMASTERS,** from "Parenthood as Crisis," *Marriage and Family Living*    177

"Viewed in this conceptual system, married couples find the transition to parenthood painful because the arrival of the first child destroys the two-person or pair pattern of group interaction and forces a rapid reorganization of their life into a three-person or triangle group system."

8.2    **DIANA BAUMRIND,** from "Child Care Practices Anteceding Three Patterns of Preschool Behavior," *Genetic Psychology Monographs*    184

"Parents of the most competent and mature boys and girls (Pattern I children) were notably firm, loving, demanding, and understanding. Parents of dysphoric and disaffiliative children (Pattern II children) were firm, punitive, and unaffectionate. Mothers of dependent, immature children (Pattern III children) lacked control and were moderately loving. Fathers of these children were ambivalent and lax."

8.3    **MURRAY A. STRAUS,** from *Beating the Devil Out of Them: Corporal Punishment in American Families and Its Effects on Children*    196

"A law prohibiting spanking is unrealistic only because spanking is such an accepted part of American culture. That was also true of smoking. Yet in less than a generation we have made tremendous progress toward eliminating smoking. We can make similar progress toward eliminating spanking by showing parents that spanking is dangerous, that their children will be easier to bring up if they do not spank, and by clearly saying that a child should *never*, under any circumstances, be spanked."

8.4    **LAWRENCE KOHLBERG,** from "The Child as a Moral Philosopher," *Psychology Today*    206

"We can speak of the child as having his own morality or series of moralities.... Actually, as soon as we talk with children about morality, we find that they have many ways of making judgements which are not 'internalized' from the outside, and which do not come in any direct and obvious way from parents, teachers or even peers."

**PART FOUR**    *Societal Influences on the Family*    213

## CHAPTER 9    Family Subcultures    215

**9.1    ROBERT STAPLES,** from "Changes in Black Family Structure: The Conflict Between Family Ideology and Structural Conditions," *Journal of Marriage and the Family*    215

"Other than being opposed to unfair discrimination against any group and favoring liberal social and economic policies, blacks often hold very traditional, even conservative, attitudes on other social issues—attitudes that place them in the mainstream of American mores and folkways."

**9.2    JUDSON T. LANDIS,** from "Religiousness, Family Relationships, and Family Values in Protestant, Catholic, and Jewish Families," *Marriage and Family Living*    226

"When most of the items denoting family success were related to family religiousness, a positive association was found.... In general the positive association between family religiousness and success in family living held when analyzed by faiths—Protestant, Catholic, Jewish, and no faith."

## CHAPTER 10    Work and the Family    235

**10.1    LOIS WLADIS HOFFMAN,** from "The Decision to Work," in F. Ivan Nye and Lois Wladis Hoffman, eds., *The Employed Mother in America*    235

"The decision to be a working mother may be made thoughtfully and deliberately or so subtly that the actors involved—the decision-makers—do not know a decision has been made. Whichever is the case, the decision may be thought of as having two components—motivations and facilitators."

**10.2    PATRICIA VOYDANOFF AND ROBERT F. KELLY,** from "Determinants of Work-Related Family Problems Among Employed Parents," *Journal of Marriage and the Family*    245

"The models reveal similarities and differences in the composition and pattern of individual, work, and family demands and resources related to time shortage and income inadequacy."

## CHAPTER 11    Violence and Abuse    256

**11.1    RICHARD J. GELLES,** from "Abused Wives: Why Do They Stay?" *Journal of Marriage and the Family*    256

"[T]he answer to why women remain with their abusive husbands is not nearly as simple as the assumption that underlies the question.... [T]he decision to either stay with an assaultive spouse or to seek intervention or dissolution of a marriage is not related solely to the extent or severity of the physical assault."

11.2  **JOHN SCANZONI,** from "Family Organization and the Probability of Disorganization," *Journal of Marriage and the Family*   270

"In order to escape the joint pitfalls of exclusion and over-magnification, we need to discard the evaluative approach, i.e., what is a 'good,' 'functional,' 'succesful,' or 'efficient' family.... [I]n terms of long-range scientific and practical benefits, the largest good will be best served by taking a *theoretical* approach, viz., by asking significant theoretical questions."

## CHAPTER 12   Stress and the Family   279

12.1  **REUBEN HILL AND ELISE BOULDING,** from *Families Under Stress: Adjustment to the Crises of War Separation and Reunion*   279

"Time and time again we find families faced with circumstances that would be termed hardships by any observer, and, yet, because the circumstances are regarded differently by the family, they may not only fail to produce hardship reactions but they may serve as a stimulus to better adjustment."

12.2  **HAMILTON I. McCUBBIN AND JOAN M. PATTERSON,** from "The Family Stress Process: The Double ABCX Model of Adjustment and Adaptation," in Hamilton I. McCubbin, Marvin B. Sussman, and Joan M. Patterson, eds., *Social Stress and the Family: Advances and Developments in Family Stress Theory and Research*   293

"A (the stressor event)—interacting with B (the family's crisis meeting resources)—interacting with C (the definition the family makes of the event)—produce X (the crisis).... In the case of the families of the missing in action, many were able to trust the efforts of the United States to do what was best under the circumstances in terms of ending the war, finding and/or returning their spouses and establishing policies to help families."

## CHAPTER 13   Divorce and Remarriage   303

13.1  **FRANK F. FURSTENBERG, JR.,** from "Divorce and the American Family," *Annual Review of Sociology*   303

"In a very real sense, then, the causes of the high rate of marital instability are 'over determined' by a confluence of cultural, economic, and political change, any one of which might have brought about a significant revision of the institution of marriage. In combination, they have profoundly shaken the commitment to lifelong marriage."

13.2  **JUDITH S. WALLERSTEIN AND JOAN B. KELLY,** from "Children and Divorce: A Review," *Social Work*   312

"With reference to the new realities represented by families in which divorce has occurred, it is important to rethink many traditional concepts of child development, psychopathology, and intervention theory and develop theoretical formulations appropriate to newly emerging family structures."

13.3   **E. MAVIS HETHERINGTON, MARTHA COX, AND ROGER COX,** from "Effects of Divorce on Parents and Children," in Michael E. Lamb, ed., *Nontraditional Families: Parenting and Child Development*   327

"[D]ivorce cannot be viewed as an event occurring at a single point in time; it represents an extended transition in the lives of parents and children."

# PART FIVE  *Aging Families*  337

## CHAPTER 14   Postparental Families   339

14.1   **MICHAEL J. SPORAKOWSKI AND GEORGE A. HUGHSTON,** from "Prescriptions for Happy Marriage: Adjustments and Satisfactions of Couples Married for 50 or More Years," *The Family Coordinator*   339

"The stages seen as most satisfying [for the marriage] were the childbearing, preschool and aging stages. Satisfactions in the first two related to children and how they added meaning to the marriage. The aging stage meant more time together, travel and activities which they did not previously have sufficient time for."

14.2   **LILLIAN E. TROLL,** from "Grandparents: The Family Watchdogs," in Timothy H. Brubaker, ed., *Family Relationships in Later Life*   349

"If grandparents are really family watchdogs, they would not have to work hard at their mission in highly integrated families, even though they might or might not partake of social interactions. Where family boundaries are permeable and there is little distinction between kin and nonkin, grandparents could share the task of watching that all goes well."

## CHAPTER 15   Older Families and Death   360

15.1   **TIMOTHY H. BRUBAKER,** from *Later Life Families*   360

"Specifically, 'later life families' refers to families who are beyond the child-rearing years and have begun to launch their children.... The emphasis is on the *remaining members* of the family of orientation *after* the children have initiated their own families of procreation."

15.2   **ELISABETH KÜBLER-ROSS,** from *On Death and Dying*   370

"If a patient has had enough time... and has been given some help in working through the previously described stages, he will reach a stage during which he is neither depressed nor angry about his 'fate.'"

*Acknowledgments*   378

*Index*   381

# PART ONE

# *Foundations of Marriage and the Family*

**Chapter 1** Definitions of the Family  3

**Chapter 2** Theoretical Approaches to the Study of the Family  32

# On the Internet . . .

## Sites appropriate to Part One

The American Association for Marriage and Family Therapy (AAMFT) is the largest organization in the world that promotes the well-being of individuals, couples, and families through the marriage and family therapy profession.

>   http://www.aamft.org/

The American Association of Family and Consumer Sciences (AAFCS) is a professional organization that promotes professional development for those working with families and children in a broad range of professions.

>   http://www.aafcs.org/

The American Sociological Association (ASA) is a professional organization that supports and encourages research and theory development about family-related issues.

>   http://www.asanet.org/

The National Council on Family Relations (NCFR) is a professional organization that provides a forum for family researchers, educators, and practitioners to share in the development and dissemination of knowledge about families and family relationships, establishes professional standards, and works to promote family well-being.

>   http://www.ncfr.com/

# CHAPTER 1 Definitions of the Family

## 1.1 WILLIAM J. LEDERER AND DON D. JACKSON

### *The Origins of Marriage and the Family—And Their Disintegration in the Modern World*

This selection is from one of the early books on marital communication, *The Mirages of Marriage* by William J. Lederer and Don D. Jackson (W. W. Norton, 1968). Although the book is over 30 years old, it discusses concepts regarding the origins of the family that remain relevant today. The book in general, and the chapter from which this selection was excerpted in particular, was most popular in the late 1960s and early 1970s because of its thought-provoking concepts and readability. Prior to his retirement, Lederer was a freelance writer for magazines, newspapers, and television. He has been a writer in residence at Harvard University, and he was a member of the board of directors of the Mental Research Institute in Palo Alto, California, a major institution focusing on the study of the family from a systems perspective.

Jackson was a founder and director of the Mental Research Institute in Palo Alto, California. He also served as an associate clinical professor at the Stanford University School of Medicine. Another well-known book by Jackson is *Pragmatics of Human Communication: A Study of Interactional Patterns, Pathologies, and Paradoxes,* coauthored with Paul Watzlawick and Janet Helmick Beavin (Faber, 1968).

**Key Concept:** origins of marriage and the family

At the beginning of man's existence, over a million years ago, it seems that members of the human race procreated in the same random manner as almost all other animals do. A female and a male met by chance, and if both had a strong sexual drive, they copulated. After a short period of intimacy, the male wandered off to continue his usual activities—hunting and fighting. Several months later, the female perhaps noticed that she was pregnant. It is probable that for many millennia pregnancy was not associated with the sex act. Furthermore, in those ancient days (as in some of the more impoverished rural nations today), the condition of pregnancy probably did not diminish the daily activities of the female until the point of actual delivery. When labor pains began, the female assumed as comfortable a position as possible—wherever she happened to be—and gave birth to the infant. Perhaps within a day or two she was foraging for food as usual, with the additional burden of nursing and caring for the child. The father was totally uninvolved and didn't know his own child.

After almost an aeon, human beings (most likely the females of the species) learned that certain fruits and grains and vegetables could be cultivated and stored for the winter months. Small gardens were started, and shelters were built nearby. Probably the females tended the gardens and built the shelters. Gradually these females must have gathered together in groups, clustering their temporary homes near one another, and the first community developed. The male still was the hunter and the warrior, probably roaming wherever game was most plentiful during the spring and summer months, and during his wanderings copulating with any female he might happen to fancy. But the female, under the necessity of rearing children, accumulated the food to last through the winter, developed skill at turning animal hides into protective clothing, maintained fires, and created shelters. It is probable, therefore, at least in the northern countries, that itinerant males migrated toward the communities of females sometime in the late autumn.

With warm weather, the males wandered off again, stopping at the abodes of females in a random fashion. Finally, in some groups, the association between sex and childbirth became known. But still the human species continued the random sexual pattern. It is likely that the first human social group consisted of women who learned to help each other during labor and take turns at minding the children.

Under this social system there was no concern about paternity. Eventually, probably because of the invention of tools and the further development of agriculture, men began to spend more time around the camp and a simple social group evolved in which they played a fixed part. A primitive law, or taboo, slowly formed, which forbade mating in directly ascending and descending lines of consanguinity—in other words, the incest taboo developed. We find this taboo among peoples and races all over the world; it is probably the first socio-marital regulation imposed by man upon himself. The origins of the incest taboo have been discussed at length by anthropologists, but none have found undebatable answers. It is possible that after generations of loose social organization, man acquired some general understanding of heredity, but this is not an easy assumption since most diseases of proven genetic causation occur only about once in a population of ten thousand unless both parents carry the offending gene. It is not difficult, however, to see how an incest taboo would simplify and strengthen the social structure by allowing relatives to band together into a "clan," whose members could trust each other and support each other in fights or other mutual endeavors. The ban against incest allowed males to avoid battles over their own sisters and mothers and to have a common link with other males (brothers-in-law). Since evidence indicates that polygamy and polyandry were common among primitive people, the early family units would have been different from those we know today and would have consisted of several women with a relatively close tie to one another and a looser tie to one or more men. Even today, in some African tribes, there is no word for "mother," but the child uses the word "auntie" for a number of women. An older man, perhaps his actual grandfather, is the male whom the child respects, and "father" as such does not exist. These ties reflect the fact that the younger men are mobile, while older men and the women stay at camp.

There is evidence that man existed for many thousands of years without clothing; the need for warmth was another factor which slowly led to the development of settled communities. In order to keep warm, he had traditionally been forced to migrate with the seasons. Some groups, such as the Australian bushmen, eventually located an agreeable climate and a large land mass suitable for foraging, and they were able to establish permanent settlements. Evidence derived from studies of the bushmen indicates that a particular kind of social organization was probably necessary for the migration and survival of the human race in early times. The men had to forage for game and yet find a camp when the hunt was over or women could not become impregnated and perpetuate the race. The long period of gestation in the human animal made possible the absence of men for considerable periods of time without a resulting decline in the birth rate.

Since the life-span of primitive man was probably less than thirty years (man's life-span was approximately thirty-seven years in Roman days), it was advantageous to mate indiscriminately. A man could thus be the father of many children by a number of women, instead of waiting as much as twelve to eighteen months for one woman to become fecund again. (Probably less than half of the children survived infancy.) If twenty men went on a hunting and foraging expedition and only five returned, there were at least four women for each survivor to impregnate in the service of the tribe. Objects relating to fertility rites have been found by anthropologists among almost all primitive and nomadic people studied; thus, it seems likely that man took great interest in the survival of the race at an early date in his history.

Today we may see indiscriminate mating as immoral and crude, but it was necessary for the preservation of the species under primitive conditions of life. The larger the gene pool from which an offspring emerged, the more likely he was to possess adaptive potentialities. When, by chance, "bad" genes (that is, those transmitting characteristics not favorable to survival in a particular environment) were inherited from mother or father, the offspring usually did not survive for long, so there was a tendency for these characteristics not to be perpetuated.

Another factor must have entered the picture at some point many thousands of years ago. Changing atmospheric and soil conditions made possible the advent of tall grasses; shelter and food became more available within a given geographical area, and with the domestication of animals and especially with the acquisition of control over fire, a "camp" could be maintained for relatively long periods of time.

Consider now in a speculative fashion the kind of organization which such circumstances might require. Women tied down by childbirth and child rearing would be likely to remain close to the camp. Men would hunt but return to the camp, either at nightfall (for protection and warmth) or after longer periods of hunting. Individuals would begin to have for their neighbors, though to a lesser extent, the kind of feeling that a mother has for her child. People would be regarded as belonging in one of two categories—those whom one knew and those whom one didn't know. The latter probably were killed whenever possible, but gradually larger groups collected where the land would support them. And as their numbers increased, people found it necessary to develop tolerance for one another.

About this time, speech probably developed. The utterance of vocal noises appears to have evolved as one method available to primitive man for finding his camp and identifying his own kind. Thus, the rudiments of human speech probably derived from crude calls which identified the location of the camp and gradually came to indicate danger or success in hunting by varying inflections of tonality. Differences in vocalization also distinguished one tribe from another, and probably promoted a developing sense of clan membership.

As long as society remained primitive, the relationship between married male and female was a practical one: *the family unit was a unit for physical survival.* Almost everyone in it had to work long and hard. A male and a female who became partners and had children normally had greater chances for survival and more advantages than they would have had if they had stayed alone. The first young children were a survival liability, but as they grew up the original "couple" became a group—with all of its members participating in the survival activities. "Love" was not important. In primitive vocabularies there was no word for "love."

It was not until the Middle Ages that the word "love" (in the sense in which it is used today) became current. Communities developed under the protection of the nobles in their great castles. The lady of a castle assumed the same prestigious position as her husband, the lord. Other people did the work, but the lady of the castle had leisure time to learn to read and practice the arts.

Usually she was more educated than her husband, and if she had duties, they were light and principally administrative. Having so much spare time, she often became egocentric, and she began to adorn herself.

She also became bored.

When the Crusades began in the eleventh century, many of the nobles went off to war, leaving their wives at home. The men who did not go on the Crusades tried to amuse the ladies; they wooed them usually with extramarital sex in mind. During this period there arose the phenomenon of the troubadour, usually a noble, who went from castle to castle to entertain. These troubadours sang songs and ballads about "romance" to entertain the lady of the castle.

There is much literature that suggests that sex outside of marriage became the fashion with these ladies. Probably these married women were the aggressors and initiators in these sex activities. The women were bored. They were intellectually and artistically superior to their husbands, and probably resented the inferior, nonproductive position into which they had been forced by a male-dominated society. *Extramarital passion was defined by them as "love."* ...

Here we have the genesis of "romantic" love. Like most human beliefs, attitudes, and ways of behaving, it grew out of the *social conditions* and requirements of an era, and represented an adjustment to these conditions. In turn, it influenced the conditions themselves, and triggered a series of changes which exert influence on attitudes and behavior even today.

The phenomenon of "romance" grew even stronger when there were powerful female monarchs on the throne—for example, Queen Elizabeth and later Queen Victoria in Great Britain. The romantic environment was utilized *during the courting of the female by the male*, but after marriage the male became dominant, even tyrannical. Romantic love had nothing to do with married love—which was something else—and still is.

This romance-before-marriage tradition was brought to the American Colonies from England. But in America its practice was not restricted to the elite. The romantic courtship became a common custom, largely because of the scarcity of women in the pioneer days. This early shortage had an enormous influence on American male-female relationships, an influence that still lingers. In pioneer days males competed for the few females, using romantic-love behavior as a persuader. Also, the widespread belief (whether true or not) that the male was stronger, more vigorous, more courageous, and more aggressive than the female placed emphasis, both directly and indirectly, on romantic love. The few females for whom the pioneers competed appeared "small and helpless." They had to be "protected" by the males. This view reinforced romantic attitudes *before marriage.*

During the periods of World War I and World War II, a revolution occurred in the relationship between men and women. Women learned that they could do almost anything men could do—as well as, and in many instances better. It was realized that women live longer, are healthier, have a higher threshold of pain than men, and can successfully compete with men scholastically.

This realization offered to women a new spectrum of satisfactions and opportunities, based in large measure on an improved self-image, which had long been denied them. For them it indicated the end of the primarily male-dominated and male-structured society. The modern woman in the first half of the twentieth century desired equality in every way, beginning with sex and the vote.

At about the same time, contraceptive devices were perfected. Now woman could be man's equal not only in society, in business, and in scholarship, but also in sexual convenience; the sex act could be enjoyed by both without the woman's having to fear an unwanted pregnancy.

In past centuries in Western society, it has been considered important for a bride to be a virgin, whereas this condition seldom was required of the male, or even considered desirable. Today, though people may pay lip service to the idea of the virgin bride, in practice it is not generally considered important. Evidence from [sexologist Alfred] Kinsey and other authorities indicates that during the past thirty years women have practiced premarital sexual relations at an increasing rate.

Probably promiscuity has always been common in certain lower socio-economic groups, but in the upper middle class it was considered relatively rare until twenty years ago; at least it was not as obvious. The desire for extramarital intercourse has been increased by the advent of mass-communication media, particularly television and advertising. These have tended to make sex—both in and out of marriage—appear to be the most important thing in the lives of most Americans. The effect of the growing sex emphasis is shown, for example, in the fact that in the year 1962 in California 57,000 babies were born to "child-mothers" twelve to eighteen years old.

Thousands of high-school students are being married annually. In California, one third of these are in the ninth and tenth grades. A great many of these couples marry not because they wish to, but because the girl is pregnant. The frequency of premarital intercourse among these California high-school students has considerable significance because it indicates a corresponding trend among adults—a trend less clearly reflected in statistics concerning adult women, despite their greater opportunities for sexual activity, because they have easy access to contraceptives and sexual information usually unavailable to their teen-age counterparts.

Two forces remain to be considered in this survey of the history of marriage. The first is religion: When the Holy Roman Empire was at its peak, the Church exerted control over all facets of human life in Western Europe by means of canonical law. The most stringent canonical laws concerned marriage. For many ages marriage laws and customs had been civil, but then the Church moved in and took control. The first step was to make marriage a Holy Sacrament, for in the New Testament there is no proviso for this.

The hold of the Church for many centuries was so complete throughout Western Europe that almost everyone believed and accepted anything (religious or nonreligious) which came from Rome. One breach occurred in the sixteenth century with the discoveries of Copernicus. His declaration that the planets, including the earth, revolve about the sun, that the earth is *not* the center of the universe, *as the Church maintained,* was heard throughout Europe. More and more, men of learning doubted some of the edicts which came from Rome. Also, with the emergence of the Protestant Churches, Roman Catholic control over many aspects of life was reduced. It became possible for the elite to divorce without having the Pope's permission.

The growing disbelief in the Church's infallibility also resulted in time in the rejection of the Church's definition of male and female characteristics, including the evil nature of woman and the natural superiority of man.

Another force which influences marriage is economics. Until the nineteenth century, the European family was a unit of economic survival. Most people lived on the land or maintained family industries. The larger the family, the more hands there were to work at home. This arrangement may have been hard on the wife, but no one seemed to care about that in the male-dominated society.

In 1769 the first great economic-technological explosion began. With the development of the modern steam engine by James Watt, an economic metamorphosis was initiated which led to corresponding changes in family life and marriage. The steam engine made factories possible, and the factories took the husband out of the home, keeping him away all day and often into the night. The full burden of maintaining the home and family life fell upon the woman. Hitherto, she had at least been able to depend on her husband to discipline the older children and to make major household decisions. In his absence, she was forced to assume almost all of the responsibility for the family.

The construction of factories also affected marriage in another way. It caused families to move from their rural homes, where they could always live off the land in times of depression, into cities and slums which provided no place to forage for food or to grow it. Workers and their families were crowded in the slum areas. Homes were small (often consisting of one room) and unheated; children had no place either to work or to play, and they were exposed to more contagious illnesses. At the age of eight they too went to work in the factories. Children longed for the day when they could leave their parents' shabby quarters, and the family was splintered in a fashion unheard of in rural communities.

The effects of slum living on family life were calamitous. The mother suffered the humiliation and despair of seeing her children grow hungry, ill, or quarrelsome. She was prevented from performing her usual nurturing role without a continuous, exhausting struggle. The slums and factories also brought humiliation to the father. Pay was so low and depressions were so frequent that he could not provide for his children or his wife. Unable to fulfill their traditional roles adequately, parents coped with hardship and disillusionment in the various ways which are common to human beings under stress. Some became lethargic and pretended not to care; some deserted the family rather than face utter failure; some stayed and continued the struggle, often at the price of illness, bitterness, and chronic fear. Women began to work and seek more education so that they could help ensure adequate care for themselves and their children when their husbands could not. Men began to seek new ways to maintain their dominance and self-respect in the home. At that time, English law, from which our own family law derives, gave the wife and mother no legal protection—let alone community property. Women in such a legally helpless condition learned to distrust men and began to seek ways to look out for themselves. According to some authorities many of these women moved to the United States as contract wives and subsequently influenced the development of American family structure along more egalitarian lines.

During this era, which lasted approximately a hundred years, we find the disintegration of the traditional home. For centuries in Western Europe the traditional home was congruent with a particular form of marriage. With the fracturing of the customary roles in the home, the institution of marriage—inevitably—also came into serious question.

In Western culture the male had always been dominant over the female. The "real man" was the individual who could use heavy tools, could hunt, and was a good physical fighter. Physical strength, having been the basis of survival, also placed men in the positions of power: they made the rules and decisions. But after the Industrial Revolution a man's value began to be measured in terms of his technical skill and intellectual productivity, as shown by the amount of money he made. And as the twentieth century moved on, the female was able to develop the same skills and intellectual powers, and make money almost as well as the man. In the United States today, the women control and spend more money than do the men.[1] In other words, as men's roles became less dependent upon physical strength and more related to skill and intellect, they also became more accessible to women. Birth control made it increasingly possible for both men and women to seek new avenues of expression. To women, with their increased education in nondomestic areas, the new male role seemed attractive. By contrast, the traditional female roles often were regarded as unchallenging and servile—perhaps less because of their inherent nature than because of their association with the concept of women as inferior beings capable of filling only these roles and no others.

Drastic changes in family life were inevitable. One such major change has completely altered marital expectations and behavior: marriage has become more than a purely functional process. People today seldom enter marriage *because it will help them survive physically,* or because it is generally more advantageous for a male and female to join in a collaborative partnership than to live alone.

The relationship problems evinced in complex industrialized societies have led some people to wish for the "good old days" when social and sexual roles were rigidly defined by the society and just as rigidly enforced. Also, one often hears: "If the youngsters had more *real* problems to worry about, they'd stay out of trouble."

Both of these nostalgic sentiments are based on some truth. In more primitive societies—those social groupings in which sheer physical survival is the consciously understood central focus of communal living—active collaboration with others and submergence of the individual interests to group interests become a necessity. Quarreling and separation such as occur in divorce or desertion are threats to individual survival and are controlled by the group in its own interest. In these societies, the socialization process is such that individual needs are adjusted to group needs. Indeed this adjustment is the goal of socialization and education in all societies; but in modern civilizations the variety of conflicting divergent groups makes it impossible for an individual to gear his needs and aims to those of all groups. The groups which capture his allegiance, or the allegiance of his parents, generally determine his social behavior.

In modern industrial society, couples facing a crisis affecting survival often stick together, only to separate when the emergency has passed.

The battle for survival in modern societies is usually a battle for emotional survival and the tools of war are correspondingly psychological, aimed at maiming the enemy's self-esteem or causing him shame rather than at killing him.

In such psychological warfare (for example, the battle of the sexes between spouses), it is difficult to decide who is the winner and who is the loser. There may be other parties in the picture operating unwittingly in subtle ways (the mother-in-law gets most of the blame), so that it is difficult to name the players without a program.

The institution of marriage has failed to adapt itself sufficiently to current requirements. The constant battle of the sexes and the family turmoil raging today are evidence of the haphazard efforts of individuals to reconcile their traditional role images with current realities. With little help from any social quarter, men and women are fighting lonely battles to find their place in the sun. Plagued by guilt and uncertainty, they struggle to discover their "identity" yet are unable to *accept* themselves if they do catch a glimpse of their genuine needs, desires, and goals. For what they glimpse is not what they have been conditioned to believe is "good" or "right" according to age-old systems of beliefs, developed on the basis of requirements which died at the time of the Industrial Revolution.

The man who, through education and training, has learned to find his greatest fulfillment in reading or art or hairstyling or general scholarship rather than in athletic or business competition, must find ways to reconcile his preference with many age-old images regarding "masculinity." The college-educated woman who finds happiness and self-respect in professional achievement has the task of reconciling her learned needs and preferences with the "feminine" image which continues to define womanliness in terms of domestic and mothering abilities.

Today both sexes can perform *most* social functions equally well, and the rigid social resistance to role diffusion is becoming a genuine frustration to those who seek self-expression in roles outside the boundaries of their defined sex roles.

Members of the younger generation today often shock and frighten their parents and grandparents by their apparent determination to break through traditional role designations. But it is a major task of this and future generations to find solutions to the sex-role problems which their parents have left unresolved. The extreme manifestations of what parents see as sex-role confusion—such as boys dressing more like girls, girls dressing more like boys, and the increase in homosexuality—frighten parents because they cannot imagine a future different from the past they have known....

In summary, marriage used to be an institution for the *physical* survival and well-being of two people and their offspring. This function gave rise to a particular rule-governed structure suitable to the situation. Today, except in time of war or accident, the struggle for survival in industrialized societies does not require purely physical strength. Instead, we have primarily the struggle for

**11**

*William J. Lederer and Don D. Jackson*

*psychological* and *emotional* survival. The family unit is the natural unit for human survival regardless of what the hazard is. But so far, the changes in the structure, form, and processes of marriage have been too few and too unsystematic to cope with the new psychological and emotional problems. Marriage still is an anachronism from the days of the jungle, or at least from the days of small farms and home industries.

Divorce, marital strife, desertion, and emotional and physical illness are a few symptoms of this cultural lag in the institution of marriage, and they seem to be on the increase. We cannot return to the "simple" life of an agricultural or primitive community in this atomic, industrial age; we must modify our outmoded attitudes, beliefs, and institutions to accommodate current social realities.

Marriage is still a necessary institution. But it must be adjusted to new social and economic conditions. Above all, the new roles and relationships of men and women must be recognized. It is not surprising that an anachronistic social institution cannot function; nevertheless, it is tragic that so many marriages fail and so little is being done about it.

## NOTES

1. Women own more than half of all stocks traded on the New York Stock Exchange.

## 1.2   ERNEST W. BURGESS

# *The Family as a Unity of Interacting Personalities*

The following selection is from "The Family as a Unity of Interacting Personalities," *The Family* (March 1926). Originally given as a speech during the 1926 meeting of the American Sociological Association, the article demonstrates the emergence of thinking of the family as a system. In it Ernest W. Burgess describes family types of the early twentieth century. The now-famous term coined by Burgess first appeared in this article when he describes the family as a "unity of interacting persons."

Burgess is widely known as one of the founding pioneers in the scientific study of the family. Each year the National Council on Family Relations gives an award to an outstanding family scientist in his memory.

**Key Concept:** the family as a system

Nine years ago I gave for the first time a course on the family. There was even then an enormous literature in this field. But among all the volumes upon the family, ethnological, historical, psychological, ethical, social, economic, statistical, radically realist, or radically idealist, there was to be found not a single work that even pretended to study the modern family as behavior or as a social phenomenon. It has been studied as a legal institution but it had not been studied as a subject of natural science, *i.e.* (as Professor Park once said of the newspaper), in the way in which the biologist studies the potato bug.[1] So far as I know, the description by Professor Thomas of the large family group among the Polish peasants was the first study of the family as a living being rather than as a dead form.[2]

Because of this lack of social psychological studies of the family, the work of the course was planned upon two principles. The first was to select from the literature of psychiatry, psychology, social psychology, and sociology, statements of concepts that seemed to have a bearing upon research in family life, as sexual instinct, maternal sentiment, wish for response, monogamy as in the

*13*

mores, birth control as a folkway, family conflict, accommodation, and assimilation. The second was to assemble, from all possible sources, case studies of family life. These were taken from the works of ethnologists, from histories of manners and customs, from biography and autobiography, from fiction, from drama, from records of social agencies, from any source where realistic pictures of family life might be secured. In addition, my students have contributed several hundred case studies, which often, with more or less intimate detail, describe their own families.

In reading these cases, reflecting upon them, and seeking to analyze them, certain facts began to emerge and finally to crystallize in rather clear form. The first was that in spite of the undoubtedly great differences between individual families or between family life in various cultural groups, there was a family type in general. In the last analysis, the essential characteristics of the family were found to be everywhere the same. And what are these characteristics? The whole body of familial sentiments which naturally and inevitably grow out of and maintain the relationships of husband and wife and parents and children. The role of the mother, for instance, we immediately recognize as basically the same, despite the apparent superficial differences in the care of children among Eskimos, Turks, or Englishmen.

My next discovery was a sudden perception of the tremendous difference between the modern family and the family of the past. How many of us realize how modern a phenomenon is the small family of father, mother, and children emancipated from the control of the wider kinship group of grandparents, uncles, aunts, and cousins? Do we perceive that it is to be found as a typical specimen perhaps only in cities, and particularly in the urbanized areas of our very largest American cities? The small family group in apartment houses or residential hotels is, no doubt, the most notorious illustration of effectual detachment from the claims of kinship. The absence in the city home of "the spare bedroom," that famous institution of the country-side, serves as a convenient defense against invading relatives.

At the same time, the family in modern life is undergoing changes and modifications which can hardly be appreciated or understood except in the perspective of the past or by an opportunity for comparison with a contemporary organization of the large family in process of disintegration, such as China affords. But, as the large family was organized in the interests of the older generation to resist change, and so to perpetuate the family pattern, the modern family is exposed to change since it begins in a certain sense anew with every marriage and is thus at the mercy of the new romantic notions of the younger generation.

In contrasting the small family of these city areas with the kinship or large family group—whether in ancient Israel, Greece, or Rome, or in contemporary India, Japan, or China, or even with the large peasant family of Poland or Russia, or with the kinship clans of American rural communities—differences are at once apparent. The large family group tends in every culture to be impressed in one standardized form; while within the same culture the small family tends to exhibit a variety of patterns. Already in American society are to be found the following patterns classified by the size of family: the childless family or the so-called "companionate"; the one-child family; the two-child family; the family with three or more children. And these are not merely biological or economic classes, they are in large part determined by custom, or by new fashions in the folkways. Dr. Mowrer[3] has even classified areas of the city by types of family life, the non-family areas with their Hobohemian and Bohemian centers; areas of the so-called emancipated family in the rooming-house regions; the patriarchal family areas of the immigrant colonies; the equalitarian family areas of apartment house districts; and finally, in the so-called dormitory suburbs that new type of family where the husband leaves for down-town before the children are awake and returns after they are asleep, the modern matriarchal family, or perhaps more accurately, the matricentric family. This correlation between cultural areas of the city and types of family life is no fortuitous coincidence. It suggests the ways in which family life is related to the ecology of the city. The pattern of family life develops under certain life conditions and thrives only in conformity with the folkways and mores of the local community.

Next I found peculiarly revealing a classification of families by the pattern of personal relationships between husband and wife and parents and children. Two contrasted patterns soon presented themselves: the highly integrated family and the unintegrated or loosely integrated family. These in turn might be subdivided into several varieties. Upon analysis it was found that the highly integrated family possessed one or more of the following traits: elaborate ritual, rigorous discipline, sentimental interdependence; stimulating co-operative activities or objectives; while the unintegrated or loosely integrated family had little or no ritual, exerted slight control either through discipline or sentimental attachment and its members were only in small degree unified by common family aims to which individual purposes were subordinated. The typical orthodox Jewish family has in marked degree all the traits that are positive for the highly integrated family. The Puritan family, stigmatized by the younger generation as the Puritanical family, is a conspicuous illustration of integration through the characteristics of rigorous discipline and dominant family objectives.

This study of the patterns of personal relationships in family life led directly to the conception of the family as a unity of interacting persons. By a unity of interacting personalities is meant a living, changing, growing thing. I was about to call it a superpersonality. At any rate the actual unity of family life has its existence not in any legal conception, nor in any formal contract, but in the interaction of its members. For the family does not depend for its survival on the harmonious relations of its members, nor does it necessarily disintegrate as a result of conflicts between its members. The family lives as long as interaction is taking place and only dies when it ceases....

The family is even more than an interaction of personalities. In this interaction, the family develops a conception of itself. When this conception of familial relations is recognized by the community, the family acquires an institutional character. This is what is meant by the family as a social institution. A family that had no conception of its rôle in the community, or of the responsibilities of its individual members would not be an institution, perhaps not even a family. It is just these natural relationships of family life, the obligations and responsibilities spontaneously assumed in family interaction, which the community seeks first through custom and then through law to define, to make contractual, and to enforce. But everywhere, and always, by those who are dealing with problems of family life it is paramount to recognize that the family as a reality exists in the interaction of its members and not in the formalities of the law with its stipulations of rights and duties....

Th[e] definition of the person as an individual with status has thrown a flood of light upon family interaction. The members of the family do react to each other as individuals and that is important. But they react to each other as persons and that is also important. For every person has, with more or less awareness, a conception of his rôle, not only in society, but in all groups of which he is a member. Not only does the person have a lively conception of his own rôle in the family, but he has a sense of the rôles of all the other members of the family and notions of what family life is or ought to be. The rôles of the good father, the good mother, and the good child enter powerfully in determining the conception which each member holds of his place in the world of family life.

In a stable, homogeneous society, ideas of family life and the rôles of its different members are relatively fixed and constant. In a changing society composed of heterogeneous elements, familial attitudes are almost inevitably in a state of flux. Instead of a common pattern of family life intrenched in tradition and crushing out all impulse to variation by the sheer weight of universal conformity, our American society presents what at first sight seems to be a chaotic conglomeration of every conceivable pattern of family organization and disorganization, from the patriarchal kinship groups of our Southern Mountain highlands to the free unions of our Greenwich Villages. Hardly a day passes but the public is shocked and outraged by some new form of wild and reckless behavior, particularly of youth in revolt no longer regulated by customary controls.

But these random and aimless variations away from the basic pattern of family life are not, as some believe, an indication of the future of family life and sexual relationships. They are only the symptoms in the present, as in similar times in the past, that society is undergoing change. When an equilibrium is re-established a new pattern of family life will emerge, better adapted to the new situation, but only a different variety of the old familiar pattern of personal relationships in the family.

The general currents of the social influences affecting the family can, however, be outlined. They were ably presented in a paper by Professor Ernest R. Groves[4] read before this group last year in Chicago. The passing of man's dominance, the emancipation of woman, and her entrance into all fields of economic, social, and civic life, parenthood by choice, the transition from the homestead family to the home in the small apartment or the hotel—these are only a few of the influences affecting family interaction in new and disturbing ways. More intangible but even more dynamic are the subtle changes taking place in our conception of the family and of the rôle of its members. It is only by contrast that we realize the revolutionary nature of the changes in our attitudes....

In his penetrating paper, Professor Groves gave a particularly illuminating explanation of the influence of conflicting conceptions of family life. The modern husband conceives the rôle which his wife should play in the family in the likeness of his mother (a sociological adaptation of the theory of the mother image) while the wife thinks of her rôle as a realization of some embodiment of the new woman. What family can be found in which this very natural divergence in family ideals has not been the crux of a conflict, perhaps slight or perhaps severe, and how interesting it would be to know the different solutions that have been worked out?

The following excerpts from a case studied by one of our graduate students depict the influence upon family life of conflicting patterns of family ideals. It will be called the Marx family, not because that is its name but because it suggests the German ancestry of the father. The father, like so many parents, acquired his notions of the rôle of parents and children from the family pattern in which he was reared.

> In the early eighties the Marx family, consisting of the paternal grandparents and a son, a child of two, emigrated from Germany to Cincinnati, Ohio. There the grandfather worked as a teamster and in a few years as a teaming contractor. The oldest son, the Mr. Marx of our small family group, at twelve worked with his father as a teamster during the heavy season. Another son and daughter were soon added to the family and the economic struggle became severe. At the age of fourteen he was taken out of school and set to work ten or twelve hours a day. His wages were given over to his father, and he was "glad to have a dime to spend on the Fourth of July." At the age of eighteen he joined the cavalry in the Spanish American War and saw active service later in the Philippines. Returning overland after his discharge, he stopped in a small town to visit a friend. There he met Mrs. Marx and married her.

This picture of the paternal family pattern, while not detailed, suggests the characteristic features of the German-American immigrant family: the exercise of the paternal authority, rigorous discipline, the subordination of the individual members to the aim of the economic security and success of the family. A brief sketch of family history will bring us down to date for a description of family interaction at the present time.

> Since his father died soon after his marriage, Mr. Marx and his bride moved to Cincinnati taking over the dwindling contracting business. His mother had grown rather harsh and melancholic during his absence and in every way he tried to defer to her wishes and render her the respect and obedience due to one who had done so much for him. In accordance with her wishes the first child was named Wilhelm (William). Four years later Henry came and only a year later, Joseph. At the outbreak of the World War Mr. Marx enlisted and was in camp near Columbus where the family took up its abode. Late in 1919 he was honorably discharged. He immediately took a commission in the National Guard commanding a cavalry troop stationed in a small city where the widowed maternal grandmother lived.
>
> Mr. Marx noticed that William had begun to grow rapidly during his absence and this continued until now he is six feet tall and only sixteen. At the same time Mr. Marx noticed that he was "acting up," was becoming lazy, was failing in school, and avoided strangers. He played with smaller boys and disobeyed his mother who gave up in despair and began to rely on the whippings administered by his father. These had little effect and William left school and went to work. Since then he has lost every job he has held after a few weeks or a month. He continues to dress slovenly, to loaf, and to disobey. William is the family problem; they have all come to take a hand in discussing him and in saying what he should do.

*Chapter 1*
*Definitions*
*of the Family*

Mr. Marx conceived his rôle as the head of the family according to his mental picture of himself as taking his father's place. His military experience but confirmed his belief in the efficacy of what Professor Thomas has called the ordering and forbidding technique.

> Mr. Marx is quite open and objective, saying what he thinks, occupied with the concrete happenings of family life and its immediate plans. He tries to dominate the family and especially to control William. The father believes in doing what you are told, in respecting your elders and superiors, and in venerating the common virtues of honesty, thrift, and industry as the sum and substance of the way of life. He is frequently heard quoting something that he did as a boy or that his parents did or expected of him. Mr. Marx attempts to "put over" his father's family idea but fails. He apparently does not find himself capable of adjusting himself to any other plan of family control; the army and his military training saw to that. Denied contacts with middle class men that would give him some conception of other family patterns, he is helpless and vainly struggles toward an impossible goal.

The maternal pattern of family life and the rôles appropriate to it are derived from the girlhood life of Mrs. Marx.

> Mrs. Marx told the writer about her own home life as a young woman and as a girl but she does not speak of it much in the family circle. Nevertheless it is very potent in the formation of her attitudes, and these attitudes remain in conflict with attitudes of her husband to the present day. Democratic family life, independence, initiative, and mutual respect on equal terms of all the members of the family, are the American notions she carries over from her girlhood family life.
> Mrs. Marx is more introspective than any other member of the family. She worries about being a failure, thinks about death and imagines all sorts of calamities that might happen to the family. She looks for spiritual values, liberty, artistic expression (she finds that her violin helps more than anything else to make life worth living). To raise her boys to be good and noble men is her idea of success in life and because they do not seem to be turning out right she feels that she is a failure. Moreover, she feels helpless to change the family situation.

The oldest son, William, has already been termed the "family problem." He has all the problems of the boy of the awkward age and others in addition. Existing in the family as an outcast, he attempts to find a social world outside the home in which his wishes may be expressed.

> William is sensitive about his stature, secretive, avoiding the society of others. He has a very decided feeling of inferiority and seeks the company of boys young enough to look up to him or at least not old enough to torment him. He is virtually an outcast from the family at present and goes his own way as much as he can. He says little but so far as his actions indicate he sees life as getting food and shelter with the least effort possible. His "bumming around" and disobedience bring on a conflict usually ending in violence on the part of Mr. Marx. His parents marvel that he has not taken to the road and become a bum. Bill takes it all without resisting but continues to disobey. Mrs. Marx expressed her opinion to the writer that it galls her to see this and that if she were a boy his size she would fight back even though defeat was inevitable. Bill has evidently been beaten so often that all the

"fight" has been taken out of him, and lacking a satisfactory status in the family he has nothing to protect by fighting back. He has accepted the rôle of the "dog" —without a bit of spirit—whipped and defeated already in life, accepting a mean, hand-to-mouth existence.

The two younger brothers, Henry and Joseph, exhibit marked temperamental differences, but time does not permit a description of their personal traits nor an account of their attitude of superiority to their older brother.

The status of the different members of the family is disclosed quite unmistakably by the seating at meals.

> Each has his position at table, Henry at the right and Joseph at the left of their father, William at his mother's left. There is indication of status in the seating arrangement: (1) Mr. Marx; (2) Mrs. Marx; (3) Henry; (4) Joseph; (5) William. Their attitude toward their places is one of "rights" and they feel disturbed if they are made to sit anywhere else, except for a guest.

The interpretation made in this case study of the Marx family life follows:

> One is struck in studying the family that it is not one family but three. Mr. Marx's family lives on through him and the patterns that it conformed to persist. While the family lived with the paternal grandmother this was probably the dominant pattern in the family life. During the taste of independence offered by Mr. Marx's absence, the maternal family's pattern, that of freedom and mutual respect developed. With the father's return a conflict arose between the paternal and maternal pattern, conflict made more intense by the training the father had received in the army. The children began to assert their own "rights" and to resent the paternal discipline. The family pattern which the children drew from their associates was formulated in the processes of interaction which took place between them and the parents. This may be called the third family pattern. At any rate three distinct patterns are to be found existing in the attitudes of father, mother and children, and more important is the fact that they have not been integrated into a single, more or less consistent and harmonious, resultant pattern upon which successful family life could be built. Hence family control is labelled "anarchy"—the family as a group is disorganized. Three family patterns are in conflict, that of the father's family, that of the mother's family, and that of the children's group of associates. All of the patterns have failed to realize adequate expression.

This case is only one among many that might have been selected to illustrate the effect on family life of conflicting rôles. Like any case study it raises more questions than it answers. Among all the many questions that might be asked, one interests me the most. What is going on in the inner life of William? What changes are taking place in his conception of himself and of his attitude toward his father that may lead him to rebel, or to escape, or to go insane? But the case at any rate does indicate the possibilities for research of an analysis of family life in terms of family patterns and rôles....

For the study of human nature, personality, and groups like the family, the basic reality is just this social image, this conception of one's rôle in the family, in the congenital group and in the community. Intimate studies of family life reveal that the actual problems of human beings center, in general, around the struggle to realize our conceptions of our rôles—as was vividly illustrated by the case of the Marx family. Any program of treating this case, to be even intelligent, not to say successful, would lie not in assessing the proportionate share of the blame upon Mr. Marx, or upon Mrs. Marx, or upon William, but in an understanding of their attitudes in the light of each one's conception of his rôle in family life7.

For it is in his social images, his memories, his wishes, his dreams, his illusions, his faiths that a human being really lives. Take from him his social images of motherhood and brotherhood, of truth and justice, of immortality and God, and life would not be worth living. Yet, for these social images, the so-called illusions of home and country, friendship and honor, humanity and right, man has always been willing to put forth the utmost effort, to make the most heroic sacrifices, even to life itself.

However, in dealing with human rôles as the social reality of personality, it is necessary to regard them not as absolutes, but as relative to the social situation. Changes in life conditions render time-honored rôles obsolete. Where is the grandmother with her black bonnet of the last generation? Where is the ideal that a woman's place is confined to the home? Why is it that the rôle which made the mother as a girl the belle of the village leaves her old-fashioned daughter a wall-flower at a dance? Why is it that the father who in the country was the center of all the activities of the family, economic and cultural, seems in many city homes to be reduced to the negative rôle of saying "no" to the plans of the other members of the family?

Then too, even the personal rôles of family life may become so formal and mechanical that they lose the spontaneity and the human quality that originally and essentially belonged to them. "Are Parents People?" is the impertinent phrasing of this question in the title of a recent motion picture. Or a similar reaction against the formalism that may ossify familial rôles and sentiments was some time ago expressed in the flippant lines of a ragtime song, "They say the family is an institution, but who wants to live in an institution?" It is well to realize that even the least institutional of institutions may become so impersonal and mechanical as to take on the characteristics of a secondary instead of a primary group.

The scientific study of the family is still in its infancy. I have attempted briefly and I know inadequately to touch on certain of the aspects of family life that, in the studies which we have made, have seemed to be important for future research. These are: first, to push further the effort to describe, analyze, and classify the patterns of family life; second, to recognize that the family as a going concern depends more on the natural unity that arises and develops through the personal interaction of its members than upon any attempt to enforce the family obligations which the law imposes; and third, to test the assumption that the family as a reality inheres in the conception which society and its members have of it and of their rôles as husbands and wives, parents and children.

# NOTES

1. *The City,* page 97.
2. Thomas, W. I.: *The Polish Peasant in Europe and America,* vol. I–II.
3. Mowrer, Ernest R.: *Family Disorganization* (to be published).
4. *American Journal of Sociology,* September, 1925.

1.3    IRA L. REISS

# The Universality of the Family: A Conceptual Analysis

One of the most difficult challenges in the study of the family is developing a definition of the concept of "family" that is relevant to all family forms. This task was hotly debated during the latter part of the tumultuous 1960s, as many of America's basic values were being challenged and revised. Ira L. Reiss was a professor of sociology at the University of Iowa when he wrote "The Universality of the Family: A Conceptual Analysis," *Journal of Marriage and the Family* (November 1965), from which this selection has been excerpted. In it, Reiss offers theoretical ideas that can move the reader toward a definition of the family. Currently a professor emeritus at the University of Minnesota at Minneapolis, Reiss has also been director of the Family Study Center at the University of Minnesota since 1969. Reiss was one of the most prolific family scholars during the 1960s. Although many people think of Reiss in terms of his research on premarital sexual permissiveness, he is a family theorist who has provided a wealth of theoretical and empirical information on the American family system.

**Key Concept:** definition of the family

During the last few decades, a revived interest in the question of the universality of the family has occurred. One key reason for this was the 1949 publication of George Peter Murdock's book *Social Structure*.[1] In that book, Murdock postulated that the nuclear family was universal and that it had four essential functions which it always and everywhere fulfilled. These four functions were: (1) socialization, (2) economic cooperation, (3) reproduction, and (4) sexual relations. Even in polygamous and extended family systems, the nuclear families within these larger family types were viewed as separate entities which each performed these four functions.

The simplicity and specificity of Murdock's position makes it an excellent starting point for an investigation of the universal functions of the human family. Since Murdock's position has gained support in many quarters, it should be examined carefully. Brief comments on Murdock's position appear in the literature, and some authors, such as Levy and Fallers, have elaborated their opposition.[2] The present paper attempts to go somewhat further, not only in testing Murdock's notion but in proposing and giving evidence for a substitute position. However, it should be clear that Murdock's position is being used merely as an illustration; our main concern is with delineating what, if anything, is universal about the human family.

The four functions of the nuclear family are "functional prerequisites" of human society, to use David Aberle's term from his classic article on the topic.[3] This means that these functions must somehow occur for human society to exist. If the nuclear family everywhere fulfills these functions, it follows that this family should be a "structural prerequisite" of human society, i.e., a universally necessary part of society.[4] The basic question being investigated is not whether these four functions are functional prerequisites of human society—almost all social scientists would accept this—but whether these four functions are necessarily carried out by the nuclear family. If these functions are not everywhere carried out by the nuclear family, then are there any functional prerequisites of society which the nuclear family or any family form does fulfill? Is the family a universal institution in the sense that it always fulfills some functional prerequisite of society? Also, what, if any, are the universal structural features of the family? . . .

## A TEST OF MURDOCK'S THESIS

One of the cultures chosen for the test of Murdock's thesis is from his own original sample of 250 cultures—the Nayar of the Malabar Coast of India. In his book, Murdock rejected Ralph Linton's view that the Nayar lacked the nuclear family.[5] Since that time, the work of Kathleen Gough has supported Linton's position, and Murdock has accordingly changed his own position.[6] . . .

The matrilineage is particularly strong among the Nayar, and a mother with the help of her matrilineage brings up her children. Her husband and "lovers" do not assist her in the raising of her children. Her brother typically assists her when male assistance is needed. Assistance from the linked lineages where most of her lovers come from also substitutes for the weak husband role. Since many Nayar women change lovers rather frequently, there may not even be any very stable male-female relation present. The male is frequently away fighting. The male makes it physiologically possible for the female to have offspring, but he is not an essential part of the family unit that will raise his biological children. In this sense, sex and reproduction are somewhat external to the family unit among the Nayar. Very little in the way of economic cooperation between husband and wife occurs. Thus, virtually all of Murdock's functions are outside of the nuclear family. However, it should be noted that the socialization of offspring function is present in the maternal extended family system. Here, then, is a society that seems to lack the nuclear family and, of necessity, therefore, the four functions of this unit. Even if we accept Gough's view that the "lovers" are husbands and that there really is a form of group marriage, it is still apparent that the separate husband-wife-child units formed by such a group marriage do not here comprise separately functioning nuclear families.

One does not have to rely on just the Nayar as a test of Murdock. Harold E. Driver, in his study of North American Indians, concludes that in matrilocal extended family systems with matrilineal descent, the husband role and the nuclear family are often insignificant.[7] It therefore seems that the relative absence of the nuclear family in the Nayar is approached particularly in other similar matrilineal societies. Thus, the Nayar do not seem to be so unique. They apparently demonstrate a type of family system that is common in lesser degree.

... A family system which is not mother-centered is the Israeli Kibbutz family system as described by Melford Spiro.[8] Here the husband and wife live together in a communal agricultural society. The children are raised communally and do not live with their parents. Although the Kibbutzim are only a small part of the total Israeli culture, they have a distinct culture and can be considered a separate society by the Aberle definition cited above. They have been in existence since 1909 and thus have shown that they can survive for several generations and that they have a self-sufficient system of action. The function which is most clearly missing in the Kibbutz family is that of economic cooperation between husband and wife. In this communal society, almost all work is done for the total Kibbutz, and the rewards are relatively equally distributed regardless of whether one is married or not. There is practically no division of labor between husbands and wives as such. Meals are eaten communally, and residence is in one room which requires little in the way of housekeeping.

Here, too, Murdock denies that this is a real exception and, in the letters to the author referred to above, contends that the Kibbutzim could not be considered a society. Murdock's objection notwithstanding, a group which has existed for over half a century and has developed a self-sufficient system of action covering all major aspects of existence indeed seems to be a society by almost all definitions. There is nothing in the experience of the Kibbutzim that makes it difficult to conceive of such groups existing in many regions of the world or, for that matter, existing by themselves in a world devoid of other people. They are analogous to some of the Indian groups living in American society in the sense that they have a coherent way of life that differs considerably from the dominant culture. Thus, they are not the same as an average community which is merely a part of the dominant culture....

There are other societies that are less extreme but which still create some difficulty with Murdock's definition of the nuclear family. Malinowski, in his study of the Trobriand Islanders, reports that except for perhaps nurturant socialization, the mother's brother rather than the father is the male who teaches the offspring much of the necessary way of life of the group.[9] Such a situation is certainly common in a matrilineal society, and it does place limits on the socialization function of the nuclear family *per se*. Further, one must at least qualify the economic function in the Trobriand case. The mother's brother here takes a large share of the economic burden and supplies his sister's family with half the food they require. The rigidity of Murdock's definition in light of such instances is apparent. These examples also make it reasonable that other societies may well exist which carry a little further such modifications of the nuclear family. For example, we find such more extreme societies when we look at the Nayar and the Kibbutz.

Some writers, like Nicholas Timasheff, have argued that the Russian experience with the family evidences the universality of the nuclear family.[10] While it is true that the Communists in Russia failed to abolish as much of the old family system as they wanted to, it does not follow that this demonstrates the impossibility of abolishing the family. In point of fact, the family system of the Israeli Kibbutz is virtually identical with the system the Russian Communists desired, and thus we must admit that it is possible for at least some groups to achieve such a system. Also, the Communists did not want to do away with the family *in toto*. Rather, they wanted to do away with the patriarchal aspects of the family, to have marriage based on love, easy divorce, and communal upbringing of children. They ceased in much of this effort during the 1930's when a falling birth rate, rising delinquency and divorce rates, and the depression caused them to question the wisdom of their endeavors. However, it has never been demonstrated that these symptoms were consequences of the efforts to change the family. They may well have simply been results of a rapidly changing social order that would have occurred regardless of the family program. Therefore, the Russian experience is really not evidence pro or con Murdock's position. . . .

Overall, it appears that a reasonable man looking at the evidence presented above would conclude that Murdock's position is seriously in doubt. As Levy and Fallers have said, Murdock's approach is too simplistic in viewing a particular structure such as the nuclear family as always, in all cultural contexts, having the same four functions.[11] Robert Merton has said that such a view of a very specific structure as indispensable involves the erroneous "postulate of indispensability."[12] Certainly it seems rather rash to say that one very specific social structure such as the nuclear family will always have the same consequences regardless of the context in which it is placed. Surely this is not true of specific structures in other institutions such as the political, religious, or economic. The consequences of a particular social structure vary with the socio-cultural context of that structure. Accordingly, a democratic bicameral legislative structure in a new African nation will function differently than in America; the Reform Jewish Denomination has different consequences in Israel than in America; government control of the economy functions differently in England than in Russia.

The remarkable thing about the family institution is that in so many diverse contexts, one can find such similar structures and functions. To this extent, Murdock has made his point and has demonstrated that the nuclear family with these four functions is a surprisingly common social fact. But this is quite different from demonstrating that this is always the case or necessarily the case. It should be perfectly clear that the author feels Murdock's work has contributed greatly to the advancement of our knowledge of the family. Murdock is used here because he is the best known proponent of the view being examined, not because he should be particularly criticized.

A safer approach to take toward the family is to look for functional prerequisites of society which the family fulfills and search for the full range of structures which may fulfill these functional prerequisites. At this stage of our knowledge, it seems more valuable to talk of the whole range of family structures and to seek for a common function that is performed and that may be essential to human society. What we need now is a broad, basic, parsimonious definition that would have utility in both single and cross-cultural comparisons.[13] We have a good deal of empirical data on family systems and a variety of definitions—it is time we strove for a universal definition that would clarify the essential features of this institution and help us locate the family in any cultural setting.

Looking over the four functions that Murdock associates with the nuclear family, one sees that three of them can be found to be absent in some cultures. The Nayar perhaps best illustrate the possibility of placing sex and reproduction outside the nuclear family. Also, it certainly seems within the realm of possibility that a "Brave New World" type of society could operate by scientifically mating sperm and egg and presenting married couples with state-produced offspring of certain types when they desired children.[14] Furthermore, the raising of children by other than their biological parents is widespread in many societies where adoption and rearing by friends and relatives is common.[15] Thus, it seems that sex and reproduction may not be inexorably tied to the nuclear family.[16]

The third function of Murdock's which seems possible to take out of the nuclear family is that of economic cooperation. The Kibbutz is the prime example of this. Furthermore, it seems that many other communal-type societies approximate the situation in the Kibbutz.

The fourth function is that of socialization. Many aspects of this function have been taken away from the family in various societies. For example, the Kibbutz parents, according to Spiro, are not so heavily involved in the inculcation of values or the disciplinary and care-taking aspects of socialization. Nevertheless, the Kibbutz parents are heavily involved in nurturant socialization, i.e., the giving of positive emotional response to infants and young children. A recent book by Stephens also reports a seemingly universal presence of nurturance of infants.[17] It should be emphasized that this paper uses "nurturance" to mean not the physical, but the emotional care of the infant. Clearly, the two are not fully separable. This use of the term nurturant is similar to what is meant by "expressive" role.[18] Interestingly enough, in the Kibbutz both the mother and father are equally involved in giving their children nurturant socialization. All of the societies referred to above have a family institution with the function of nurturant socialization of children. This was true even for the extreme case of the Nayar.

The conception of the family institution being developed here has in common with some other family definitions an emphasis on socialization of offspring. The difference is that all other functions have been ruled out as unessential and that only the nurturant type of socialization is the universal function of the family institution. This paper presents empirical evidence to support its contention. It is important to be more specific than were Levy and Fallers regarding the type of socialization the family achieves since all societies have socialization occurring outside the family as well as within. It should be noted that this author, unlike Murdock, is talking of *any* form of family institution and not just the nuclear family.

As far as a universal structure of the family to fulfill the function of nurturant socialization is concerned, it seems possible to set only very broad limits, and even these involve some speculation. First, it may be said that the structure of the family will always be that of a primary group. Basically, this position rests on the assumption that nurturant socialization is a process which cannot be adequately carried out in an impersonal setting and which thus requires a primary type of relation.[19] The author would not specify the biological mother as the socializer or even a female, or even more than one person or the age of the person. If one is trying to state what the family must be like in a minimal sense in any society—what its universally required structure and function is—one cannot be too specific. However, we can go one step farther in specifying the structure of the family group we are defining. The family is here viewed as an institution, as an integrated set of norms and relationships which are socially defined and internalized by the members of a society. In every society in the world, the institutional structure which contains the roles related to the nurturant function is a small kinship structured group.[20] Thus, we can say that the primary group which fulfills the nurturant function is a kinship structure. Kinship refers to descent—it involves rights of possession among those who are kin. It is a geneological reckoning, and people with real or fictive biological connections are kin.[21]

This specification of structure helps to distinguish from the family institution those non-kin primary groups that may in a few instances perform nurturant functions. For example, a nurse-child relation or a governess-child relation could, if carried far enough, involve the bulk of nurturant socialization for that child. But such a relationship would be a quasi-family at best, for it clearly is not part of the kinship structure. There are no rights of "possession" given to the nurse or the child in such cases, and there is no socially accepted, institutionalized, system of child-rearing involving nurses and children. In addition, such supervisory help usually assumes more of a caretaking and disciplinary aspect, with the parents themselves still maintaining the nurturant relation.

Talcott Parsons has argued, in agreement with the author's position, that on a societal level, only kinship groups can perform the socialization function.[22] He believes that socialization in a kin group predisposes the child to assume marital and parental roles himself when he matures and affords a needed stable setting for socialization. Clearly other groups may at times perform part of the nurturant function. No institution in human society has an exclusive franchise on its characteristic function. However, no society exists in which any group other than a kinship group performs the dominant share of the nurturant function. Even in the Israeli Kibbutz with communal upbringing, it is the parents who dominate in this area....

In summation then, following is the universal definition of the family institution: *The family institution is a small kinship structured group with the key function of nurturant socialization of the newborn.*...

# EVIDENCE ON REVISED CONCEPTION

The evidence to be examined here relates to the question of whether the definition proposed actually fits all human family institutions. Three types of evidence are relevant to test the universality of the proposed definition of the family. The first source of evidence comes from a cross-cultural examination such as that of this article. All of the cultures that were discussed were fulfilling the proposed functional prerequisite of nurturant socialization, and they all had some sort of small kinship group structure to accomplish nurturant socialization. The author also examined numerous reports on other cultures and found no exception to the proposed definition. Of course, other functions of these family groups were present in all instances, but no other specific universally present functions appeared. However, the author hesitates to say that these data confirm his position because it is quite possible that such a cross-cultural examination will reveal some function or structure to be universally *present* but still not universally *required*. Rather, it could merely be universally present by chance or because it is difficult but not impossible to do away with. . . .

One type of evidence that is relevant concerns the effect of maternal separation or institutional upbringing on human infants. To afford a precise test, we should look for a situation in which nurturant socialization was quite low or absent. Although the Kibbutzim have institutional upbringing, the Kibbutz parents and children are very much emotionally attached to each other. In fact, both the mother and father have expressive roles in the Kibbutz family, and there is a strong emphasis on parent-child relations of a nurturant sort in the few hours a day the family is together.

A better place to look would be at studies of children who were raised in formal institutions or who were in other ways separated from their mothers. Leon J. Yarrow has recently published an excellent summary of over one hundred such studies.[23] For over 50 years now, there have been reports supporting the view that maternal separation has deleterious effects on the child. The first such reports came from pediatricians pointing out physical and psychological deterioration in hospitalized infants. In 1951, Bowlby reviewed the literature in this area for the World Health Organization and arrived at similar conclusions.[24] More recent and careful studies have made us aware of the importance of distinguishing the effects of maternal separation from the effects of institutionalization. Certainly the type of institutional care afforded the child is quite important. Further, the previous relation of the child with the mother before institutionalization and the age of the child are important variables. In addition, one must look at the length of time separation endured and whether there were reunions with the mother at a later date. Yarrow's view is that while there is this tendency toward disturbance in mother separation, the occurrence can best be understood when we learn more about the precise conditions under which it occurs and cease to think of it as inevitable under any conditions. In this regard, recent evidence shows that children separated from mothers with whom they had poor relationships displayed less disturbance than other children. Further, infants who were provided with adequate mother-substitutes of a personal sort showed much less severe reactions. In line with the findings on the Kibbutz, children who were in an all-day nursery gave no evidence of serious disturbance.

Many studies in the area of institutionalization show the importance of the structural characteristics of the institutional environment. When care is impersonal and inadequate, there is evidence of language retardation, impairment of motor functions, and limited emotional responses toward other people and objects.[25] Interestingly, the same types of characteristics are found among children living in deprived family environments.[26] One of the key factors in avoiding such negative results is the presence of a stable mother-figure in the institution for the child. Individualized care and attention seem to be capable of reversing or preventing the impairments mentioned. Without such care, there is evidence that ability to form close interpersonal relations later in life is greatly weakened.[27] ...

## SUMMARY AND CONCLUSIONS

A check of several cultures revealed that the four nuclear family functions that Murdock states are universally present were often missing. The nuclear family itself seems either absent or unimportant in some cultures. An alternate definition of the family in terms of one functional prerequisite of human society and in terms of a broad structural prerequisite was put forth. The family was defined as a small kinship structured group with the key function of nurturant socialization of the newborn. The nurturant function directly supports the personality system and enables the individual to become a contributing member of society. Thus, by making adult role performance possible, nurturant socialization becomes a functional prerequisite of society.

... It is theoretically possible that a society could bring up its entire newborn population in a formal institutional setting and give them nurturance through mechanical devices that would reassure the child, afford contact, and perhaps even verbally respond to the child. In such a case, the family as defined here would cease to exist, and an alternate structure for fulfilling the functional requirement of nurturant socialization would be established. Although it is dubious whether humans could ever tolerate or achieve such a means of bringing up their children, this logical possibility must be recognized. In fact, since the evidence is not conclusive, one would also have to say that it is possible that a society could bring up its offspring without nurturance, and in such a case also, the family institution as defined here would cease to exist. The author has argued against this possibility by contending that nurturance of the newborn is a functional prerequisite of human society and therefore could never be done away with. However, despite a strong conviction to the contrary, he must also admit that this position may be in error and that it is possible that the family as defined here is not a universally required institution. There are those, like Barrington Moore, Jr., who feel that it is largely a middle-class sentimentality that makes social scientists believe that the family is universal.[28] It is certainly crucial to test further the universality of both the structural and functional parts of this definition and their interrelation.

The definition proposed seems to fit the existing data somewhat more closely than Murdock's definition. It also has the advantage of simplicity. It affords one a definition that can be used in comparative studies of human society. Further, it helps make one aware of the possibilities of change in a society or an institution if we know which functions and structures can or cannot be done away with. In this way, we come closer to the knowledge of what Goldenweiser called the "limited possibilities" of human society.[29] If nurturance in kin groups is a functional and structural prerequisite of society, we have deepened our knowledge of the nature of human society for we can see how, despite our constant warfare with each other, our conflicts and internal strife, each human society persists only so long as it meets the minimal nurturant requirements of its new members. This is not to deny the functions of social conflict that Coser and others have pointed out, but merely to assert the importance of nurturance.[30]

## NOTES

1. George P. Murdock, *Social Structure,* New York: Macmillan, 1949.
2. Marion J. Levy, Jr. and L. A. Fallers, "The Family: Some Comparative Considerations," *American Anthropologist,* 61 (August 1959), pp. 647–651.
3. David F. Aberle *et al.,* "The Functional Prerequisites of a Society," *Ethics,* 60 (January 1950), pp. 100–111.
4. *Ibid.*
5. Murdock, *op. cit.,* p. 3.
6. For a brief account of the Nayer, see: E. Kathleen Gough, "Is the Family Universal: The Nayer Case," pp. 76–92 in *A Modern Introduction to the Family, op. cit.* It is interesting to note that Bell and Vogel, in their preface to Gough's article on the Nayer, contend that she supports Murdock's position on the universality of the nuclear family. In point of fact, Gough on page 84 rejects Murdock and actually deals primarily with the marital and not the family institution. See also: *Matrilineal Kinship,* ed. by David M. Schneider and Kathleen Gough, Berkeley: U. of California Press, 1961, Chaps. 6 and 7. A. R. Radcliffe-Brown was one of the first to note that the Nayer lacked the nuclear family. See his: *African Systems of Kinship and Marriage,* New York: Oxford U. Press, 1959, p. 73.
7. Harold H. Driver, *Indians of North America,* Chicago: U. of Chicago Press, 1961, pp. 291–292.
8. Melford E. Spiro, *Kibbutz: Venture in Utopia,* Cambridge, Mass.: Harvard U. Press, 1956; and Melford E. Spiro, *Children of the Kibbutz,* Cambridge, Mass.: Harvard U. Press, 1958.
9. Bronislaw Malinowski, *The Sexual Life of Savages in North-Western Melanesia,* New York: Harvest Books, 1929.
10. Nicholas S. Timasheff, "The Attempt to Abolish the Family in Russia," pp. 55–63 in Bell and Vogel, *op. cit.*
11. Levy and Fallers, *op. cit.*
12. Robert K. Merton, *Social Theory and Social Structure,* Glencoe, Ill.: Free Press, 1957, p. 32.

13. Zelditch attempted to see if the husband-wife roles would be differentiated in the same way in all cultures, with males being instrumental and females expressive. He found general support, but some exceptions were noted, particularly in societies wherein the nuclear family was embedded in a larger kinship system. Morris Zelditch, Jr., "Role Differentiation in the Nuclear Family: A Comparative Study," in Parsons and Bales, *op. cit*. The Kibbutz would represent another exception since both mother and father play expressive roles in relation to their offspring.
14. Aldous Huxley, *Brave New World,* New York: Harper & Bros., 1950.
15. See: *Six Cultures: Studies in Child Rearing,* ed. by Beatrice B. Whiting, New York: John Wiley, 1963. Margaret Mead reports exchange of children in *Coming of Age in Samoa,* New York: Mentor Books, 1949. Similar customs in Puerto Rico are reported in David Landy, *Tropical Childhood,* Chapel Hill: U. of North Carolina Press, 1959.
16. Robert Winch, in his recent textbook, defines the family as a nuclear family with the basic function of "the replacement of dying members." In line with the present author's arguments, it seems that the actual biological production of infants can be removed from the family. In fact, Winch agrees that the Nayar lack the family as he defined it because they lack a permanent father role in the nuclear family. See: *The Modern Family,* New York: Holt, 1963, pp. 16, 31, and 750.
17. William N. Stephens, *The Family in Cross Cultural Perspective,* New York: Holt, Rinehart & Winston, 1963, p. 357. Stephens discusses the universality of the family in this book but does not take a definite position on the issue. See Chapter 1.
18. Zelditch, *op. cit.,* pp. 307–353.
19. The key importance of primary groups was long ago pointed out by Charles Horton Cooley, *Social Organization,* New York: Scribners, 1929.
20. The structural definition is similar to Levy and Fallers, *op. cit.*
21. Radcliffe-Brown, *op. cit.*
22. Parsons, *op. cit.*
23. Leon J. Yarrow, "Separation from Parents During Early Childhood," pp. 89–136 in *Review of Child Development,* ed. by Martin L. Hoffman and Lois W. Hoffman, New York: Russell Sage Foundation, 1964, Vol. 1.
24. John Bowlby, *Maternal Care and Mental Health,* Geneva: World Health Organization, 1951.
25. Yarrow, *op. cit.,* p. 100.
26. *Ibid.,* p. 101–102.
27. *Ibid.,* p. 106.
28. Barrington Moore, Jr., *Political Power and Social Theory,* Cambridge, Mass.: Harvard U. Press, 1958, Chap. 5.
29. Alexander A. Goldenweiser, *History, Psychology, and Culture,* New York: Alfred A. Knopf, 1933, esp. pp. 45–49.
30. Lewis Coser, *The Functions of Social Conflict,* Glencoe, Ill.: Free Press, 1956.

CHAPTER 2 # Theoretical Approaches to the Study of the Family

### 2.1 CARLFRED BRODERICK AND JAMES SMITH

# The General Systems Approach to the Family

Perhaps no other theoretical orientation has had as profound an impact on the marriage and family discipline as general systems theory. This theory originated in the natural sciences, but in the 1960s social scientists began to apply its tenets to human systems, such as the family. Family scholars readily embraced the theoretical approach, and much empirical research ensued.

This selection is from "The General Systems Approach to the Family," by Carlfred Broderick and James Smith, which was published in Wesley R. Burr et al.'s edited book *Contemporary Theories About the Family, vol. 2* (Free Press, 1979). It represents an attempt by Broderick and Smith to organize and apply systems concepts to describe the family system in a logical manner. Broderick, an educator, researcher, theorist, and therapist, has been a professor in the department of sociology at the University of California, Los Angeles, since 1971. Broderick has also been an associate professor at Pennsylvania State University. He has held many offices in national organizations related to the discipline of marriage and the family, and he has been a prolific contributor to the field. Many of his works have been translated from English into other languages.

**Key Concept:** family systems theory

# THE FEATURES OF A SYSTEM

The primary unit of analysis for a systems theorist is, of course, the system. Systems have been variously defined, but the most generic (and most often quoted) definition is Hall and Fagan's: "A system is a set of objects together with relationships between the objects and between their attributes" (1956).

Buck (1956) and others have criticized this definition as excluding nothing and therefore as giving no information. Nonetheless, it may serve as a place to begin.

### The Definition of Boundaries

Implicit in the Hall and Fagan definition is the existence of a boundary that delineates the elements belonging to the system and those belonging to its environment. As a general rule, it makes sense to select a boundary such that the units inside the system have a higher level of interaction among themselves than with units outside the system. In such living systems as the family, however, boundaries are more than arbitrarily chosen and passively observed lines of demarcation. In their classic study of family systems Kantor and Lehr (1975) refer to the energy devoted to the process of boundary maintenance (a process they label "bounding"). Through bounding, external elements seen as hostile to system goals and policies are actively filtered out, while those seen as beneficial to the pursuit of system goals and policies may be actively sought out and incorporated. Similarly, members may be discouraged or encouraged in their outside contacts and in extreme cases may be expelled from the system....

Once the boundaries have been identified and the system set off from its surrounding environment, it is possible to classify each particular system on a continuum from *open* to *closed*, based on the permeability of its boundaries. Families may be characterized as more open if members have a relatively high level of exchange with the outside environment and more closed if they keep more to themselves. A considerable body of research has demonstrated that a family's degree of openness is a structural variable of both theoretical and practical significance....

### The Designation of Units

In applying Hall and Fagan's definition of a system to the family, the second task is to identify the "objects" that make up the system. Scholars have taken two different approaches to this problem. The more obvious is to designate each member as a unit. When this approach is taken, it immediately calls attention to the fact that families do not maintain a constant membership over time.

In a single day it would not be unusual for every single member to leave the company of other members for a period of hours as they pursue their various activities. The children leave for school or to play with friends. The husband and often the wife leave for work. Various members leave to pursue recreational activities or do errands, and each returns on his or her own time schedule. Thus from hour to hour the number of family members who are available to interact with each other shifts dramatically.

If a broader temporal perspective is chosen, with years rather than hours as the units, the same fluidity of membership can be observed. Family ranks are swollen with the birth or adoption of children, with relatives moving in, with reconciliation after a separation or remarriage after a divorce, with the return of a member after a long period away at school or at war or at prison or in the hospital. Similarly the family may shrink through death, separation, desertion, or the subtraction of children who grow up and leave home....

Using this approach, it is clear that one of the main dimensions along which families vary is their size. Bossard and Boll (1956) and others have suggested that large family systems are structurally so different from small family systems that they should be considered separately in making any generalizations about how family systems operate. Implicit also in this model of fluctuating membership is the importance of categorizing families according to how flexible or rigid their structure is, that is, how smoothly they are able to adjust to all of the entrances and exits across family boundaries....

Whatever the particulars, all such approaches attempt to avoid the analytic challenges posed by shifting memberships. Members may come and go as they please without much disturbing the system of roles or player parts. The advantage of this strategy is that it permits analysis of a wide variety of families within a common framework. Its disadvantage, of course, is precisely its insensitivity to the process of expansion and contraction that is one of the central issues of families as viewed from the member-as-unit perspective.

**The Specification of Relationships**

Having discussed boundaries and the designation of the units in the family system, Hall and Fagan's definition still requires us to address the issue of specifying the nature of the relationships among the units. This takes us to the very heart of systems theory.

When a stimulus from the environment enters a system it is called *input*. When the system emits any response back into the environment it is called *output*. The central concern of systems theory is what happens to the input as it is processed by the system on its way to becoming an output. The process of transformation as the stimulus passes through the system is governed by what systems theorists call (reasonably enough) *rules of transformation*. Family theorists who take a systems perspective (such as Jackson, 1967) are more likely to refer simply to *family rules*. These rules, in effect, prescribe the familial response to any of a very wide range of possible inputs.

It is not reasonable to expect, however, that every family should have in its repertoire a rule to cover every possible situation. System theorists are keenly interested in the response of a system to this type of challenge. When a family finds itself facing a novel and unanticipated situation for which it lacks a ready response, it is said in systems jargon to lack the *requisite variety* to process the input appropriately. In such circumstances a family, depending upon its internal structure, may simply be immobilized or even break down altogether, or on the other hand it may marshal its resources to innovate a new response, suitable to the occasion. This generation of a new rule of transformation is called *morphogenesis*, a highly important concept which will occupy our attention in greater detail below.

A common response to a new stimulus under conditions of insufficient variety is to fall back on a stock residual response (such as punting in football when you don't know what else to do). Studies of child abuse suggest that some such mechanism may be involved in these unhappy cases. The parents perceive the child as engaging in some behavior that they do not know how to deal with. Lacking the requisite variety of rules to deal with the problem appropriately, they resort to the only fallback response in their repertoire, violence.

Systems theorists are concerned with family rules at several levels. In fact, the concept that levels of rules may exist in a kind of hierarchy is one of the unique contributions of the systems perspective.

## HIERARCHIES OF RULES

… In the following pages we shall focus primarily at the level of the family as the system with members as units and community as environment. The family could as well be viewed as an undifferentiated unit in a larger social system or as the environment for individuals considered as systems. It should be clear from the start then that our choice of levels is arbitrary and that studying the rules of transformation at higher or lower levels of the strata hierarchy might be equally useful.

### Temporal/Logical Hierarchies

Often the rules of transformation of a system are quite complex and involve whole sequences of rules, subrules, and sub-subrules. The temporal and logical sequences of steps by which these complex rules may be applied to any given input constitute a hierarchy of rules, which we have labeled temporal/logical.

In the simplest case there is only a temporal hierarchy, a simple sequence of steps that must occur in a given order to produce the output. For example, the newspaper may be routinely taken in and divided or circulated among members in a prescribed fashion, then picked up by the twelve-year-old son and put in a pile in the garage to be turned in to the scout troop as a part of a commitment to recycling. The routine does not vary from day to day. There are no decision points to deal with.

In most cases rules are more complex than that, of course. There may be many points at which decisions must be made as to the direction in which the process will proceed. Rules at this point take the form: If A then X, but if not A then Z. The hierarchies of rules can get very complex in these cases. Many readers will recognize that computer programs are neither more nor less than the spelling out of logical and temporal hierarchies of rules. Systems theorists commonly use computer programs to attempt to simulate the rules of real systems. They feel they have succeeded if they can get the computer to generate the same outputs as the living system generates from a specified set of inputs. Such simulations have played an important part in advancing the understanding of economic and ecological systems....

### Hierarchies of Feedback and Control

A[n]... even more intriguing hierarchical arrangement of rules can be observed in the structure of feedback and control within systems. A system may be characterized as having feedback if it has the ability to perceive its own output at one point as input at some subsequent point. As we shall see in detail below, a system's capability to monitor its own progress toward a set goal, to correct and to elaborate its response, and even to change its goals depends upon the complexity of its feedback structure. A system without such a capability is intrinsically static.

*Level 1: Simple Feedback.* At the simplest level, feedback consists of a circular process by which an output is subsequently processed as an input. The result of this loop depends upon the particular rules of transformation interior to the system. It could generate an escalating spiral of amplification of the original input. When this occurs it is called a *positive* or *deviation amplifying* feedback loop. For example, suppose a family were subjected to some external stress which, according to the rules of transformation in the family, resulted in internal dissension. This output may very well feed back into the system as further stress, which evokes more dissension, and so forth, in an escalating spiral of conflict. Were this the only mechanism at work, there would be no way to dampen the spiral until the system itself was destroyed.

A *negative* or *deviation dampening* feedback loop is one in which the rules of transformation tend to dampen any variation in initial input. In this case an externally induced crisis might bring the family closer together, which in turn reduces the crisis....

All intrafamily power struggles may be thought of as examples of this type of feedback. Watzlawick, Beavin, and Jackson (1967) differentiate *symmetrical* power struggles of the attack—counter attack—etc. variety and *complementary* power struggles of the attack—resist—etc. variety. Both constitute positive feedback loops and if left unchecked by any higher control mechanism will escalate until the system itself is damaged.

Inherent in such models of family interaction is the assumption that the members react reflexively to each other, their responses unmediated by considerations of family goals or policies. There is evidence that some families actually do interact at this level (Broderick, 1975, 1977). Such families may be viewed as seriously deficient in their structure, and this style of interaction is associated with marital instability and negative child outcomes.

*Level 2: Cybernetic Control.* At least one additional level of complexity in feedback structure appears to be necessary for stable system operation. This second level is sometimes referred to as the level of cybernetic control. The output from the system feeds back to a monitoring unit. There it is compared to some criterion such as a family standard, goal, or policy, and an adjustment is made in the system intended to correct any deviation from that criterion. The key is in the word "intended." At Level 1 a negative feedback loop has the effect of correcting a response, but no one and nothing is in charge of seeing to it that a given criterion is met. At Level 2 the system can at least choose between alternative rules of transformation that are in the system repertory. For example, parents may respond to their daughter's return from a date positively or negatively depending on whether she conformed to family policy in the time she arrived, the condition she was in, and so forth. These family policies may be called meta-rules....

Dean Black (1971) has developed another interesting variation on the basic Level-2 feedback model which demonstrates the flexibility of this approach. He took as his goal explaining the fluctuations in marital morale over the family life cycle using a systems approach. In our previous examples the basic structural feature of the model was a positive feedback loop between the partners. Runaway escalation was subject to control by the partners as they compared their own potential responses with some set of values, policies, or beliefs about the costs of each response to them. In Black's model the potential runaway feedback loop is between one partner (the husband) and another element in his environment (his job). The control unit is the other partner (the wife). However,... the control unit is also subject to inputs from the environment and must process these as well as inputs from the other elements in the system.... Black posits a rule of transformation in the business system that rewards employees for giving priority to their jobs and investing time in them. This feeds into a rule of transformation in the husband. The rule is to respond to rewards as the laws of operant conditioning suggest he should and to invest more and more time, energy, and priority in his work. In this model the wife's role is to be the control subsystem responding to her husband's tendency to invest more and more in his occupation (and hence less and less in his marriage) by countering with corrective action calculated to maintain his involvement in the marriage. As long as she functions in this way, her husband balances his investments between his work and his marriage. When an input from outside the marital system (namely a child) intrudes upon the wife by placing unnegotiable demands upon her, this immobilizes her as an agent of control, and the husband–job spiral is unrestrained until the children grow up a little. This model makes traditional, sex-linked role assumptions, which may offend the contemporary eye. It is an empirical question, however, as to whether it could explain adequately the observed variation in marital morale over the life cycle.

Level-2 control, by its very nature, can only switch from one set of available rules of transformation to another. At this level a system cannot learn or innovate. As noted, if it lacks a response appropriate to the input we say it lacks requisite variety; that is, it does not have an adequate variety of rules of transformation to accommodate all of the variety of inputs it is receiving.

For example, a parent may have a basic rule of transformation that dictates that a child's obedience should be rewarded and his or her disobedience punished. But suppose a child attempts suicide, becomes an addict, has a psychotic break, or runs away and doesn't come back. Many parents in those situations are immobilized because they have no rule in their repertory for processing this unprecedented behavior. It is at such points that families seek ways to increase their variety of rules for response. This shift to altogether new rules of transformation (as contrasted to simply switching from one to another as circumstances dictate) is called *morphogenesis* in the systems literature and *meta-change* or Level-2 change in the family process literature (Watzlawick *et al.*, 1974). In our system it constitutes the third level of feedback structure.

*Level 3: Morphogenesis.* From what has been said it will be clear that, just as Level-2 feedback was based upon an evaluation of Level-1 output, so Level-3 feedback is based on an evaluation of Level-2 output. A family comes to perceive that its usual range of corrective responses to unacceptable family outputs is not working. When this becomes clear, family members may react in different ways. Some will talk to friends, bartenders, hairdressers, and teachers to try to find alternative responses. Some take courses, enroll in workshops, read books, or seek professional counseling. This latter group has attracted the most attention from social scientists, because social scientists give courses, run workshops, write books, and do counseling. Most of the writing on change at this level is about therapeutically induced change.

Yet it could be argued that in some circumstances divorce, attempted suicide, mental illness, psychosomatic illness, desertion, adultery, and intrafamilial murder might all be considered innovative responses to inputs for which a family lacks any adequate response in the present repertory. The crucial issue is not the ethical attractiveness of the new response but that it is new—an innovative effort to set the family back upon a course toward its goals in the face of repeated failures while using customary approaches.

*Level-4 Feedback: Reorientation or Conversion.* At Levels 2 and 3 the system monitors its progress toward its goals. At Level 2 it selects from among its preprogrammed options those rules of transformation that seem to produce the best response (that is, the response that most closely approximates the criterion). At Level 3, failure to achieve an adequate approximation leads to changes in the very structure of the system, as old rules of transformation are abandoned and new rules forged. But in neither case are the fundamental goals of the system challenged. Families are, however, capable of this order of change.

Little has been done to study dramatic reorientations such as occurs when a black Baptist family becomes Muslim or a Protestant family converts to Judaism or members of a Catholic family become Jehovah's Witnesses. Religious conversions are not the only system reorientations that have these qualities. Secular movements such as unions, scouting, and peace movements can also capture families. The investigation of these change phenomena requires before-and-after studies, and so is seldom attempted. Yet even post hoc analyses of these phenomena might shed light on the nature of family systems and the circumstances and preconditions that lead to this highest order of change. According to some systems theorists it is one of the characteristics of hierarchies that the highest levels are more difficult to capture, measure, and understand.

# APPLICATIONS OF THE SYSTEMS PERSPECTIVE...

**Courtship: The Founding of a Family System**

The problem of how a man and woman pass from the status of unconnected stranger to tightly interconnected units in a relatively closed marital and familial system has intrigued students of courtship for decades.

As in the formation of any other system at least three issues have to be addressed: (1) How do the units come initially to have a higher rate of interaction with each other than with other units in the new environment; (2) how are boundaries set up and maintained around this fledging unit; and (3) how is the internal structure (rules of transformation, hierarchies of control, etc.) established and elaborated? In order for this inquiry to be profitable it must be demonstrated not only that these questions help one to organize and interpret much of the work on courtship process but also that it raises new and important questions as a theoretical perspective....

*Establishing Boundaries.* In our culture even the most preliminary and tentative form of male–female interaction, the date, is concerned with boundaries, albeit ephemeral ones. A date is, among other things, an agreement to become a boundary-maintaining unit for a few hours. It is bad form to pay too much attention to anyone but your date, and abandoning a date or coming home with another person is considered rude and insulting. Reciprocally, others are expected to observe the boundary and refrain from attempting to cut in on another person's partner. On the other hand it is equally clear that, when the date is over, so is the claim.

If a couple moves from casual, intermittant dating to seeing each other regularly, both they and others, explicitly or implicitly, begin to behave as though the couple had established a boundary that operates between dates as well. To some extent this "just happens" without the necessity of real decision making; that is, from a systems perspective, the boundaries grow stronger through a simple Level-1 positive feedback loop. Partly, this process is maintained by the members of the pair employing cybernetic or Level-2 mechanisms. One partner may object that the other is taking too much for granted or alternatively complain that the person is "cheating" on the relationship. This brings us to the third issue that must be dealt with in the process of systems formation.

*The Formation and Elaboration of Internal Structure.* The formation of internal structure in the courtship process has remained unstudied, although Bolton (1961) alludes to it. Therefore the series of steps involved in the evolution of couple policies and rules can only be guessed.

Systems theory itself suggests that the process of courtship might be viewed as the elaboration of hierarchical feedback structure. The initial stages of system development might very well take place at a simple circular feedback level of organization. That is, internalized role behavior and external circumstances might bring a couple together and escalate them into a primitive system without much planning, monitoring, or evaluating against criteria.

Early on, however (and with many individuals from the very beginning), the couple must develop a Level-2 cybernetic system capable of monitoring its own behavior, establishing and mobilizing joint efforts in pursuit of joint goals (however transitory), and so forth. Finally, however, unless they find themselves moved along toward marriage in a more or less mindless fashion, they need also to develop morphogenic capabilities to shift from one Level-2 state to another and to generate new responses in pursuit of pair goals. To the extent that the shift from the single to the married state involves a major reorientation in basic goals and life-style for one or the other, it might even be that Level-4 system feedback would be required to make the change. In the majority of cases, however, it could be argued that the sequence of steps is too well preprogrammed to require any major reorientation in shifting from one status to another. In any case, it can be seen that courtship provides an exceptionally good example of the relevance of the systems model to social phenomena....

*Sequential Patterns of Interaction.* Much of life can be conceptualized as a series of events related to each other in complex temporal patterns. Almost always we observe the processes of feedback at work in our everyday experiences. Yet social scientists have not been conceptually or technically equipped to deal with these phenomena. Developmental theory is a partial exception. Yet in our view that approach handles the escalation (or dampening) of courtship spirals, of family crisis, and of conflict descriptively and awkwardly, lacking adequate conceptual tools. In this, family scholars are far behind neighboring disciplines, such as economics and international relations, where systems approaches have been utilized profitably for decades. The concepts of feedback loops, temporal hierarchies, escalation, and dampening are well understood in these contexts....

*Boundary Maintenance.* The function of maintaining systems boundaries has received attention from several perspectives, but in no other framework does it play the crucial role that it does in system analysis. Particularly in the case of family systems, the evidence is convincing that whether boundaries are relatively open or closed is a crucial determinant of systems effectiveness. At a more sophisticated level, whether they are competent to filter in external inputs in a manner healthy to the system appears to be a crucial issue. Therapists who work at the boundary of family systems have paid more attention to this issue than others, but family scholars are getting into the matter....

Although systems theory, like other theories, still has many areas in which work must be done, the chief problem is not with the theory but with the application. The fact is that we know very little about the family as a system. Its system parameters have certainly not been specified and calibrated (let alone measured) in a degree to even approximate the level of precision required by much of the systems literature. We have done many studies on family power but understand little about the process of control in families. With the exception of the work by Kantor and Lehr and a few others, we have done almost no work on the process of boundary maintenance or on the rules of transformation that convert family inputs into family outputs. We have not mapped the interior structure of families in any detail. It is not possible to get systems answers unless we ask systems questions.

# REFERENCES

BLACK, K. D. **1971** "A systems approach to the development of the marital relationship." Unpublished Doctoral Dissertation, Pennsylvania State University.

BOLTON, C. D. **1961** "Mate selection as the development of a relationship." *Marriage and Family Living,* 23: 234–240.

BOSSARD, J. H. S. AND E. S. BOLL **1956** *The Large Family System.* Philadelphia: University of Pennsylvania Press.

BRODERICK, C. B. **1975** "Power in the government of families." In R. E. Cromwell and D. H. Olson (eds.), *Power in Families.* New York: Sage Publications.

BRODERICK, C. B. **1977** "Fathers." *The Family Coordinator* 26: 269–275.

BUCK, R. C. **1956** "On the logic of general behavior systems theory." In H. Feige and M. Seriven (eds.), *Minnesota Studies in the Philosophy of Science,* Vol. I, *The Foundations of Science and the Concepts of Psychology and Psychoanalysis.* Minneapolis: University of Minnesota Press.

HALL, A. D. AND R. E. FAGAN **1956** "Definition of systems." Revised introductory chapter of *Systems Engineering.* New York: Bell Telephone Laboratories. Reprinted from *General Systems* 1: 18–28.

JACKSON, D. D. **1967** "The individual and the larger contexts." *Family Process* 6: 139–47.

KANTOR, D. AND LEHR, W. **1975** *Inside the Family.* San Francisco: Jossey-Bass.

WATZLAWICK, P.; J. BEAVIN AND D. JACKSON **1967** *Pragmatics of Human Communication.* New York: Norton.

WATZLAWICK, P.; J. H. WEAKLAND AND R. FISCH **1974** *Change.* New York: Norton.

## 2.2 DAVID H. OLSON, DOUGLAS H. SPRENKLE, AND CANDYCE S. RUSSELL

# Circumplex Model of Marital and Family Systems

The circumplex model of marital and family systems is a direct outgrowth of the tremendous popularity of the application of general systems theory to the scientific study of the family. The circumplex model, developed by David H. Olson, has become a widely used family system model. Hundreds of research studies have utilized the model since it was first introduced. Also, the vast majority of courses that examine family theory introduce students to this model to teach them to think systemically about families. The following selection is from a paper about this model by Olson, Douglas H. Sprenkle, and Candyce S. Russell entitled "Circumplex Model of Marital and Family Systems: I. Cohesion and Adaptabililty Dimensions, Family Types, and Clinical Applications," *Family Process* (April 1979).

Olson is a professor of family social science at the University of Minnesota in St. Paul. Sprenkle was a professor of child development and family studies at Perdue University when this article was written. Russell was a professor of family and child development at Kansas State University at that time. Olson has received several national awards for his theory and research contributions to the field of marriage and the family. This selection introduces many of the basic tenets of the circumplex model and explains how it could be utilized in clinical settings.

**Key Concept:** family systems theory

## INTRODUCTION

In the last decade, a plethora of concepts has emerged describing marital and family dynamics. Many of these terms originated in the field of family therapy. While many of the concepts appear unrelated, most attempt to describe a circumscribed domain of marital and family interaction. General systems theory (von Bertalanffy, 1; Buckley, 3) has provided a central underlying base for many of these formulations. However, little attempt has been made to integrate these concepts conceptually or to place them within a systematic model.

The purpose of this paper is to delineate two aspects of marital and family behavior, *cohesion* and *adaptability,* that appear as underlying dimensions for the multitude of concepts in the family field. These two dimensions have emerged from an inductive conceptual clustering rather than from an empirical clustering based on factor analysis. Family cohesion and family adaptability are then organized into a circumplex model that, in turn, facilitates the identification of 16 types of marital and family systems. The 16 types will be described, and their clinical usefulness discussed. The ultimate purpose of the circumplex model is to facilitate bridging the gaps that often exist among theorists, researchers and practitioners (9)....

### Conceptual Definition and Significance of Family Cohesion

The definition of family cohesion used in this model has two components; *the emotional bonding members have with one another and the degree of individual autonomy a person experiences in the family system.* At the extreme of high family cohesion, *enmeshment,* there is an overidentification with the family that results in extreme bonding and limited individual autonomy. The low extreme, *disengagement,* is characterized by low bonding and high autonomy from the family. It is hypothesized that a *balanced* degree of family cohesion is the most conducive to effective family functioning and to optimum individual development....

Some specific variables that can be used to assess the degree of family cohesion are: *emotional bonding, independence, boundaries, coalitions, time, space, friends, decision-making,* and *interests* and *recreation....* It is hypothesized that when the levels of cohesion are balanced, there will be a more functional balance of the issues identified and the family will deal more effectively with situational stress and developmental change. Because of differences in cultural norms, it is possible for some families to operate at these extremes without problems. However, these extreme patterns are more problematic in the long run for most families who are acculturated to the norms in this society....

It is no historical accident that most of these recent concepts were developed by psychiatrists working with clinic families. These family therapists, working within a general systems orientation, have been primarily describing families of schizophrenics. While the originators of these concepts shared a common interest in family oriented treatment and a focus on families of schizophrenics, they each developed their own terminology—even when the professionals were working in the same town or, indeed, the same building. For example, the extreme of family togetherness was described by Wynne et al. (16) as "pseudo-mutuality," by Bowen (2) as "undifferentiated family ego mass," by Stierlin (15) as "binding," and by Reiss (11) as "consensus-sensitive families."...

Historically, Wynne et al. (16) were among the first to note that some families, particularly those with a schizophrenic, have a predominant concern with fitting together at the expense of developing personal identities. They described this process as *pseudo-mutuality;*

> In pseudo-mutuality the subjective tension aroused by divergence or independence of expectations, including the open affirmation of a sense of personal identity, is experienced as not merely disruption of that particular transaction but as possibly demolishing the entire relation. [16, 207]

Stierlin (15) clarified the struggle to balance separateness and togetherness in families by identifying two opposing forces, centripetal and centrifugal. High family cohesion can be viewed as *centripetal force* pulling family members toward one another into an intellectual and emotional "oneness." This cohesiveness is contrasted with the *centrifugal force,* which pulls family members away from the family system. He identifies three transactional modes that characterize parent-adolescent relationships. Two of these modes (binding and delegating) are centripetal and the third (expelling) is centrifugal. These modes are generally functional for families but become dysfunctional when they are inappropriately timed or excessively intense so that only one extreme predominates. He proposes, in essence, that a family system operates most effectively when these two opposing forces operate in a more or less balanced manner.

Considerable interest in extremely high family cohesion continues, as witnessed by recent articles in the literature (Schaffer, 13; Hoffman, 4; Karpel, 5; Klugman, 6). Hoffman describes the dysfunctional nature of enmeshed or too richly cross-joined family systems. Minuchin calls attention to the point, often overlooked, that dyadic groupings have difficulty functioning in enmeshed family systems because of interference from another (third or fourth) party: "Dyadic transactions rarely occurred. They became triadic or group transactions that promoted a sense of vagueness and confusion in all family members" (7, p. 248).... [W]eak family coalitions or parent-child coalitions characterize disengaged or enmeshed family systems, respectively. A strong marital coalition correlates with balanced family cohesion....

Karpel (5) has recently proposed a model that describes how individuals can deal with the duality of distance (the "I") and relation (the "We") and how they would vary on the stages of maturity (immature, transitional, and mature). In the immature stage, individuals deal with distance by being unrelated or with relation by pure fusion. Only in the mature stage can individuals maintain both relation (through dialogue) and distance (through individuation). The importance of this "I" versus "We" balance in mature relationships is emphasized in that individuation and dialogue facilitate each other.

... [T]he conceptual review of the literature from various fields demonstrates that the cohesion dimension is an important aspect of both ad hoc and family groups. The relevance of the dimension to several social science disciplines provides a type of cross-validation of its salience and significance. The most recent interest in the dimension has come, however, from family therapists who have developed numerous concepts that relate primarily to the extreme ends of the dimension. Cohesion, therefore, is one of the two central dimensions for developing the circumplex model of marital and family systems....

## Conceptual Definition and Significance of Family Adaptability

The definition of adaptability used in this paper is: *the ability of a marital/family system to change its power structure, role relationships, and relationship rules in response to situational and developmental stress.* The assumption is that an adaptive system requires balancing both morphogenesis (change) and morphostasis (stability).

The specific variables that are of interest in terms of this dimension are: *family power structure* (assertiveness and control) *negotiation styles, role relationships* and *relationship rules,* and *feedback* (positive and negative)....

Basically, the most viable family systems are those in the two central levels of the adaptability dimension. It is hypothesized that when there is a more free-flowing *balance* between morphogenesis and morphostasis, there will be a mutually assertive style of communicating; equalitarian leadership; successful negotiation; positive and negative feedback loops; role sharing and role-making; and rule-making, with few implicit rules and more explicit rules. Conversely, more dysfunctional family systems will fall at either extreme of these variables....

## Sixteen Types of Marital and Family Systems

The circumplex model proposed in this paper was intuitively derived and has been empirically validated in two separate studies by Russell (12) and Sprenkle and Olson (14). The types were developed by classifying the two dimensions into four levels: very low, low to moderate, moderate to high, and very high. This 4x4 matrix forms 16 cells, each of which identifies one possible type (see Figure 1).

In labeling these types we tried to avoid value-laden terminology, i.e., clinical terms or clinical types of families (schizophrenic, delinquent, neurotic). The two descriptive terms for each type are related to the level of adaptability and cohesion, respectively. The terms are intended to describe the underlying dynamics of a marital or family system.

Although it is empirically and conceptually possible that all 16 types realistically describe some couples and families, it is assumed that the four central and four extreme types are the most common. It is assumed that the other eight types are *dynamically* less frequent because if a couple or family is extreme on one dimension, they will also tend to be extreme on the other dimension.

Figure 1 identifies the 16 types in the circumplex model. The four types in the central area reflect balanced levels of both adaptability and cohesion and are seen as most functional to individual and family development. The four extreme types reflect very high or low levels of adaptability and cohesion and are seen as most dysfunctional to individual and family development.

The central area, which represents moderate cohesion and adaptability, is seen as most functional and indicates a balance on both dimensions....

Although it is generally assumed that the central area of the model is most functional to individual and family development over time, it is possible that extreme family types can be functional at some times for families. For example, extreme cohesion in a family might be functional in the short run after they have experienced a crisis—such as the loss of a family member—or after a significant addition—such as the birth of a child. However, if this pattern of relating becomes the predominant style across the various stages of the family life cycle, it could become problematic for one or more of the family members. For example, the extreme family type of being *rigidly enmeshed* might be functional for taking care of an infant, but it would be less functional when the child becomes an adolescent....

**Four Balanced Types: Open Systems**

Based on the design of the model and the scaling of the dimensions, the four types in the center circle (*flexible separateness, flexible connectedness, structured connectedness,* and *structured separateness*) represent more functional marital and family systems. An open system is distinguished by the ability of individuals to *experience* and *balance* the extremes of being independent from and connected to their families. Individual family members have the freedom to be more alone or connected to each other as they wish. However, they seldom remain at either extreme for long periods of time.

The model is *dynamic* in that it assumes that changes can occur in family types over time. Families are free to move in any direction that the situation, stage of the family life cycle, or socialization of family members may require. A retrospective look at a family known to one of the authors illustrates the dynamic nature of the model.

Steve and Sally were both raised in rather traditional homes. Three years after they were married, they became parents for the first time, and Sally resigned from her teaching job. Because of the dependency needs of their son and their own desire for mutual support in this transition period, they developed a moderately high, but not extreme, level of family cohesion. Also, their upbringing led them to be moderately low, but not rigid, on the adaptability dimension. They were comfortable with a rather traditional husband-dominant power structure and segregated role relationship, preferring the relative security of these established patterns to the ambiguities of continually negotiating them. Using the current model, we would classify their family type as *structurally connected,* an option that seemed to be satisfying to them at the time.

When Sally's and Steve's son became a teenager, Sally started pursuing a career, and both parents experienced a good deal of "consciousness raising" about sex roles through the media and through involvement in several growth groups. Because of their son's needs for more autonomy at this age, as well as the parents' separate career interests, they began operating at a lower level of cohesiveness, moving from being connected to being more separated.

Furthermore, the family power structure shifted from being husband-dominant to a more shared pattern. Sally exercises much more control in the relationship than previously, and the couple is struggling, almost on a weekly basis, to redefine the rules and role relationship that will govern their relationship. Although they occasionally yearn for the security of their earlier more structured relationship, both find excitement and challenge in this more flexible

**FIGURE 1**

*Sixteen Possible Types of Marital and Family Systems Derived from the Circumplex Model*

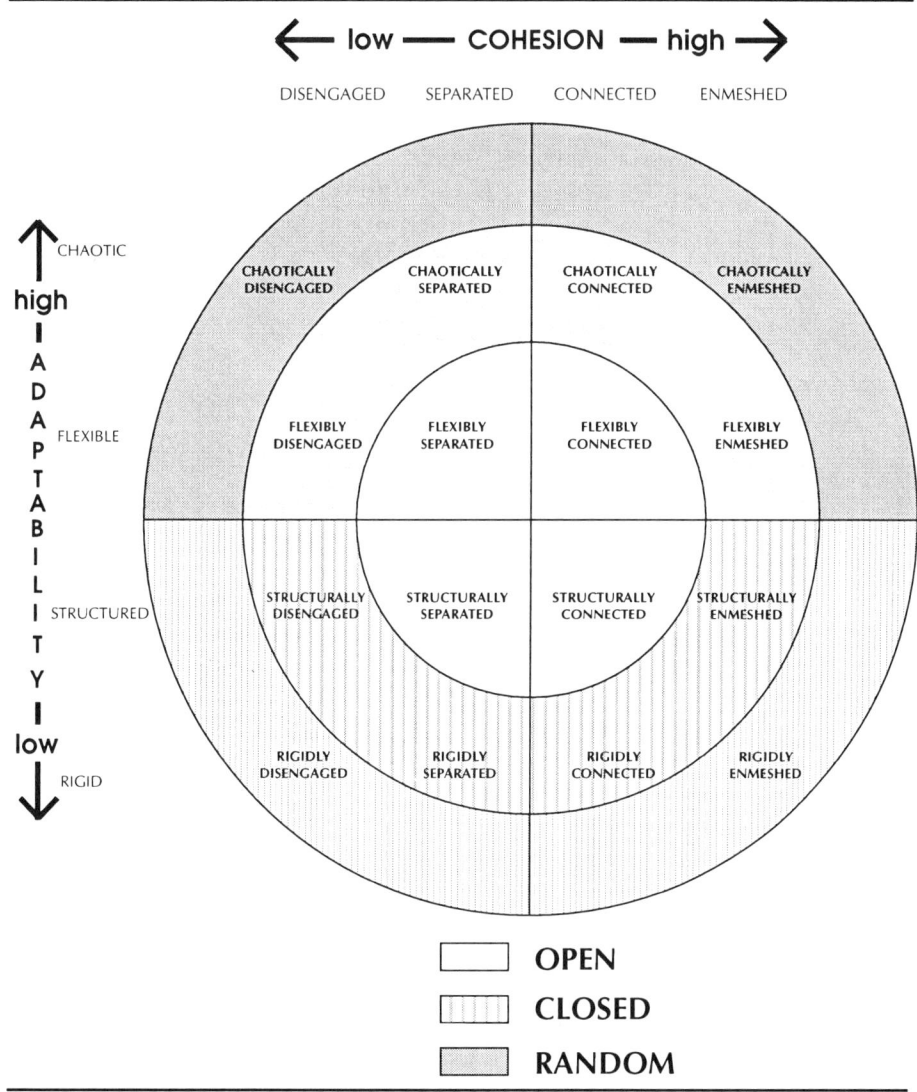

relationship style. In short, *flexibly separated* best describes their current family organizational pattern.

This brief case history illustrates the dynamic nature of the model, which allows for movement within reasonable limits. It also seeks to recognize diverse values and legitimize the diverse organizational ideals of families. None of the four types in the inner circle is designated as "the ideal" at any given stage of the family life cycle, but all are more functional than the extreme types.

**Four Extreme Types**

The four extreme types in the outer circle are seen as least functional to individual and family development: *chaotically disengaged, chaotically enmeshed, rigidly enmeshed,* and *rigidly disengaged.* Families in these categories can be described by the extremes of family cohesion and adaptability.

In defining these four extreme types, we believe that these behaviors are continuous with functional behavior but represent an exaggerated version of it. Even the pioneer family therapists were impressed with the fact that "normal" families displayed some of the same behavior, albeit limited, as the clinical families they were describing as dysfunctional. The current typology makes this connection explicit, i.e., *chaotically disengaged* is an exaggerated form of the *flexibly separated* type.

Second, we have endeavored to avoid developing a classification system for families based upon individual psychology. We have tried to go beyond the crude practice of using the symptoms of one family member to characterize a family, such as a "delinquent family" or a "schizophrenic family." Third, we tried to select terms with a less value-laden history than the types just mentioned.

Finally, we tried to create a classification system that might be useful to clinicians in determining treatment goals for a wide variety of clients. Many family categories or clinical labels, e.g., embroilment, extraordinary mutual involvement, have been of limited value to therapists since (a) the labels were designed to apply primarily to families with one specific difficulty (e.g., schizophrenia); (b) they are unidimensional, most frequently centering on the cohesiveness dimension alone; and (c) they assume a simple linear continuum from more of the property to less of the property, one end of the continuum representing functional behavior and the other dysfunctional.

There are a wide variety of ways in which extreme types of couples and families encounter problems. First, one family member may want more cohesion or adaptability than the other family member(s). For example, a common problem with divorcing couples is that one partner wants more closeness and the other more individual autonomy, i.e., freedom. They are really at opposite ends of the cohesion dimension. Often, as they struggle to maintain these extreme postures, they sometimes flip positions. This could be interpreted to mean that they are not satisfied with either extreme all the time but really want to have both closeness and freedom. The balance between having closeness at times and also having individual freedom is often what both want. The problem is working on finding the best balance for both of them in terms of what they want individually and what their partner can tolerate. Although couples have some difficulty knowing what they want, they have more difficulty learning how to achieve these goals in their relationship. Napier (8) describes in greater detail the struggle that divorcing couples have in dealing with their conflicting needs for closeness and separateness.

A second problem encountered by couples is that *both* partners are at the extreme on one or both dimensions. For example, if both partners are at the disengaged extreme, they are often afraid to be close. They rigidly try to maximize their autonomy. Couples who are emotionally enmeshed with each other are often afraid of developing their own autonomy because it might mean losing the approval and love of their partner. Both of these couples need to experience and learn that it is possible to have both closeness and autonomy and that these are not mutually exclusive experiences....

### Indicators of Family Cohesion: Clinical Assessment

... In doing the general classification of a marital or family unit, it is important to consider each member, each dyadic unit, other combinations of family units, and the entire system. It is also important to remember that all family members or dyadic units in the family will not be classified in an identical manner. In fact, one dyadic unit might exhibit behavior that is opposite from the other dyadic units on the dimensions of cohesion and adaptability. This is naturally the kind of diagnostic information that can be useful to a therapist.

It is also important to remember that this is a general and subjective assessment based on an individual's self-report. Although this method does provide interesting subjective data, it should be expected that individuals within the same family may see things differently and that these reports may not be equivalent to a more objective assessment (10). Because of the difference among family members' reports and behaviors, it is necessary to make some judgment on where to place a given couple or family on each scale.

Once an assessment is done for each area, it then becomes possible to develop an overall assessment for the couple or family. Families very low on cohesion are described as *disengaged*, moderately low as *separated*, moderately high as *connected*, and very high as *enmeshed* (see Figure 1). Again, there are no absolute guidelines, but couples with extremely low cohesion in six or more areas would be considered disengaged on cohesion. Conversely, couples with six or more areas in the extremely high region would be considered enmeshed on cohesion. Couples or families dealing with most of these areas in the central areas would represent those who have a more balanced orientation to individual autonomy and family cohesion....

### Indicators of Family Adaptability: Clinical Assessment

As we discussed in regard to the dimension of family cohesion, it is possible operationally to define and assess adaptability both clinically and empirically. The following discussion will focus on how a clinical assessment can be made using the variables of *assertiveness* and *control, discipline, negotiation style, role relationships, relationship rules,* and *system feedback*....

Once a clinical assessment is made for each of these seven variables, a therapist will then have both an overall assessment of a family's adaptability and a specific breakdown for each variable. If a couple or family is high, moderate, or low on five or more of these variables, the therapist derives a *modal* pattern for the couple or family. The extremes of family chaos and family rigidity are typically most problematic for both individual and family functioning. Variables that fall into these extremes are, therefore, of considerable clinical interest and value because they are often problematic. The treatment goal would be to facilitate movement on these problematic areas to make them less extreme....

### Diagnosis and Treatment Planning

Once a clinical assessment has been made of a couple or family on both the cohesion and adaptability dimensions, it is possible to place the couple or family into one of the sixteen cells of the circumplex model (Figure 1). As previously mentioned, couples and families in the four extremes will often have the most difficulty as a system, whereas those in the central areas usually experience less difficulty as a unit. It is possible that the marital, parental, and sibling subsystems within some families occupy different regions in the circumplex model. Treatment goals would naturally have to take these dynamics into account.

In addition to the general assessment on both dimensions, the therapist also has specific information on the nine variables related to cohesion and the seven variables related to adaptability. This information can aid a therapist in deciding what areas might be the most beneficial to focus on in treatment.

Once the diagnostic assessment is made, the therapist can begin to formulate *treatment goals.* If a couple or family is extreme on either cohesion or adaptability, the model suggests that the family would function more adequately in a more moderate degree on that dimension. Clinically it has been found useful to try to move a couple or family only *one* level on a dimension. This can be done on one dimension or on both dimensions. If too dramatic a change is imposed on the system, such as moving a chaotic family to a structured one, the family will often resist or do a dramatic shift to the opposite extreme....

The decision of what dimension and what specific variables related to that dimension require change is one that needs to be made by the therapist in consultation with the couple or family. Therapists differ greatly in the extent to which they involve the family in the decision regarding the treatment goals. However, we believe that it is therapeutically useful to share the diagnostic assessment with the family and involve them actively in the decision regarding the specific goals of treatment on both the two dimensions and on the specific variables related to each dimension.

While the circumplex model is useful for diagnosing family functioning on the dimensions of cohesion and adaptability and for deciding on treatment goals on these two dimensions, the model does *not* specify what therapeutic *techniques* will be most helpful in achieving these goals. Techniques are for the most part atheoretical and can be used regardless of the therapist's theoretical orientation. The therapist must, therefore, select from the techniques with which she or he is familiar and use those that are likely to be most effective in achieving the treatment goals for the couple or family.

# REFERENCES

1. BERTALANFFY, L. VON, *General Systems Theory*, New York, George Braziller, 1968.
2. BOWEN, M., "The Family as the Unit of Study and Treatment," *Am. J. Orthopsychiat.* 31: 40–60, 1960.
3. BUCKLEY, W., *Sociology and Modern Systems Theory*, Englewood Cliffs, New Jersey, Prentice Hall, 1967.
4. HOFFMAN, L., "'Enmeshment' and the Too Richly Cross-Joined System," *Fam. Proc.* 14: 457–468, 1975.
5. KARPEL, M., "Individuation: From Fusion to Dialogue," *Fam. Proc.* 15: 65–82, 1976.
6. KLUGMAN, J., "Enmeshment and Fusion," *Fam. Proc.* 15: 321–323, 1976.
7. MINUCHIN, S., *Families and Family Therapy*, Boston, Harvard University, University Press, 1974.
8. NAPIER, A. Y., "The Rejection-Intrusion Pattern: A Central Family Dynamic," *J. Marr. Fam. Couns.* 4: 5–12, 1978.
9. OLSON, D., "Bridging Research Theory and Application: The Triple Threat in Science," in Olson, D. H. (Ed.) *Treating Relationships*, Lake Mills, Graphic Publishing, 1976.
10. _____, "Insiders' and Outsiders' View of Relationships: Research Strategies," in G. Levinger, and H. L. Raush, (Eds.) *Close Relationships*, Amherst, Mass., University of Massachusetts Press, 1978.
11. REISS, D., "Varieties of Consensual Experience. I. A Theory for Relating Family Interaction to Individual Thinking," *Fam. Proc.* 10: 1–27, 1971a.
12. RUSSELL, C., "Circumplex Model of Family Systems. III: Empirical Evaluation with Families," *Fam. Proc.* 18: 29–45, 1979.
13. SCHAFFER, H. R., "The Too Cohesive Family: A Form of Group Pathology," *Int. J. Soc. Psychol.* 10: 266–275, 1964.
14. SPRENKLE, D. and OLSON, D., "Circumplex Model of Marital Systems IV: Empirical Study of Clinic and Non-Clinic Couples," *J. Marr. Fam. Counsel.* 4: 59–74, 1978.
15. STIERLIN, H., *Separating Parents and Adolescents*, New York, Quadrangle, 1974.
16. WYNNE, L. et al., "Pseudo-Mutuality in the Family Relations of Schizophrenics," *Psychiatry*, 21: 205–222, 1958.

## 2.3 GEORGE C. HOMANS

# Social Behavior as Exchange

This selection is from "Social Behavior as Exchange," by George C. Homans, *The American Journal of Sociology* (May 1958). This theoretical piece is a pioneering effort by Homans in which he applies concepts traditionally found in the field of business (e.g., profits, rewards, and costs) to interpersonal relationships. When the article was originally published, this "exchange theory" was a remarkably fresh idea that was readily embraced by the social science community. Exchange theory continues to be widely utilized and studied in contemporary teaching and research about marriage and the family. This selection introduces and outlines Homans's ideas about exchange theory and discusses how it can be a useful theoretical framework for studying families and relationships. Homans, an expert on the behavior of small social groups such as the family, was a professor of sociology at Harvard University when he wrote this article.

**Key Concept:** exchange theory

*I* have come to think that [it would be beneficial to adopt]... the view that interaction between persons is an exchange of goods, material and nonmaterial. This is one of the oldest theories of social behavior, and one that we still use every day to interpret our own behavior, as when we say, "I found so-and-so rewarding"; or "I got a great deal out of him"; or, even, "Talking with him took a great deal out of me." But, perhaps just because it is so obvious, this view has been much neglected by social scientists. So far as I know, the only theoretical work that makes explicit use of it is Marcel Mauss's *Essai sur le don*, published in 1925, which is ancient as social science goes.[1] It may be that the tradition of neglect is now changing and that, for instance, the psychologists who interpret behavior in terms of transactions may be coming back to something of the sort I have in mind.[2]

An incidental advantage of an exchange theory is that it might bring sociology closer to economics—that science of man most advanced, most capable of application, and, intellectually, most isolated. Economics studies exchange carried out under special circumstances and with a most useful built-in numerical measure of value. What are the laws of the general phenomenon of which economic behavior is one class?

In what follows I shall suggest some reasons for the usefulness of a theory of social behavior as exchange and suggest the nature of the propositions such as a theory might contain.

## AN EXCHANGE PARADIGM

I start with the link to behavioral psychology and the kind of statement it makes about the behavior of an experimental animal such as the pigeon.[3] As a pigeon explores its cage in the laboratory, it happens to peck a target, whereupon the psychologist feeds it corn. The evidence is that it will peck the target again; it has learned the behavior, or, as my friend Skinner says, the behavior has been reinforced, and the pigeon has undergone *operant conditioning*. This kind of psychologist is not interested in how the behavior was learned: "learning theory" is a poor name for his field. Instead, he is interested in what determines changes in the rate of emission of learned behavior, whether pecks at a target or something else.

The more hungry the pigeon, the less corn or other food it has gotten in the recent past, the more often it will peck. By the same token, if the behavior is often reinforced, if the pigeon is given much corn every time it pecks, the rate of emission will fall off as the pigeon gets *satiated*. If, on the other hand, the behavior is not reinforced at all, then, too; its rate of emission will tend to fall off, though a long time may pass before it stops altogether, before it is *extinguished*. In the emission of many kinds of behavior the pigeon incurs *aversive stimulation*, or what I shall call "cost" for short, and this, too, will lead in time to a decrease in the emission rate. Fatigue is an example of a "cost." Extinction, satiation, and cost, by decreasing the rate of emission of a particular kind of behavior, render more probable the emission of some other kind of behavior, including doing nothing. I shall only add that even a hard-boiled psychologist puts "emotional" behavior, as well as such things as pecking, among the unconditioned responses that may be reinforced in operant conditioning. As a statement of the propositions of behavioral psychology, the foregoing is, of course, inadequate for any purpose except my present one.

We may look on the pigeon as engaged in an exchange—pecks for corn —with the psychologist, but let us not dwell upon that, for the behavior of the pigeon hardly determines the behavior of the psychologist at all. Let us turn to a situation where the exchange is real, that is, where the determination is mutual. Suppose we are dealing with two men. Each is emitting behavior reinforced to some degree by the behavior of the other. How it was in the past that each learned the behavior he emits and how he learned to find the other's behavior reinforcing we are not concerned with. It is enough that each does find the other's behavior reinforcing, and I shall call the reinforcers—the equivalent of the pigeon's corn—*values*, for this, I think, is what we mean by this term. As he emits behavior, each man may incur costs, and each man has more than one course of behavior open to him.

This seems to me the paradigm of elementary social behavior, and the problem of the elementary sociologist is to state propositions relating the variations in the values and costs of each man to his frequency distribution of behavior among alternatives, where the values (in the mathematical sense) taken by these variable[s] for one man determine in part their values for the other.[4]

I see no reason to believe that the propositions of behavioral psychology do not apply to this situation, though the complexity of their implications in the concrete case may be great indeed. In particular, we must suppose that, with men as with pigeons, an increase in extinction, satiation, or aversive stimulation of any one kind of behavior will increase the probability of emission of some other kind. The problem is not, as it is often stated, merely, what a man's values are, what he has learned in the past to find reinforcing, but how much of any one value his behavior is getting him now. The more he gets, the less valuable any further unit of that value is to him, and the less often he will emit behavior reinforced by it.

## THE INFLUENCE PROCESS

We do not, I think, possess the kind of studies of two-person interaction that would either bear out these propositions or fail to do so. But we do have studies of larger numbers of persons that suggest that they may apply, notably the studies by Festinger, Schachter, Back, and their associates on the dynamics of influence. One of the variables they work with they call *cohesiveness*, defined as anything that attracts people to take part in a group. Cohesiveness is a value variable; it refers to the degree of reinforcement people find in the activities of the group. Festinger and his colleagues consider two kinds of reinforcing activity: the symbolic behavior we call "social approval" (sentiment) and activity valuable in other ways, such as doing something interesting.

The other variable they work with they call *communication* and others call *interaction*. This is a frequency variable; it is a measure of the frequency of emission of valuable and costly verbal behavior. We must bear in mind that, in general, the one kind of variable is a function of the other.

Festinger and his co-workers show that the more cohesive a group is, that is, the more valuable the sentiment or activity the members exchange with one another, the greater the average frequency of interaction of the members.[5] With men, as with pigeons, the greater the reinforcement, the more often is the reinforced behavior emitted. The more cohesive a group, too, the greater the change that members can produce in the behavior of other members in the direction of rendering these activities more valuable.[6] That is, the more valuable the activities that members get, the more valuable those that they must give. For if a person is emitting behavior of a certain kind, and other people do not find it particularly rewarding, these others will suffer their own production of sentiment and activity, in time, to fall off. But perhaps the first person has found their sentiment and activity rewarding, and, if he is to keep on getting them, he must make his own behavior more valuable to the others. In short, the propositions of behavioral psychology imply a tendency toward a certain proportionality between the value to others of the behavior a man gives them and the value to him of the behavior they give him.[7]

Schachter also studied the behavior of members of a group toward two kinds of other members, "conformers" and "deviates."[8] I assume that conformers are people whose activity the other members find valuable. For conformity is behavior that coincides to a degree with some group standard or norm, and the only meaning I can assign to *norm* is "a verbal description of behavior that many members find it valuable for the actual behavior of themselves and others to conform to." By the same token, a deviate is a member whose behavior is not particularly valuable. Now Schachter shows that, as the members of a group come to see another member as a deviate, their interaction with him—communication addressed to getting him to change his behavior—goes up, the faster the more cohesive the group. The members need not talk to the other conformers so much; they are relatively satiated by the conformers' behavior: they have gotten what they want out of them. But if the deviate, by failing to change his behavior, fails to reinforce the members, they start to withhold social approval from him: the deviate gets low sociometric choice at the end of the experiment. And in the most cohesive groups—those Schachter calls "high cohesive-relevant"—interaction with the deviate also falls off in the end and is lowest among those members that rejected him most strongly, as if they had given him up as a bad job. But how plonking can we get? These findings are utterly in line with everyday experience....

## PROFIT AND SOCIAL CONTROL

Though I have treated equilibrium as an observed fact, it is a fact that cries for explanation. I shall not, as structural-functional sociologists do, use an assumed equilibrium as a means of explaining, or trying to explain, why the other features of a social system should be what they are. Rather, I shall take practical equilibrium as something that is itself to be explained by the other features of the system.

If every member of a group emits at the end of, and during, a period of time much the same kinds of behavior and in much the same frequencies as he did at the beginning, the group is for that period in equilibrium. Let us then ask why any one member's behavior should persist. Suppose he is emitting behavior of value $A_1$. Why does he not let his behavior get worse (less valuable or reinforcing to the others) until it stands at $A_1 - \Delta A$? True, the sentiments expressed by others toward him are apt to decline in value (become less reinforcing to him), so that what he gets from them may be $S_1 - \Delta S$. But it is conceivable that, since most activity carries cost, a decline in the value of what he emits will mean a reduction in cost to him that more than offsets his losses in sentiment. Where, then, does he stabilize his behavior? This is the problem of social control.[9]

**TABLE 1**

*Percentage of Subjects Changing Toward Someone in the Group*

|  | Agreement | Mild Disagreement | Strong Disagreement |
|---|---|---|---|
| High attraction.... | 0 | 12 | 44 |
| Low attraction.... | 0 | 15 | 9 |

Mankind has always assumed that a person stabilizes his behavior, at least in the short run, at the point where he is doing the best he can for himself under the circumstances, though his best may not be a "rational" best, and what he can do may not be at all easy to specify, except that he is not apt to think like one of the theoretical antagonists in the *Theory of Games*. Before a sociologist rejects this answer out of hand for its horrid profit-seeking implications, he will do well to ask himself if he can offer any other answer to the question posed. I think he will find that he cannot. Yet experiments designed to test the truth of the answer are extraordinarily rare.

I shall review one that seems to me to provide a little support for the theory, though it was not meant to do so. The experiment is reported by H. B. Gerard, a member of the Festinger-Schachter team, under the title "The Anchorage of Opinions in Face-to-Face Groups."[10] The experimenter formed artificial groups whose members met to discuss a case in industrial relations and to express their opinions about its probable outcome. The groups were of two kinds: high-attraction groups, whose members were told that they would like one another very much, and low-attraction groups, whose members were told that they would not find one another particularly likable.

At a later time the experimenter called the members in separately, asked them again to express their opinions on the outcome of the case, and counted the number that had changed their opinions to bring them into accord with those of other members of their groups. At the same time, a paid participant entered into a further discussion of the case with each member, always taking, on the probable outcome of the case, a position opposed to that taken by the bulk of the other members of the group to which the person belonged. The experimenter counted the number of persons shifting toward the opinion of the paid participant.

The experiment had many interesting results, from which I choose only those summed up in Tables 1 and 2. The three different agreement classes are made up of people who, at the original sessions, expressed different degrees of agreement with the opinions of other members of their groups. And the figure 44, for instance, means that, of all members of high-attraction groups whose initial opinions were strongly in disagreement with those of other members, 44 per cent shifted their opinion later toward that of others.

In these results the experimenter seems to have been interested only in the differences in the sums of the rows, which show that there is more shifting

**TABLE 2**

*Percentage of Subjects Changing Toward the Paid Participant*

|  | Agreement | Mild Disagreement | Strong Disagreement |
|---|---|---|---|
| High attraction.... | 7 | 13 | 25 |
| Low attraction.... | 20 | 38 | 8 |

toward the group, and less shifting toward the paid participant, in the high-attraction than in the low-attraction condition. This is in line with a proposition suggested earlier. If you think that the members of a group can give you much —in this case, liking—you are apt to give them much—in this case, a change to an opinion in accordance with their views—or you will not get the liking. And, by the same token, if the group can give you little of value, you will not be ready to give it much of value. Indeed, you may change your opinion so as to depart from agreement even further, to move, that is, toward the view held by the paid participant.

So far so good, but, when I first scanned these tables, I was less struck by the difference between them than by their similarity. The same classes of people in both tables showed much the same relative propensities to change their opinions, no matter whether the change was toward the group or toward the paid participant. We see, for instance, that those who change least are the high-attraction, agreement people and the low-attraction, strong-disagreement ones. And those who change most are the high-attraction, strong-disagreement people and the low-attraction, mild-disagreement ones.

How am I to interpret these particular results? Since the experimenter did not discuss them, I am free to offer my own explanation. The behavior emitted by the subjects is opinion and changes in opinion. For this behavior they have learned to expect two possible kinds of reinforcement. Agreement with the group gets the subject favorable sentiment (acceptance) from it, and the experiment was designed to give this reinforcement a higher value in the high-attraction condition than in the low-attraction one. The second kind of possible reinforcement is what I shall call the "maintenance of one's personal integrity," which a subject gets by sticking to his own opinion in the face of disagreement with the group. The experimenter does not mention this reward, but I cannot make sense of the results without something much like it. In different degrees for different subjects, depending on their initial positions, these rewards are in competition with one another: they are alternatives. They are not absolutely scarce goods, but some persons cannot get both at once.

Since the rewards are alternatives, let me introduce a familiar assumption from economics—that the cost of a particular course of action is the equivalent of the foregone value of an alternative[11]—and then add the definition: Profit = Reward − Cost.

Now consider the persons in the corresponding cells of the two tables. The behavior of the high-attraction, agreement people gets them much in the way of acceptance by the group, and for it they must give up little in the way of personal integrity, for their views are from the start in accord with those of the group. Their profit is high, and they are not prone to change their behavior. The low-attraction, strong-disagreement people are getting much in integrity, and they are not giving up for it much in valuable acceptance, for they are members of low-attraction groups. Reward less cost is high for them, too, and they change little. The high-attraction, strong-disagreement people are getting much in the way of integrity, but their costs in doing so are high, too, for they are in high-attraction groups and thus foregoing much valuable acceptance by the group. Their profit is low, and they are very apt to change, either toward the group or toward the paid participant, from whom they think, perhaps, they will get some acceptance while maintaining some integrity. The low-attraction, mild-disagreement people do not get much in the way of integrity, for they are only in mild disagreement with the group, but neither are they giving up much in acceptance, for they are members of low-attraction groups. Their rewards are low; their costs are low too, and their profit—the difference between the two—is also low. In their low profit they resemble the high-attraction, strong-disagreement people, and, like them, they are prone to change their opinions, in this case, more toward the paid participant. The subjects in the other two cells, who have medium profits, display medium propensities to change.

If we define profit as reward less cost, and if cost is value foregone, I suggest that we have here some evidence for the proposition that change in behavior is greatest when perceived profit is least. This constitutes no direct demonstration that change in behavior is least when profit is greatest, but if, whenever a man's behavior brought him a balance of reward and cost, he changed his behavior away from what got him, under the circumstances, the less profit, there might well come a time when his behavior would not change further. That is, his behavior would be stabilized, at least for the time being. And, so far as this were true for every member of a group, the group would have a social organization in equilibrium.

I do not say that a member would stabilize his behavior at the point of greatest conceivable profit to himself, because his profit is partly at the mercy of the behavior of others. It is a commonplace that the short-run pursuit of profit by several persons often lands them in positions where all are worse off than they might conceivably be. I do not say that the paths of behavioral change in which a member pursues his profit under the condition that others are pursuing theirs too are easy to describe or predict; and we can readily conceive that in jockeying for position they might never arrive at any equilibrium at all.

## DISTRIBUTIVE JUSTICE

Yet practical equilibrium is often observed, and thus some further condition may make its attainment, under some circumstance, more probable than would the individual pursuit of profit left to itself. I can offer evidence for this further condition only in the behavior of subgroups and not in that of individuals. Suppose that there are two subgroups, working close together in a factory, the job of one being somewhat different from that of the other. And suppose that the members of the first complain and say: "We are getting the same pay as they are. We ought to get just a couple of dollars a week more to show that our work is more responsible." When you ask them what they mean by "more responsible," they say that, if they do their work wrong, more damage can result, and so they are under more pressure to take care.[12] Something like this is a common feature of industrial behavior. It is at the heart of disputes not over absolute wages but over wage differentials—indeed, at the heart of disputes over rewards other than wages.

In what kind of proposition may we express observations like these? We may say that wages and responsibility give status in the group, in the sense that a man who takes high responsibility and gets high wages is admired, other things equal. Then, if the members of one group score higher on responsibility than do the members of another, there is a felt need on the part of the first to score higher on pay too. There is a pressure, which shows itself in complaints, to bring the *status factors,* as I have called them, into line with one another. If they are in line, a condition of *status congruence* is said to exist. In this condition, the workers may find their jobs dull or irksome, but they will not complain about the relative position of groups.

But there may be a more illuminating way of looking at the matter. In my example I have considered only responsibility and pay, but these may be enough, for they represent the two kinds of things that come into the problem. Pay is clearly a reward; responsibility may be looked on, less clearly, as a cost. It means constraint and worry—or peace of mind foregone. Then the proposition about status congruence becomes this: If the costs of the members of one group are higher than those of another, distributive justice requires that their rewards should be higher too. But the thing works both ways: If the rewards are higher, the costs should be higher too. This last is the theory of *noblesse oblige,* which we all subscribe to, though we all laugh at it, perhaps because the *noblesse* often fails to *oblige.* To put the matter in terms of profit: though the rewards and costs of two persons or the members of two groups may be different, yet the profits of the two—the excess of reward over cost—should tend to equality. And more than "should." The less-advantaged group will at least try to attain greater equality, as, in the example I have used, the first group tried to increase its profit by increasing its pay.

I have talked of distributive justice. Clearly, this is not the only condition determining the actual distribution of rewards and costs. At the same time, never tell me that notions of justice are not a strong influence on behavior, though we sociologists often neglect them. Distributive justice may be one of the conditions of group equilibrium....

## SUMMARY

The current job of theory in small-group research is to make the connection between experimental and real-life studies, to consolidate the propositions that empirically hold good in the two fields, and to show how these propositions might be derived from a still more general set. One way of doing this job would be to revive and make more rigorous the oldest of theories of social behavior—social behavior as exchange.

Some of the statements of such a theory might be the following. Social behavior is an exchange of goods, material goods but also non-material ones, such as the symbols of approval or prestige. Persons that give much to others try to get much from them, and persons that get much from others are under pressure to give much to them. This process of influence tends to work out at equilibrium to a balance in the exchanges. For a person engaged in exchange, what he gives may be a cost to him, just as what he gets may be a reward, and his behavior changes less as profit, that is, reward less cost, tends to a maximum. Not only does he seek a maximum for himself, but he tries to see to it that no one in his group makes more profit than he does. The cost and the value of what he gives and of what he gets vary with the quantity of what he gives and gets. It is surprising how familiar these propositions are; it is surprising, too, how propositions about the dynamics of exchange can begin to generate the static thing we call "group structure" and, in so doing, generate also some of the propositions about group structure that students of real-life groups have stated.

In our unguarded moments we sociologists find words like "reward" and "cost" slipping into what we say. Human nature will break in upon even our most elaborate theories. But we seldom let it have its way with us and follow up systematically what these words imply.[13] Of all our many "approaches" to social behavior, the one that sees it as an economy is the most neglected, and yet it is the one we use every moment of our lives—except when we write sociology.

## NOTES

1. Translated by I. Cunnison as *The Gift* (Glencoe, Ill.: Free Press, 1954).
2. In social anthropology D. L. Oliver is working along these lines, and I owe much to him. See also T. M. Newcomb, "The Prediction of Interpersonal Attraction," *American Psychologist*, XI (1956), 575–86.
3. B. F. Skinner, *Science and Human Behavior* (New York: Macmillan Co., 1953).
4. *Ibid.*, pp. 297–329. The discussion of "double contingency" by T. Parsons and E. A. Shils could easily lead to a similar paradigm (see *Toward a General Theory of Action* [Cambridge, Mass.: Harvard University Press, 1951], pp. 14–16).
5. K. W. Back, "The Exertion of Influence through Social Communication," in L. Festinger, K. Back, S. Schachter, H. H. Kelley, and J. Thibaut (eds.), *Theory and Experiment in Social Communication* (Ann Arbor: Research Center for Dynamics, University of Michigan, 1950), pp. 21–36.

6. S. Schachter, N. Ellertson, D. McBride, and D. Gregory, "An Experimental Study of Cohesiveness and Productivity," *Human Relations,* IV (1951), 229–38.
7. Skinner, *op. cit.*, p. 100.
8. S. Schachter, "Deviation, Rejection, and Communication," *Journal of Abnormal and Social Psychology,* XLVI (1951), 190–207.
9. Homans, *op. cit.*, pp. 281–301.
10. *Human Relations,* VII (1954), 313–25.
11. G. J. Stigler, *The Theory of Price* (rev. ed.; New York: Macmillan Co., 1952), p. 99.
12. G. C. Homans, "Status among Clerical Workers," *Human Organization,* XII (1953), 5–10.
13. *The White-Collar Job* (Ann Arbor: Survey Research Center, University of Michigan, 1953), pp. 115–27.

# PART TWO

# *Mate Selection and Marriage*

**Chapter 3**   Premarital Relationships   65

**Chapter 4**   Theories of Mate Selection   90

**Chapter 5**   Marital Adjustment   122

**Chapter 6**   Marital Role Satisfaction   140

# On the Internet . . .

## Sites appropriate to Part Two

The Coalition for Marriage, Family and Couples Education (CMFCE) is dedicated to bringing information about skill-based marriage education courses to the public.

    http://www.smartmarriages.com/

The Association for Couples in Marriage Enrichment (A.C.M.E.) is a group of couples who believe in marriage, know that a good marriage takes work, and understand that communication is essential to an enriched marriage.

    http://home.swbell.net/tgall/acme.htm

# CHAPTER 3 Premarital Relationships

## 3.1 WILLARD WALLER

## *The Rating and Dating Complex*

There are few introductory courses in the study of marriage and the family that do not examine the dating and courtship process. One classic theory of dating and courtship is the "principle of least interest." Willard F. Waller developed this theory during the early part of the twentieth century. Waller, a professor of sociology at Barnard College and an active member of the American Sociological Society, was a pioneer in the scientific study of dating and courtship patterns in America.

In this selection from "The Rating and Dating Complex," *American Sociological Review* (October 1937), Waller offers his basic assumptions about the courtship process. It is interesting to note that many of Waller's premises still hold true today. Although this piece was written over 60 years ago, there are many similarities in the observations that Waller made about society then as compared to contemporary society.

**Key Concept:** dating and courtship

Courtship may be defined as the set of processes of association among the unmarried from which, in time, permanent matings usually emerge. This definition excludes those associations which cannot normally eventuate in marriage—as between Negro and white—but allows for a period of dalliance and experimentation. In the present paper we propose to discuss the customs of courtship which prevail among college students.

Courtship practices vary from one culture group to another. In many cultures marriage eventuates from a period of sexual experimentation and trial unions; in others the innocence of the unmarried is carefully guarded until their wedding day. In some cultures the bride must be virginal at marriage; in others this is just what she must not be. Sometimes the young are allowed no liberty of choice, and everything is determined for them by their elders. Sometimes persons marry in their own age group, but in other societies older men pre-empt the young women for themselves. Although there are endless variations in courtship customs, they are always functionally related to the total configuration of the culture and the biological needs of the human animal. It is helpful to remember that in a simple, undifferentiated, and stable society a long and complex process of choosing a mate is apparently not so necessary or desirable as in our own complex, differentiated, and rapidly changing society.[1]

The mores of courtship in our society are a strange composite of social heritages from diverse groups and of new usages called into existence by the needs of the time. There is a formal code of courtship which is still nominally in force, although departures from it are very numerous; the younger generation seems to find the superficial usages connected with the code highly amusing, but it is likely that it takes the central ideas quite seriously. The formal code appears to be derived chiefly from the usages of the English middle classes of a generation or so ago, although there are, of course, many other elements in it.

The usual or intended mode of operation of the formal mores of courtship—in a sense their "function"—is to induct young persons into marriage by a series of progressive commitments. In the solitary peasant community, in the frontier community, among the English middle classes of a few decades back, and in many isolated small communities in present-day America, every step in the courtship process has a customary meaning and constitutes a powerful pressure toward taking the next step—is in fact a sort of implied commitment to take the next step. The mores formerly operated to produce a high rate of marriage at the proper age and at the same time protected most individuals from many of the possible traumatic experiences of the courtship period.

The decay of this moral structure has made possible the emergence of thrill-seeking and exploitative relationships. A thrill is merely a physiological stimulation and release of tension, and it seems curious that most of us are inclined to regard thrill-seeking with disapproval. The disapproving attitude toward thrill-seeking becomes intelligible when we recall the purpose of such emotional stirrings in the conventional mores of courtship. Whether we approve or not, courtship practices today allow for a great deal of pure thrill-seeking. Dancing, petting, necking, the automobile, the amusement park, and a whole range of institutions and practices permit or facilitate thrill-seeking behavior. These practices, which are connected with a great range of the institutions of commercialized recreation, make of courtship an amusement and a release of organic tensions. The value judgment which many lay persons and even some trained sociologists pass upon thrill-seeking arises from the organizational mores of the family—from the fact that energy is dissipated in thrills which is supposed to do the work of the world, i.e., to get people safely married.

The emergence of thrill-seeking furthers the development of exploitative relationships. As long as an association is founded on a frank and admitted barter in thrills, nothing that can be called exploitative arises. But the old mores of progressive commitment exist, along with the new customs, and peculiar relationships arise from this confusion of moralities. According to the old morality a kiss means something, a declaration of love means something, a number of Sunday evening dates in succession means something, and these meanings are enforced by the customary law, while under the new morality such things may mean nothing at all—that is, they may imply no commitment of the total personality whatsoever. So it comes about that one of the persons may exploit the other for thrills on the pretense of emotional involvement and its implied commitment. When a woman exploits, it is usually for the sake of presents and expensive amusements—the common pattern of "gold-digging." The male exploiter usually seeks thrills from the body of the woman. The fact that thrills cost money, usually the man's money, often operates to introduce strong elements of suspicion and antagonism into the relationship.

With this general background in mind, let us turn to the courtship practices of college students. A very important characteristic of the college student is his bourgeois pattern of life. For most persons, the dominant motive of college attendance is the desire to rise to a higher social class; behind this we should see the ideology of American life and the projection of parents' ambitions upon children. The attainment of this life goal necessitates the postponement of marriage, since it is understood that a new household must be economically independent; additional complications sometimes arise from the practice of borrowing money for college expenses. And yet persons in this group feel very strongly the cultural imperative to fall in love and marry and live happily in marriage.

For the average college student, and especially for the man, a love affair which led to immediate marriage would be tragic because of the havoc it would create in his scheme of life. Nevertheless, college students feel strongly the attractions of sex and the thrills of sex, and the sexes associate with one another in a peculiar relationship known as "dating." Dating is not true courtship, since it is supposed not to eventuate in marriage; it is a sort of dalliance relationship. In spite of the strength of the old morality among college students, dating is largely dominated by the quest of the thrill and is regarded as an amusement. The fact that college attendance usually removes the individual from normal courtship association in his home community should be mentioned as a further determinant of the psychological character of dating.

In many colleges, dating takes place under conditions determined by a culture complex which we may call the "rating and dating complex." The following description of this complex on one campus is probably typical of schools of the sort:

> X College, a large state-supported school, is located in a small city at a considerable distance from larger urban areas. The school is the only industry of the community. There are few students who live at home, and therefore the interaction of the young is but little influenced by the presence of parents. The students

of this college are predominantly taken from the lower half of the middle classes, and constitute a remarkably homogeneous group; numerous censuses of the occupations of fathers and of living expenses seem to establish this fact definitely. Nevertheless, about half of the male students live in fraternities, where the monthly bill is usually forty-five or fifty dollars a month, rarely as high as fifty-five. There is intense competition among the fraternities. The desire for mobility of class, as shown by dozens of inquiries, is almost universal in the group and is the principal verbalized motive for college attendance.

Dating at X College consists of going to college or fraternity dances, the movies, college entertainments, and to fraternity houses for victrola dances and "necking"; coeds are permitted in the fraternity parlors, if more than one is present. The high points of the social season are two house parties and certain formal dances. An atypical feature of this campus is the unbalanced sex ratio, for there are about six boys to every girl; this makes necessary the large use of so-called "imports" for the more important occasions, and brings it about that many boys do not date at all or confine their activities to prowling about in small industrial communities nearby; it also gives every coed a relatively high position in the scale of desirability; it would be difficult to say whether it discourages or encourages the formation of permanent attachments. Dating is almost exclusively the privilege of fraternity men, the use of the fraternity parlor and the prestige of fraternity membership being very important. Freshman men are forbidden by student tradition to have dates with coeds.[2]

Within the universe which we have described, competition for dates among both men and women is extremely keen. Like every other process of competition, this one determines a distributive order. There are certain men who are at the top of the social scramble; they may be placed in a hypothetical Class A. There are also certain coeds who are near the top of the scale of dating desirability, and they also are in Class A. The tendency is for Class A men to date principally Class A women. Beneath this class of men and women are as many other classes as one wishes to create for the purposes of analysis. It should be remembered that students on this campus are extremely conscious of these social distinctions and of their own position in the social hierarchy. In speaking of another student, they say, "He rates," or "He does not rate," and they extend themselves enormously in order that they may rate or seem to rate.

Young men are desirable dates according to their rating on the scale of campus values. In order to have Class A rating they must belong to one of the better fraternities, be prominent in activities, have a copious supply of spending money, be well-dressed, "smooth" in manners and appearance, have a "good line," dance well, and have access to an automobile. Members of leading fraternities are especially desirable dates; those who belong to fraternities with less prestige are correspondingly less desirable. I have been able to validate the qualities mentioned as determinants of campus prestige by reference to large numbers of student judges.

The factors which appear to be important for girls are good clothes, a smooth line, ability to dance well, and popularity as a date. The most important of these factors is the last, for the girl's prestige depends upon dating more than anything else; here as nowhere else nothing succeeds like success. Therefore the clever coed contrives to give the impression of being much sought after even if she is not. It has been reported by many observers that a girl who is called to the telephone in the dormitories will often allow herself to be called several times, in order to give all the other girls ample opportunity to hear her paged. Coeds who wish campus prestige must never be available for last minute dates; they must avoid being seen too often with the same boy, in order that others may not be frightened away or discouraged; they must be seen when they go out, and therefore must go to the popular (and expensive) meeting places; they must have many partners at the dances. If they violate the conventions at all, they must do so with great secrecy and discretion; they do not drink in groups or frequent the beer-parlors. Above all, the coed who wishes to retain Class A standing must consistently date Class A men.

Cressey has pointed out that the taxi-dancer has a descending cycle of desirability. As a new girl in the dance hall, she is at first much sought after by the most eligible young men. Soon they tire of her and desert her for some newer recruit. Similarly the coed has a descending cycle of popularity on the campus which we are describing, although her struggle is not invariably a losing one. The new girl, the freshman coed, starts out with a great wave of popularity; during her freshman year she has many dates. Slowly her prestige declines, but in this case only to the point at which she reaches the level which her qualities permanently assure her. Her descent is expedited by such "mistakes," from the viewpoint of campus prestige, as "going steady" with one boy (especially if he is a senior who will not return the following year), by indiscretions, and by too ready availability for dates. Many of the girls insist that after two years of competitive dating they have tired of it and are interested in more permanent associations.

This thrill-dominated, competitive process involves a number of fundamental antagonisms between the men and the women, and the influence of the one sex group accentuates these. Writes one student informant, a girl, "Wary is the only word that I can apply to the attitude of men and women students toward each other. The men, who have been warned so repeatedly against coeds, are always afraid the girls are going to 'gold-dig' them. The coeds wonder to what degree they are discussed and are constantly afraid of being placed on the black list of the fraternities. Then too they wonder to what extent they can take any man seriously without being taken for a 'ride'." Status in the one-sex group depends upon avoiding exploitation by the opposite sex. Verbatim records of a number of fraternity "bull sessions" were obtained a few years ago. In these sessions members are repeatedly warned that they are slipping, those who have fallen are teased without mercy, and others are warned not to be soft. And almost all of the participants pretend a ruthlessness toward the opposite sex which they do not feel.

This competitive dating process often inflicts traumas upon individuals who stand low in the scale of courtship desirability. "While I was at X College," said a thirty year old alumnus, "I had just one date. That was a blind date, arranged for me by a friend. We went to the dorm, and after a while my girl came down and we were introduced. She said, 'Oh, I'm so sorry. I forgot my coat. I'll have to go get it.' She never came down again. Naturally I thought, 'Well what a hit I made!'" We have already seen that nonfraternity men are practically excluded from dating; it remains to note that many girls elect not to date rather than take the dates available to them. One girl writes as follows: "A girl's choice of whom to fall in love with is limited by the censorship of the one-sex group. Every boy that she dates is discussed and criticized by the other members of the group. This rigid control often keeps a girl from dating at all. If a girl is a member of a group in which the other girls are rated higher on the dating scale than she, she is often unable to get dates with boys who are considered desirable by her friends. In that event she has to decide whether to date the boys that she can and choose girl friends who would approve, or she must resign herself to not dating."

Since the class system, or gradient of dating desirability on the campus, is clearly recognized and adjusted to by the students themselves, there are interesting accommodations and rationalizations which appear as a result of inferior status. Although members of Class A may be clearly in the ascendant as regards prestige, certain groups of Class B may contest the position with them and may insist upon a measuring stick which will give them a favorable position. Rationalizations which enable Class D men and women to accept one another are probably never completely effective.

The accommodations and rationalizations worked out by one group of girls who were toward the bottom of the scale of campus desirability are typical. Four of these girls were organized in one tightly compact "bunch." All four lived off campus, and worked for their room and board. They had little money to spend for clothes, so there was extensive borrowing of dresses. Members of the group co-operated in getting dates for one another. All of them accepted eleventh hour invitations, and probably realized that some stigma of inferiority was attached to such ready availability but they managed to save their faces by seeming very reluctant to accept such engagements, and at length doing so as a result of the persuasion of another member of the bunch. The men apparently saw through these devices, and put these girls down as last minute dates, so that they rarely received any other invitations. The bunch went through "dating cycles" with several fraternities in the course of a year, starting when one of the girls got a date with one member of the fraternity, and ending, apparently when all the girls had lost their desirability in that fraternity.

Partly as result of the unbalanced sex ratio, the boys of the group which we are discussing have a widespread feeling of antagonism toward the coeds. This antagonism is apparently based upon the fact that most of the male students are unable to date with coeds, at least not on terms acceptable to themselves. As a result of this, boys take great pride in the "imports" whom they bring in for house parties, and it is regarded as slightly disgraceful in some groups to date a coed for one of the major parties. Other men in the dateless group take on the role of misogynists—and read Schopenhauer.

During the winter term the preponderance of men assures to every coed a relatively high bargaining power. Every summer witnesses a surprising reversal of this situation. Hundreds of women school teachers flock to this school for the summer term, and men are very scarce; smooth, unmarried boys of college age are particularly scarce. The school-teachers are older than the boys; they have usually lost some of their earlier attractiveness; they have been living for some months or years within the school-teacher role. They are man-hungry, and they have a little money. As a result, there is a great proliferation of highly commercialized relations. The women lend their cars to their men friends, but continue to pay for repairs and gasoline; they take the boys out to dinner, treat them to drinks, and buy expensive presents for them. And many who do not go so far are available for sex relations on terms which demand no more than a transitory sort of commitment from the man.

The rating and dating complex varies enormously from one school to another. In one small, coeducational school, the older coeds instruct the younger that it is all right for them to shop around early in the year, but by November they should settle down and date someone steadily. As a result, a boy who dates a girl once is said to "have a fence around her," and the competition which we have described is considerably hampered in its operation. In other schools, where the sex ratio is about equal, and particularly in the smaller institutions, "going steady" is probably a great deal more common than on the campus described. It should be pointed out that the frustrations and traumas imposed upon unsuccessful candidates by the practice of "going steady" (monopolistic competition) are a great deal easier to bear than those which arise from pure competition. In one school the girls are uniformly of a higher class origin than the boys, so that there is relatively little association between them; the girls go with older men not in college, the boys with high school girls and other "townies." In the school which is not coeducational, the dating customs are vastly different, although, for the women at least, dating is still probably a determinant of prestige.

True courtship sometimes emerges from the dating process, in spite of all the forces which are opposed to it. The analysis of the interaction process involved seems to be quite revealing. We may suppose that in our collegiate culture one begins to fall in love with a certain unwillingness, at least with an ambivalent sort of willingness. Both persons become emotionally involved as a result of a summatory process in which each step powerfully influences the next step and the whole process displays a directional trend toward the culmination of marriage; the mores of dating break down and the behavior of the individuals is governed by the older mores of progressive commitment. In the fairly typical case, we may suppose the interaction to be about as follows: The affair begins with the lightest sort of involvement, each individual being interested in the other but assuming no obligations as to the continuation of the affair. There are some tentatives of exploitation at the beginning; "the line" is a conventionalized attempt on the part of the young man to convince the young woman that he has already at this early stage fallen seriously in love with her—a sort of exaggeration, sometimes a burlesque, of coquetry—it may be that each person, by a pretence of great involvement, invites the other to rapid sentiment-formation —each encourages the other to fall in love by pretending that he has already done so. If either rises to the bait, a special type of interaction ensues; it may be that the relation becomes exploitative in some degree and it is likely that the relationship becomes one in which control follows the principle of least interest, i.e., that person controls who is less interested in the continuation of the affair. Or it may be that the complete involvement of the one person constellates the other in the same pattern, but this is less likely to happen to happen in college than in the normal community processes of courtship.

If both persons stand firm at this early juncture, there may ensue a series of periodic crises which successively redefine the relationship on deeper levels of involvement. One form which the interaction process may assume is that of "lover's quarrels," with which the novelists have familiarized us. A and B begin an affair on the level of light involvement. A becomes somewhat involved, but believes that B has not experienced a corresponding growth of feeling, and hides his involvement from B, who is, however, in exactly the same situation. The conventionalized "line" facilitates this sort of "pluralistic ignorance," because it renders meaningless the very words by means of which this state of mind could be disclosed. Tension grows between A and B, and is resolved by a crisis, such as a quarrel, in which the true feelings of the two are revealed. The affair, perhaps, proceeds through a number of such crises until it reaches the culmination of marriage. Naturally, there are other kinds of crises which usher in the new definition of the situation.

Such affairs, in contrast to "dating," have a marked directional trend; they may be arrested on any level, or they may be broken off at any point, but they may not ordinarily be turned back to a lesser degree of involvement; in this sense they are irreversible. As this interaction process goes on, the process of idealization is re-enforced by the interaction of personalities. A idealizes B, and presents to her that side of his personality which is consistent with his idealized conception of her; B idealizes A, and governs her behavior toward him in accordance with her false notions of his nature; the process of idealization is mutually re-enforced in such a way that it must necessarily lead to an increasing divorce from reality. As serious sentimental involvement develops, the individual comes to be increasingly occupied, on the conscious level at least, with the positive aspects of the relationship; increasingly he loses his ability to think objectively about the other person, to safeguard himself or to deal with the relationship in a rational way; we may say, indeed, that one falls in love when he reaches the point where sentiment-formation overcomes objectivity.

The love relationship in its crescendo phase attracts an ever larger proportion of the conative trends of the personality; for a time it may seem to absorb all of the will of the individual and to dominate his imagination completely; the individual seems to become a machine specially designed for just one purpose; in consequence, the persons are almost wholly absorbed in themselves and their affair; they have an *egoisme à deux* which verges upon *folie à deux*. All of these processes within the pair-relationship are accentuated by the changes in the attitude of others, who tend to treat the pair as a social unity, so far as their association is recognized and approved.

# NOTES

1. James G. Leyburn quotes an old-fashioned Boer mother who said, "I am sick of all this talk of choosing and choosing.... If a man is healthy and does not drink, and has a good little handful of stock, and a good temper, and is a good Christian, what great difference can it make to a woman which man she takes? There is not so much difference between one man and another." (*Frontier Folkways*, p. 129.) Such an attitude was possible in Boer society as it is not in ours.
2. Folsom, who has studied this same process, has come to essentially similar conclusions concerning the exclusion of certain persons from the dating process: "This factor is especially prominent in state universities with a vigorous fraternity culture and social stratification. Such institutions are attended by students from an unusually wide range on the social scale; there is a tendency to protect one's social ranking in college through a certain snobbishness, and there is also a great drive toward social climbing. Fraternities are important agencies in this struggle for prestige. The fraternities and sororities apply considerable pressure to the 'dating' of their members. One gets merits, whether formally recorded or not, for dating with a coed of a high-ranking fraternity, demerits for association with a non-fraternity person. The net result of this competition might seem to be to match each person with one of fairly equal rank, as happens in society in general. But there is another result. It is to discourage matching altogether among the lower ranks. The fire of competitive dating burns hot at the top, smoulders at the bottom. The low-ranking student often has more to gain by abstaining from dating than from dating with a person of his own rank." (J. K. Folsom, *The Family*, p. 341.)

## 3.2 MARGARET MEAD AND RHODA METRAUX

# *Marriage in Two Steps—A Proposal*

The following selection is from Margaret Mead and Rhoda Metraux's book *A Way of Seeing* (McCall, 1970). In that book, Mead and Metraux offered ideas that could be considered radical for the time of its publication. They suggested that the early stages of heterosexual relationships should not focus on procreation. In effect, they were among the early advocates of childless cohabitation until such a time that couples felt sufficiently responsible and ready for parenthood. Although the ideas presented in this article may seem normative by today's standards, they were quite controversial when they were first offered.

Mead, a noted anthropologist, was known throughout the world as a humanitarian and an expert in numerous areas, including family structure, mental health, ecology, and the growth, change, and structure of cultures. Much of Mead's life was spent doing field research in foreign cultures. However, she was most adept at anticipating many of the changes in American culture by projecting her data. Metraux was a research associate of Mead's who had expertise in writing and editing as well as in the field of anthropology. Metraux was a fellow of the American Anthropological Association and the Social Science Research Council. She received many grants from the National Institute of Mental Health and the National Science Foundation.

**Key Concept:** marital adjustment

*T*he June bride evokes memory pictures of her mother and her mother's mother as just such a happy girl, caught between tears and laughter. The newest bridegroom, describing his difficulties, awakens memories of other crises, each story a different one, and yet in its happy outcome the same.

For everyone taking part in a wedding each small event, like the solemn ritual of marriage itself, binds the generations in the shared belief that what has been true and lasting in the past is true and lasting today and will remain so safely across time. On such occasions sentiment and loving hope for the young couple—these two who are entering the most important relationship of their adult lives—join in renewing our faith in traditional forms. This, we believe, is how families begin.

But in the cool light of everyday experience a different picture emerges. As a society we have moved—and are still moving—a long way from the kinds of marriage our forefathers knew and believed in. We still define marriage as essentially an adult relationship. But now, in a period in which full participation in adult life is increasingly delayed, the age of first marriage for boys as well as girls has been declining steadily. And although people can look forward to longer years of vigorous maturity, young couples are entering parenthood not later than in the past, but even earlier.

We still believe that marriage entails financial responsibility. Yet we indulge in endless subterfuge to disguise the economic dependency of the majority of very young marriages. Significantly, we have devised systems of loans and insurance to ease our financial burden of seeing children through years of higher education. However, we have not invented any form of insurance to cover the care of children born of student marriages or born to teen-aged parents who are struggling to find themselves. If we encourage these young marriages, as in fact we do, then we must think more clearly about the long-term economic problems for which we, as parents, may have to take some responsibility.

We still believe that marriage is the necessary prelude to responsible parenthood even though, in every social class, pregnancy is to an increasing extent preceding marriage. We still strongly believe that children born of a marriage should be wanted. In the past, this meant accepting the birth of children no matter what the number and circumstances; but today, with existing methods of conception control, every child could be a chosen child.

We still believe that the continuity of the family, based on marriage, is fundamental to our way of life and to the well-being of every individual child. Yet there is clear evidence of the fragility of marriage ties, especially among very young couples who become parents before they know each other as husband and wife.

The disparities are plain to see and the outlook is unpromising. We might expect this to force us to recognize how great are the discrepancies between our expectations, based on tradition, and what is happening to young American families. The truth is, we have not really faced up to the many conflicts between belief and experience, precept and practice, in our current, muddled style of marriage. It is not enough to say, "Yes, marriage patterns are changing." What we have not fully realized is that we do not have to stand by helplessly while change sweeps over us, destroying our hopes for a better life for our children.

Instead, we can look steadily at the changes that have brought us where we are.

We can ask, "How can we invest marriage forms with new meaning?"

We can move toward a reconciliation of belief and practice that is consonant with our understanding of good human relationships.

Of course, there is no simple way of defining the changes that have already taken place, but two things are crucial in the contemporary situation —our attitude toward sex and our attitude toward commitment. Today, I am convinced, most Americans have come to regard sex, like eating and sleeping, as a natural activity. We lean toward the belief that people who are deprived of sex will be tense and crotchety, and perhaps unreliable in their personal relationships. We have come to believe also that asking physically mature young people to postpone sex until their middle twenties is neither fair nor feasible. And as we have learned to deal more evenhandedly with boys and girls most of us have ceased to believe in any double standard of morality. This is in keeping with our belief that sex, like marriage and parenthood, should involve social equals who are close in age. When the age gap widens—when the man is much older than the woman or the woman older than the man—we disapprove. And although we may not express our doubts, we do not have very high expectations for eventual happiness when two people must bridge wide differences in upbringing. We believe that young people should learn about sex together, as equals. But this means that both are likely to be equally inexperienced. Our emphasis, in the ideal, is on spontaneity. It is this combination of beliefs, together with our continuing certainty that sex is safe only in marriage, that has fostered —that has, in fact, forced—our present acceptance of very young marriage.

But in accepting early marriage as the easiest solution to the problem of providing a sex life for everyone, we confront new difficulties. No matter how many books adolescent boys and girls have read or how freely they have talked about sex, they actually know very little about it and are very likely to bungle their first serious sex relations. Certainly this is not new; an unhappy honeymoon all too often has been a haunting prelude to marriage. What is new is that the young husband and wife are as yet inexperienced in living through the initial difficulties that can enter into any important adult relationship of choice. They are, for example, inexperienced in making friends and living through the give-and-take that adult friendships require. Young men today rarely know how to make friends with girls; and girls, looking for mates, are unlikely to be much interested in a man as a friend. Heterosexual friendships therefore are postponed until after marriage, and then entered into only with other married couples. Thus friendship, which ideally should precede marriage and help the young man and woman better understand the adjustments that any adult relationship requires, now comes too late to help a first marriage.

Inexperience is one hazard. But it becomes especially hazardous because we also believe that no one should be trapped in a final mistake. Individuals as they grow and develop are permitted to change their jobs and occupations, to move from one part of the country to another, to form new associations and develop new interests that bring them into contact with new people. And as part of our expectation that people change as they grow, most of us have come also to accept the idea of divorce. When a marriage does not work out, most of us believe, each partner should have another chance to start over again with a different man or a different woman. We believe in commitment, but we do not believe that commitments are irrevocable.

But divorce also is a hazard. It is true that for two adults without children who now find that they cannot carry out a commitment made at an earlier stage of their lives, divorce can be an end and a beginning; but because of the role children play in the present style of marriage, divorce becomes a widespread hazard. For whereas in the past a man, and especially a woman, might marry in order to have children, now having a child validates marriage. Pregnancy often precedes marriage, and even where it does not, the style is to have a child quickly. It is as if having a child sets the seal of permanence on a marriage that is in truth far from permanent, and that at this stage is still in the making.

The child thus becomes a symbol. This use of a child is out of keeping with our belief that each person should be valued as an individual for his own sake. And when the marriage breaks down, the child is sacrificed to the changed needs of the man and woman, who are acting not as parents but as husband and wife. The child—a person in his own right, growing toward the future—stands as a symbol of an unreal past.

Perhaps we can catch a glimpse of what we might make of marriage and parenthood if we think in terms of a new pattern that would both give young couples a better chance to come to know each other and give children a better chance to grow up in an enduring family. Through what steps might this be accomplished?

It should be said at once that changes as important as those involved in creating a new style of marriage can never be brought about through the actions of a few people, or even all the members of a single group. In a democracy as complex as ours, in which one must always take into account a great diversity of religious, regional, class and national styles, success will depend on contributions made by all kinds of people. Ideas will arise out of discussions in the press, from the pulpits of churches, on television, in the agencies of government, in the theater and in community organizations. Some will come from those whose work brings them face-to-face with the failures of the present system and who are aware of the urgent need for new forms. Some will be shaped by the actual experiments in which lively, imaginative young people are engaging. And still others will arise out of the puzzlement and questions of the people who listen to the suggestions made by all those who are trying to become articulate about the issues. Out of all these discussions, carried on over a period of time, there will, I hope, evolve the kind of consensus that will provide the basis for a new marriage tradition. We are still a long way from the point at which we can consider the new tradition in such pragmatic terms as its formal social framework—in law and religious practice. No one, it should be clear, can write a prescription or make a blueprint for a whole society.

What I am doing here is advancing some ideas of my own as one contribution to an ongoing discussion. First I shall outline the goals that I personally hope we may reach.

I should like to see us put more emphasis upon the importance of human relationships and less upon sex as a physiological need. That is, I would hope that we could encourage a greater willingness to spend time searching for a congenial partner and to enjoy cultivating a deeply personal relationship. Sex then would take its place within a more complex intimacy and would cease to be sought after for itself alone.

I should like also to see children assured of a lifelong relationship to both parents. This, of course, can only be attained when parents themselves have such a relationship. I do not mean that parents must stay married. As long as early marriage remains a practice, it must be assumed that some marriages—perhaps many marriages—will break down in the course of a lifetime of growth, mobility and change. But I should like to see a style of parenthood develop that would survive the breaking of the links of marriage through divorce. This would depend on a mutual recognition that coparenthood is a permanent relationship. Just as brother and sister are irrevocably related because they share the same parents, so also parents are irrevocably related because they share the same child. At present, divorce severs the link between the adult partners and each, in some fashion, attempts—or sometimes gives up the attempt—to keep a separate contact with the children, as if this were now a wholly individual relationship. This need not be.

Granting the freedom of partners to an uncongenial marriage to seek a different, individual commitment within a new marriage, I would hope that we would hold on to the ideal of a lifetime marriage in maturity. No religious group that cherishes marriage as a sacrament should have to give up the image of a marriage that lasts into old age and into the lives of grandchildren and great-grandchildren as one that is blessed by God. No wholly secularized group should have to be deprived of the sense that an enduring, meaningful relationship is made binding by the acceptance, approval and support of the entire society as witnesses.

At the same time, I believe, we must give greater reality to our belief that marriage is a matter of individual choice, a choice made by each young man and woman freely, without coercion by parents or others. The present mode of seeking for sex among a wide range of partners casually, and then, inconsistently, of accepting marriage as a form of "choice" arising from necessity, is a deep denial of individuality and individual love. In courtship, intensity of feeling grows as two people move toward each other. In our present system, however, intensity of feeling is replaced by the tensions arising from a series of unknown factors: Will pregnancy occur? Is this the best bargain on the sex market? Even with sexual freedom, will marriage result? Today true courtship, when it happens, comes about in spite of, not because of, the existing styles of dating and marrying.

These goals—individual choice, a growing desire for a lifelong relationship with a chosen partner and the desire for children with whom and through whom lifelong relationships are maintained—provide a kind of framework for thinking about new forms of marriage. I believe that we need two types of marriage, one of which can (though it need not) develop into the other, each with its own possibilities and special forms of responsibility.

The first type of marriage may be called an *individual marriage*, binding together two individuals only. It has been suggested that it might be called a "student" marriage, as undoubtedly it would occur first and most often among students. But looking ahead, it would be a type of marriage that would also be appropriate for much older men and women; so I shall use the term individual marriage. Such a marriage would be a licensed union in which two individuals would be committed to each other as individuals for as long as they wished to remain together, but not as future parents. As the first step in marriage, it would not include having children.

In contrast, the second type of marriage, which I think of as *parental marriage*, would be explicitly directed toward the founding of a family. It would be not only a second type but also a second step or stage, following always on an individual marriage and with its own license and ceremony and kinds of responsibility. This would be a marriage that looked to a lifetime relationship with links, sometimes, to many people.

In an individual marriage the central obligation of the boy and girl or man and woman to each other would be an ethical, not an economic, one. The husband would not be ultimately responsible for the support of his wife: if the marriage broke up, there would be no alimony or support. The husband would not need to feel demeaned if he was not yet ready, or was not able, to support his wife. By the same token, husband or wife could choose freely to support the other within this partnership.

Individual marriage would give two very young people a chance to know each other with a kind of intimacy that does not usually enter into a brief love affair, and so it would help them to grow into each other's life—and allow them to part without the burden of misunderstood intentions, bitter recriminations and self-destructive guilt. In the past, long periods of engagement, entered into with parental consent, fulfilled at least in part the requirement of growing intimacy and shared experience. But current attitudes toward sex make any retreat to this kind of relationship impossible. In other societies, where parents chose their children's marriage partners, the very fact of meeting as strangers at the beginning of a lifelong relationship gave each a high sense of expectancy within which shared understanding might grow. But this is an impossible option for us because of our emphasis upon personal choice and our unwillingness to insist on maintaining a commitment that has failed.

Individual marriage in some respects resembles "companionate marriage" as it was first discussed in the 1920's and written about by Judge Ben Lindsey on the basis of his long experience in court with troubled young people. This was a time when very few people were ready as yet to look ahead to the consequences of deep changes in our attitude toward sex and personal choice. Today, I believe, we are far better able to place young marriage within the context of a whole lifetime.

Individual marriage, as I see it, would be a serious commitment, entered into in public, validated and protected by law and, for some, by religion, in which each partner would have a deep and continuing concern for the happiness and well-being of the other. For those who found happiness it could open the way to a more complexly designed future.

Every parental marriage, whether children were born into it or adopted, would necessarily have as background a good individual marriage. The fact of a previous marriage, individual or parental, would not alter this. Every parental marriage, at no matter what stage in life, would have to be preceded by an individual marriage. In contrast to individual marriage, parental marriage would be hard to contract. Each partner would know the other well, eliminating the shattering surprise of discovery that either one had suffered years of mental or physical illness, had been convicted of a serious crime, was unable to hold a job, had entered the country illegally, already had children or other dependents, or any one of the thousand shocks that lie in wait for the person who enters into a hasty marriage with someone he or she knows little about. When communities were smaller, most people were protected against such shocks by the publication of the banns. Today other forms of protection are necessary. The assurance thus given to parents that their son or daughter would not become hopelessly trapped into sharing parenthood with an unsuitable mate also would serve as a protection for the children, not yet born.

As a couple prepared to move from an individual to a parental marriage they also would have to demonstrate their economic ability to support a child. Instead of falling back on parents, going deeply into debt or having to ask the aid of welfare agencies, they would be prepared for the coming of a child. Indeed, both might be asked to demonstrate some capacity to undertake the care of the family in the event one or the other became ill. Today a girl's education, which potentially makes her self-sustaining, is perhaps the best dowry a man can give his son-in-law so he will not fall prey to the gnawing anxiety of how his family would survive his death. During an individual marriage, designed to lead to parental marriage, a girl, no less than a boy, might learn a skill that would make her self-supporting in time of need.

Even more basic to the survival of a marriage, however, is the quality of the marriage itself—its serenity, its emotional strength, its mutuality. Over long years we have acquired a fund of experience about good marriages through the inquiries made by adoption agencies before a child is given permanently to adoptive parents. Now, if we wished to do so, we could extrapolate from this experience for the benefit of partners in individual marriages but not yet joined in parenthood and for the benefit of infants hoped for but not yet conceived. And in the course of these explorations before parental marriage the ethical and religious issues that sometimes are glossed over earlier could be discussed and, in a good relationship, resolved. Careful medical examinations would bring to light present or potential troubles and, beyond this, would help the couple to face the issue: What if, in spite of our desire for a family, having a child entails a serious risk to the mother, or perhaps the child? What if, in spite of a good prognosis, we, as a couple, cannot have a child? And then, even assuming that all such questions have been favorably resolved, it must not be forgotten that in all human relationships there are imponderables—and the marriage will be tested by them.

As a parental marriage would take much longer to contract and would be based on a larger set of responsibilities, so also its disruption would be carried out much more slowly. A divorce would be arranged in a way that would protect not only the two adults but also the children for whose sake the marriage was undertaken. The family, as against the marriage, would have to be assured a kind of continuity in which neither parent was turned into an angry ghost and no one could become an emotional blackmailer or be the victim of emotional blackmail.

Perhaps some men and women would choose to remain within individual marriage, with its more limited responsibilities; having found that there was an impediment to parental marriage, they might well be drawn into a deeper individual relationship with each other. And perhaps some who found meaningful companionship through parenthood would look later for more individualized companionship in a different kind of person.

By dignifying individual relationships for young people we would simultaneously invest with new dignity a multitude of deeply meaningful relationships of choice throughout life. First and foremost, we would recognize parenthood as a special form of marriage. But we would also give strong support to marriage as a working relationship of husband and wife as colleagues and as a leisure relationship of a couple who have not yet entered into or who are now moving out of the arduous years of multiple responsibilities. By strengthening parenthood as a lasting relationship we would keep intact the link between grandparents, parents and children. Whether they were living together or were long since divorced, they would remain united in their active concern for their family of descendants. The acceptance of two kinds of marriage would give equal support, however, to the couple who, having forgone a life with children, cherish their individual marriage as the expression of their love and loyalty.

The suggestion for a style of marriage in two steps—individual marriage and marriage for parenthood—has grown out of my belief that clarification is the beginning of constructive change. Just as no one can make a blueprint of the future, so no one can predict the outcome of a new set of practices. We do know something about the unfortunate direction in which contemporary marriage is drifting. But we need not simply continue to drift. With our present knowledge, every child born can be a child wanted and prepared for. And by combining the best of our traditions and our best appraisal of human relations, we may succeed in opening the way for new forms of marriage that will give dignity and grace to all men and women.

## 3.3 CARL A. RIDLEY, DAN J. PETERMAN, AND ARTHUR W. AVERY

# *Cohabitation: Does It Make for a Better Marriage?*

One question that seems to cause curiosity in every generation of family scholars is whether or not cohabitation among unmarried heterosexual couples is good preparation for marriage. In this selection from the highly readable research article "Cohabitation: Does It Make for a Better Marriage?" *The Family Coordinator* (April 1978), Carl A. Ridley, Dan J. Peterman, and Arthur W. Avery offer a framework that identifies major types of cohabiting relationships. They also discuss the personal and relationship characteristics of people in each type of cohabiting relationship and offer pros and cons for each type of relationship as well. Although over 20 years old, this article has endured the test of time and continues to be relevant today in helping couples, therapists, and researchers to understand motivations for premarital cohabitation.

When this article was written, Ridley was a professor in and chair of the Department of Child Development and Family Relations at the University of Arizona; Peterman was a practicing clinical psychologist at the Mid-Coast Mental Health Center in Rockland, Maine; and Avery was the associate chair and professor in charge of the graduate program in the Department of Home and Family Life at Texas Tech University in Lubbock, Texas.

**Key Concept:** premarital cohabitation

*I*n the classroom and in counseling, individuals persist in their desire to know if living with their boyfriend or girlfriend will prepare them better for a satisfying marital relationship in the future. In addition, a common question in counseling is: "My girlfriend/boyfriend and I have been dating for a while and... ah, well, we were wondering what, ah,... you think about people living together before marriage?" As counselors and educators, our initial response to such an inquiry is to clarify the nature of the question and the feelings that underly it. Beyond that, however, we often find ourselves saying, "Well,... sometimes living together before marriage can provide positive experiences that will better prepare you for marriage, whereas other times living together is simply a matter of convenience for the individuals involved and is not likely to provide a better foundation for marriage."

No doubt all of us have witnessed cohabiting relationships which have proven particularly valuable for the individuals involved. The partners have learned to be more aware of their needs, more open and honest in their communication, more accepting of their own strengths and weaknesses and those of their partner, and perhaps more aware of the reciprocity necessary for maintaining satisfactory heterosexual relationships. Unfortunately, we have also seen situations where cohabiting relationships, not unlike some marital relationships, have been sources of constant misunderstanding, frustration, and resentment for the persons involved. Interactions of this type where one or both partners leave the relationship with a loss of self-esteem and a lack of self-confidence in their ability to maintain relationships with the opposite sex are not likely to encourage successful heterosexual relationships in the future.

Based on an understanding of our students and clients, then, we need to determine the likely benefits and costs of a cohabiting relationship. Unfortunately, as Blaine (1975) so aptly pointed out, "no scientifically valid survey has yet been made which shows the effect of living together beforehand upon marriage" (p. 32). As is frequently the problem, we are forced as counselors and teachers to advise individuals without having sufficient information on the issue at hand.

Despite the general lack of careful empirical study on the effects of living together before marriage on later marital success, it seems reasonable to conclude from the available evidence that not all cohabiting relationships have the same impact on individuals. In an initial attempt to describe the differential impact of cohabitation on the individuals involved, the authors focused their attention on a recent study by Peterman, Ridley, and Anderson (1974) that describes the background, personal, and interpersonal characteristics of cohabiting college students. It was apparent from a review of these findings that there is not a single type of cohabitation relationship, but rather several different types. In one type, both partners perceive themselves as well-adjusted and see the relationship as a positive learning experience. In another type, however, one or both partners see themselves as not well-adjusted and perceive the relationship as a source of dissatisfaction.

A basic assumption of this paper is that cohabiting relationships are not inherently good or bad for the persons involved, but rather they have the potential to be both depending on the goals, expectations, and skills of the cohabiting individuals. In the following section, several types of cohabiting relationships are discussed in the hope that by recognizing individual and relationship characteristics associated with positive cohabiting experiences and comparing those to characteristics associated with negative cohabiting experiences, we will be better able to assess the likely impact of a cohabiting experience on those who seek our counsel.

# TYPES OF COHABITING RELATIONSHIPS

Four commonly observed types of cohabiting relationships are described in terms of their potential value as marriage preparation experiences for the individuals involved. The major objective of this typology is to identify and explain some of the general discernable themes of cohabiting relationships, not to describe numerous individual relationship variations. The typology is based on an integration of information from existing research on cohabitation (e.g., Henze & Hudson, 1974; Lyness, Note 1; Macklin, Note 2; Peterman, et al., 1974) as well as on clinical observations....

*"Linus Blanket"*. The first type of cohabiting relationship described here, "Linus Blanket," is characterized by what appears to be an overwhelming need for one member of the pair to have a relationship with *someone*, with little apparent regard for whom, or under what conditions. To have someone to be with, even though he or she may treat you badly, is better than not having anyone at all. It seems that the need to feel secure through a relationship makes it virtually unimportant to evaluate the circumstances of relationship formation, the motivations of the partner, or the conditions surrounding relationship continuation. Thus, the primary goal of this relationship is one of emotional security. For example, the insecure partner (male or female) in this situation comes across as a clinging vine. When interacting with others, this individual typically stays physically close to the partner, depends on him/her to carry the conversation, and when the individual speaks, comments revolve primarily around the partner. So long as the more secure partner does not feel trapped in this situation and their behavior remains predictable, the insecure partner's basic needs are likely to be met. The fragility of this relationship seldom leads to the type of interaction between partners that increases the development of interpersonal skills important for maintaining heterosexual relationships. The insecure person attempts to elicit interaction with the secure partner which can be interpreted as self-confirming. Negative statements made to the insecure person (frequently in the form of criticisms) are often interpreted as a severe questioning of his or her self-worth. The result is that the more secure person perceives and/or acts as if the partner is fragile ("can't take criticism") and that they cannot "rock the boat" without hurting their partner and the relationship.

Since it is through the constructive handling of disagreements that internal relationship changes take place (e.g., Raush, Barry, Hertel, & Swain, 1974), the more secure partner is often forced into accepting the relationship as it is or leaving it. If the relationship is maintained, open communication and successful problem solving do not take place and thus the experience does not serve as "practice" for improving the skills of the partners. Continued interaction is likely to be ritualized following traditional lines of male-female role behavior. In this case, the "Linus Blanket" relationship provides an opportunity to learn sex role stereotyped behaviors. When a "Linus Blanket" type relationship terminates, the insecure individual typically suffers a loss of self-esteem which neutralizes much of the potential gain of having lived with someone in an intimate relationship.

*"Emancipation"*. Peterman, et al. (1974), found that more than 75 percent of the "repeating" cohabiting males and females (those with more than one cohabiting experience) reported that their longest cohabiting experience lasted less than six months. Two relatively distinct types of cohabiting relationships appeared typical of this group—"Emancipation" and "Convenience." Although the "Emancipation" type of cohabiting relationship was apparent for both males and females, perhaps the clearest example of this pattern was found among Catholic females who started cohabiting early in their college years and maintained a pattern of short duration but frequent cohabiting relationships (Peterman, et al., 1974). It was concluded that these females must be experiencing pulls, pushes, and resistances to becoming involved in cohabiting relationships. Such resistances may reside primarily in socialization to strict sexual standards from family and church which deny guilt-free participation in sexualized heterosexual relationships. The restrictions seem to be countered by internal pushes to loosen external controls and to demonstrate increased freedom by becoming sexually active. Peer pressures which typically support a liberalized set of sexual norms place the Catholic females in a potentially double binding situation. The double bind develops something like this: peer pressure and the desire for more self control result in her becoming involved in a cohabiting situation. The subtle guilt feeling of "doing something wrong," however, makes it difficult for her to become actively involved in the cohabiting situation and ultimately forces her exit. Once out of the relationship, the pulls and pushes reassert themselves and the cycle repeats itself. In an attempt to determine the effect of this type of cohabiting situation on the female, a general principle originating in Gestalt therapy provides an interesting perspective. Namely, when someone is carrying around extensive "unfinished business," it is difficult to function adequately in the here and now. The "unfinished business" in the "Emancipation" type of cohabiting relationship continues to encourage cohabiting relationships while a value system does not support it. Tenuous involvement in the cohabiting relationship does not allow for the type of practice necessary to improve interaction skills. When the pattern is left unchecked, reasons for exit from the relationship are rarely understood and result in confusion and self-doubt on the part of both partners. Should the cohabiting experiences serve the purpose of helping the person work through the value-behavior discrepancy, then the increased self-knowledge would be reflected in better preparation for future heterosexual relating.

*"Convenience"*. A third type of cohabiting relationship, "Convenience," is perhaps best exemplified in the short duration cohabiting relationship of freshmen or sophomore males. This cohabiting situation allows the male to have regularized sexual contact and the luxuries of domestic living without the responsibilities of a committed relationship. The performance of many of the domestic tasks falls to the female simply because she is thought to be more skilled and/or has been socialized to perform them. His major task is to keep the female interested in the relationship when it appears that she is putting more into the relationship than he is. If he can maintain this type of relationship, and most do not, he is probably exhibiting a fairly high interpersonal skill level even though the inequity of the relationship may seem somewhat unjust. This

type of cohabiting situation provides a rich opportunity for both the male and the female to learn the idea of reciprocity—mutual giving and getting in a relationship. She can learn that unconditional giving can have limited long-range payoff and that assessments of what one is giving and getting are important in certain contexts. At times it appears that the female is trying to make the male so dependent on her that he would not think of leaving the relationship. At other times, it appears she is simply fitting into the culturally prescribed role for women. It appears that the male is getting much practice at strategic interaction by trying to maintain his freedom to interact with others (keeping his options open), but at the same time presenting to his partner a high level of involvement in the cohabiting relationship. Generally, he seems to learn a great deal about the day-to-day aspects of domestic life (role behavior) and at least some exchange skills. His guarded openness serves the purpose of preventing the type of involvement that escalates the relationship toward a premature commitment.

Although it may appear from the above description that the male is getting the better end of the deal, it should be noted that both the male and female are learning important aspects of "survival" within intimate relationships— even though this learning may be painful for one or both of them. Although the authors have found from their experience that this situation is most typical with the male in the convenience role, the situation is sometimes reversed with a more assertive female forming and maintaining the relationship primarily for its convenience qualities. Future research will be needed to determine if this type of heterosexual interaction early in the college years makes it more difficult to make permanent commitments later in life.

*"Testing".* Individuals who are in the "Testing" type of cohabiting relationship are typically well-adjusted people (lacking extensive past grievances or major individual problems) who exhibit a higher than average interpersonal skill level upon entrance into a cohabiting relationship. Macklin (1974) suggests that one of the most difficult tasks in a cohabiting relationship is to form a good intimate relationship while at the same time maintaining individuality and autonomy. The mutuality-autonomy issue seems to surface primarily when the individuals involved have met their security needs and are motivated to try out a quasi-committed relationship with the intent being to learn more about themselves and complex intimate relationships. When their basic needs have been met, they are then able to move outside their own skin and become interested in the well-being of their partner. This willingness to get to know one's partner facilitates deeper reciprocal levels of self-disclosure. In a sense, the partners seem to use the relationship to get to know more about themselves —their likes and dislikes, and to learn more about how intimate relationships of this type apparently lead to a deeper level of self-understanding for both individuals. However, when the relationship solidifies too quickly—prior to the development of individual interests and preferences—the partners feel overinvolved and dependent on the relationship with the accompanying sense of loss of identity (Macklin, Note 2).

The combination of perceived loss of identity and high relationship cohesiveness *without* commitment increases the probability that many "Testing" relationships will terminate at this juncture. If the mutuality-autonomy issue is handled successfully, the relationship may develop in one of three directions:

1. The relationship can terminate because the primary objectives for its formation (of which they may or may not have been aware) have been accomplished (increased self-understanding within a relationship context and increased knowledge of day-to-day intimate living).

2. The relationship can become an enduring cohabiting relationship similar to a marriage relationship, but without formal commitment and the ever-present possibility of terminating the relationship. The effects on the relationship of a lack of formal commitment and the availability of alternative sources of gratification is as yet unclear. It might be suggested that the persons involved would have to possess sufficient interpersonal skills to maintain this type of relationship without experiencing continuous crises through attempts to establish relationship predictability.

3. Another direction the relationship could take is for the goal to be extended from increasing self-understanding within the relationship context to developing a marital relationship which would involve further testing of compatibility and the ability to work together. If the cohabiting experience demonstrated to the couple that they could not work together, the relationship would likely terminate. If compatibility testing were positive, escalation toward marriage would be likely.

The authors have taken a special interest in the termination of those "Testing" relationships which are less traumatic for the participants with the idea that much can be learned about the acquisition of interpersonal skills and marriage preparation under these conditions. Although it is unclear why some terminations are as easy as they are, some information is available that may help to explain it:

1. Most of the individuals in "Testing" relationships have had a rich dating history in which the outcome was a confirmation of their desirability to the opposite sex and a developed repertoire of interpersonal skills.

2. Cohabitation was a small step from their previous experiences in terms of the degree of involvement and complexity of the heterosexual relationship. Although frequently not at a conscious level, participants had ordered their experiences with increased complexity so that cohabitation was only different from previous involvements in degree, not type. Thus, they were largely prepared for what would be required of them in a complex cohabiting situation. It has been hypothesized that heterosexual relationship termination (including cohabitation termination) will be traumatic when the involvement that is being terminated is very different from the previous level of involvement. It is when this gap exists that the relationship is most "potent" in terms of its positive or negative impact on the participants. For example, termination of a cohabiting relationship would be more traumatic when the highest level of previous involvement had been "casual dating" than when the previous involvement had been "going steady."

3. Another factor which cushions the impact of termination is that "Testing" cohabitors typically have a fairly extensive network of like and opposite sex relationships (Peterman, et al., 1974) that provide friends at termination and a pool of possible eligibles for future involvement. Rather than being alone in

their loss, they have friends to talk to and to become involved with and the known ability to start new heterosexual involvements when desired.

4. Lastly, they exhibit a high interpersonal skill level at termination by "closing the door" to the relationship. When termination was the result of unresolved problems, each partner knew what went wrong and how they contributed to the problem.

In short, the major potential advantage of a cohabiting relationship is its structural complexity. The potential extensive demands of a cohabiting relationship, in particular a "Testing" type of relationship, more closely approximate marital demands than any other courtship pattern. Thus, if individuals have experience in which gradual increments of interpersonal skills were learned, cohabitation can be an ideal situation for "trial marriage" and for learning the complexity of intimate relationship functioning. However, if preparatory experiences have not occurred, cohabitation tends to result in: (a) social isolation, and (b) solidification of non-adaptive interactional patterns within the cohabiting relationship.

## IMPLICATIONS

It should be apparent at this point that a specific answer to the question of whether cohabitation makes for a better marriage is as yet unavailable. With a knowledge of the cohabitation typology presented here *and* an accurate understanding of the persons involved, however, it should be easier to assess the potential effects of cohabitation on the individuals. In order to do this effectively, several important factors must be considered, including (a) partners' motivations for cohabiting, (b) partners' expectations for the cohabiting experience, (c) partners' personal and interpersonal needs and goals, (d) partners' interpersonal skill levels, (e) the present status of the relationship (e.g., level of commitment), (f) the effects of the partners' previous heterosexual experiences, and (g) the support structure of the partners' interpersonal networks.

Fortunately, much of this information can be obtained either through personal interaction or observation of the individuals involved. Although it is obvious that there are wide individual differences in these areas, as a general rule it appears that cohabiting relationships are likely to provide positive learning experiences and better preparation for marriage when the participants: (a) have as cohabitation goals, greater self-understanding within a heterosexual context and increased knowledge of day-to-day aspects of intimate living, (b) have realistic and mutually agreed upon expectations for the cohabiting experience, (c) do not have strong "deficiency" needs for emotional security (e.g., "Linus Blanket") or a residue of past grievances and/or unfinished business (e.g., "Emancipation"), (d) have higher interpersonal skill levels (e.g., the ability to openly and honestly express their feelings, the ability to understand and accept their partner, and the ability to mutually solve problems), (e) have had a relationship where the present degree of involvement closely approximates that of a cohabiting relationship (e.g., steady dating rather than casual dating), (f) have a rich dating history resulting in positive self-perceptions in terms of their desirability to the opposite sex, and (g) have a fairly extensive network of like and opposite sex relationships where important needs are being met....

## SUMMARY AND CONCLUSIONS

The degree to which cohabiting experiences prepare individuals for marriage depends in part on the needs, goals, motivations, and competence of the persons involved. It would seem unfortunate to conclude that cohabitation is inherently good or bad preparation for marriage, but rather it should be viewed as having the potential for both, with the characteristics of the individuals and the relationship being of critical importance in determining the long-range effects of cohabitation.

Educators and counselors can discuss the concept of living together before marriage with the openness and objectivity with which they discuss other premarital heterosexual experiences. They can outline the personal skills and abilities which individuals typically require in order to function effectively in marriage as well as how certain types of cohabiting arrangements can facilitate growth in these areas. One such area where a cohabiting experience can prepare individuals for marriage involves sex roles and sex role expectations. With changing socialization patterns, sex role structures and expectations of husbands and wives are no longer as clearly defined as they once were. As Peterman (1975) noted:

> Partners must now work out a role differentiation to suit their own unique personal and pair characteristics rather than simply following models handed down by tradition. To do so requires replacing romantic myth by a capacity to be more aware of one's own needs, learning habits of openness, practicing becoming accurately empathic, acquiring information and technique in human sexuality, ridding oneself of sexist attitudes, and so forth. (p. 40–41)

Lee (1975) expressed another potential positive outcome of cohabitation: "The essence of marriage is commitment, the contract and the concern shared by the couple. If they express these mutual responsibilities as living together without formal marriage, it is likely that when the formal promises are made the marriage will have greater endurance" (p. 41). The authors have argued that living together before marriage may also result in unpredictable or clearly negative consequences: "If living together is undertaken as a trial of compatibility motivated by curiosity rather than by commitment, the results are likely to be as whimsical and unpredictable as the curiosity of the participants" (p. 41).

In summary, the guidelines presented in the previous section—linked to the cohabitation typology outlined earlier—hopefully will serve as a first step toward increasing our understanding of how cohabitation affects preparation for marriage. Future research is sorely needed, however, to further clarify the types of cohabiting relationships, the degree to which couples might move from one type to another, and to identify the person and relationship characteristics that play an important role in determining the long-range effects of living together before marriage.

# NOTES

1. Lyness, J. F. Open marriage among former cohabitants: "We have met the enemy: Is it us?" Manuscript submitted for publication, 1976.
2. Macklin, E. D. *Unmarried Heterosexual Cohabitation on the University Campus*. Unpublished manuscript, Cornell University, 1974.

# REFERENCES

Blaine, G. B. Does living together before marriage make for a better marriage? *Medical Aspects of Human Sexuality*, 1975, **9**, 32–39.

Henze, L. F., & Hudson, J. W. Personal and family characteristics of cohabiting and non-cohabiting college students. *Journal of Marriage and the Family*, 1974, **36**, 722–727.

Lee, R. V. Does living together before marriage make for a better marriage? *Medical Aspects of Human Sexuality*, 1975, **9**, 41–44.

Peterman, D. J. Does living together before marriage make for a better marriage? *Medical Aspects of Human Sexuality*, 1975, **9**, 39–41.

Peterman, D. J., Ridley, C. A., & Anderson, S. M. A comparison of cohabiting and non-cohabiting college students. *Journal of Marriage and the Family*, 1974, **36**, 344–354.

Raush, H. L., Barry, W. A., Hertel, R. K., & Swain, M. A. *Communication, conflict and marriage*. New York: Jossey-Bass, 1974.

# CHAPTER 4 Theories of Mate Selection

### 4.1 ALAN C. KERCKHOFF AND KEITH E. DAVIS

## *Value Consensus and Need Complementarity in Mate Selection*

Mate selection was never more popular an area of study for family scholars than in the late 1950s and early 1960s. In this selection from "Value Consensus and Need Complementarity in Mate Selection," *American Sociological Review* (June 1962), Alan C. Kerckhoff and Keith E. Davis offer a theoretical understanding of mate selection as a series of filtering processes that ultimately lead to marriage. This article was an early attempt to integrate some of the prevailing ideas about mate selection into one comprehensive theory. In essence, the theory suggests that successful filtering through the sociological concepts of endogamy followed by homogamy and finally heterogamy leads to the selection of a mate.

Kerckhoff was a professor of sociology at Duke University in Durham, North Carolina, when he teamed with Davis of Princeton University to formulate this paper. Kerckhoff had a brilliant career as a family scholar and received numerous honors, awards, and visiting scholar positions.

**Key Concept:** mate selection

*Alan C. Kerckhoff and Keith E. Davis*

One of the continuing interests in family research has been the attempt to define the factors which lead to a lasting relationship between a man and a woman. The two major concerns in such research have been with the process through which mates are chosen and the characteristics of mates which are predictive of "success" in the marital relationship. A considerable body of knowledge has been assembled based on data gathered in both the premarital and postmarital periods. Although there have been somewhat inconsistent results at times, the most general conclusion suggested by these data is that individuals who are similar to each other are most likely to choose each other as mates and are most likely to be successful in the relationship. Similarities have been noted in a large number of characteristics such as area of residence, socioeconomic level, religious affiliation and activity, and many kinds of attitudes and values. This tendency toward homogamy in mate selection, however, is not the only tendency noted in the literature. A strong case has been made, for instance, for the proposition that heterogamy or complementarity of personality needs is an important principle of selection. [Robert F.] Winch has indicated that those variables normally associated with the theory of homogamy in mate selection simply define the "field of eligibles" from which each individual then chooses a mate who is likely to complement himself on the personality level.

The present study is intended as a contribution to this body of knowledge. The major innovation it introduces is a longitudinal perspective during the selection period so that further knowledge of the actual selection process is gained. This is in contrast to most of the earlier studies which have compared a number of cases at a single point in time. The present study attempts to examine the relationship between progress in the mate selection process in the premarital period and measures of homogamy and complementarity.

# METHOD

In October, 1959 an attempt was made to enlist the cooperation of a number of women students at Duke University as participants in this study. This was done both through calling a meeting for this purpose and through making the study instruments available in the dormitories. Women who were engaged, pinned or "seriously attached" were asked to participate. The latter term was used to refer to those who were seriously considering marriage even though not actually pinned or engaged. Since the women were told that the man would be asked to take part also, we assume the group was limited to those who were fairly confident of the relationship. The women filled out an extended questionnaire (including materials not reported here) and gave us the names and addresses of their fiancés or boy-friends. The same questionnaire was sent to the men by mail. One hundred and sixteen women filled out the questionnaire, and 103 of their boy-friends returned completed questionnaires. In May of 1960 both members of the 103 couples on whom we had complete October data were sent another short questionnaire. Data for the present report on 94 couples were derived from these returns.

Four factors were considered in the analysis. The dependent variable was the degree of movement toward a permanent union between October and May. The two independent variables were: (a) the degree of consensus between the man and woman on family values, and (b) the degree of need complementarity. In addition, the length of time the couple had been going together was used as a control variable since it was expected that the relationship of either or both of the independent variables with the dependent variable might differ at different stages of the mate selection process.

Two hypotheses guided the analysis:

(1) Degree of value consensus is positively related to progress toward a permanent union.

(2) Degree of need complementarity is positively related to progress toward a permanent union.

The variables were measured as follows:

*Progress toward a permanent union.* In May the subjects were asked: "Is the relationship (between you two) different from what it was last fall when you filled out the first questionnaire?" There were three possible responses: "Yes, we are farther from being a permanent couple," "No, it is the same," and "Yes, we are nearer to being a permanent couple." Since only twelve gave the first response, the sample was divided into those who said they were *closer* to being a permanent couple (56 couples) vs. all others (38 couples). This factor will be referred to as "progress toward permanence."

*Value consensus.* Bernard Farber's "index of consensus" was used for this purpose. As in Farber's original work, both members of the couple were asked (in October) to rank order ten standards by which family success might be measured. The rank correlation between the two sets of rankings was the index of consensus....

*Need complementarity.* William Schutz's FIRO-B scales were used in the October questionnaire. There are six of these scales consisting of nine items each. Each scale is concerned with one of the content variables which Schutz calls "inclusion," "control," and "affection," and each is also concerned with either the desire to have others act in some way toward one's self or the desire to act in some way toward others. These two directions are called "wanted" and "expressed" by Schutz. Before computing the complementarity scores for each couple, the scalability of the six scales was tested. It was found that it was necessary to reduce the size of the scales to five items each in order to arrive at equal-sized scales which met the scaling criteria for both men and women separately. Using the scale scores on the six five-item scales, need complementarity was computed using Schutz's formula for what he calls "reciprocal compatibility." The formula is $rk_{ij} = |e_i - w_j| + |e_j - w_i|$ where $e_i$ and $w_i$ are the expressed and wanted scores of the man and $e_j$ and $w_j$ are the expressed and wanted scores of the woman. A separate rk was computed for each need area (inclusion, control, and affection). Since the scale scores varied from 0 to 5, it was possible for rk to assume values of from 0 to 10, lower values indicating greater complementarity....

*Length of association.* For the purposes of this analysis, couples were divided into approximately equal groups, the "long-term" group having gone together for 18 months or more, the "short-term" group having gone together less than 18 months.

## RESULTS

Since the dependent variable was a dichotomy and since the independent variables could not be assumed to be more than ordinal scales, the form of analysis used was the test of significance of the difference in the proportions of couples showing progress toward permanence in the categories defined by the hypotheses. In all tests, the distributions of cases on the independent and control variables were dichotomized as close to the median as possible. One-tailed tests were used.

When the simple relationships between the independent and the dependent variables were tested, only that between value consensus and progress in the relationship proved to be statistically significant at the .05 level or better. Two of the measures of complementarity (inclusion and control) approached this level of significance, however, and the third relationship was in the predicted direction.... Although these findings lead to the tentative acceptance of the first hypothesis and the rejection of the second, further analysis presents a somewhat different picture.

As we have noted, all four of the differences... are in the predicted direction. It may also be argued that *if* the two hypotheses being tested are true, we should find a general pattern of relationships among the categories of couples defined by a combination of the two types of independent variables (homogamy and complementarity). This pattern should be: HH>Mixed>LL. (Since the original hypotheses did not include a statement about the relative importance of the two independent variables, there is no basis for predicting a difference between the HL and LH cases within the Mixed category.)... [W]ith one exception, this pattern is found in each of the combinations of value consensus with one of the complementarity measures.

In all three sets of comparisons, the difference between the HH and the LL cases approaches significance. Although this... does not provide unequivocal support for the hypotheses, it does present a rather consistent pattern of relationships which may be derived from those hypotheses.

The introduction of the control variable of length of association provides even more information about the adequacy of the hypotheses.... In all four cases, the introduction of the control variable points up a difference in the pattern for short-term and long-term couples. Most interesting is the fact that the pattern is consistently different for value consensus and the three measures of need complementarity.

The relationship between value consensus and progress toward permanence is still significant for the short-term couples as it was for the total sample. However, for the long-term couples, although the direction of the relationship remains the same, the degree of significance falls even below the .10 level. On the other hand, when the relationships between progress toward permanence and the three measures of complementarity are examined, the reverse is true. For the short-term couples there is no hint of a relationship between complementarity and progress toward permanence. But for the long-term couples the relationship is significant at the .02 level in the inclusion area and at the .05 level in the control area. In the affection area the direction of the relationship is the same, but it is not statistically significant.

Although it had originally been considered necessary to control for length of association while examining the relationship between the independent and dependent variables, the particular pattern of relationships which was found had not been hypothesized. The original hypotheses simply dealt with the overall relationship between progress toward permanence and value consensus and the three measures of complementarity. Thus, it is not possible to state that the original hypotheses were clearly either confirmed or denied by the data, although value consensus was significantly related to progress toward permanence for the total sample.

## DISCUSSION

If we accept the pattern of relationships discussed above as significant for the research enterprise, two further issues remain: (a) How do we interpret or explain the pattern of relationships noted? (b) How does this research fit into the body of knowledge about the process of mate selection?

Turning to the first question, it is necessary to argue on a somewhat *ad hoc* basis since the specific pattern of relationships found had not been explicitly predicted. However, the pattern does fit rather well with some earlier work in the field of inquiry. It was noted above that Winch speaks of the "field of eligibles" from which one presumably chooses a spouse who complements one's personality needs. In his discussion of the concept "field of eligibles" Winch says:

> There is a set of variables upon which homogamy has been shown to function: race, religion, social class, broad occupational grouping, location of residence, income, age, level of education, intelligence, etc. It is my opinion that these variables function to select for each of us the sort of people with whom we shall be most likely to interact, to assure that the people with whom we otherwise associate are more or less like us with respect to that set of variables and also with respect to cultural interests and values.

Although neither this particular passage nor others in Winch's writings make the point explicit, he seems to be lumping social structure variables and attitude and value variables together in his discussion. The expectation that the two kinds of variables would be highly correlated is a reasonable one, but, we would argue, further understanding of the selection process might be gained if we examined the concept "field of eligibles" more closely.

The present study indicates that such a blanket statement concerning the homogamy variables may give a misleading image of the mate selection process. The homogamy variable discussed above is value consensus. However, other measures of homogamy were also made in this study, such as education, religion, and father's occupation. It is of interest to note that such social categories did not discriminate effectively among the couples. That is, the subjects of this study were very homogamous with respect to social attributes. On the other hand, the use of the more individual measure of values reported here led to a much clearer discrimination among the couples,... although even here the degree of homogamy is notable.

Thus, a different kind of homogamy is evidently represented by family value consensus than by similarity in social characteristics. Evidently the couples of the present study had *already* limited their field of eligibles with respect to social characteristics but were far from having limited it with respect to value consensus.

This leads us to the tentative suggestion that there are various "filtering factors" operating during the mate selection period. The social attributes presumably operate at an early stage, but values and needs are more clearly operative later on.

Our data do not fit neatly into the logic of a serial set of filtering factors, however. If they did, and if we assume that social attributes, value consensus, and complementarity operate in that order, we would expect a significantly higher proportion of high value consensus couples in the long-term group, since many of the low consensus couples would have broken up (been filtered out) in the early stages of courtship. This is not the case. What we do find is that *if* the couple survives the earlier stages despite having low value consensus, they are more likely than short-term low consensus couples to progress toward permanence, and this greater likelihood is largely explained by the variable of complementarity.

This may be seen in part from the fact that long-term low consensus couples show progress more often than short-term low consensus couples (.538 *vs* .350). If the low consensus couples are sorted according to *both* length of association *and* one measure of complementarity, however, it is even more striking.... In the case of each measure of complementarity, there is a negligible difference in the short-term row but a very sizeable difference in the long-term row. Thus, complementarity evidently does have a differential effect in long-term and short-term low consensus couples. What remains unspecified is the mechanism through which some short-term low consensus couples manage to stay together.

However, even if this question were answered adequately, our data raise another question about the order of influence of these filtering factors, namely: How does it happen that the filtering effects of need complementarity are not noticeable until the later stages of courtship? Although our data do not provide a wholly satisfactory answer to this question either, some light may be shed on the issue. One of the measures used in the October questionnaire was the other half of Farber's "Index of Marital Integration," the measure of value consensus being the first half. This second measure involves the rating of one's self and of one's partner on a set of personality characteristics. Some of these characteristics are "negative," such as "irritable," "stubborn," "easily excited," etc. Scores are computed for each person according to the number and intensity of such negative personality traits he attributes to his partner. If we sum the two scores for the couple, we have a measure of negative person perceptions in the couple or what Farber calls "an index of role tension."

When we analyze these scores according to the length of association, we find that short-term couples have much lower scores than long-term couples. That is, short-term couples were less likely to attribute negative personality characteristics to each other than were long-term couples. Also, there is a greater tendency for the person perception scores of short-term couples to become *more* negative between October and May, even when we hold original scores constant. This seems to be in keeping with the point so often stressed in the literature that couples go through a period of idealization and perception distortion which may lead to disillusionment (or "reality shock") at a later date.

In the light of our other findings, we would interpret this to mean that the short-term couples were likely to be responding to an idealized version of the love object which would make the effectiveness of any personality complementarity less probable. They were responding to a stylized role relationship rather than to another personality. Not until the idealization is destroyed can they interact at the more realistic level of personality, and only then can need complementarity "make a difference" in the relationship.

We may now turn to our other question: How does this research fit into the body of knowledge about the process of mate selection? First, the research gives added support for both the homogamy and complementarity theories, and it provides a tentative statement of the relationship between these two during the selection process.

Second, rather than simply comparing married or engaged couples with a random pairing of other individuals in order to show greater complementarity in the couples, this study attempts to demonstrate that complementarity "makes a difference" in the actual selection process. So far as we know, this is the first time such a longitudinal perspective has been provided.

Third, this is the first study of mate selection in which paper and pencil measures have pointed to a significant contribution of complementarity in the selection process. One of the criticisms of Winch's work has been that his measures were not adequately freed of rater bias. On the other hand, one of Winch's criticisms of other attempts to test the importance of complementarity with paper and pencil instruments has been that such instruments are not sufficiently sensitive to tap the relevant need area. Although there may be some disagreement over the adequacy of our operational definitions of the needs involved, the fact remains that this study has been more successful in showing a contribution of complementarity than any other of its kind.

Finally, although the present study has added to our knowledge, it still leaves many unanswered questions which are also left unanswered by earlier studies. One of the most critical of these is the question of the importance or the salience of the needs being studied. In order for complementarity to make much of a difference in the selection process, one would expect that the needs involved must be of some importance to the individuals. Neither the present study nor the earlier ones has provided a means of determining the salience of the needs. It would be possible with the present measuring devices to use the intensity dimension of Guttman scaling as a measure of salience, but with such a small sample the simultaneous control of another variable in addition to those already included would not be feasible.

## SUMMARY

We have reported on the findings of a study in which measures of value consensus and need complementarity have been shown to be related to a sense of progress toward permanence during a seven-month interval in the mate selection period. Although only value consensus was related to progress toward permanence for the sample as a whole, when the sample was divided into long-term and short-term couples, value consensus was related to progress for the short-term couples and two of three measures of complementarity were related to progress for the long-term couples. These findings are interpreted as indicating that a series of "filtering factors" operate in mate selection at different stages of the selection process. Our data generally support the idea that social status variables (class, religion, etc.) operate in the early stages, consensus on values somewhat later, and need complementarity still later. Our interpretation of the delay in the operation of the complementarity factor is that such personality linkages are often precluded by the unrealistic idealization of the loved one in the early stages of courtship.

4.2 ROBERT F. WINCH

# *Another Look at the Theory of Complementary Needs in Mate-Selection*

In the 1950s Robert F. Winch created a stir among family scholars when he presented empirical evidence suggesting that need complementarity is the major driving force that motivates a person to select a mate. Numerous studies resulted that largely refuted Winch's claim. However, Winch continued to publish data that supported his contentions, and lively debate in the academic community ensued. By offering this theory, Winch created an awareness of the need for research in the area of mate selection, a need that family scholars rallied to address. This selection from "Another Look at the Theory of Complementary Needs in Mate-Selection," *Journal of Marriage and the Family* (November 1967) provides an overview of Winch's theory of complementary needs in mate selection and updates how the theory evolved in the 10 or so years after it was originally presented.

Winch was a professor of sociology at Northwestern University in Evanston, Illinois, when he wrote this article. Prior to his death in 1977, he was prolific in his research and publications on family-related issues and was honored by numerous professional organizations for his contributions to the field.

**Key Concept:** mate selection

## INTRODUCTION

The purpose of this paper is to review the theory of complementary needs in mate-selection and to indicate the direction in which the theory has recently been developing.

From 1954 through 1958 the writer and his associates published several papers and a book on the theory of complementary needs in mate-selection. Very simply, the theory begins with the observation that in the United States mate-selection has been shown to be largely homogamous with respect to age, race, religion, social class, education, location of previous residence, and previous marital status. It has been proposed that these variables define for each individual a field of eligible spouse-candidates and that there remains the task of accounting for mate-selection within the field of eligibles. Toward this objective the theory of complementary needs offers the following hypothesis: In mate-selection each individual seeks within his or her field of eligibles for that person who gives the greatest promise of providing him or her with maximum need gratification.

## THE ORIGINAL TEST OF THE THEORY

In 1950, 25 young married couples served as test subjects for the theory. At the time of testing, one or both members of each couple were undergraduate students. In 1950 a considerable number of veterans of World War II were still completing their education, and a considerable number of the husbands in this study were veterans. An effort was made to obtain couples as soon after marriage as possible. No couple had been married more than two years; the median couple had been married for one. At the time of being interviewed no couple had children.

The data-gathering procedure employed two interviews and a projective test. The main interview (called a "need interview") was based on nearly 50 open-ended questions. Each question was designed to elicit information on the intensity of one of the needs or traits, i.e., to give an indication as to the strength of the need in the person being interviewed and the manner in which that person went about obtaining gratification for the need or expressing the trait. For example, to elicit information about the subject's hostile need (n Hos), he was asked the following:

> Let us suppose that you have entered a crowded restaurant, have stepped in line, have waited your turn, and presently someone enters and steps in front of you in line. What would you do? Has this ever happened to you? When was the last time this happened? Tell me about it.

A second interview sought to uncover the subject's perceptions concerning the salient relationships in his life and how he saw these as being related to his psychic and social development. In particular, he was asked to recount from his earliest memories the history of his relationships with his parents and siblings, as well as those in school and peer group. The third procedure was an abridged (ten-card) version of the Thematic Apperception Test, wherein a person is presented with a somewhat ambiguous picture concerning which he is asked to tell a story.

From each of these three sets of information a separate set of ratings was developed. For each instrument at least two raters were employed.

The theory was interpreted as predicting two types of complementariness:

*Type I.* The same need is gratified in both person A and person B but at very different levels of intensity. A negative interspousal correlation is hypothesized. For example, it is hypothesized that if one spouse is highly dominant, the other will be very low on that need.

*Type II.* Different needs are gratified in *A* and *B*. The interspousal correlation may be hypothesized to be either positive or negative, contingent upon the pair of needs involved. For example, it is hypothesized that if one spouse is highly nurturant, the other will be found to be high on the succorant (or dependent) need.

Statistical analysis of the results came out in the hypothesized direction, and the data were interpreted as providing adequate, though not overwhelming, support for the theory of complementary needs in mate-selection.

Qualitative analysis of the same 50 persons suggested that there were two principal psychological dimensions underlying the various needs: (1) nurturance-receptivity, or a disposition to give versus a disposition to receive, and (2) dominance-submissiveness....

## SUBSEQUENT EFFORTS BY OTHERS TO TEST THE THEORY

Unfortunately no one has ever replicated the original study. For a time the literature bristled with articles purporting to be tests of the theory, and it seemed that the more categorical the claims of the authors in this regard, the less directly their results actually bore on the theory.

There is one probably very significant difference between the original study and all subsequent studies of complementary needs in mate-selection of which the author is aware. In the original study each test subject was interviewed about his need-pattern and then his answers were assessed by two or more trained analysts, whereas all subsequent studies of which the author is aware used some paper-and-pencil test in which the subject assessed himself. Some critics of the original study have made the seemingly absurd observation that the analysts on the mate-selection study were probably more subjective in their ratings (and hence less valid) than would have been the subjects themselves. How can it be reasoned that the analysts would be more concerned whether Subject 17, whom they did not know, was rated high or low on need dominance, say, than Subject 17 himself? It is this author's view that the frequently observed disposition of test subjects (like human beings generally) to portray themselves in a favorable light biases their responses.

In 1954 Allen Edwards published the Personal Preference Schedule (PPS), a paper-and-pencil test designed to measure fifteen of the needs that had been postulated and nominally defined by [Henry] Murray. By name ten of the fifteen needs in the PPS were similar with or cognate to those used in the Winch study. Presumably this fact encouraged a considerable number of social scientists to think that an easy way to duplicate the Winch study was to use the PPS. The fact is that no evidence was presented to show that the Edwards test was valid either by means of a behavioral or a peer-rating criterion. Undaunted by this fact, a very considerable number of studies have purported to have tested the theory of complementary needs by means of the PPS.

Other ways in which subsequent studies have failed to be true replications include: extraneous variables (when all of the variables of the PPS are used, more than half of the resulting matrix of correlations involves variables not even proposed by name in the original study), incomplete concept of complementariness (a good many studies have ignored what is designated above as type II complementariness), and inappropriate subjects (instead of a sample of newly married couples selected in order to have complementariness at its presumed maximum, various studies used dating couples, couples married ten to thirty years, couples belonging to one unspecified church, and couples selected in such a way that they could be called only a "grab" sample).

Perhaps one should expect that if the theory were a really good one, then even with poor samples and even with a very questionable instrument the results should support the theory. In the original study, the support was visible though not overwhelmingly strong. In the subsequent studies, the general result was to show no correlation between members of couples and such correlation as did appear was more often in the direction of similarity than of complementarity.

## CRITICISMS OF THE THEORY

Several thoughtful critiques of the theory have been published. Irving Rosow is the author of the first of these to come to this writer's attention. Beginning with the observation that the theory had applicability to other social groups as well as to marital dyads, Rosow went on to point out that Winch's statement of the theory did not make clear at what level the needs were hypothesized to be functioning, i.e., whether at the overt or behavioral level or at some covert or perhaps even unconscious level. The locus of gratification he saw as another problem; by this is meant the question of what happens to the expression of a need within the marriage if the person is obtaining gratification of that need outside the marriage, or if the gratification of that need is being frustrated outside the marriage. Perhaps Rosow's most important criticism of the theory is that it does not provide criteria for determining which needs are complementary; a further difficulty, he says, is that in many cases similarity of need may be as compatible and as functional as complementarity.

[George] Levinger has proposed some remedies for the difficulties posed by Rosow. The former writer has suggested an operation that he believes removes the conceptual ambiguity between complementarity and similarity of needs. He advocates having the testing procedure concentrate on gratification derived from within the marital relationship in order to remove the problem about the locus of gratification, and he sees the formulation of needs by [William C.] Schutz as clarifying the idea of complementarity by offering the more limited idea of compatibility. Another proposal, about which more will be said below, is that of Tharp, who advocates substituting the sociological concept of role for the psychological concept of need.

# DEVELOPMENTS BEARING ON A REFORMULATION OF THE THEORY

Two studies have contributed to the development and refinement of the theory of complementary needs. [Alan] Kerckhoff and [Keith E.] Davis have studied a sample of undergraduates who were "engaged, pinned or 'seriously attached' " and concluded that there was a sequence of filtering factors such that first individuals sort out each other by characteristics of social background (social class, religion, etc.), later by consensus on familial values (place in the community, having healthy and happy children, etc.), and still later by need complementarity. It is perhaps worth noting that this is the first time the theory of complementary needs received support from a study using a paper-and-pencil test; that test was not the Edwards PPS but Schutz's FIRO-B, each scale of which deals with the desire of the respondent to act toward others with respect to inclusion, control, and affection and also to have the others act towards him with respect to the same three variables.

A very interesting development comes from an application of the theory of complementary needs in a context other than that of mate-selection. [Eric A.] Bermann has been studying the stability of dyadic relationships among female students at the University of Michigan. He dealt with three categories of undergraduate women: student nurses, women residents of a cooperative house, and residents of a sorority house. He determined that membership in each category involved a set of norms distinctive from each of the others. That is, his investigation revealed that a nursing student is expected to be friendly, gregarious, affiliative, abasing, to suppress concern about any bodily ailments she might experience, and to be low on dependent needs as well as needs for recognition. This set of norms may be regarded as defining part of the role of the student nurse. Normative traits contributing to a definition of the role of the resident of the cooperative house were that she should be politically progressive and active, rebellious, sorority-shunning, avoid the constraints of conventional dormitories, and be a member of a religious or ethnic minority, of urban residence, highly intellectual, achieving, autonomous, non-deferent, aggressive, non-abasing, and individualistic. The only norm Bermann lists as pertaining to the role of the sorority girl is that of emitting highly dominant behavior.

Bermann reports on a study of 44 pairs of roommates in a dormitory for nursing students. Of these, 22 pairs were rated by themselves and by peers as highly stable pairs, whereas the other 22 were rated as being of low stability. As in Winch's study, interviews provided the basis for assessing the needs of the subjects; the questions designed to elicit data about needs were open-ended. The protocols of the interviews were coded for nine needs: dominance, deference, exhibition, aggression, abasement, nurturance, succorance, achievement, and affiliation.

Bermann sought to predict the stability of pairs of roommates on the basis of the relationship between the pattern of needs of one girl in each pair to the pattern of her roommate. To do this, he used role theory and the theory of complementary needs to generate competing hypotheses. Using role theory, he reasoned that if both roommates were close to the ideal specified by the appropriate set of norms—in the case of student nurses, if both were friendly, abasing, etc.—each would serve the other as an object of identification with a resulting solidarity that would bind the two roommates into a stable relationship. From this reasoning he inferred, e.g., that, if both should be low on the need to dominate, the pair should be stable (since low dominance was found to be an element in the definition of the role of student nurse). Using the theory of complementary needs, however, Bermann reasoned, as was done in Winch's study of mate-selection, that a more solidary relationship should exist where one was high and the other low on dominance (type I complementariness). More formally, Bermann hypothesized (1) that compatibility with respect to role is predictive of stability, (2) that complementariness of needs is predictive of stability, and (3) that both of these predictors considered together predict stability better than either does when taken separately. Generally, Bermann's data supported all of these propositions. Need complementarity predicted stability, but role compatibility predicted it better. Bermann's index of total compatibility, which is a combination of need complementarity and role compatibility, was the most effective predictor of stability.

## SOME THOUGHTS ON A REFORMULATION OF THE THEORY

The theory of complementary needs is a psychological theory in that it refers to the actor's personality, conceived as the organization of a set of needs and traits. Role theory is a sociological theory in that its referent is a role, which is the product of the consensus of some collectivity. What Bermann has done is to show that the psychological *plus* the sociological theory is better than either of these standing alone.

Before attempting to integrate the significance of these findings and formulations, it may be useful to distinguish a bit more explicitly between role and personality. Very simply, the distinction is seen as follows. Role directs our attention to behaviors and attitudes that are appropriate to a situation, irrespective of the actor, whereas personality directs our attention to behaviors and attitudes that are characteristic of the actor, irrespective of the situation. As Bermann has shown, both role and personality may be stated in terms of needs.

How can Bermann's results, obtained from studying pairs of girls rooming together, bear on the marital dyad? In the general statement of the theory of complementary needs, the sex of the actor is not significant; the gender of the actor became significant in Winch's study because he placed the test of the theory in the context of mate-selection.

This writer would argue that the theoretically significant feature is not whether the members of the dyad are of the same or different sexes but whether their roles are or are not differentiated. The student nurses were enacting identical roles; there is always some difference between the familial roles of men and women because of the fact that women bear and nurse children. The degree to which roles of the sexes are differentiated beyond this inescapable consideration varies from one societal and cultural context to another. Elsewhere the present writer has argued that the degree of differentiation of sex roles varies inversely with the use of nonhuman power.

Beyond the point of initial attraction, at which differences between the sexes tend to be emphasized, the Kerckhoff-Davis study shows that during the filtering process prospective mates are selecting each other as they find that they participate in the same subculture. After that, according to Kerckhoff and Davis, selection occurs on the basis of complementarity. But is this complementarity of personality or of role or of both?

Before trying to answer the foregoing question, the writer must pause for a slight detour. It has been noted above that the study of complementary needs concluded with the proposal that there were two underlying dimensions of complementariness: nurturance-receptivity and dominance-submissiveness. Subsequent reflection leads the writer to the view that those same data revealed a third dimension that was not quite as well determined as the other two but seems, nevertheless, to be conceptually distinct from them. This dimension may be called "achievement-vicariousness." In the theory of complementary needs, it will be recalled, it makes no difference which spouse is high on needs pertaining to which end of any of these three dimensions—if one spouse is high on one, e.g., nurturance, the other spouse is predicted to be low on that need and to be high on its complement, in this case, receptivity.

As we try to incorporate role theory into the above formulation, the first question is whether or not any of these variables enters into the specification of the role of husband or of wife. If so, what bearing would this have? It seems justified to assert that the traditional public image of the husband-father in the American middle class represents him as the dominant member of the family and as being strongly oriented to achievement. The wife-mother is traditionally portrayed as nurturant but as having the children as the objects of her nurturance; also she is traditionally seen as deriving vicarious gratification from the achievements of her husband.

If these statements of role-specification are correct (or to the extent that they are correct), it does follow that the variables of Winch's study of mate-selection can be related to roles that are familial, including marital. At this point it is useful to recall that roles, through what Gross *et al.* call the "norm-senders," put a strain on personality to conform to the specifications of the roles. To the extent that one sees that one's need-pattern (personality) is consistent with present and prospective roles, one can feel comfortable and adjusted. But where personality is inconsistent with role(s)—e.g., the succorant or submissive or non-achievement-oriented husband—there is room for regarding oneself a misfit and for developing intrapsychic conflict. Placed in the present context, the Bermann study suggests a hypothesis:

> A pair of spouses who are attracted to each other on the basis of complementary needs will be a less stable pair if the complementariness is counter to role-specification than if it is consistent with role-specification.

The point here is that, where personality and role are mutually consistent, this state of affairs should not generate intrapsychic conflict, while the pair of actors should find that their relationship is given normative support. On the other hand, where personality is in conflict with role, each actor is put in a situation to suffer intrapsychic conflict (unless each accepts a self-definition as a deviant) and the marital relationship is open to criticism on normative grounds.

Perhaps an example is in order. Let us assume there are two persons, $A$ and $B$, in a dyadic relationship. $A$ is high on dominance and low on submissiveness; $B$ has the opposite need-pattern. At this point we do not specify which is male, which is female. With respect to needs they are complementary on this dimension. Accordingly, the theory of complementary needs predicts they are more likely to select each other as mates than a pair in which both are dominant or both are submissive. (And of course the theory of complementary needs purports to predict only mate-selection, not marital happiness nor marital stability.) With respect to role what is the situation? If we are given the information that they are members of a society wherein the male role is defined as dominant and the female role submissive, then we are part of the way home. If, in addition, we learn that $A$ is the male and $B$ the female, we conclude that their need-complementariness on the dominance-submissiveness dimension is consistent with their role-specifications. Then, on the basis of the hypothesis derived from the Bermann study, we might predict that this relationship would be a relatively stable one. Of course if we were told that $B$ was the man and $A$ the woman, the prediction about their being attracted to each other would still stand but the prediction about the stability of their marriage would be reversed. This case has been oversimplified for heuristic purposes; one would not be justified in predicting either mate-selection or marital stability on only this narrow view of the two parties.

The next step in the prediction of mate-selection and marital stability would seem to be the further analysis of marital and other familial roles. It is not clear whether or not it is desirable to continue working with the needs and traits used by Winch and by Bermann. The latter has shown that, to a limited extent at least, such variables may be used as elements of both personality and of role and thus can be used to integrate the two kinds of theory. It is in contemplating further, even exhaustive, analysis of marital and other familial roles where there arises some uncertainty as to just how adequately such an analysis can be made in terms of, or translated into, needs and traits. Some idea of the task can be seen from the following examples taken from a list of components of marital roles derived from a middle-class sample by Hurvitz: performer of domestic chores; companion of spouse; friend, teacher, and guide of offspring; sexual partner; and model for offspring. The present author has previously published the following list of conceptually derived components or marital subroles:

- progenitor or progenitrix
- father or mother (nurturer, disciplinarian, socializer, model)
- position conferrer (provider of position in society for self, spouse, offspring)
- emotional gratifier
- sexual partner

The list of five subroles shown just above is intended to be universal, or culture-free, although precisely how they are defined is of course specified in each culture. For the specific setting of the American middle class, the following might be added:

- host or hostess
- home manager
- companion in leisure

Presumably the task of translating such subroles into needs is to analyze (a) how the spouses complement each other with respect to these subroles and (b) the needs involved in such complementariness.

There are two further ideas to be taken into account in suggesting a possible direction for the analysis of marital roles. First, there will be variation from one society to another and from one segment to another within even moderately differentiated societies as to the number and nature of the subroles relating spouses to each other. In general, the more functional the nuclear family is, the greater will be the number of such subroles. Second, the importance of complementary needs as a mate-selective criterion appears to vary inversely with the functionality of the extended family. It may be surmised that the relevance of complementary needs to marital stability is also inversely related to the functionality of both the nuclear and extended family forms. In other words, in societal contexts where the family—extended and/or nuclear—is highly functional, the resulting subroles are important; it should follow that the more important such subroles are, the less importance the culture will give to the idiosyncratic needs of the individual. In middle-class America, where the extended family appears to be relatively nonfunctional and where the functions of the nuclear family also tend toward the low end, love can exist as a criterion for mate-selection and its absence as a criterion for marital dissolution. Hence it is reasoned that complementariness of needs, as a basis for such love, tends to assume importance with respect to both mate-selection and marital stability in family systems of low functionality, whereas role compatibility tends to assume importance for both the selection and retention of mates in more functional family systems.

One final consideration not to be lost sight of is that with the passage of time very significant changes take place in roles and in gratifications and frustrations, and quite possibly in need-patterns. As we follow a couple from their period of engagement into early marriage with its concomitants of occupational demands for the man and domestic demands for the wife-mother into middle and later years when their offspring have been launched and the breadwinner retires, it is obvious that the roles are modified and energy-levels changed and aspirations modified.

# SUMMARY

Twenty-five recently married young couples were examined by means of two lengthy interviews and a projective technique in order to provide a test of the theory of complementary needs in mate-selection. The data were interpreted as providing some support of the theory. Originally two dimensions of complementariness were induced from the data: nurturance-receptiveness and dominance-submissiveness. Subsequently a third has been proposed: achievement-vicariousness. A spate of non-replicative tests based on the PPS has provided no support for the theory; however, Kerckhoff and Davis' study based on Schutz's FIRO-B has shown a culturally homogenizing filtering process followed by mate-selection on the basis of complementary needs. Whether or not replication of the study of mate-selection would provide additional support of the theory remains an unanswered question.

In a study of roommates in a dormitory of nursing students, Bermann has strongly suggested the advisability of adding the concept of role compatibility to that of need complementarity; he showed that the stability of pairs of roommates could be predicted better by using both concepts together than by using either singly.

## 4.3 BERNARD I. MURSTEIN

# Stimulus—Value—Role: A Theory of Marital Choice

Toward the end of the 1960s a stage-type theory of mate selection was offered by psychologist Bernard I. Murstein. This selection is from Murstein's "Stimulus—Value—Role: A Theory of Marital Choice," *Journal of Marriage and the Family* (August 1970). In this paper, Murstein outlines three stages in the process of mate selection: stimulus, value, and role. In explaining his theory, Murstein considers several variables and hypotheses to explain progress in courtship. Among the variables considered are sex drive, self-concept, physical attraction, and role complementarity. This theory has been a popular one for nearly 30 years, as students of the family have embraced it as a meaningful way to gain insights into the mate selection process.

Murstein has been a professor of psychology at Connecticut College in New London, Connecticut, since 1963. He has written numerous books and articles about love, interpersonal attraction, sexual intimacy, marital choice, and marriage.

**Key Concept:** mate selection

[T]he present lacunae in the field of marital choice may be attributed to the lack of a comprehensive detailed theory and the absence of a sustained program of research to test the various postulates of the theory. Some of the important questions which have either been ignored or only briefly treated include the following: (1.) How do people get acquainted in the first place so that value similarity has a chance to operate? (2.) Why should people like others who have similar values? (3.) Do individuals marry those who are perceived as similar or do they sometimes marry perceived "opposites?" (4.) Do all people succeed in marrying in accordance with their needs? (5.) Do people marry on the basis of actual role-compatibility or *imagined* role-compatibility? (6.) What is the role in marital choice of such variables as "self-esteem," "neuroticism" and "sexual drive?" (7.) Are the perceptions and behavior of both men and women of equal importance in determining marital choice?

To attempt to answer these and other questions regarding marital choice, the author proposes to build on the pioneering efforts of earlier researchers by formulating a three-stage theory of marital choice called Stimulus—Value—Role (SVR). The three stages refer to the chronological sequence of the development of the relationship....

# SVR THEORY

SVR theory holds that in a relatively "free choice" situation as exists in the United States, most couples pass through three stages before deciding to marry. These stages will be defined and discussed in detail, but first the locus of the potential marital encounter merits some discussion.

### "Open" and "Closed" Fields

An "open" field encounter refers to a situation in which the man and woman do not as yet know each other or have only a nodding acquaintance. Examples of such "open field" situations are "mixers," presence in a large school class at the beginning of the semester, and brief contacts in the office. The fact that the field is "open" indicates that either the man or the woman is free to start the relationship or abstain from initiating it, as they wish. . . .

# "STIMULUS" STAGE

In the "open field," an individual may be drawn to another based on his perception of the other's physical, social, mental or reputational attributes and his perception of his own qualities that might be attractive to the other person. Because initial movement is due primarily to non-interactional cues not dependent on interpersonal interaction, these are categorized as "stimulus" values.

### Qualities of Other

In the absence of other information, the attraction of the other will often depend on visual and auditory cues. The other may look beautiful, have a sexy voice, or may be "too old," "just right," or "too young." However, the attractiveness of the other person may be established even *prior* to the first meeting, on the basis of information that he satisfies the system of values held by the perceiver. Furthermore, an individual may be viewed as physically unstimulating yet possess compensating stimulus attributes. The rugged but ugly football tackle may attract a physically appealing woman because his stimulus impact as a virile, glamorous hero, as well as his promising financial prospects, may more than compensate for a forbidding physiognomy. Moreover, knowing that a man is a medical intern of a certain age and of the "right" religion may make him a desirable person for a woman to invite to a soirée.

In sum, in the first stage, perception of the other comprises the appreciation of all perceptions of the prospective partner, both sensate and non-sensate, which do not necessitate any kind of meaningful interaction. This stage is of crucial importance in the "open field," for, if the other person fails to provide sufficient reinforcement of one's value system at this stage, further contact is not sought. While the "prospect" in question might potentially be a highly desirable person with compatible values, the individual—foregoing opportunities for further contact—never finds this out. In consequence, it would appear that physically unattractive individuals are at a considerable handicap.

If marital choice depended only on the attractiveness of the other, we would have a largely unmarried population since everyone would be drawn towards the relatively few highly attractive persons. The fact that the vast majority of persons do marry points out the necessity of considering at least two other factors: the person's own evaluation of how attractive he is to the other, and the conceptualization of marital choice as a kind of exchange-market phenomenon.

**Perception of Self**

As a function of his previous experiences, the individual builds up an image of himself in terms of his attractiveness to the opposite sex. If he sees himself as highly attractive, he is more likely to approach a highly attractive prospective partner than if he sees himself as unattractive. In actuality, we may suppose that each individual's self-concept covers a series of different aspects and that a person might think of himself as adequate in some aspects and inadequate in others. There is some evidence, however (Kiesler and Baral, in press), which suggests that even experiences which reduce self-esteem but which do not deal specifically with members of the opposite sex tend to influence subsequent "dating approaches" to the opposite sex.

Another factor to consider within the area of self-perception is the "fear of failure." Some individuals will avoid approaching attractive persons because they fear rejection, whereas others shrug off repeated rejections by a single person or different individuals without apparent damage to their self-esteem. The exact nature of the relationship between self-esteem and "fear of failure" remains to be clarified by future research, but it seems likely that both are highly important in determining approach behavior towards others....

During the first moments of contact, the individual may attempt to supplement his visual impression of the other with information regarding the other's role in society, professional aspirations, and background. Persons attracted to each other, thus, are likely to be balanced for the total weighted amalgam of stimulus characteristics even though, for a given trait, gross disparities may exist. Men, for example, tend to weigh physical attractiveness in a partner more than women do, whereas women give greater weight to professional aspiration in the partner; accordingly, although physical attraction may play a leading role, it is hypothesized that the weighted pool of stimulus attractions that each possesses for the other will be approximately equal if individuals are to progress into the second stage of courtship....

*Hypothesis 1. As a result of "bargaining," pre-marital couples will show greater than chance similarity with respect to physical attraction, whether objectively or subjectively measured....*

## "VALUE" STAGE

Assume for the moment that mutual "stimulus" attraction has occurred between a young man and woman at a "mixer" dance, and that they sit down and talk to each other. They are now entering the second stage, that of "value comparison." Unlike the "stimulus" stage in which attributes of the partner are evaluated without any necessary interpersonal contact, the value comparison stage involves the appraisal of value compatibility through verbal interaction. The kinds of values explored through discussion are apt to be much more varied than those possible in the "stimulus" stage. The couple may compare their attitudes towards life, politics, religion, sex, and the role of men and women in society and marriage. The fact that the couple is now interacting also permits more continuous and closer scrutiny of physical appearance, as well as other important factors such as temperament, "style" of perceiving the world, and ability to relate to others.

It is possible that closer appraisal of physical qualities and temperament will lead to a changed opinion regarding the desirability of the partner, and this may result in an attempt to terminate the contact as soon as gracefully possible. If contact has been made on the basis of strong stimulus attraction, however, it is more likely that the couple will remain in the second stage, continuing to assess the compatibility of their values.

Should the couple find that they hold similar value orientations in important areas, they are apt to develop much stronger positive feelings for each other than they experienced in the "stimulus" stage. One reason for this is that when an individual encounters another who holds similar values, he gains support for the conclusion that his own values are correct; his views are given social validation (Berscheid and Walster, 1969). Further, many values are intensely personal and are so linked to the self-concept that rejection of these values is experienced as rejection of the self, and acceptance of them implies validation of the self. Providing we have a reasonably positive self-image, we tend to be attracted to those persons whom we perceived as validating it. Also, perceived similarity of values may lead to the assumption that the other likes us, and there is empirical evidence that we like those individuals whom we think like us (Berscheid and Walster, 1969).

Last, we may note that persons who have similar values are likely to engage in similar activities and, thus, reward each other by validating each other's commitment to the activity. Moreover, because these activities are similar, they are apt to have similar reward value in the world at large, thus, further drawing the couple together since they share equal status in their milieu.... [I]ndividuals of equal standing in attractiveness are most apt to be drawn to each other because of their equal ability to reward each other. In sum, the holding of similar values should be a major factor in drawing two individuals together. Our second hypothesis, therefore, is:

*Hypothesis 2. Individuals considering marriage tend to show greater than chance similarity with regard to their hierarchy of values concerning marriage....*

## "ROLE" STAGE

There are many tasks which face the couple in the "role" stage before they move into marriage. Rapoport (1963) has listed nine of these, but the limitations of the type of data collected by the author as well as a somewhat different conceptual framework dictate limiting the analysis to three broad areas: perceived role "fit," personal adequacy, and sexual compatibility.

Concerning role "fit," it may be noted that as the couple's relationship ripens, the members increasingly confide in each other and, thus, become aware of a broader range of each other's behavior than heretofore. They may also become more cognizant of what they desire in a future spouse, and more consciously compare these expectations with their perception of the partner. They also become increasingly aware of the impact that their own behavior has on the partner and whether he considers these behaviors to be appropriate. Mutual role "fit" should be mutually rewarding and result in a desire to assure the continuity of satisfaction by putting the relationship on a more or less permanent basis through marriage.

A second task is to take the measure of one's own personal adequacy and that of a partner since, for example, moodiness, inability to make decisions, dislike of the self, and neuroticism may be high costs to bear in marriage. The third task involves the necessity of attaining sexual compatibility whether by achieving a good sexual relationship in practice or by agreement as to the degree of sexuality which will be expressed during the "role" stage prior to marriage. Throughout the three areas, it will be seen that the roles of men and women are not only often dissimilar, but often of unequal importance to courtship progress (henceforth called CP). Before considering these three areas, however, the utilization of a formal criterion of the progress of the relationship in the "role" stage will be described....

## TASK 1: ROLE "FIT"

### Is the Partner Perceived to Be Similar or Opposite to the Self?

... [R]esearch on marital choice has offered lukewarm support to the homogamy principle and even less support to the principle of complementary needs. SVR theory, as described so far, has been in accord with the homogamy principle with respect to the "stimulus" and "value" stages. Role similarity, however, is not necessarily advantageous during the "role" stage of courtship. The explanation for the lack of usefulness of role-homogamy lies in a basic distinction between values and roles.

Values are experienced by most persons as part and parcel of the "self" whereas roles, although they may serve as goals, are often *means* to goals. Should the goals change, therefore, the roles may also change. The wife may play the role of the loving homemaker so long as she enjoys the rewards of appreciation and affection from her spouse. If she learns that her husband is about to divorce her, however, she may exchange this role for that of "the woman scorned." Since roles are often behavioral means to an end, it is possible that, in some instances, role-similarity may impede the goals of one or both partners. Suppose that both husband and wife desire to essay the role of homemaker and neither wishes to enter the business world. The result is no family income. It is clear, therefore, that what is important is the compatibility of roles with goals, not whether roles are homogamous or complementary.

An individual's ideal-self may be termed a goal more than a role since it is an end he strives towards rather than a part he actually plays. In similar vein, the goal he sets for his partner is embodied in his concept of ideal-spouse. The extent to which an individual is currently able to meet his personal goals is measured by his self ideal-self discrepancy, and the perceived fulfillment of his expectation for his partner is determined by the discrepancy between his perception of partner and his concept of ideal-spouse.

To understand why role satisfaction for some individuals is associated with perceived similarity of self to the partner while for others it involves perceived dissimilarity, we must consider four perceptual concepts: self, ideal-self, perceived partner and ideal-spouse. Consider first the relationship of the concept of ideal-spouse to ideal-self. It is to be expected that these variables should be highly correlated because idealized expectations in marriage are generally similar for most of the individuals within the same culture.

The perception of the partner should also be relatively highly correlated with the perceptions of both ideal-spouse and ideal-self in a society such as ours which emphasizes free choice. The "dating" structure, after all, encourages "shopping around" until some tangible approximation of the ideal is discovered. The slightly lower expected correlations of the perceived partner with ideal-self and with ideal-spouse compared to the ideal-spouse, ideal-self correlation should merely reflect the fact that the partner, no matter how strongly admired, never quite reaches the ideal. In any event, we should expect that the perceptions of partner, ideal-self, and ideal-spouse, should be highly correlated with one another....

Focusing on the question of perceived similarity to the partner, it is proposed that, if the individual is highly satisfied with himself as determined by a high correlation between the self and ideal-self and, if it is true, as has been earlier proposed, that the concepts of ideal-self, ideal-spouse, and perceived partner are highly intercorrelated, then it follows that the individual will attempt to marry someone whom he perceives as highly similar to himself.

If, however, the subject is highly dissatisfied with himself (low self, ideal-self correlation), he will still want to marry someone close to his ideal-self and ideal-spouse since, as noted earlier, these variables are largely determined by stereotyped normative values acquired in the process of culturalization. The difference between high and low self-acceptance persons with respect to these aforementioned variables, therefore, would not be expected to be very large; accordingly, the fact that the self is unlike the ideal-self will also result in the self being unlike the ideal-spouse and perceived partner. To the extent that the low self-acceptance person succeeds in meeting a reasonable facsimile of his ideal-spouse, therefore, he will tend to perceive that person as less similar to himself than would be the case for the high self-acceptance person. The perception of the partner as relatively similar or dissimilar to the self is, thus, largely a derivative of the position of the self with respect to the trinity of desiderata, the ideal-self, ideal-spouse, and perceived partner.... Our formal hypothesis for this event is as follows:

*Hypothesis 3. Couples with high self-acceptance (HSA) view their partner as significantly more similar to themselves than couples with low self-acceptance (LSA)....*

### Perceptual Congruency, Perceptual Accuracy, and Courtship Progress

The more "A" likes "B," the more he discloses his private world to "B." In a "dating" situation, such a disclosure is rewarding to "B" because it marks him as worthy of receiving intimate information and, accordingly, raises his self-esteem. Moreover, the receipt of intimate information from "A" encourages "B" to reciprocate by offering information at equal levels of intimacy. This theoretical sequence of events has recently received solid empirical verification in the work of Worthy *et al.* (1969).

Once engaged in mutual disclosures, the tendency is for couples to proceed to continuously more intimate cycles of rewarding disclosure. The act of disclosure is not only rewarding to the listener, but may serve as a cathartic agent for the discloser who himself gains a feeling of acceptance and other rewards from the attention of the other. Individuals who attain even deeper levels of mutual disclosure, therefore, should make good CP, whereas those who do not reach these levels are more apt to flounder in their courtship.

In addition, the level of disclosure reached should have a profound effect on the perception of the partner and on the individual's own perceptual world. Because they have attained deeper levels of disclosure, couples destined to make good CP should become more accurate in predicting each other's self and ideal-self concepts. Also, because disclosure to a friend usually meets acceptance, it increases liking by the discloser; hence, couples reaching an intimate level of disclosure should manifest considerable perceptual congruence between their concept of ideal-spouse and their perception of their partner. The following two predictions are made therefore:

*Hypothesis 4. Couples who show good CP were able to make more accurate predictions of the partner's self and ideal-self at the beginning of the study (six months earlier) than were poor CP couples....*

*Hypothesis 5. Couples who make good CP showed greater compatibility between their conception of ideal-spouse and their perception of the partner than couples making poor CP....*

*Hypothesis 6. Perceived compatibility as derived from intra-perceptions (perceptions stemming from the same person) is significantly greater than compatibility as derived from inter-perceptions (perceptions stemming from both members of the couple)....*

## PERSONALITY ADEQUACY

An individual's self-acceptance and neuroticism determine his attractiveness to his partner for several reasons. First, there is less cost in relating to a non-neurotic, HSA person than to an inadequate, LSA one because the former makes fewer unreasonable demands on the relationship and his demands, when made, are apt to be more logical and easily satisfied. Also, such an individual is more apt to come closer to the model of the ideal-spouse and to have high social stimulus value in the eyes of others.

In a study on friendship which seems applicable here, Kipnis (1961) has pointed out yet another function of interpersonal relationships. She found that an individual begins a friendship (and by extension I apply her results to courtship as well) so that his self-esteem may rise as a consequence of the new relationship. To the extent that the relationship does not yield this reward, there is a considerable probability that the friendship will be terminated.

If personal adequacy is an asset, however, it seems logical that highly adequate individuals will not be satisfied with persons less adequate than themselves because of the higher cost of relating to them and because rewards in terms of possible gains in self-acceptance are likely to be smaller. They will, therefore, tend to reject these individuals at such time as the disparity in adequacy becomes manifest. The result is that couples who progress to the stage of serious courtship may be expected to have similar self-acceptance and neuroticism scores. Given the occurrence of occasional mis-matchings, it could be predicted that, with the passage of time, individuals who differ widely in personal adequacy are more likely to experience disparate degrees of profit from the relationship. They are more likely to break up, therefore, than are those with similar degrees of adequacy. We may, therefore, formulate the following three hypotheses:

*Hypothesis 7. Individuals tend to choose partners whose level of self-acceptance is similar to their own....*

*Hypothesis 8. Individuals tend to choose partners whose level of neuroticism is similar to their own....*

*Hypothesis 9. Individuals are more likely to make good CP when they are going with a partner of comparable neuroticism than when they are courting a person with a dissimilar degree of neuroticism....*

## Choosing as Opposed to "Settling" for a Partner

One sometimes gains the impression from the literature on marital choice that everyone sets out to seek a partner who can fulfill one's personal needs, and that somehow or other each individual more or less manages to find a partner admirably or maliciously suited for himself; hence, some psychiatrists (Kubie, 1956; Mittelman, 1944) assume that even neurotics seek each other out. From the conception expressed here that "personal adequacy" is attractive because of both its high reward value and low cost, a rather different conclusion is reached. Individuals possessing the greater number of assets and the fewest liabilities should be able to choose partners appropriately suited to them with a greater probability of success than those who are quite low in marital assets and high in liabilities; consequently, despite the rationalizing process which would tend to force an individual to view his prospective spouse as close to his heart's desire, it is predicted that LSA and/or neurotic persons, for example, should experience less satisfaction with the "steady" or fiancé(e) than HSA and/or non-neurotic persons.[1] Whereas HSA persons "choose" each other because each represents the potential for profitable experiences for the other, LSA persons are more apt to "settle" for each other for want of a better alternative.

*Hypothesis 10. HSA individuals are more likely to perceive their partners as approaching their concept of ideal-spouse than are LSA individuals....*

## SEX-DRIVE

Although much attention has been given to the concepts of role and value in the literature on marital choice, there has been little concern with drives and in particular, the sex-drive. Drive is defined here as "A tendency initiated by shifts in physiological [or psychological] balance to be sensitive to stimuli of a certain class and to respond in any of a variety of ways that are related to the attainment of a certain goal" (English and English, 1958:163–164). Drives function in a similar manner to values in that, for a given drive, the more similar the intensity of that drive for each member of the couple, the more compatible the couple. The reason why similarity of sex-drive is rewarding is that it leads to a similar desire for frequency of sexual contacts and to an optimum ratio of desire for sex to participation in sex.

*Hypothesis 11. Couples going together exhibit a greater than chance similarity of sexual drive level....*

*Hypothesis 12. Couples in which the male sex-drive is high will show less role-compatibility and less CP than couples in which the male sex-drive is low. Women making good CP will, however, manifest a higher average orgasm-rate than poor CP women....*

*Hypothesis 13. Men with high sex-drives are significantly less accurate in their estimate of how their partners perceive them, and how their partners perceive themselves, than are low sex-drive men....*

# THE GREATER IMPORTANCE OF THE MAN IN COURTSHIP

From the dawn of recorded time, men have manifested greater control over their partner's behavior than have women. In the United States, even as late as the nineteenth century, men had the power to deny women full legal status, political franchise, and equal economic opportunity (Murstein, 1970). Currently, most of these inequities have been greatly reduced, but it is nevertheless true that economic and social power is still disproportionately distributed by sex, with the average woman still less powerful than the average man.

From the point of view of our marital bargaining model, the effect is that the cost of abstaining from marriage is greater for women than for men. The status of the unmarried woman is lower than that of the unmarried man and her economic skills are apt to be inferior and, hence, less rewarded in the market. To compound the difficulty for women, the age difference between marriageable men and women, the women's shorter age range of marriageability, and their longer life-span put them in greater supply and in less demand than men. The effect of this greater power of men is that, in courting situations, the man is:

> ... the one who usually takes the most active role. He often is the one who actively initiates the relationship by asking for a date. He also is more often the one who is the first to commit himself to the relationship and who, in the everyday aspects of the courtship, decides about such activities as dinner arrangements, movies, and dances. The woman occupies the more passive role as the recipient of the man's wooing. She is not as likely to manifest signs of disturbance during the courtship simply because she has less role-prescribed need to initiate the contact and to make decisions.... If she accepts the man as a legitimate suitor, he is expected to shoulder most of the interpersonal responsibilities from that point on (Murstein 1967:450).

The result is that although the greatest likelihood of good CP occurs when both members of a couple possess the same degree of neuroticism, the impact of neuroticism for the relationship when only one member is neurotic should be greater when the neurotic partner is the man.

*Hypothesis 14. Courtship progress is impaired more by neuroticism in the man than by neuroticism in the woman....*

*Hypothesis 15. Confirmation of the man's self and ideal-self concepts through the perceptions of his girlfriend will be followed six months later by good CP, whereas confirmation of the woman's self and ideal-self concepts by the perceptions of her boyfriend will not be as strongly associated with good CP....*

*Hypothesis 16. Good CP women will a) predict their boyfriends' selves and ideal-selves better than poor CP women, and, b) the association between predictive accuracy and CP will be greater for women than for men....*

*Hypothesis 17. The intra-perceptual congruencies (the tendency for any two perceptual sets of a person to coalesce) of good CP men should be significantly higher than for poor*

*CP men. Since the perceptions of women have less of a determining significance, the intra-perceptual congruencies of good CP women should not differ significantly from those of poor CP women....*

## TWO TESTS OF CHRONOLOGICAL SEQUENCE

We have essentially completed our description of the chief "stimulus," "value," and "role" variables. However, we have not as yet dealt with the relationship of these variables to each other apart from noting that, chronologically, "stimulus" variables precede "value" variables in importance, which in turn precede the effective operation of "role" variables. This, of course, is only relatively true, since information regarding the prospective partner in all three areas becomes available from the beginning of the relationship. However, the likelihood that certain kinds of information will be more readily available in specific stages of the relationship suggests that a successive filtering process occurs. "Stimulus" variables should be most operative during the initial phases of the relationship and least operative during the engagement period, since by that time those couples of disparate stimulus attractiveness are likely to have broken off their relationship. The comparison of values through verbal interaction should not be a powerful factor in initial "dating" since a certain amount of time is required for them to be expressed. Conversely, value similarity should not be strongly operative in relationships of long duration because by that time couples with strong value differences are likely to have separated.

Role-relationship variables should be most operative during the last stages of the relationship prior to marriage. Because it takes a long time to acquire information about them, they should be virtually inoperative in the early stages of the relationship and only moderately operative during the middle stages of the relationship. The author has collected sufficient data to test two hypotheses regarding the effectiveness of "stimulus" and "value" variables at different chronological periods of the courtship process.

*Hypothesis 18. As a "stimulus" variable, the degree to similarity of physical attractiveness between a couple should not differentiate those individuals making good CP from those making poor CP during the "role" stage of courtship....*

*Hypothesis 19. Because "value consensus" is a second-stage variable, it should not differentiate between couples making good and poor CP when progress is measured during the "role" phase of the relationship....*

## TWO IMPORTANT FACTORS NOT MEASURED

Before closing, it is necessary to describe two important factors in marital choice which were not studied empirically but which are important targets for future research. The first of these is the strength of the "desire to marry." To the extent that this variable is experienced as a drive-state, the importance of the other factors such as assets in the marriage market and role-compatibility should be lessened. On the other hand, to the extent that marriage is seen as a distant or arbitrary goal, the necessity of the existence of a near perfect compatibility before considering marriage is increased. This variable accounts for the fact that marriage is not entered into simply because of the compatibility between two people. Marriage, as a status, has a value in its own right which may be considered as the summation of positive and negative aspects as seen by the potential candidate.

The presence of the same degree of compatibility for a medical student and his fiancée and for the skilled factory worker and his fiancée would have rather different implications. The student would most likely weigh the facilitative and disruptive effects of marriage on the attainment of the M.D. degree. He also might consider whether the choices available at the present moment might be as wide as those available later when, as a practicing physician, his assets in marital bargaining would be considerably elevated. This time-perspective would probably not weigh as heavily with the factory worker who does not anticipate as great a shift in his rank in the marital market with the passage of time.

The second factor necessitating future research is the determination of how marital choice develops in a "closed field." In a "closed field" such as, for example, a classroom seminar, individuals experience a certain amount of non-stereotyped interaction regardless of whether they are drawn to each other. The effect is to weaken the influence of stimulus variables on marital choice and to maximize the influence of the second-stage or verbal-interaction variables; thus, the individual who might never have been approached in an "open field" because she is of modest physical attraction may become quite attractive to her co-worker in the office as a result of luncheon conversations in the cafeteria which reveal her intelligence, sensitivity, and the similarity of her value-orientation to his own.

It is not meant to imply that, under these conditions, physical attraction completely loses its valence. Rather, the face that the second-stage variables are given such a favorable opportunity to operate may serve to counterbalance discrepancies in physical attraction. Marriages arising as the result of "closed field" contacts may be more harmonious in later years than those arising in "open field" situations. Physical beauty wanes with age and to the extent that this variable played a part in marital selection and continues to play a part in marital satisfaction, it might contribute to lessened satisfaction with age.

# CONCLUSIONS

Nineteen hypotheses relating to SVR theory were tested empirically and all of the hypotheses received at least moderate support. As predicted, partners possessed similar physical attractiveness and value similarity as consequences of successful passage through the "stimulus" and "value" stages of courtship. In the "role" stage, it was shown that perceived similarity or complementarity is not *per se* as important in understanding marital choice as is the self-acceptance of the perceiver. High self-accepting individuals were much more apt to perceive their partner as similar than low self-accepting ones. Accuracy in predicting the partner was associated with good CP as was perceived fulfillment of ideal-spouse expectations in the partner. Because pre-marital couples do not have much opportunity to experience each other in a wide variety of roles, it was predicted and verified that imagined role-compatibility would greatly exceed actual role-compatibility.

Investigation of mental health showed, as predicted, that high self-accepting persons tended to pair with high self-accepting persons and neurotics with neurotics. When "normals" and neurotics paired, poor CP was more likely to result than when members of a couple possessed similar degrees of neuroticism. Also, in accordance with exchange theory, individuals with high self-acceptance, thereby possessing greater marital assets than individuals with low self-acceptance, were able to obtain partners closer to their expectations than were low self-accepting persons.

In the area of sex, it was predicted and confirmed that individuals of similar strength of sex-drive would tend to pair, and that the man with a high sex-drive would pose a greater threat to the viability of the relationship than the man with a low sex-drive. High-drive men, indeed, possessed less role-compatibility, were less accurate perceivers of their girlfriends, and made poorer CP compared with low-drive men. For women, no similar relationships were found except that, as expected, good CP women showed greater sex-drive than poor CP women.

The greater importance of the man compared to the woman in determining CP was testified to by the fact that neuroticism in men was more inimical to CP than neuroticism in women. Further, men's greater importance as perceptual targets was evidenced by the fact that confirmation of men's self and ideal-self concepts lead to good CP, and the women's ability to predict their boyfriends' self and ideal-self concepts was also related to good CP. In addition, men's intra-perceptual congruence also assured good CP. On the other hand, confirmation of the woman's self concept, her boyfriend's ability to predict her self concept, and her tendency towards intra-perceptual congruency were not related to CP. Contrary to expectation, however, confirmation of and prediction of woman's ideal-self concept was related to good CP.

Last, some sequence effects related to SVR theory were tested. As predicted, physical attraction, a "stimulus" variable, did not relate to CP in the "role" stage and the same was true of value similarity which was described as a "value" stage variable.

Although the data offer considerable support for SVR theory, the author is aware that consistency of the theory with existing data is not sufficient to validate it. It merely proves that the theory is tenable. Future research should determine whether the findings reported can be replicated and whether alternative models will also account for the findings reported here equally well or perhaps even better.

# NOTES

1. My research data show that these two variables are moderately correlated (r=.57; reliability of measures was between .80 and .90).

# REFERENCES

Berscheid, E. and E. H. Walster. 1969. Interpersonal Attraction. Reading, Mass.: Addison-Wesley.

English, H. B. and A. C. English. 1968. A Comprehensive Dictionary of Psychological and Psychoanalytical Terms. New York: David McKay.

Kiesler, S. B. and R. L. Baral (in press). "The search for a romantic partner: the effects of self-esteem and physical attractiveness on romantic behavior." In K. Gergen and D. Marlowe (eds.), Personality and Social Behavior. Reading, Massachusetts: Addison-Wesley (in press).

Kipnis, D. 1961. "Changes in self-concepts in relation to perceptions of others." Journal of Personality 29:449–465.

Kubie, L. S. 1956. "Psychoanalysis and marriage: practical and theoretical issues." Pp. 10–43 in Victor E. Eisenstein (ed.), Neurotic Interaction in Marriage. New York: Basic Books.

Mittelman, B. 1944. "Complementary neurotic reactions in intimate relations." Psychoanalytic Quarterly 13:479–491.

Murstein, B. I. 1967. "The relationship of mental health to marital choice and courtship progress." Journal of Marriage and the Family 29:447–451.

Murstein, B. I. 1970. "Love, sex and marriage throughout history." Unpublished manuscript, Connecticut College.

Rapoport, R. 1963. "Normal crises, family structure and mental health." Family Process 2:68–80.

Worthy, M., A. L. Gary and G. M. Kahn, 1969. "Self disclosure as an exchange process." Journal of Personality and Social Psychology, 13, 59–63.

# CHAPTER 5 Marital Adjustment

## 5.1 HARVEY J. LOCKE AND KARL M. WALLACE

# *Short Marital-Adjustment and Prediction Tests: Their Reliability and Validity*

Many people would agree that accurate predictions of the success of a marriage would be valuable information. Imagine if there were an instrument that could tell every couple who wished to get married whether or not their union would last. Not only did Harvey J. Locke and Karl M. Wallace attempt to predict marital adjustment, but they tried to do it with as short a test as possible. In the following selection from "Short Marital-Adjustment and Prediction Tests: Their Reliability and Validity," *Marriage and Family Living* (August 1959), Locke and Wallace explain how they determined reliability and validity for a 15-item marital adjustment test and for a 35-question marital prediction test. They defined marital adjustment as the accommodation of a husband and wife to each other at a given time, while marital prediction forecasted marital adjustment in the future. Up to the time of this study, marital adjustment and prediction tests contained up to 246 questions. By lowering the number of items while still maintaining the integrity of the test, Locke and Wallace reduced the amount of time individuals needed for taking the test as well as the time required for scoring it.

This article was published several years before the women's liberation movement began to gain momentum and before divorce statistics began to climb. When this article was published, Locke was at the University of Southern California and had already published his book *Predicting Adjustment in Marriage: A Comparison of a Divorced and a Happily Married Group*. Wallace was at Los Angeles State College when this paper was written.

**Key Concept:** marital adjustment

This study is an attempt to develop short, but reliable, and valid, marital-adjustment and prediction tests. Marital adjustment is accommodation of a husband and wife to each other at a given time. Marital prediction is forecasting the likelihood of marital adjustment at a future time.

Before considering the reliability and validity of the short tests, we shall discuss the length of previous tests, the study design, and the sample.

# PREVIOUS TESTS

The first attempt to measure marital success by a numerical score was made by Hamilton.[1] He used a relatively short test composed of only thirteen items. More recent tests of marital adjustment and prediction have used a very large number of items. The length of these tests is their main disadvantage.

The Burgess-Wallin Marital-Success Schedule contains 89[2] numbered items, but several of these have multiple subitems.[3] Counting the multiple subitems, it requires answers to a possible maximum of 246 questions.[4] Enumerating items on this basis, the Terman Happiness Test contains 75 items;[5] the modified Terman-Oden test contains 103 items.[6] The Locke Marital-Adjustment Test contains 50 items.[7] The Karlsson Index of Marital Satisfaction used 40 items.[8] The Burgess-Cottrell Marital-Adjustment Test contains 26 items.[9]

The various marital-prediction tests contain the following number of items, if all questions in multiple items are counted: Burgess-Wallin, 133;[10] Terman, 182;[11] Terman-Oden, 180,[12] Locke, 155 for men and 158 for women;[13] Karlsson, 94 for men and 102 for women;[14] and Burgess-Cottrell, 195.[15]

It seems to the authors that by using only the most basic or fundamental items the length of marital-adjustment and prediction tests might be reduced without any appreciable loss in reliability and validity. As early as 1941, the same viewpoint was expressed in a study sponsored by the Social Science Research Council.[16]

# THE STUDY DESIGN

The hypothesis of the study was that reliable and valid adjustment and prediction tests can be constructed by using a limited number of the most significant items taken from studies made prior to this one.

The specific purposes of the study were: (1) to critically review marital-prediction studies in order to select the most basic or fundamental items; (2) to utilize these items, with minor modifications, in the construction of short marital-adjustment and prediction tests; and (3) to test the reliability and validity of these by applying them to a new sample.

First, adjustment and prediction items, which had proved significant in the original studies, were recorded. Then those items were selected which (1) had the highest level of discrimination in the original studies, (2) did not duplicate other included items, and (3) would cover the important areas of marital adjustment and prediction as judged by the authors.

Fifteen items were selected for the adjustment test, and thirty-five for the prediction test. The possible scores for the adjustment test ranged from 2–158 points; for the prediction test the score ranged from 0–532 for men, and from 0–502 for women.

# THE SAMPLE

A sample representative of the general married population was not needed, for the only purpose of this study was to see if reliable and valid short tests could be constructed. However, if it were to be used either in counseling or for research, it would be most applicable to a middle class group. The social characteristics of the 118 husbands and 118 wives in the present sample were quite similar to those of the Burgess-Cottrell and the Terman samples. The husbands and wives were not related spouses and, consequently, the sample represents 236 marriages.

The sample was a predominantly young,[17] native-white,[18] educated,[19] Protestant,[20] white-collar and professional,[21] urban group.[22] The families were predominantly childless or had only one child.[23] Mean length of marriage was

## TABLE 1
### Marital-Adjustment Test

1. Check the dot on the scale line below which best describes the degree of happiness, everything considered, of your present marriage. The middle point, "happy," represents the degree of happiness which most people get from marriage, and the scale gradually ranges on one side to those few who are very unhappy in marriage, and on the other, to those few who experience extreme joy or felicity in marriage.

| 0 | 2 | 7 | 15 | 20 | 25 | 35 |
|---|---|---|----|----|----|----|
| • | • | • | •  | •  | •  | •  |
| Very Unhappy | | | Happy | | | Perfectly Happy |

State the approximate extent of agreement or disagreement between you and your mate on the following items. Please check each column.

| | Always Agree | Almost Always Agree | Occasionally Disagree | Frequently Disagree | Almost Always Disagree | Always Disagree |
|---|---|---|---|---|---|---|
| 2. Handling family finances | 5 | 4 | 3 | 2 | 1 | 0 |
| 3. Matters of recreation | 5 | 4 | 3 | 2 | 1 | 0 |
| 4. Demonstrations of affection | 8 | 6 | 4 | 2 | 1 | 0 |
| 5. Friends | 5 | 4 | 3 | 2 | 1 | 0 |
| 6. Sex relations | 15 | 12 | 9 | 4 | 1 | 0 |
| 7. Conventionality (right, good, or proper conduct) | 5 | 4 | 3 | 2 | 1 | 0 |
| 8. Philosophy of life | 5 | 4 | 3 | 2 | 1 | 0 |
| 9. Ways of dealing with in-laws | 5 | 4 | 3 | 2 | 1 | 0 |

10. When disagreements arise, they usually result in: husband giving in   0  , wife giving in   2  , agreement by mutual give and take   10
11. Do you and your mate engage in outside interests together? All of them   10  , some of them   8  , very few of them   3  , none of them   0  .
12. In leisure time do you generally prefer: to be "on the go" —-, to stay at home —-? Does your mate generally prefer: to be "on the go" —-, to stay at home —-? (Stay at home for both, 10 points; "on the go" for both, 3 points; disagreement, 2 points.)
13. Do you ever wish you had not married? Frequently   0  , occasionally   3  , rarely   8  , never   15
14. If you had your life to live over, do you think you would: marry the same person   15  , marry a different person   0  , not marry at all   1  ?
15. Do you confide in your mate: almost never   0  , rarely   2  , in most things   10  , in everything   10  ?

5.6 years for husbands and 5.3 years for wives. Cases married less than one year were excluded. We now turn to the question of reliability and validity.

The short marital-adjustment test [is shown in Table 1.]

[See box for the] short marital-prediction test.

# RELIABILITY AND VALIDITY OF THE MARITAL-ADJUSTMENT TEST

The reliability coefficient of the adjustment test, computed by the split-half technique and corrected by the Spearman-Brown formula, was .90. Thus the short adjustment test has high reliability.

Forty-eight of the 236 subjects were known to be maladjusted in marriage. Extensive case data corroborated this for thirty-one of the persons, twenty-nine of whom were clients of the American Institute of Family Relations. Eleven more cases were recently divorced, and six were separated, making a total of twenty-two males and twenty-six females in the maladjusted group. This group of forty-eight was matched for age and sex with forty-eight persons in the sample judged to be exceptionally well-adjusted in marriage by friends who knew them well.

---

### Marital-Prediction Test

1. Circle the number which represents the highest grade of schooling which you had completed at the time of your marriage:
   1 2 3 4 5 6 7 8     1 2 3 4         1 2 3 4     1 2 3 4
   Grade School     High School     College     Postgraduate
        (0)              (5)          (10)         (20)

2. Check the number which represents your age at the time of marriage: 19  and under  0 , 20–24  H,2;W,5  ; 25–30  10  ; 31 and over  8 .

3. How long did you "keep company" with your mate before marriage? (check) 1 to 3 months  0  ; 3 to 6 months  2  ; 6 months to 1 year  4  ; 1 to 2 years  7  ; 2 to 3 years  10  ; 3 years or longer  15 .

4. How long had you known your mate at the time of your marriage? (check) 1 to 3 months  0  ; 3 to 6 months  2  ; 6 months to 1 year  4  ; 1 to 2 years  7  ; 2 to 3 years  10  ; 3 years to 5 years  15  ; 5 years or longer  20  ; since childhood  25 .

5. My father and mother (check) both approved my marriage  15  ; both disapproved my marriage  0  ; father disapproved  H,0;W,5  ; mother disapproved  5 .

6. My childhood and adolescence, for the most part, were spent in: (check) open country  20  ; a town of 2,500 population or under  15  ; a city of 2,500 to 10,000  10  ; 10,000 to 50,000  3  ; 50,000 and over  0 .

7. Did you ever attend Sunday school or other religious school for children and young people? (check) Yes  ; no  H,5;W0 . If answer is yes, at what age did you stop attending such a school? Before 10 years old  H,5;W,0  ; 11 to 18 years  H,15;W,10  ; 19 and over  H,25;W,20  ; still attending  H,25;W,20 .

8. Religious activity at time of marriage: (check) never attended church  0  ; attended less than once per month  3  ; once per month  H,8;W,5; twice  H,12;W,7  ; three times  H,15;W,10  ; four times  H,15;W,10   more than four times  H,15;W,10 .

9. Indicate the number of your friends of the same sex before marriage: (check) almost none  0  ; a few  H,5;W,10  ; several  H,10;W15 ; many  H,15;W,20 .

10. Before your marriage how much conflict was there between you and your father? (check) None  H,25;W,20  ; very little  H,20;W,15  ; moderate  H,15;W,10  ; a good deal  H,5;W,3  ; almost continuous  0 .

11. Before your marriage how much attachment was there between you and your father? (check) None  0  ; very little  5  ; moderate  7  ; a good deal  H,15;W,10  ; very close  H,25;W,15 .

12. Before your marriage how much conflict was there between you and your mother? (check) None  H,25;W,20  ; very little  H,20;W,15  ; moderate  H,15;W,10  ; a good deal  H,5;W,3  ; almost continuous  0 .

13. Before your marriage how much attachment was there between you and your mother? (check) None  0  ; very little  5  ; moderate  7  ; a good deal  H,15;W,10  ; very close  H,25;W,15 .

*(Continued on next page)*

14. Give your appraisal of the happiness of your parents' marriage: (check) very happy  45  ; happy  30  ; about averagely happy  15  ; unhappy  3  ; very unhappy  0  .
15. My childhood on the whole was: (check) very happy  55  ; happy  20  ; about averagely happy  10  ; unhappy  3  ; very unhappy  0  .
16. In my childhood I was (check) punished severely for every little thing  0  ; was punished frequently  2  ; was occasionally punished  10  ; rarely  15  ; never  15  .
17. In my childhood the type of training in my home was: (check) exceedingly strict  5  ; firm but not harsh  20  ; usually allowed to have my own way  5  ; had my own way about everything  3  ; irregular (sometimes strict, sometimes lax)  0  .
18. What was your parents' attitude toward your early curiosities about birth and sex? (check) Frank and encouraging  15  ; answered briefly  10  ; evaded or lied to me  3  ; rebuffed or punished me  0  ; I did not disclose my curiosity to them  5  .
19. My general mental ability, compared to my mate's is: (check) very superior to his (hers)  0  ; somewhat greater  H,5;W,0  ; about equal  H,15;W,20  ; somewhat less  H,5;W,10  ; considerably less  0  .
20. Before marriage what was your general attitude toward sex? (check) One of disgust and aversion  0  ; indifference  H,0;W,5  ; interest and pleasant anticipation  15  ; eager and passionate longing  H,5;W,0  .
21. Do you often feel lonesome, even when you are with other people? (check) Yes  0  ; No  5  ; ?  2  .
22. Are you usually even-tempered and happy in your outlook on life? Yes  20  ; No  0  ; ?  9  .
23. Do you often feel just miserable? (check) Yes  0  ; No  7  ; ?  3  .
24. Does some particular useless thought keep coming into your mind to bother you? (check) Yes  0  ; No  5  ; ?  2  .
25. Do you often experience periods of loneliness? (check) Yes  0  ; No  10  ; ?  4  .
26. Are you in general self-confident about your abilities? (check) Yes  5  ; No  0  ; ?  2  .
27. Are you touchy on various subjects? (check) Yes  0  ; No  6  ; ?  2  .
28. Do you frequently feel grouchy? (check) Yes  0  ; No  8  ; ?  3  .
29. Do you usually avoid asking advice? (check) Yes  0  ; No  5  ; ?  2  .
30. Do you prefer to be alone at times of emotional stress? (check) Yes  0  ; No  5  ; ?  2  .
31. Do your feelings alternate between happiness and sadness without apparent reason? (check) Yes  0  ; No  6  ; ?  2  .
32. Are you often in a state of excitement? (check) Yes  0  ; No  5  ; ?  2  .
33. Are you considered critical of other people? (check) Yes  0  ; No  8  ; ?  3  .
34. Does discipline make you discontented? (check) Yes  0  ; No  7  ; ?  3  .
35. Do you always try carefully to avoid saying anything that may hurt anyone's feelings? (check) Yes  10  ; No  0  ; ?  4  .

The mean adjustment score for the well-adjusted group was 135.9, whereas the mean score for the maladjusted group was only 71.7. This difference was very significant, for the critical ratio was 17.5.

Only 17 per cent of the maladjusted group achieved adjustment scores of one hundred or higher, whereas 96 per cent of the well-adjusted group achieved scores of one hundred or more.

The above figures indicate that this short marital-adjustment test clearly differentiates between persons who are well-adjusted and those who are maladjusted in marriage. It is evident, therefore, that the test has validity, since it seems to measure what it purports to measure—namely, marital adjustment.

## RELIABILITY AND VALIDITY OF THE MARITAL-PREDICTION TEST

The reliability coefficient of the prediction test, computed by the split-half technique and corrected by the Spearman-Brown formula, was .84. This coefficient is approximately the same as that of other longer tests.

The most exacting measure of the validity of a marital-prediction test would require a longitudinal study over a period of several years. Since this was not feasible, the prediction scores were correlated with the adjustment scores for the 236 husbands and wives. For the total sample, the coefficient of correlation between the prediction and adjustment scores was .47.

Interestingly enough, this correlation is almost identical with those obtained in both the Burgess-Cottrell and the Terman studies. Burgess and Cottrell obtained a correlation of .48 between the adjustment and prediction scores for their couples.[24] Terman and his associates obtained correlations between the happiness and prediction scores of .54 for husbands and .47 for wives.[25]

## CONCLUSIONS

The foregoing data confirm the hypothesis tested in this study: namely, that marital-adjustment and marital-prediction tests, constructed with a relatively small number of basic and fundamental items, achieve results approximately comparable with the longer and more complex adjustment and prediction tests.

With the short tests, measurement or prediction of marital adjustment can be accomplished with approximately the same accuracy in a few minutes as ordinarily would require an hour or more with the longer ones.

These findings also raise a question: Can short tests of all types, which use a few of the most basic and discriminating items, profitably replace the long ones in current use? Further research is needed to answer this question.

## NOTES

1. Gilbert V. Hamilton, *A Research in Marriage*, New York: Albert and Charles Boni, 1929, pp. 60–76.
2. One of these was not numbered.
3. It was sometimes difficult on multiple-answer questions to decide when an item should be counted as separate.
4. Ernest W. Burgess and Paul Wallin, *Engagement and Marriage*, Philadelphia: J. B. Lippincott Company, 1953, pp. 485–502. For wives it was 242.
5. Lewis M. Terman, et. al., *Psychological Factors in Marital Happiness*, New York: McGraw-Hill Book Company, 1938, p. 50. For wives it was 71.
6. Lewis M. Terman and Melita H. Oden, *Genetic Studies of Genius, Vol. IV, The Gifted Child Grows Up*, Palo Alto: Stanford University Press, 1947, pp. 431–33. For wives it was 106.
7. Harvey J. Locke, *Predicting Adjustment in Marriage: A Comparison of a Divorced and a Happily Married Group*, New York: Henry Holt and Company, 1951, pp. 48–52.
8. Georg Karlsson, *Adaptability and Communication in Marriage: A Swedish Prediction Study of Marital Satisfaction*, Uppsala, Sweden: Almqvist and Wiksells, Boktrycheri Aktiebolag, 1951, pp. 95–99 and question 53 on pp. 171–72. For wives it was 40.
9. Ernest W. Burgess and Leonard S. Cottrell, *Predicting Success or Failure in Marriage*, New York: Prentice-Hall, 1939, pp. 64–65.

10. Ernest W. Burgess and Paul Wallin, *op. cit.*, pp. 801–808.
11. Lewis M. Terman, *et. al., op. cit.*, pp. 122–41, 260–64, 352–55.
12. Lewis M. Terman and Melita H. Oden, *op. cit.*, pp. 419–29.
13. Harvey J. Locke, *op. cit.*, pp. 319–38.
14. Georg Karlsson, *op. cit.*, pp. 136–49.
15. Ernest W. Burgess and Leonard S. Cottrell, *op. cit.*, pp. 420–29.
16. Paul Horst, Editor, *The Prediction of Personal Adjustment,* New York: Social Science Research Council, 1941, Chapter 6.
17. Mean age of husbands was twenty-nine years; wives, thirty years.
18. Eighty-one per cent of subjects' fathers were native-white Americans; 15 per cent were born in Northern European countries.
19. Seventy per cent had some college training; 42 per cent of husbands and 32 per cent of wives had graduated from college; mean years of education was fifteen for husbands and fourteen for wives.
20. Seventy-three per cent were Protestant; 11 per cent Catholic; 5 per cent Jewish; and 11 per cent no church affiliation.
21. Fifty-four per cent of husbands engaged in professional, sales, and semiprofessional occupations; 58 per cent of wives listed occupation as housewife, and the majority of the remainder were in clerical, skilled, and semiskilled occupations.
22. All cases were from Los Angeles.
23. Forty per cent of husbands and 48 per cent of wives had no children; 39 per cent of husbands and 27 per cent of wives had only one child.
24. Ernest W. Burgess and Leonard S. Cottrell, *op. cit.*, p. 286.
25. Lewis M. Terman, *et. al., op. cit.*, p. 360.

5.2 WILLIAM STEPHENS

# Predictors of Marital Adjustment

Marital prediction studies have confirmed that there are certain marriages that will almost certainly fail. If you are very young, have not known your prospective partner very long, have been divorced already, subscribe to a different religion and have an educational background that is different from your prospective partner, and have parents who are divorced, chances are your marriage will not be successful. Yet couples marry every day regardless of these facts. This raises the question of how much marital prediction research has really helped society.

In the following selection from William Stephens's "Predictors of Marital Adjustment," published in his edited book *Reflections on Marriage* (Thomas Y. Crowell, 1968), Stephens concedes that some variables are simply correlated with failed marriages and may not really explain why marriages do not succeed. He has more confidence in some of the other predictors and their ability to forecast the viability of certain marriages. Ultimately, he suggests, the couple must collect all the information that is available to them and decide how strong their commitment to be married is and how long it will last. Stephens published *Reflections on Marriage* while at Florida Atlantic University.

**Key Concept:** marital adjustment

*A* life insurance company, in issuing policies and setting premium rates, is guided by actuarial tables. Given a few facts about a prospective customer, the company "knows the odds" that this person will live a specified number of years. If he is twenty years old, the chances that he will still be alive thirty years from now are fairly good. If he is forty-five, the chances are less good. Other factors, aside from age, enter into the calculus of life expectancy. Women, as a group, live longer than do men. Healthy persons live longer than do diabetics and cardiac patients. Accountants live longer than do steeplejacks.

Life expectancy, then, can be predicted. For a particular individual, the prediction may fall wide of the mark. But for large groups of people, the actuarial tables do well enough to enable the insurance companies to stay in business. Even for the single individual, the predictors have something significant to say.

They give a probabilistic—if not a certain—knowledge of the future. They tell you the odds.

Using the actuarial model, one can also say something about the life expectancy of marriages. One cannot predict with certainty about a particular marriage. Neither can we quote precise odds. However, we do have evidence that certain types of people are more apt to make successful marriages, are less prone to divorce, than are other types. The marital adjustment studies point to numerous signs. If, for a certain prospective marriage, the signs are generally good, that marriage stands an excellent chance for success. If the signs are generally negative, the future of that marriage looks bleak.

Suppose that you are a girl, and a boy has just proposed to you. Suppose further that in the interval between the proposal and your "yes" or "no" you could be as coldly rational as the insurance company executive. In this unlikely event, the marital adjustment studies have something to say to you:

1. If you are very young you should wait a few years before getting married. As people grow older, their chances of making a successful marriage increase.
2. If you have known him for a long time—and still want to marry him—your chances of success are better than if the period of acquaintanceship, prior to marriage, is short.
3. If your beloved is divorced, the chances are fair that he will get divorced again—from you.
4. If you and he are religious, this is a good sign. If you are both of the same faith, this also augurs well.
5. The more education you (and he) have had, the better your chances for a good marriage.
6. If your parents are happily married, this is a good sign. The odds improve if your fiance's parents are also happily married.

These are just a few of the predictors. There are many more, and they will be discussed presently.

## THE STUDIES

... [S]tudies... have documented various social-background correlates of marital adjustment. These studies were done over the past forty years. With two exceptions, they were conducted in this country. Aside from a few studies of divorce, based on court records, all derive from interviews and questionnaires —survey data. In any given study, various traits of a person or a married couple—age at marriage, religion, brothers and sisters, residence, education, and so on—are correlated with an index of marital adjustment. Indices of marital adjustment (marital happiness, success of the marriage, or what have you) are of three types. (1) A few studies use ratings. A couple is rated, by the researcher or by an acquaintance, as to whether their marriage is successful (i.e., adjusted, "good") or unsuccessful (maladjusted, "bad"). (2) Many a study uses divorce. Some marriages within the sample have ended in divorce; others have not. The assumption is that, on the whole, the nondivorced marriages have been more successful than the others that did end in divorce. Allowance is made for a certain percentage of "errors"; in particular, miserable but stable marriages that go on and on. (3) The third type of marital adjustment index is questionnaire-based. A sample of couples is given a standard list of questions to answer. The questions ask, in one form or another, and in relation to various aspects and areas of married life: "How are you getting along?" A couple answers the questionnaire; the answers are scored, using a standard scoring key and scaling convention; and thereby the couple is assigned a score on degree of marital adjustment.

All these indices are admittedly crude, tainted with an unknown amount of measurement error. They do, I think, permit certain conclusions which are likewise crude: cautious statements as to the presence and direction of associations; statements that permit a large margin for error. If, for example, we find that people who marry young have a higher divorce rate than do other people who marry when they are older, this gives us some basis for concluding that age at marriage has something to do with subsequent marital adjustment. If this same correlation turns up in eleven separate studies (as is the case), done in different places at different times, using a variety of marital adjustment indices, our conclusion would seem even better-grounded. It may be that age at marriage, in itself, is not a determinant of marital adjustment. Still, it would seem to be a trustworthy actuarial sign: if you marry young, your chances of success are somewhat diminished since, in the past, early-marrying people have been more prone to divorce, and have scored relatively badly on marital adjustment tests.

Actually, the persuasiveness of the evidence varies somewhat, from one predictor to the next. For some, like age at marriage, findings from all studies agree.[1] For level of education, on the other hand: most study findings return a positive correlation with marital adjustment; but a few do not. Along with agreement between studies, the danger of systematic bias must be taken into account. Some of these correlations might, conceivably, have nothing to do with marital adjustment. Take, for example, the finding that divorce predicts divorce; a divorced man, if he remarries, is more likely (than a previously unmarried person) to get divorced. Perhaps divorced men really are poor risks. Or perhaps they are merely people who are better able to break out of a marriage, once it has gone sour. In other words, readiness to seek divorce might be the controlling variable here; not ability to make a good marriage.

In general, I think, the greatest danger of systematic bias lies with the studies that use questionnaire-based marital adjustment indices. These are, of course, subject to distortion: lying, positive thinking, viewing-with-rose-colored-glasses on the part of questionnaire respondents. Some respondents are, no doubt, more candid than are others. For some predictors, individual differences in respondent-honesty could produce positive correlations with the questionnaire-based marital adjustment test scores. Take the finding that persons who report their parents were happily married tend to report that they too are happily married. Exaggeration, in a positive direction, by a certain fraction of the sample could have produced this correlation.

This sort of danger is alleviated, to some degree, by two characteristics of the data. (1) For some of the predictors, such as age at marriage and place of residence, it is hard to imagine how untruthful questionnaire responses could produce this sort of systematic bias. (2) For a given predictor, evidence typically comes from many studies; some of these employ the marital adjustment tests, but others use divorce as the index of marital adjustment. Information on divorce does not come from questionnaires; hence it cannot be influenced by respondent-lying. If the same effect holds up across both types of studies, confidence in the data increases.

We are now ready to review seventeen predictors. I have grouped them into three classes—A, B, and C—on the basis of an admittedly arbitrary judgment as to the persuasiveness of the supporting evidence. In the Class A predictors I have the highest confidence. For the Class B predictors, evidence seems a bit less persuasive. With the Class C predictors I am still impressed, but still less confident. The judgment is based on the two criteria that were just discussed: extent of agreement between studies, and a guess as to the danger of systematic bias.

### Class-A Predictors

**1. Age at Marriage:** Eleven studies here, and they all agree. Five find early marriages more prone to divorce. The other six find early-marrying persons scoring relatively low on marital adjustment tests. (Burgess and Cottrell 1939; Bernard 1934; Burchinal 1960; Christensen and Meissner 1953; Hart and Shields 1926; King 1952; Locke 1951; Landis and Landis 1958; Monahan 1953; Rountree 1964; Terman 1938.) What is an "early" marriage? What is too young? Perhaps about eighteen for girls, and twenty for men. However, the general trend across the studies is: up to the late twenties at least, the older you are, the better your chances.

**2. Length of Acquaintanceship:** The longer you've known him, the longer you have gone together, the longer the engagement: the better your chances. Six studies, all agreeing. (Burgess and Cottrell 1939; King 1952; Locke 1951; Locke and Karlsson 1952; Popenoe and Neptune 1938; Terman 1938.) How long is long enough? Date him for at least a year; but the longer the better.

**3. Premarital Pregnancy:** Don't let it happen to you. (Christensen and Meissner 1953; Geismar and La Sorte 1963; Rountree 1964.)

**4. Religiosity:** An atheist is a relatively poor risk. Eight studies suggest this; there is one dissenter. (Kirkpatrick 1937.) The index of religiosity is, generally, frequency of church attendance; also used [is] Sunday school attendance, formally belonging to a church, and stating (or not stating) a religious preference on the marriage license application. (Burgess and Cottrell 1939; Burchinal 1955; Chesser 1957; King 1952; Landis 1946, 1949; Locke 1951; Schroeder 1938.) Also, marriages performed by a minister, priest, or rabbi stand a better chance that those joined by a Justice of the Peace. (Burgess and Cottrell 1939; Christensen and Meissner 1953; Schroeder 1938.)

**5. Similarity of Faith:** Mixed-faith marriages: Catholic-Protestant, Catholic-Jew, Protestant-Jew; these show higher divorce rates than do same-faith marriages. Nine studies, all agreeing. (Chancellor and Monahan 1955; Gordon 1946; Kirkpatrick 1937; Landis 1949; Vernon 1960; Vincent 1959; Monahan and Chancellor 1955; Monahan and Kephart 1954; Weeks 1943.)

**6. Social Class:** It is best not to be poor. Fourteen studies return a positive correlation between social class (signified by income or by husband's occupation) and a marital adjustment index. (Burgess and Cottrell 1939; Census 1953; Christensen and Meissner 1953; Goode 1956; Hamilton 1929; Kephart 1955; King 1952; Land 1932; Locke 1951; Monahan 1955; Roth and Peck 1951; Schroeder 1938; Weeks, 1943; Williamson 1952.) Two studies find no relationship. (Bernard 1934; Terman 1938.) The one nation-wide study, done by the Census Bureau, returns an impressive correlation between income and divorce rate. On the subject of occupations: two old studies find that travelling men, whose occupations take them away form home a good deal, are also poor risks. (Burgess and Cottrell 1939; Land 1932.) Beware of travelling salesmen, railroad men, transcontinental truck drivers.

What of social class differences: a rich girl marries a poor man, or vice versa? Two studies indicate that this, also, may be a negative predictor. (Kirkpatrick 1937; Roth and Peck 1951.)

**Class-B Predictors**

**7. Level of Education:** If we merely view the studies that use marital adjustment tests or ratings, there is no relationship to speak of. Three of these return a positive correlation between years of schooling and marital adjustment. (Burgess and Cottrell 1939; Landis 1946; Terman 1938.) One shows a weak negative correlation. (Hamilton 1926.) Three show no relationship at all. (Bernard 1934; Kirkpatrick 1937; Geismar and La Sorte 1963.) The eight studies that use divorce, however, all agree: the more years of schooling, the lower the divorce rate. (Census 1953; HEW 1957; Glick 1957; Glick and Carpenter 1958; Locke 1951; Monahan 1961; Schroeder 1938; Terman and Oden 1947.) A number of them are based on nation-wide probability samples. It looks as if there is something here.

**8. Previous Divorce:** Past divorce is a predictor of future divorce, upon remarriage. Five studies agree. (Census 1949; Christensen and Meissner 1953; Monahan 1952, 1953, 1958.) There is one dissenter. (Locke 1951.) Two more studies use something other than divorce to indicate marital adjustment: Geismar and La Sorte (a marital adjustment rating), and Locke and Klaussner (a marital adjustment test). Both find that previously divorced *grooms* represent a poor risk; but this is *not* true for previously divorced *brides*.

**9. Divorced Parents:** Children of divorced parents tend to score low on marital adjustment tests. (Burgess and Cottrell 1939; Hamilton 1926.) They are more apt to get divorced or separated. (Landis 1955; Schroeder 1938.) Geismar and La Sorte, using marital adjustment ratings, found that divorced parents represented a negative predictor for grooms (again), but not for brides.

In six more studies, *happiness of parents' marriage* (as judged by the respondent) correlates positively with scores on marital adjustment tests. (Burgess and Cottrell 1939; Hamilton 1929; Locke and Karlsson 1952; Popenoe and Wicks 1937; Terman 1938; Terman and Buttenwiser 1935.) There is one dissenting study. (Locke 1951.)

There is an impressive mass of data here. Agreement is high. But systematic bias may be a real factor.

**10. Where They Will Live:** Live in the country or in a small town; don't live in the city. (Census 1958; Burgess and Cottrell 1939; Carter and Plateris 1963; Christensen and Meissner 1953.)

**11. Parents' Approval:** Get it first. Four studies all agreeing. Either the old folks really know something, or parental objections generate a self-fulfilling prophecy effect. (Burgess and Wallin 1953; King 1952; Locke 1951; Locke and Karlsson 1951.)

**12. Sociability:** People who report they (and/or the spouse) are joiners, have "lots of friends," are "popular": these persons tend to score high on the marital adjustment tests. (Burgess and Cottrell 1939; Burgess and Wallin 1953; King 1952; Locke 1951; Locke and Karlsson 1952; Terman and Oden 1947.)

**Class-C Predictors**

**13. Differences in Age:** If the groom is much older—or much younger—than the bride: this looks as if it may be a negative predictor. Five studies find this negatively correlated with marital adjustment; two studies report no association (Christensen and Meissner 1953; Burgess and Cottrell 1939; Geismar and La Sorte 1963; King 1952; Kirkpatrick 1937; Locke 1951; Terman 1938.) What is "much older?" perhaps five years or more. It is hard to say, given the low degree of consensus among studies.

**14. Brothers and Sisters:** Being an only child, without brothers or sisters: this looks as if it may be a negative predictor. Two studies assert that it is. (Burgess and Cottrell 1939; Terman 1938.) A third study disagrees. (Kirkpatrick 1937.) A fourth returns mixed results (Hall 1965.)

**15. Relationship with Parents:** In two old studies, persons who report they had a lot of conflict with their parents tend to have low marital adjustment scores. (Terman 1938; Burgess and Cottrell 1939.)

**16. The Relationship Before Marriage:** This seems to be one indicator of how the couple will get along after they are married. If the engagement relationship is tempestuous and strife-torn, chances are the marriage will be too. (Burgess and Wallin 1944; Locke 1951; Geismar and La Sorte 1963.)

**17. Mental Health:** In three studies, an index of mental health correlates positively with an index of marital adjustment. (Burchinal 1957; Eshleman 1965; Robbins and O'Neal 1958.)

Clifford Kirkpatrick (1963) has made an even more extensive literature review. He cites still more predictors. Generally, these are the type that I would place in "Class C" or below; the supporting evidence, in my view, is not impressive. Here are some examples, all positive predictors: the wife is pretty; they are in good health; they are similar in personality and values and have common interests.

# DISCUSSION

The picture that emerges is: a great many variables correlate with marital adjustment indices; and, as is typical of survey data, the correlations generally are rather weak. It is impossible to firmly establish the relative importance of all these variables: which are really important, which do not particularly matter. I would guess that no single predictor counts for very much; but all the predictors, taken together, definitely count for something. The seventeen predictors, given above, could be used as a checklist. Thus, for a contemplated marriage: if the signs are unfavorable on only two of the predictors, this is very good, because it means that the signs are favorable with respect to the other fifteen. If, on the other hand, the prospective marriage rates bad on ten of the predictors, this is reason to pause.

Needless to say, this long list of variables still leaves much unaccounted for. No doubt the most crucial events, the interpersonal mechanisms on which marriages actually succeed and fail, are hardly touched by the survey data. We have, in a sense, been examining surface phenomena; the data, as they have been used here, contribute little to any deeper understanding of causal mechanisms. If one is willing to interpret further and to speculate, it is possible to employ questionnaire data in a quest for understanding....

One more general conclusion: the data seem to say that conventional people and conventional marriages stand the best chance. Girls: marry a Rotarian who is active in his church, who gets on well with his parents, who has never been divorced, who is about your age, whom you have known for years. Don't get pregnant first. Don't marry without your parents' blessings. Don't marry until you are out of school. Marry your own kind, *vis à vis* religion and social class position. And stay out of big cities.

Conceivably, all these precepts are spurious. The entire conventionality effect might be one huge, ramified case of systematic bias. Perhaps it merely happens that conventional people are less willing to seek divorce, and less able to face the truth about their marriages when they take marital adjustment tests. Perhaps, but I think not.

# NOTES

1. Agree, that is, as to the *direction* of the association. Agreement as to the strength of the association or the shape of the curve is, of course, too much to ask.

# REFERENCES

JESSIE BERNARD, "Factors in the Distribution of Success in Marriage," *American Journal of Sociology,* XL (1934), 49–60.

LEE G. BURCHINAL, "Research on Young Marriage: Implications for Family Life Education," *The Family Life Coordinator,* IX (1960), 6–24.

BUREAU OF THE CENSUS SERIES P-20 NO. 23, March 4, 1949. "Marital Status, Number of Times Married, and Duration of Present Marital Status: April, 1948."

*U.S. Census of Population: 1950. Vol IV, Special Reports,* Part 5, Chapter 5, 1953.

———, *Current Population Reports,* Series 20, No. 87, November 14, 1958.

ERNEST W. BURGESS and LEONARD S. COTTRELL, *Predicting Success or Failure in Marriage* (New York: Prentice-Hall, Inc., 1939).

ERNEST W. BURGESS and HARVEY J. LOCKE, *The Family* (New York: American Book Co., 1945).

ERNEST W. BURGESS and PAUL WALLIN, "Marriage Adjustment and Engagement Adjustment," *American Journal of Sociology,* XLIX (1944), 324–30.

———, *Engagement and Marriage* (Philadelphia: Lippincott, 1953).

HUGH CARTER and ALEXANDER PLATERIS, "Trends in Divorce and Family Disruption," *HEW Indicators,* September 1963.

LORING CHANCELLOR and THOMAS MONAHAN, "Religious Preference and Interreligious Mixtures in Marriages and Divorces in Iowa," *American Journal of Sociology,* LXI (1955), 233–39.

HAROLD T. CHRISTENSEN and HANNA H. MEISSNER, "Studies in Child Spacing: III-Premarital Pregnancy as a Factor in Divorce," *American Sociological Review,* XVIII (1953), 641–44.

EUSTACE CHESSER, *The Sexual, Marital, and Family Relationships of the English Woman* (New York: Roy, 1957).

RAYMOND J. CORSINI, "Understanding and Similarity in Marriage," *Journal of Abnormal and Social Psychology,* LII (1956), 327–32.

———, "Multiple Predictors of Marital Happiness," *Marriage and Family Living,* XVIII (1956), 240–42.

LEONARD W. FERGUSON, "Correlates of Marital Happiness," *Journal of Psychology,* VI (1938), 285–94.

LUDWIG L. GEISMAR and MICHAEL A. LA SORTE, "Factors Associated with Family Disorganization," *Marriage and Family Living* (1963), 479–81.

PAUL C. GLICK, *American Families* (New York: Wiley, 1957).

PAUL C. GLICK and HUGH CARPENTER, "Marriage Patterns and Educational Level," *American Sociological Review,* XXIII (1958), 294–300.

WILLIAM J. GOODE, *After Divorce* (Glencoe, Ill.: Free Press, 1956).

ALBERT I. GORDON, *Intermarriage* (Boston: Beacon Press, 1964).

EVERETT HALL, "Ordinal Position and Success in Engagement and Marriage," *Journal of Individual Psychology,* XXI (1965), 154–58.

GILBERT V. HAMILTON, *A Research in Marriage* (New York: A. & C. Boni, 1929).

HORNELL HART and WILMER SHIELDS, "Happiness in Relation to Age at Marriage," *Journal of Social Hygiene,* XII (1926), 403–8.

JEROLD S. HEISS, "Interfaith Marriage and Marital Outcome," *Marriage and Family Living,* XXIII (1961), 228–33.

WILLIAM K. KEPHART, "Occupational Level and Marital Disruption," *American Sociological Review,* XX (1955), 456–65.

CHARLES E. KING, "A Research Technique of Marital Adjustment Applied to a Southern Urban Minority Population Group," *Factors Making For Success or Failure in Marriage Among 466 Negro Couples in a Southern City* (Ph.D. thesis, University of Chicago, 1951).

———, "The Burgess-Cottrell Method of Measuring Marital Adjustment Applied to a Nonwhite Southern Urban Population," *Marriage and Family Living,* XIV (1952), 280–85.

CLIFFORD KIRKPATRICK, "Factors in Marital Adjustment," *American Journal of Sociology,* XLIII (1937), 270–83.

———, *The Family: As a Process and Institution* (New York: Ronald, 1963).

CLIFFORD KIRKPATRICK and JOHN COTTON, "Physical Attractiveness, Age, and Marital Adjustment," *American Sociological Review,* XVI (1951), 81–86.

JUDSON T. LANDIS, "Marriages of Mixed and Non-mixed Religious Faith," *American Sociological Review,* XIV (1949), 401–7.

———, "The Pattern of Divorce in Three Generations," *Social Forces,* XXXIV (1955), 213–16.

———, "Social Correlates of Divorce or Nondivorce among the Unhappy Married," *Marriage and Family Living* (1963), 178–83.

JUDSON T. LANDIS and MARY G. LANDIS, *Building a Successful Marriage* (New York: Prentice-Hall, 1958).

RICHARD O. LANG, "A Study of the Degree of Happiness or Unhappiness in Marriage," Quoted in Burgess and Cottrell, *Predicting Success or Failure in Marriage.* (Master's Thesis, University of Chicago, 1932).

HARVEY J. LOCKE, "Predicting Marital Adjustment by Comparing a Divorced and a Happily Married Group," *American Sociological Review,* XII (1947), 187–91.

———, *Predicting Adjustment in Marriage* (New York: Holt, 1951).

HARVEY J. LOCKE and GEORG KARLSSON, "Marital Adjustment and Prediction in Sweden and the United States," *American Sociological Review,* XVII (1952), 10–17.

HARVEY J. LOCKE and WILLIAM J. KLAUSNER, "Marital Adjustment of Divorced Persons in Subsequent Marriages," *Sociology and Social Research,* XXX (1948), 97–101.

HARVEY J. LOCKE and MURIEL MACKEPRANG, "marital Adjustment and the Employed Wife," *American Journal of Sociology,* LIV (1949), 536–38.

THOMAS P. MONAHAN, "How Stable are Remarriages?, *American Journal of Sociology,* LVIII (1952), 280–88.

———, "Does Age at Marriage Matter in Divorce?, *Social Forces,* XXXII (1953), 81–87.

———, "Divorce by Occupation Level," *Marriage and Family Living,* XVII (1955), 322–24.

———, "The Changing Nature and Instability of Remarriages," *Eugenics Quarterly,* V (1958), 73–85.

———, "Educational Achievement and Family Stability," *Journal of Psychology,* LV (1961), 253–63.

THOMAS P. MONAHAN and LOREN E. CHANCELLOR, "Statistical Aspects of Marriage and Divorce by Religious Denomination in Iowa," *Eugenics Quarterly*, II (1955), 162–73.

THOMAS P. MONAHAN and WILLIAM KEPHART, "Divorce and Desertion by Religious and Mixed Religious Groups," *American Journal of Sociology*, LIX (1954), 454–65.

PAUL POPENOE and D. W. NEPTUNE, "Acquaintance and Betrothal," *Social Forces*, XVI (1938), 552–55.

PAUL POPENOE and DONNA WICKS, "Marital Happiness in Two Generations," *Mental Hygiene*, XXI (1937), 218–23.

LEE N. ROBINS and PATRICIA O'NEAL, "Marital History of Former Problem Children," *Social Problems*, V (1958), 347–58.

JULIUS ROTH and ROBERT F. PECK, "Social Class and Social Mobility Factors Related to Marital Adjustment," *American Sociological Review*, XVI (1951), 478–86.

GRISELDA ROUNTREE, "Some Aspects of Marriage Breakdown in Britain During the Last Thirty Years," *Population Studies*, XVIII (1964), 147–63.

CLARENCE W. SCHROEDER, "Divorce in a City of 100,000 Population" (Ph.D. Thesis, University of Chicago, 1938, Private Edition; distributed by Bradley Polytechnic Institute Library, Peoria, Ill., 1939).

LEWIS M. TERMAN et al., *Psychological Factors in Marital Happiness* (New York: McGraw-Hill, 1938).

LEWIS M. TERMAN and PAUL BUTTENWISER, "Personality Factors in Marital Incompatibility," *Journal of Social Psychology*, VI (1935), 143–71.

LEWIS M. TERMAN and MELITA H. ODEN, *The Gifted Child Grows Up: Twenty-five Years' Follow-up of a Superior Group* (Stanford, Calif.: Stanford University Press, 1947).

U.S. DEPARTMENT OF HEALTH, EDUCATION and WELFARE, *Vital Statistics—Special Reports*, Vol. 45, No. 12 (September 9, 1957).

GLENN M. VERNON, "Interfaith Marriages," *Religious Education*, LV (1960), 261–64.

CLARK E. VINCENT, "Intefaith Marriages: Problem or Symptom?", in Jane C. Zahn (ed.), *Religion and the Face of America* (University Extension, University of California, 1959).

PAUL WALLIN, "Religiosity, Sexual Gratification, and Marital Satisfaction," *American Sociological Review*, XXII (1957), 300–5.

H. ASHLEY WEEKS, "Differential Divorce Rates by Occupation," *Social Forces*, XXI (1943), 334–37.

ROBERT C. WILLIAMSON, "Economic Factors in Marital Adjustment," *Marriage and Family Living*, XIV (1952), 298–300.

# CHAPTER 6 Marital Role Satisfaction

## 6.1 ROBERT O. BLOOD, JR., AND DONALD M. WOLFE

# *The Power to Make Decisions*

Robert O. Blood, Jr., and Donald M. Wolfe's power-of-decision-making scale was used extensively in studies of the family in the 1960s and 1970s. This selection was excerpted from their 1960 book *Husbands and Wives: The Dynamics of Married Living* (Free Press). The book made a significant impact on the study of marriage and family because it gave researchers a consistent tool from which to draw conclusions as family life changed from 1960 to 1980. As more women began taking home paychecks, power and decision making changed dramatically. Women began to rival men in deciding how the family would spend money. It was discovered that income was a serious determinant of the balance of power in marriages.

Blood (b. 1921) wrote or cowrote the books *Marriage*, with Margaret Blood (Free Press, 1969), *Love Match and Arranged Marriage* (Free Press, 1967), *Northern Breakthrough* (Wadsworth, 1962), and *The Family* (Free Press, 1972). He began his career as a college professor and became a marriage counselor in private practice. He was a Fulbright research scholar at Tokyo Educational University in 1958, and he spent part of his career at the University of Michigan in Ann Arbor, Michigan.

Wolfe is presently a professor of organizational behavior in the School of Management at Case Western Reserve University. He completed his doctoral degree in 1960 at the University of Michigan, where he and Blood wrote *Husbands and Wives*. His publications have appeared in journals such as the *Journal of Black Studies* and the *Organization Development Journal*.

**Key Concept:** marital roles

No change in the American family is mentioned more often than the shift from one-sided male authority to the sharing of power by husband and wife. Perhaps no change is more significant, either. The balance of power between husband and wife is a sensitive reflection of the roles they play in marriage—and, in turn, has many repercussions on other aspects of their relationship.

*Power and Authority.* Power may be defined as the potential ability of one partner to influence the other's behavior. Power is manifested in the ability to make decisions affecting the life of the family.

Authority is closely related to power. Authority is legitimate power, i.e., power held by one partner because both partners feel it is proper for him to do so. The family authority pattern is prescribed by the society at large in such forms as: "the man should be the head of the house"—or "husbands should not dictate to their wives."

Power, on the other hand, refers to the way in which husbands and wives actually deal with each other. Caspar Milquetoast, as a man, may be supposed to have considerable authority, but in practice he exercises very little power. Power and authority do not necessarily coincide....

## THE CONTEMPORARY PATTERN OF POWER

In order to measure the precise balance of power between husbands and wives one would have to assess their influence in all the family decisions which had ever been made—or at least all those which had been made over a considerable period of time. Such an exhaustive undertaking would exceed the capacities of husbands' and wives' memories.

Since a complete record of decisions is unobtainable, any study of marriage must rely on a sample of decisions to represent the larger whole. In this study, eight decisions were selected to provide an estimate of the relative balance of power between husband and wife.

The eight decisions are:

1. What job the husband should take.
2. What car to get.
3. Whether or not to buy life insurance.
4. Where to go on a vacation.
5. What house or apartment to take.
6. Whether or not the wife should go to work or quit work.

7. What doctor to have when someone is sick.
8. How much money the family can afford to spend per week on food.

These eight were selected because they are all relatively important (compared to deciding whether to go to a movie tonight). They are also questions which nearly all couples have to face. (This is why no questions were asked relating to children.) Only three per cent of the couples at most answered any question in hypothetical terms (the three per cent who had never bought a car and the similar number who hadn't yet taken a vacation). The remaining criterion for these questions was that they should range from typically masculine to typically feminine decisions—but should always affect the family as a whole.

It was assumed in advance that contemporary husbands and wives would often talk things over in the process of arriving at a decision. Even a patriarchal husband may consult his wife as one source of opinion and one factor to be taken into consideration while he makes up his mind. The crucial question is not who takes part in the discussion but who makes the final decision. To get this information the lead-in statement to the battery of questions was as follows:

"In every family somebody has to decide such things as where the family will live and so on. Many couples talk such things over first, but the *final* decision often has to be made by the husband or the wife. For instance, who usually makes the final decision about... ?"

In order to provide comparable answers, the respondents were given a choice of "husband always," "husband more than wife," "husband and wife exactly the same," "wife more than husband," and "wife always" as response categories.

**Who Decides?**

The wives' answers to the eight questions are shown in Table 1 with the items arranged in order of decreasing male participation.

Two decisions are primarily the husband's province (his job and the car), two the wife's (her work and the food), while all the others are joint decisions in the sense of having more "same" responses than anything else. Even the wife's working turns out to be a quite middling decision from the standpoint of the mean score, leaving only the food expenditures preponderantly in the wife's hands. Only the two male decisions are made more than half the time by a particular partner.

*Sex Roles.* The distribution of decisions by sex is not surprising. The husband's work is his chief role in life. From it he derives his greatest sense of well-being or malaise, and there he invests the greatest part of his energies. His work is so one-sidedly important to him that almost all the wives leave him alone for his final decision.

Automobiles are associated with the mechanical aptitude of males (Scheinfeld, 1943). Moreover, a large proportion of the driving in the United States is done by males, giving them added interest in the choice of car.

**TABLE 1**

*Allocation of Power in Decision-Making Areas (731 Detroit Families)*

| WHO DECIDES? | DECISION | | | | | | | |
|---|---|---|---|---|---|---|---|---|
| | Husband's job | Car | Insurance | Vacation | House | Wife's work | Doctor | Food |
| (5) Husband always | 90% | 56% | 31% | 12% | 12% | 26% | 7% | 10% |
| (4) Husband more than wife | 4 | 12 | 11 | 6 | 6 | 5 | 3 | 2 |
| (3) Husband and wife exactly the same | 3 | 25 | 41 | 68 | 58 | 18 | 45 | 32 |
| (2) Wife more than husband | 0 | 2 | 4 | 4 | 10 | 9 | 11 | 11 |
| (1) Wife always | 1 | 3 | 10 | 7 | 13 | 39 | 31 | 41 |
| N.A. | 2 | 1 | 2 | 3 | 1 | 3 | 3 | 3 |
| Total | 100 | 99 | 99 | 100 | 100 | 100 | 100 | 99 |
| Husband's mean power* | 4.86 | 4.18 | 3.50 | 3.12 | 2.94 | 2.69 | 2.53 | 2.26 |

*The mean for each column is computed on the basis of the weights shown, e.g., "husband always" = 5.

At the other extreme, meal-planning is part of the wife's role in the division of labor,... giving to the wife the major responsibility for food expenditures.

The choice of doctor falls to the wife especially often where there are dependent children in the home, so that it is associated with her role as mother. However, it also reflects the general tendency of women to play a nurturant role for the sick and helpless.

The family vacation and the choice of house are most frequently joint decisions. Is this because they most clearly affect both partners equally?

The fact that insurance decisions are made somewhat more often by the husband may reflect the technical financial questions involved. If so, the financial training involved in his money-earning role gives him extra competence.

That the husband should be more involved in his wife's job decisions than she with his is understandable. For one thing, her work is seldom her major preoccupation in life the way it is for a man. Even if she works just as many hours a week, she does not usually make the same life-long commitment to the world of work. Nor is her pay check as indispensable to the family finances (if only because it is usually smaller). In such ways the choice whether to work or not is less vital to a woman than to a man.

In addition, the wife's decision about working have repercussions on the husband. If his wife goes to work, he will have to help out more around the house. If he is a business executive, he may prefer to have her concentrate her energy on entertaining prospective clients at home. As a small businessman or independent professional, he may need her services in his own enterprise. On the other hand, regardless of his own occupation, he may want her to work in order to help him buy a house or a business or pay for the children's education.

It may be, then, that the work role is so much the responsibility of the husband in marriage that even the wife's work is but an adjunct of his instrumental leadership, leaving this decision frequently in his hands.

**The Balance of Power**

Whether families are patriarchal in general is far more important than whether they sometimes conform to patriarchal norms in a single area of decision-making. With eight questions so widely distributed between masculine and feminine roles, the Detroit families as a whole could not look very patriarchal when their answers to the whole battery of questions are totalled up. Even so, there might still be considerable variation between families, if in some the husbands consistently make the decisions while in others wives consistently do.

In actual practice, such consistency is rare. Less than one half of one per cent of the Detroit husbands make all eight decisions and a similarly small proportion of wives are all-powerful. Nevertheless such extremes do exist and exemplify the fact that it is possible to find all kinds of power-balances from the most patriarchal to the most matriarchal.

Given these eight particular questions, the aggregate balance of power falls slightly in the husband's direction. When the total scores for the eight questions, weighted as shown in Table 1, are converted into a ten-point scale reflecting the amount of influence exerted by the husband, the average score for all families is 5.09 (whereas a score of 4.00 is the equivalent of "husband and wife exactly the same").

Although families can be found varying all the way from one extreme to the other, most families bunch together around this mean score. Forty-six per cent of all the Detroit families have scores of four to six. Though slightly skewed to the husband's side in absolute terms, it seems preferable to label these as relatively equalitarian couples. This leaves twenty-two per cent with scores of seven or more who can be called relatively male-dominant and another twenty-two per cent with scores of three or less who are relatively female-dominant.[1] Even these extreme groups cluster close to the central group. This means that Detroit families, on the whole, are extraordinarily alike when it comes to the balance of decision-making.

The middle group of equalitarian marriages can be differentiated further according to whether they make most of their decisions jointly or whether they assign equal numbers of separate decisions to both partners. The former type is called "syncratic" and the latter "autonomic" (Herbst in Oeser and Hammond, 1954). Despite the fact that these four types (husband-dominant, syncratic, autonomic, and wife-dominant) are concentrated in the middle range of power, they still differ enough from each other to provide important distinctions between families in many respects.

The impression that the average Detroit marriage is properly labelled equalitarian is supported by answers to the question: "When you and your husband differ about something, do you usually give in and do it your husband's way, or does he usually come around to your point of view?" Thirty-four per cent say that they usually or always give in under these circumstances, twenty-four per cent say the husband does, but the remaining forty per cent (two per cent, no answer) give equalitarian responses. This forty per cent undoubtedly underestimates the proportion of equalitarian marriages because many wives made it entirely clear that they and their husbands agree on most things most of the time, leaving this question to apply only to marginal disagreements. When viewed against the relatively small margin of husband-winning over wife-winning cases, Detroit marriages have clearly moved a long way from nineteenth century patriarchalism.

## NOTES

1. The remaining 10 per cent are unknown because they failed to answer one or more of the eight decision questions.

## 6.2 JOHN F. CUBER AND PEGGY B. HARROFF

# The More Total View

Five categories for couples' relationships were originally proposed by John F. Cuber and Peggy B. Harroff in 1962 at the Groves Conference on Marriage and the Family in Baltimore, Maryland. Their taxonomy of marriage styles was subsequently published as "The More Total View: Relationships Among Men and Women of the Upper Middle Class," in the May 1963 issue of *Marriage and Family Living* (now referred to as the *Journal of Marriage and the Family*). These categories were included in textbooks and were for many years required learning in undergraduate family living classes. According to Cuber and Harroff, couples could be pigeonholed into one of the following types of relationships: passive-congenial, total, conflict-habituated, devitalized, and vital. It is interesting to note that although Cuber and Harroff's conclusions were based on studies of the upper middle class, the categories were usually applied to the whole population of married couples by other professionals and teachers.

Cuber and Harroff, who married in 1964, were at Ohio State University at the time their article, which is reprinted in this selection, was published. They have published a number of books, both separately and together, one of which was popular with the academic as well as the general public in the 1960s: *Sex and the Significant Americans: A Study of Sexual Behavior Among the Affluent*.

**Key Concept:** marital roles

The "field" of marriage and family now consists of an impressive array of expert findings, theories, and typologies which together purport, by implication at least, to present to the interested student and colleague a composite picture of the bi-sexual world today. A strong accent, not always so stated, in all of this is diagnostic. Within certain limits we profess to *understand* the condition of man, so to speak, in his bi-sexual nature, the traditional and emergent forms which this nature takes and something about the predicaments which he persistently gets into. We have evolved a set of concepts like "the child-centered family," "permissive parenthood," "the family cycle" and have formulated a number of theoretical models and sequences which have become almost professional clichés—"from institution to companionship," "alternative roles for women," "complementary needs"—and a plethora of analyses as to why more and more marriages are apparently impermanent. This all adds up for one who tries to see it as a gestalt to a professional diagnosis as to what "is," what is wrong—or at least troublesome—and to some extent how it might be remedied.

Something additional might presumably be gained by turning to the subjects themselves for *their* concepts and *their* diagnosis of the state of the bi-sexual world. It might be well, moreover, to find out whether the concepts of professionals are reasonably in line with laymen's own perceptions and whether the imagery of the professionals corresponds to the imagery of the subjects about the same matters. We (the professionals) might, as Bierstedt says in another connection, often be re-enacting the deaf man in Tolstoy, muttering answers to questions that no one has asked.

In the research upon which we are about to make a preliminary report, we have focused upon a select group of subjects for the purpose of securing their conceptions of reality in the man-woman world, their strivings and apathies and their own evaluation of the success or failure of their own *modus operandi*. In constructing this collective self portrait, we invented, or more accurately, adapted a type of inquiry apparently not much in use by contemporary social scientists, with the exception perhaps of some anthropologists. It could be described tersely as the unstructured, lengthy and intimate interview. In some respects it resembles a depth interview, because being unstructured, there was no way to avoid subjects' efforts at deeper self-examination, if they so chose. The important things to stress, however, are the unstructured nature of the talking-over process, leaving the subject wide latitude as to what he chose to discuss and what he chose to say about it and second, the completeness of the material reported by the subject. It would be possible in a number of instances to write a sizable book on the basis of the information we have about a given person or a given pair.

Such an undertaking, however, presents problems. First of all it presumes that one can find subjects sufficiently self-conscious about their life processes that they have intellectualizations worth talking about and second, that they are sufficiently articulate to be able to communicate such ideas effectively to someone else. Obviously, many potential subjects would be disqualified on one or another of these counts. It is also important to secure a sufficiently homogeneous group so that there would be some comparability relative to their life circumstances in order that even guarded generalization would be possible.

As the best approximation of our objectives, we settled upon a group of subjects whom most sociologists would probably designate as the upper echelons of the "Upper Middle Class." We interviewed individuals, not couples or families, although in a number of instances, both husband and wife came to be included. Since our focus was upon men and women and not upon marriage or family, we also interviewed widowed, divorced and single people in the approximate percentage in which they are found in this population. To insure further homogeneity interviewees were limited to an age span of 35 to 55 because we were more interested in mature reflection than in the immature projections of the very young and yet wanted persons in the vital years, before, as a rule, serious health or disillusionment begin to presage senility. We have interviewed in all 437 such persons.

Our rationale for this kind of selection is simply this: Since this segment of the population is highly educated, highly travelled, and widely exposed to allegedly emancipating influences, it could be presumed that they would have had occasion to observe and reflect seriously upon the man-woman world and would be relatively articulate in communicating their perceptions, evaluations and adaptations. These assumptions seemed vindicated by our actual experience in communicating with them. There were virtually no refusals; they had a great deal they wished to talk about, and by and large, were eager to talk about it.

One final criterion for selection of interviewees was observed. So much work in the social sciences has been done with relatively captive samples of people who are caught at some point of crisis in their lives, that a serious bias might thus have been introduced. We sought a non-clinical sample; that is, one limited to people not currently securing any kind of counselling or psychotherapy or having recently had any, or who were, in the opinion of the interviewers, clearly in need thereof. Obviously, such a sample is not normal by every criterion of normality, but it is at least free of some of the manifest distortion-producing influences of a crisis-caught group.

The problem of moving from data gathering to reporting is always ticklish. Many devices for content analysis of interview records have become conventional. These were not functional for us, because such techniques presume comparability of data for each subject. This we did not seek and therefore did not get. Accordingly we resorted to an informal, ideal-typical procedure in which we repeatedly reviewed and analyzed our materials looking for commonalities, generalizations and recurrent syndromes, none of which has at this point any formal statistical validity other than that it is *recurrent*. In other words, idiosyncratic data have been completely ignored in the analysis and so far as we could control it, in our own thinking and conversations about our material. We sought generalizable information, even though we knew before we started that generalizing would have to occur in non-statistical language.

Perhaps our most important finding was in the form, not of data about men and women or marriage, but a vivid and recurrent reminder that when the professional listens modestly, he can learn a great deal more from the subject than he would have had the wit to ask about, if he had approached the interview with a set of questions or hypotheses derived from prior experience. It seems to us that the most important part of this investigation consists of new concepts and hypotheses which apparently are quite familiar to the persons in this class but which for the most part, specialists have not talked about or have touched upon only obliquely.

## A TYPOLOGY OF MARRIAGES

One specific and recurrent enlightenment concerns the omnipresent problem of categories. Such familiar categories as marriage, monogamy, divorce have become in the modern world, if they have not always been so, highly diversified—or "contaminated" as some methodologists aptly put it. Persons and pairs who have one common attribute are conventionally placed in some category but often have so little in common otherwise that to hold them in a single category is a serious distortion of reality. One divorce, for example, may grow out of exploitation, irresponsibility and degeneracy and leave scars of bitterness and pathology on a number of people. In another instance a divorce may be an orderly, empathic, cooperative effort on the part of two or more people simply in order to bring their subjective experience and their legal status into more reasonable consonance. Similarly, a "stable" married pair may on the one hand be deeply fulfilled people, living vibrantly, or at the other extreme entrapped, embittered, resentful people, living lives of duplicity in an atmosphere of hatred and despair. And more important perhaps than the extremes are the wide ranges in between. The use of categories in research and theory building are, of course, essential and to some extent dissimilarities of otherwise homogeneous cases may be ignored or presumed to be randomized out. But there is no license here for the use of traditional legalistic and theological categories merely because they are convenient stereotypes and reflect comfortable similitudes about people. In short, it is a major lesson from our inquiry that more professional effort should be devoted to establishing more truly discriminating categories. One such effort is presented here.

The following taxonomy has grown out of an analysis of the testimony of those persons in our sample who have been married for at least a decade, indicated that they had never considered separation or divorce, and so far as they knew, no one, including members of the family, thought of them as other than normal American families. From their various comments, however, the following manifest differences were documented.

### Conflict-Habituated Relationships

In this husband-wife configuration there is much tension and conflict—although largely "controlled." At worst, there is some private quarreling, nagging, and "throwing up the past" of which members of the immediate family, and more rarely even close friends and relatives, have some awareness. At best, the couple is discreet and polite, "genteel about it" when in the company of others, but rarely succeeds completely in concealing it from the children—although the illusion is common among them that they do. The essence, however, is that there is awareness by both husband and wife that incompatibility is pervasive, conflict is ever-potential, and an atmosphere of equilibrated tension permeates their lives together. These relationships are sometimes said to be "dead" or "gone" but there is a more subtle valence here—a very active one. So central is the necessity for channeling conflict and bridling hostility that these imperatives structure the togetherness. Some psychiatrists have gone so far as to suggest that it is precisely the conflict and the habituated need to do psychological battle with one another which constitutes the cohesive factor which insures continuity of the marriage. Possibly so, but from a less psychiatric point of view, the overt and manifest fact of habituated attention to handling tension, keeping it chained, and concealing it, becomes the overriding life force. And it can, and does for some, last for a lifetime.

## "Devitalized" Relationships

Here the relationship is essentially devoid of zest. There is typically no serious tension or conflict and there maybe aspects of the marriage which are actively satisfying, such as mutual interest in children, property, or family tradition. But the interplay between the pair is apathetic, lifeless. There is no serious threat to the marriage. It will likely continue indefinitely, despite its numbness. It continues, and conflict does not occur in part because of the inertia of "the habit cage." Continuity is further insured by the absence of any engaging alternatives, "all things considered." Perpetuation is also reinforced, sometimes rather decisively, by legal and ecclesiastical requirements and expectations. These people quickly explain that "there are other things in life," which are worthy of sustained human effort. But the relationship *between the pair* is essentially devoid of vital meaning, essentially empty, by comparison to what it was when the mating began and what was then considered to be its *raison d'être*.

This kind of relationship is exceedingly common. Many persons in this circumstance do not accurately appraise their position because they frequently make comparisons with other pairs, many of whom are similar to themselves. This fosters the illusion that "marriage is like this—except for a few odd balls or pretenders who claim otherwise."

While these relationships lack vitality, there is "*something* there." There are occasional periods of sharing at least of something, if only memory. Formalities can have meanings. Anniversaries can be celebrated, even if a little grimly, for what they once commemorated. As one said, "Tomorrow we are celebrating the anniversary of our anniversary." Even clearly substandard sexual expression is said by some to be better than nothing, or better than a clandestine substitute. A "good man" or "good mother for the kids" may "with a little affection and occasional companionship now and then, get you by."

### Passive-Congenial Relationships

This configuration seems roughly about as prevalent as the preceding one. There is little suggestion of disillusionment or compulsion to make believe to anyone. Existing modes of association are comfortably adequate—no stronger words fit the facts. There is little conflict. They tip-toe rather gingerly over and around a residue of subtle resentments and frustrations. In their better moods they remind us that "there are many common interests" which they both enjoy. When they get specific about these common interests it typically comes out that the interests are neither very vital things nor do they involve participation and sharings which could not almost as well be carried out in one-sex associations or with comparative strangers. "We both like classical music"; "We agree completely on religious and political matters"; "We both love the country and our quaint exurban neighbors"; "We are both lawyers."

We get the strong feeling when talking with these people that they would have said the same things when they were first married—or even before. When discussing their decisions to marry, some of them gave the same rationales for that decision that they do now for their present relationship, some twenty or thirty years later. This is why we have said that they seem to be passively content, not disillusioned even though, as compared to the next type, they show so little vitality and so little evidence that the spouse is important—much less indispensable—to the satisfactions which they say they enjoy.

### Vital Relationships

It is hard to escape the word, vitality, here—vibrant and exciting sharing of some important life experience. Sex immediately comes to mind, but the vitality need not surround the sexual focus or any aspect of it. It may emanate from work, association in some creative enterprise, child rearing, or even hobby participation. The clue that the *relationship is vital* and significant derives from the *feelings of importance about it* and *that that importance is shared*. Other things are readily sacrificed to it. It is apparent, even sometimes to the superficial observer, that these people are living for something which is exciting; it consumes their interest and effort, and the particular man or woman who shares it is the indispensable ingredient in the meaning which it has.

### "Total" Relationships

The total relationship is like the vital relationship with the important addition that it is *multi-faceted*. This kind of man-woman relationship is rare in marriage or out, but it does exist and undoubtedly could exist more often than it does were men and women free of various impediments. One will occasionally find relationships in which *all* important aspects of life are mutually shared, enthusiastically participated in. It is as if neither partner had a truly private existence. Cynics and the disillusioned scoff at this, calling it "romance" and usually offering an anecdote or two concerning some such "idyllic" relationship which later lost its totality, if not its vitality too. This should not be taken to mean, however, even if accurately interpreted and reported, that the relationship had not been total at the prior time. Or it may simply be evidence of the failure of the observer to be more discriminating in the first place.

Relationships are not *made* vital, much less total, by asserting them to be so, by striving to make them so, or by deceiving the neighbors that they are so. This is not to deny, however, that the total relationship is particularly precarious; precisely because it is multi-faceted, it is multi-vulnerable as circumstances change.

This typology is offered as an illustration of some needed refinements in thinking about man-woman relationships. People involved in all five of the above relationships are (1) married and (2) stay so. (3) There is no public awareness of conflict. (4) Nor is there any offense to the most genteel standards of propriety. What, however, does one know when he has ascertained that a given pair has been married for a decade, that no one has seen them quarrel? What does he know, that is, about the life essence, the *joie de vivre?* Obviously nothing, until the pair is seen against the backdrop of some sort of taxonomy and more private facts about them are known.

# SYNOPSIS OF SOME TENTATIVE FINDINGS

Partly because our methods and inquiry have been quite unorthodox, it becomes exceedingly difficult to present the findings of the study in the customary format for reports on research. In fact, we shall say little at this time about our precise findings, because to do so in synoptical form would be to miss much of the essence of the investigation. Nevertheless, a few somewhat general and guarded general ideas, *sans* documentation, will be attempted. It should be remembered that these generalizations apply to that American subculture, the Upper Middle Class, which presumably comprises no more than nine per cent of the American population. Moreover, our sample is completely a metropolitan sample, is white, is non-clinical, and probably oversamples the upper echelons of the nine per cent. Obviously, the empirical base, being what it is, requires us to say that our generalizations should not be trusted beyond the limits of this class.

(1) Our vague hunch, by no means remotely an hypothesis, at the beginning of the study that marital relationships between men and women of middle age comprised by no means the preponderant part of man-woman *meaningful* interaction was abundantly documented. Partly *sub rosa* and partly with the open knowledge of spouses, numerous kinds and degrees of meaningful non-marital man-woman relationships abound. These are not always frankly sexual, but they are nonetheless meaningful, *important* and *central* in the lives of these people.

If we are going to understand the bisexual world better, we need to cast a larger net when drawing in our specimens for examination. Attention has usually been focused chiefly upon those institutional arrangements known as "marriage and the family." It seems to us that the focus instead should be directly upon men and women—the entire bisexual world. For many students, moreover, marriage has come to be reified as something in and of itself, many times to the rather dismal neglect and devaluation of other intensely important aspects in the total lives of mature men and women. Little has been said or written, for example, concerning the important *constructive* realities regarding divorce or about "third parties" in relationship triangles. There is a continuing preoccupation with predicting divorce and measuring the effects and causes (so-called) of divorce. As any man on the street can tell us, and probably should, the incidence of divorce has little connection with the incidence of breakdown of man-woman relationships in marriage, and deeply fulfilling man-woman relationships exist where there is no marriage at all—and may never be.

We are not maintaining that there is any error necessarily in being concerned in research and thinking with marriage and family relationships *per se*. It is the *preoccupation* and the *reification* which has narrowed the focus. To comprehend adult man-woman relationships as coterminous with marriage and family relationships is like trying to understand, say, the United States Senate simply by watching what goes on on the Senate floor. The result is a colossal naïveté. It is not so much that the existing knowledge is demonstrably wrong so far as it goes, but that it is almost child-like in its self-imposed innocence and isolation from more complete awareness.

(2) Despite the monolithic character of religious and legal sanctions concerning man-woman behavior, *individuation rather than universalism* is a preponderant condition of their man-woman world. Nor are these radical variations from person to person and pair to pair completely idiosyncratic by any means. There are numerous types and typologies and classifications which stand out. The important thing about these, however, is that they do not correspond to the typologies that are conventional in the professional literature, presumably dealing with the bisexual world in America. We are not asserting that professional opinion is wrong. An alternative possibility is that the Upper Middle Class has been insufficiently studied and may have a more distinct subculture than the professionals have apprehended. More likely, the disjuncture results from the fact that research has been, as we said before, too preoccupied with "marriage" and moralism and not enough with men and women.

(3) There is a manifest, yet at the same time subtle, amorality which forms the backdrop for the behavior of the prevailing groups in this class. At least, it would so be seen from the perspectives of, say, the Lower Middle Class. Some important philosophical considerations hinge upon this, but their refusal to be guided by other than pragmatic considerations where important decisions are concerned, is the prevailing weather in their intellectual climate. There are typically sharp contradictions between their public verbalisms and their overt conduct in almost every matter in their man-woman worlds.

(4) There is a pronounced tendency to polarize man-woman relationships over against other important valences in their life space. Not many are in-between. Mostly they function with a supremely valued or an equally extremely *de*valued conception of man-woman relationships in the total scheme of things. At the one extreme there is a pronounced asceticism, a devaluation of all aspects of the man-woman world from sex to joint problem solving, which distinctly separates them from the other group for whom all life exigencies are mediated through the inescapable and supremely important nexus of man and woman.

(5) If there is a core problem in handling the world of men and women, the nub of it is the impasse in communication between the married or otherwise related man and woman who would be presumed *a priori*, because intimate, to be in good rapport. These impasses persist despite the fact that this is a highly educated, articulate group, highly adept in social skills. We are developing an hypothesis which we think may serve to explain the characterological basis for this impasse.

(6) Viewing the matter qualitatively, the evidence forces us to an extremely depressing conclusion: there are very few qualitatively good man-woman relationships at this age in this class. Putting the matter this way, we are quite aware that we have not defined the word, "good." Pending more detailed elaboration, we may say here that by "good" we mean simply deeply satisfying man-woman relationships as appraised by the people themselves. This is meant to include the narrowly sexual as well as the more diffuse companionship and intellectual aspects of relationships. The fact of enduring marriage is in nowise to be confused with a satisfying relationship as subjectively experienced by the people in it. Further, of the good relationships that do exist, there is a surprisingly high incidence of them outside of marriage—either as enduring, relatively total as-

sociations among the unmarried, or, as is more often the case, extramarital in the sense that one or both in the pairdom are married to someone else.

These generalizations notwithstanding, the more overriding generalization about man-woman relationships in marriage is that continuity based upon "alien considerations," mere tradition, practical convenience, austere social sanctions, appear to be the rule rather than the exception, and that what we have called qualitatively good relationships are the exception rather than the rule. This has many and important implications which from time to time we plan to discuss in print and out.

# PART THREE
# *Parenthood*

**Chapter 7**  Maternal Attachment  157

**Chapter 8**  Childrearing  177

# On the Internet . . .

## Sites appropriate to Part Three

The National Association for the Education of Young Children (NAEYC) is America's largest organization of early childhood professionals devoted to improving the quality of early childhood education programs for children from birth through age eight.

    http://www.naeyc.org/

This site offers links to organizations that provide behavioral approaches to parenting and child development.

    http://www.coedu.usf.edu/behavior/
      bares.htm

The Society for Research in Child Development (SRCD) is a multidisciplinary professional association. It promotes research in the field of human development.

    http://www.journals.uchicago.edu/SRCD/
      srcdhome.html

CHAPTER 7 # Maternal Attachment

## 7.1 MARY D. SALTER AINSWORTH

## *Infant–Mother Attachment*

London psychiatrist John Bowlby's research on mother-child separation led to many subsequent studies and directions concerning infant development and child attachment to adults. One of these spin-offs was the work of Mary D. Salter Ainsworth, who answered the question, "Why are infants afraid of strangers?" Ainsworth's name has become synonymous with the strange-situation studies as described in the following selection from "Infant–Mother Attachment," which was published in *American Psychologist* in 1979. Her research quantified the amount of anxiety exhibited by infants when they were separated from their mothers for varying lengths of time and left with a person who was unknown to them. Based on observations of infant behavior, the type of maternal attachment that babies exhibited was categorized as either secure or insecure. The three types of insecure attachment were anxious, avoidant, and disoriented. Practitioners used the interpretations of this research to determine the appropriate amount of attachment for infants and mothers. For example, children who showed no reaction to their mothers' leaving were thought to be in jeopardy, and children who became overly upset were also considered to be somewhat maladapted.

Ainsworth's studies spanned several decades and became even more visible as child care became popular in the 1960s and 1970s. Studies of child-care givers and the children in their care versus mother care, which used Ainsworth's strange-situation technique to collect data, came under scrutiny by some child-development experts. Some researchers considered this technique inappropriate for studying the maternal attachment of children who attend child-care centers on a daily basis.

Ainsworth (b. 1913) has studied mother-infant attachment in England, Uganda, and the United States and has been publishing reports of these studies since the 1960s. She has taught at Johns Hopkins University and the University of Virginia. Ainsworth received all of her degrees from the University of Toronto by age 26. She has authored books with such notables as John Bowlby, and she has contributed to numerous books and journals, including the *Review of Child Development Research*. Her latest contribution was to Colin Murray Parkes and Joan Stevenson-Hyde, eds., *The Place of Attachment in Human Behavior* (Basic Books, 1982).

**Key Concept:** infant-mother attachment

Bowlby's (1969) ethological–evolutionary attachment theory implies that it is an essential part of the ground plan of the human species—as well as that of many other species—for an infant to become attached to a mother figure. This figure need not be the natural mother but can be anyone who plays the role of principal caregiver. This ground plan is fulfilled, except under extraordinary circumstances when the baby experiences too little interaction with any one caregiver to support the formation of an attachment. The literature on maternal deprivation describes some of these circumstances, but it cannot be reviewed here, except to note that research has not yet specified an acceptable minimum amount of interaction required for attachment formation.

However, there have been substantial recent advances in the areas of individual differences in the way attachment behavior becomes organized, differential experiences associated with the various attachment patterns, and the value of such patterns in forecasting subsequent development. These advances have been much aided by a standardized laboratory situation that was devised to supplement a naturalistic, longitudinal investigation of the development of infant–mother attachment in the first year of life. This *strange situation*, as we entitled it, has proved to be an excellent basis for the assessment of such attachment in 1-year-olds (Ainsworth, Blehar, Waters, & Wall, 1978).

The assessment procedure consists of classification according to the pattern of behavior shown in the strange situation, particularly in the episodes of reunion after separation. Eight patterns were identified, but I shall deal here only with the three main groups into which they fell—Groups A, B, and C. To summarize, Group B babies use their mothers as a secure base from which to explore in the preseparation episodes; their attachment behavior is greatly intensified by the separation episodes so that exploration diminishes and distress is likely; and in the reunion episodes they seek contact with, proximity to, or at least interaction with their mothers. Group C babies tend to show some signs of anxiety even in the preseparation episodes; they are intensely distressed by separation; and in the reunion episodes they are ambivalent with the mother, seeking close contact with her and yet resisting contact or interaction. Group A babies, in sharp contrast, rarely cry in the separation episodes and, in the reunion episodes, avoid the mother, either mingling proximity-seeking and avoidant behaviors or ignoring her altogether.

## COMPARISON OF STRANGE-SITUATION BEHAVIOR AND BEHAVIOR ELSEWHERE

Groups A, B, and C in our longitudinal sample were compared in regard to their behavior at home during the first year. Stayton and Ainsworth (1973) had identified a security–anxiety dimension in a factor analysis of fourth-quarter infant behavior. Group B infants were identified as securely attached because they significantly more often displayed behaviors characteristic of the secure pole of this dimension, whereas both of the other groups were identified as anxious because their behaviors were characteristic of the anxious pole. A second dimension was clearly related to close bodily contact, and this was important in distinguishing Group A babies from those in the other two groups, in that Group A babies behaved less positively to being held and yet more negatively to being put down. The groups were also distinguished by two behaviors not included in the factor analysis—cooperativeness and anger. Group B babies were more cooperative and less angry than either A or C babies; Group A babies were even more angry than those in Group C. Clearly, something went awry in the physical-contact interaction Group A babies had with their mothers, and as I explain below, I believe it is this that makes them especially prone to anger.

Ainsworth et al. (1978) reviewed findings of other investigators who had compared A–B–C groups of 1-year-olds in terms of their behavior elsewhere. Their findings regarding socioemotional behavior support the summary just cited, and in addition three investigations using cognitive measures found an advantage in favor of the securely attached.

## COMPARISON OF INFANT STRANGE-SITUATION BEHAVIOR WITH MATERNAL HOME BEHAVIOR

Mothers of the securely attached (Group B) babies were, throughout the first year, more sensitively responsive to infant signals than were the mothers of the two anxiously attached groups, in terms of a variety of measures spanning all of the most common contexts for mother–infant interaction (Ainsworth et al., 1978). Such responsiveness, I suggest, enables an infant to form expectations, primitive at first, that moderate his or her responses to events, both internal and environmental. Gradually, such an infant constructs an inner representation—or "working model" (Bowlby, 1969)—of his or her mother as generally accessible and responsive to him or her. Therein lies his or her security. In contrast, babies whose mothers have disregarded their signals, or have responded to them belatedly or in a grossly inappropriate fashion, have no basis for believing the mother to be accessible and responsive; consequently they are anxious, not knowing what to expect of her.

In regard to interaction in close bodily contact, the most striking finding is that the mothers of avoidant (Group A) babies all evinced a deep-seated aversion to it, whereas none of the other mothers did. In addition they were more rejecting, more often angry, and yet more restricted in the expression of affect than were Group B or C mothers. Main (e.g., in press) and Ainsworth et al. (1978) have presented a theoretical account of the dynamics of interaction of avoidant babies and their rejecting mothers. This emphasizes the acute approach–avoidance conflict experienced by these infants when their attachment behavior is activated at high intensity—a conflict stemming from painful rebuff consequent upon seeking close bodily contact. Avoidance is viewed as a defensive maneuver, lessening the anxiety and anger experienced in the conflict situation and enabling the baby nevertheless to remain within a tolerable range of proximity to the mother.

Findings and interpretations such as these raise the issue of direction of effects. To what extent is the pattern of attachment of a baby attributable to the mother's behavior throughout the first year, and to what extent is it attributable to built-in differences in potential and temperament? I have considered this problem elsewhere (Ainsworth, 1979) and have concluded that in our sample of normal babies there is a strong case to be made for differences in attachment quality being attributable to maternal behavior. Two studies, however (Connell, 1976; Waters, Vaughn, & Egeland, in press), have suggested that Group C babies may as newborns be constitutionally "difficult." Particularly if the mother's personality or life situation makes it hard for her to be sensitively responsive to infant cues, such a baby seems indeed likely to form an attachment relationship of anxious quality.

### Contexts of Mother–Infant Interaction

Of the various contexts in which mother–infant interaction commonly takes place, the face-to-face situation has been the focus of most recent research. By many (e.g., Walters & Parke, 1965), interaction mediated by distance receptors and behaviors has been judged especially important in the establishment of human relationships. Microanalytic studies, based on frame-by-frame analysis of film records, show clearly that maternal sensitivity to infant behavioral cues is essential for successful pacing of face-to-face interaction (e.g., Brazelton, Koslowski, & Main, 1974; Stern, 1974). Telling evidence of the role of vision, both in the infant's development of attachment to the mother and in the mother's responsiveness to the infant, comes from Fraiberg's (1977) longitudinal study of blind infants.

So persuasive has been the studies of interaction involving distance receptors that interaction involving close bodily contact has been largely ignored. The evolutionary perspective of attachment theory attributes focal importance to bodily contact. Other primate species rely on the maintenance of close mother–infant contact as crucial for infant survival. Societies of hunter–gatherers, living much as the earliest humans did, are conspicuous for very much more mother–infant contact than are western societies (e.g., Konner, 1976). Blurton Jones (1972) presented evidence suggesting that humans evolved as a species in which infants are carried by the mother and are fed at frequent intervals, rather than as a species in which infants are left for long periods, are cached in a safe place, and are fed but infrequently. Bowlby (1969) pointed out that when attachment behavior is intensely activated it is close bodily contact that is specifically required. Indeed, Bell and Ainsworth (1972) found that even with the white, middle-class mothers of their sample, the most frequent and the most effective response to an infant's crying throughout the first year was to pick up the baby. A recent analysis of our longitudinal findings (Blehar, Ainsworth, & Main, Note 1) suggests that bodily contact is at least as important a context of interaction as face-to-face is, perhaps especially in the first few months of life. Within the limits represented by our sample, however, we found that it was *how* the mother holds her baby rather than *how much* she holds him or her that affects the way in which attachment develops.

In recent years the feeding situation has been neglected as a context for mother–infant interaction, except insofar as it is viewed as a setting for purely social, face-to-face interaction. Earlier, mother's gratification or frustration of infant interest to both psychoanalytically oriented and social-learning research, on the assumption that a mother's gratification or frustration of infant instinctual drives, or her role as a secondary reinforcer, determined the nature of the baby's tie to her. Such research yielded no evidence that methods of feeding significantly affected the course of infant development, although these negative findings seem almost certainly to reflect methodological deficiencies (Caldwell, 1964). In contrast, we have found that sensitive maternal responsiveness to infant signals relevant to feeding is closely related to the security or anxiety of attachment that eventually develops (Ainsworth & Bell, 1969). Indeed, this analysis seemed to redefine the meaning of "demand" feeding—letting infant behavioral cues determine not only when feeding is begun but also when it is terminated, how the pacing of feeding proceeds, and how new foods are introduced.

Our findings do not permit us to attribute overriding importance to any one context of mother–infant interaction. Whether the context is feeding, close bodily contact, face-to-face interaction, or indeed the situation defined by the infant's crying, mother–infant interaction provides the baby with opportunity to build up expectations of the mother and, eventually, a working model of her as more or less accessible and responsive. Indeed, our findings suggest that a mother who is sensitively responsive to signals in one context tends also to be responsive to signals in other contexts....

### Using the Mother as a Secure Base from Which to Explore

Attachment theory conceives of the behavioral system serving attachment as only one of several important systems, each with its own activators, terminators, predictable outcomes, and functions. During the prolonged period of human infancy, when the protective function of attachment is especially important, its interplay with exploratory behavior is noteworthy. The function of exploration is learning about the environment—which is particularly important in a species possessing much potential for adaptation to a wide range of environments. Attachment and exploration support each other. When attachment behavior is intensely activated, a baby tends to seek proximity contact rather than exploring; when attachment behavior is at low intensity a baby is free to respond to the pull of novelty. The presence of an attachment figure, particularly one who is believed to be accessible and responsive, leaves the baby open to stimulation that may activate exploration.

Nevertheless, it is often believed that somehow attachment may interfere with the development of independence. Our studies provide no support for such a belief. For example, Blehar et al. (Note 1) found that babies who respond positively to close bodily contact with their mothers also tend to respond positively to being put down again and to move off into independent exploratory play. Fostering the growth of secure attachment facilitates rather than hampers the growth of healthy self-reliance (Bowlby, 1973).

### Response to Separation from Attachment Figures

Schaffer (1971) suggested that the crucial criterion for whether a baby has become attached to a specific figure is that he or she does not consider this figure interchangeable with any other figure. Thus, for an infant to protest the mother's departure or continued absence is a dependable criterion for attachment (Schaffer & Callender, 1959). This does not imply that protest is an invariable response to separation from an attachment figure under all circumstances; the context of the separation influences the likelihood and intensity of protest. Thus there is ample evidence, which cannot be cited here, that protest is unlikely to occur, at least initially, in the case of voluntary separations, when the infant willingly leaves the mother in order to explore elsewhere. Protest is less likely to occur if the baby is left with another attachment figure than if he or she is left with an unfamiliar person or alone. Being left in an unfamiliar environment is more distressing than comparable separations in the familiar environment of the home—in which many infants are able to build up expectations that reassure them of mother's accessibility and responsiveness even though she may be absent. Changes attributable to developmental processes affect separation protest in complex ways. Further research will undoubtedly be able to account for these shifts in terms of progressive cognitive achievements....

### Other Attachment Figures

Many have interpreted Bowlby's attachment theory as claiming that an infant can become attached to only one person—the mother. This is a mistaken interpretation. There are, however, three implications of attachment theory relevent to the issue of "multiple" attachments. First, as reported by Ainsworth (1967) and Schaffer and Emerson (1964), infants are highly selective in their choices of attachment figures from among the various persons familiar to them. No infant has been observed to have many attachment figures. Second, not all social relationships may be identified as attachments. Harlow (1971) distinguished between the infant–mother and peer–peer affectional systems, although under certain circumstances peers may become attachment figures in the absence of anyone more appropriate (see, e.g., Freud & Dann, 1951; Harlow, 1963). Third, the fact that a baby may have several attachment figures does not imply that they are all equally important. Bowlby (1969) suggested that they are not—that there is a principal attachment figure, usually the principal caregiver, and one or more secondary figures. Thus a hierarchy is implied. A baby may both enjoy and derive security from all of his or her attachment figures but, under certain circumstances (e.g., illness, fatigue, stress), is likely to show a clear preference among them.

In recent years there has been a surge of interest in the father as an attachment figure, as reported elsewhere in this issue. Relatively lacking is research into attachments to caregivers other than parents. Do babies become attached to their regular baby-sitters or to caregivers in day-care centers? Studies by Fleener (1973), Farran and Ramey (1977), and Ricciuti (1974) have suggested that they may but that the preference is nevertheless for the mother figure. Fox (1977) compared the mother and the *metapelet* as providers of security to kibbutz-reared infants in a strange situation, but surely much more research is needed into the behavior of infants and young children toward caregivers as attachment figures in the substitute-care environment.

### Consequences of Attachment

... In comparison with anxiously attached infants, those who are securely attached as 1-year-olds are later more cooperative with and affectively more positive as well as less aggressive and/or avoidant toward their mothers and other less familiar adults. Later on, they emerge as more competent and more sympathetic in interaction with peers. In free-play situations they have longer bouts of exploration and display more intense exploratory interest, and in problem-solving situations they are more enthusiastic, more persistent, and better able to elicit and accept their mothers' help. They are more curious, more self-directed, more ego-resilient—and they usually tend to achieve better scores on both developmental tests and measures of language development. Some studies also reported differences between the two groups of anxiously attached infants, with the avoidant ones (Group A) continuing to be more aggressive, noncompliant, and avoidant, and the ambivalent ones (Group C) emerging as more easily frustrated, less persistent, and generally less competent.

### Conclusion

It is clear that the nature of an infant's attachment to his or her mother as a 1-year-old is related both to earlier interaction with the mother and to various aspects of later development. The implication is that the way in which the infant organizes his or her behavior toward the mother affects the way in which he or she organizes behavior toward other aspects of the environment, both animate and inanimate. This organization provides a core of continuity in development despite changes that come with developmental acquisitions, both cognitive and socioemotional.

Chapter 7
Maternal
Attachment

## NOTES

1. Blehar, M. C., Ainsworth, M. D. S., & Main, M. *Mother–infant interaction relevant to close bodily contact.* Monograph in preparation, 1979.

## REFERENCES

Ainsworth, M. D. S. *Infancy in Uganda: Infant care and the growth of love.* Baltimore, Md.: Johns Hopkins Press, 1967.

Ainsworth, M. D. S. Attachment as related to mother–infant interaction. In J. S. Rosenblatt, R. A. Hinde, C. Beer, & M. Busnel (Eds.), *Advances in the study of behavior* (Vol. 9). New York: Academic Press, 1979.

Ainsworth, M. D. S., & Bell, S. M. Some contemporary patterns of mother–infant interaction in the feeding situation. In A. Ambrose (Ed.), *Stimulation in early infancy.* London: Academic Press, 1969.

Ainsworth, M. D. S., Blehar, M. C., Waters, E., & Wall, S. *Patterns of attachment: A psychological study of the strange situation.* Hillsdale, N.J.: Erlbaum, 1978.

Bell, S. M., & Ainsworth, M. D. S. Infant crying and maternal responsiveness. *Child Development,* 1972, *43,* 1171–1190.

Blurton Jones, N. G. Comparative aspects of mother–child contact. In N. G. Blurton Jones (Ed.), *Ethological studies of child behavior.* London: Cambridge University Press, 1972.

Bowlby, J. *Attachment and loss: Vol. 1. Attachment.* New York: Basic Books, 1969.

Bowlby, J. *Attachment and loss: Vol. 2. Separation: Anxiety and anger.* New York: Basic Books, 1973.

Brazelton, T. B., Koslowski, B., & Main, M. The origins of reciprocity: The early mother–infant interaction. In M. Lewis & L. A. Rosenblum (Eds.), *The effect of the infant on its caregiver.* New York: Wiley, 1974.

Caldwell, B. M. The effects of infant care. In M. L. Hoffman & L. W. Hoffman (Eds.), *Review of child development research* (Vol. 1). New York: Russell Sage Foundation, 1964.

Connell, D. B. *Individual differences in attachment: An investigation into stability, implications, and relationships to the structure of early language development.* Unpublished doctoral dissertation, Syracuse University, 1976.

Farran, D. C., & Ramey, C. T. Infant day care and attachment behavior toward mother and teachers. *Child Development,* 1977, *48,* 1112–1116.

Fleener, D. E. Experimental production of infant-maternal attachment behaviors. *Proceedings of the 81st Annual Convention of the American Psychological Association,* 1973, *8,* 57–58. (Summary)

Fox, N. Attachment of kibbutz infants to mother. *Child Development,* 1977, *48,* 1228–1239.

Fraiberg, S. *Insights from the blind.* New York: Basic Books, 1977.

Freud, A., & Dann, S. An experiment in group upbringing. *Psychoanalytic Study of the Child,* 1951, *6,* 127–168.

Harlow, H. F. The maternal affectional system. In B. M. Foss (Ed.), *Determinants of infant behaviour* (Vol. 2) New York: Wiley, 1963.

Harlow, H. F. *Learning to love.* San Francisco: Albion, 1971.

Konner, M. J. Maternal care, infant behavior, and development among the !Kung. In R. B. Lee & I. DeVore (Eds.), *Kalahari hunter–gatherers.* Cambridge, Mass.: Harvard University Press, 1976.

Main, M. Avoidance in the service of proximity. In K. Immelmann, G. Barlow, M. Main, & L. Petrinovich (Eds.), *Behavioral development: The Bielefeld Interdisciplinary Project.* New York: Cambridge University Press, in press.

Ricciuti, H. N. Fear and the development of social attachments in the first year of life. In M. Lewis & L. A. Rosenblum (Eds.), *The origins of fear.* New York: Wiley, 1974.

Schaffer, H. R. *The growth of sociability.* London: Penguin Books, 1971.

Schaffer, H. R., & Callender, W. M. Psychological effects of hospitalization in infancy. *Pediatrics,* 1959, *25,* 528–539.

Schaffer, H. R., & Emerson, P. E. The development of social attachments in infancy. *Monographs of the Society for Research in Child Development,* 1964, *3* (Serial No. 94).

Stayton, D. J., & Ainsworth, M. D. S. Individual differences in infant responses to brief, everyday separations as related to other infant and maternal behaviors. *Developmental Psychology,* 1973, *9,* 226–235.

Stern, D. N. Mother and infant at play: The dyadic interaction involving facial, vocal, and gaze behaviors. In M. Lewis & L. A. Rosenblum (Eds.), *The effect of the infant on its caregiver.* New York: Wiley, 1974.

Walters, R. H., & Parke, R. D. The role of the distance receptors in the development of social responsiveness. In L. P. Lipsitt & C. C. Spiker (Eds.), *Advances in child development and behavior.* New York: Academic Press, 1965.

Walters, E., Vaughn, B. E., & Egeland, B. R. Individual differences in infant–mother attachment relationships at age one: Antecedents in neonatal behavior in an urban economically disadvantaged sample. *Child Development,* in press.

7.2  MARGARET MEAD

# Some Theoretical Considerations on the Problem of Mother-Child Separation

The following selection from "Some Theoretical Considerations on the Problem of Mother-Child Separation," *American Journal of Orthopsychiatry* (July 1954) was published at a time when many theorists were conceptualizing research questions and generalizing answers to other fields of study. It was originally delivered as a speech at a professional meeting shortly after John Bowlby's study on mother-child separation was released in 1951. By this time, World War II had ended, and the family had taken on a traditional look, with father-headed households and mothers who stayed home to raise their children. Information on mother-infant attachment would have been particularly important to families at this time. In this selection, anthropologist Margaret Mead cautions researchers against making broad leaps from research results to conclusions about behavior. She also suggests a theoretical context within which research could be conducted.

Mead (1901–1978) made many significant contributions to the study of the family. She studied the male-female relationship, child development, and sexual behavior in a variety of cultures. Mead wrote 44 books and over 1,000 articles, and she is probably best remembered for her book *Coming of Age in Samoa: A Psychological Study of Primitive Youth for Western Civilisation* (William Morrow, 1928). Her other writings focus on many different topics, such as mental and spiritual health, ethics, and overpopulation. Mead was a pioneer in psychologically oriented field work and one of the founders of the "Culture and Personality School of Anthropology." Although her primary field of study was anthropology, her work has been applied extensively in the area of marriage and family relationships.

**Key Concept:** mother-child separation

*T*he publication by the World Health Organization of John Bowlby's study of mother-child separation (5) has highlighted the extreme importance of this area of research. The International Seminar on Mental Health and Infant Development held at Chichester in the summer of 1952 (24) further emphasized the extent to which findings in the field of child care may now be rapidly generalized, affecting medical practice, hospital design, and public health practices all over the world. This new capacity for the rapid dissemination and translation into practice of research findings places an extra burden of responsibility for the very careful examination of the theoretical basis of research on those of us concerned in either the research itself or the experimental translation of the research into practice. In this paper I want to consider the present status of our knowledge about mother-child separation, attempt to define some of the most immediate questions for research, and suggest the lines along which this research may perhaps be pursued most profitably.

We may first consider the type of research on which the theory has been developed. Research in the field of cultural anthropology and research in fields basic to the exercise of therapeutic skills have in common a sense of urgency on the one hand and a subject matter of great complexity on the other. Field anthropologists have never been able to wait until newer and better methods of research were devised. If we waited, our material would disappear. We have always worked on the edge of possibility, in cultures which had already come into some contact with a higher culture and which were being subjected to more European contact with every day that passed. In comparable fashion, the therapist cannot wait, because the patient now in the consulting room must be dealt with *now*. It is perhaps this combination of urgency and complexity which gives anthropological and psychiatric research other common features—a refusal to oversimplify in order to appear scientific, and a continued use of the highly trained human being as a diagnostic instrument. We have refused to give our material spurious quantification by translating subjective judgments or poor observations into numbers, as is done for instance when three judges are asked to rate poor material and the research worker then acts as if the addition of the three judges somehow alters the quality of the original observation (45). We have continued to rely on the speed of multiple observation of which human beings and human beings alone are capable, knowing that the clinical observation "the child is frightened" can be made, but that no observer or set of observers could record rapidly enough the multiple observations on which the clinician's statement is based when, using all his senses plus a stored memory of the child in previous states, allowing for respiration, pallor, tensity of muscles, direction of vision, etc., he makes the judgment on the child.

To make the statement "Charles showed more fright on his second visit," or to say "In the 'X' tribe babies make a passive adjustment to the bodies of their carriers" (25) requires thousands of such units, the utilization of an enormous number of stored memories, thousands of cross-correlations. Furthermore, all of these are made without tearing apart the texture of Charles's behavior as a whole reacting human being responding to a real situation, as is necessary if one attempts to substitute indicators of states (such as, for example, the psychogalvanic reflex) on the one hand, or to standardize stimuli, on the other, as is done in standard word-association tests. Similarly, the anthropologist must be able to observe many infants at many times in many situations—noting, remembering, recording mentally—in order finally to make the statement about "passive adjustment." Whether the observations of the clinician or the anthropologist stand up when subjected to interpretation within some wider theoretical framework which makes prediction possible—as prediction from one clinical hour to another, or form one body of observations on a culture to another body of observations on the same culture—is primarily a function of how good a clinician or how good an anthropologist the reporter is, "good" in the sense of having acquired trained and disciplined sensitivity to the particular type of phenomena being observed.

These statements may appear truistic to this audience, accustomed as clinicians to include the worker within the observation, again often unconsciously, as when a psychiatrist makes a different sort of rapid correction for a report coming from one social caseworker than he does for one coming from another, or from one psychologist rather than another. If the statement "Charles showed more fright on his second visit" comes from a worker he has found sensitive and trustworthy, it will be given immediately a weight different from that given the same statement from a less sensitive worker, while a statement from an unknown caseworker will be evaluated in terms of the psychiatrist's general judgment of the degree of precision that can be expected from caseworkers in general. Judgment on a mother's report on a child will include the psychiatrist's knowledge of the particular mother, his response to her at the moment she makes the report, and probably also something of his general theory about the accuracy of maternal reporting or the reporting of special types of mothers who have been classified as "overprotective," "compulsive," and so forth. In the same way, an anthropologist reading a field worker's statement includes the personality, training, and theoretical framework of the writer, the period of history, the size of population on which observations were made, the length of stay, etc., in evaluating his statements about such a matter as infant care....

When anthropologists work in groups, the same care which the clinician uses is exercised. Observations are analyzed in terms of what X's informant, Y, said to X; they are not merely taken at their face value. Most of our information about the way in which methods of child rearing are expressed in character formation is of this order—careful reports by trained people, actually summaries of millions of unrecorded and unrecordable observations which have been coded and correlated by the particular human being who made them. These observations stand up well when submitted to theoretical analysis or appropriate internal cross-checking for congruence. The current efforts to handle "scientifically" the importance of early child training in shaping character have attempted either to use incomparable data (Whiting, 45), putting observations made by the trained and the untrained, the interested and the uninterested, side by side; to test correspondences between single factors, i.e., breast feeding and some index of adjustment (Peterson, 29); or to use retrospective accounts of exceedingly complex behavior (Sewell, 37; Dennis, 8) in order to claim that differences in child-rearing practices have no effect. None of these attempts to test "scientifically" the hypothesis that child-rearing practices are represented in character formation has taken proper account either of the hypotheses or of the methods and theoretical structure of the anthropologists and psychiatrists who have been responsible for the research involved and its interpretation.[1] Stated broadly, the position for which I believe we have evidence we ourselves can trust is that the character formation of the child represents the child's total environmental situation (15) as it is responded to and introcepted by that child in terms of its constitution and individual life history. Neither anthropologists nor psychiatrists would expect (a) that a single activity like breast feeding would have consistent effects, (b) that the statement "the child was breast-fed" could be interpreted meaningfully unless a trained person had made a detailed study over time of the behavior of both mother and child during the breast feeding, or that (c) a mother's report several years later would indicate anything of what was actually done with enough precision to be valuable in a study of personality. Studies like those of Sewell (37) in which questionnaire results are correlated with test results need not concern us seriously to the point of arousing doubts in our own minds. They are, however, very serious in that they use inadmissible oversimplification to bring into disrepute findings on which recommendations for breast feeding, rooming-in, and self-demand feeding have been based. It is important that the unjustified claims of such research should not be permitted to becloud the climate of opinion.

The second set of researches, the experiments provided by the study of children who have been subjected to a variety of practices in institutions, have given us one valuable set of data (1, 5, 7, 33, 39, 40). It has been, I believe, effectively demonstrated that children do not thrive, in spite of good physical care, if kept as young infants in impersonal institutions, and that separation from the mother—especially at certain periods—has serious deleterious effects on the child. Retardation, failure to learn to talk, apathy, regression, and death all appear as accompaniments to institutionalization when no mother surrogate is provided.

But now let us examine where our recommendations in regard to mother-child relations have gone on the basis of these sets of materials. The institutional experiments suggest that some continuity of interpersonal contact is essential if the child is to thrive. The clinical and anthropological studies point to the great importance of the configuration of that care, both in terms of the total adults-child relationship and of the biologically given, constitutionally specified pattern of the child's development as it is involved in the different zones, modes, senses, etc. (11). Stated concretely, breast feeding provided by an angry mother or an anxious mother may differ more from that given by a relaxed happy mother than breast feeding will differ from bottle feeding given by any of these. To see the exact effects of breast feeding alone, one would need sets of identical twins in whose lives every factor except manner of feeding in infancy was held absolutely constant. The most we can do is to establish the existence of recognizable patterns, which themselves take their consistency and systematic character from the structure of *Homo sapiens* as expressed in culture, so that we can compare the general character formation of children of compulsive, overorderly, time-conscious mothers, or of children reared in societies where compulsive orderliness is manifested regularly by members of that culture as part of the formal child-rearing practices. Sensitive pediatricians are well aware that small changes in procedure will not alter to any appreciable degree the impact of the total situation on the child as long as the personality of mother or nurse is actively involved in whatever procedure is followed. We are beginning to accumulate records (Jackson, 16) of what happens when modern women with different personality configurations insist on nursing their babies or practicing natural childbirth. It is on the basis of a large number of such patterned situations that most of the new procedures recommended for child care have been based, not on simple, uncritical beliefs that breast feeding was *ipso facto* a single item which could be relied upon to produce specific good results. To state the case broadly, those who apply the current findings of psychiatry, anthropology, and child development research insist that the closer, warmer, and more frequent the mother's contact with the child, the more the mother studies the child's own rhythm and the less she imposes an external rhythm, and the better adjusted to developmental stages the child rearing is—food to chew on when there are teeth to chew with, toilet training when the child can understand and talk, etc.—the better the chance that the child will grow up in good communication with his own body and with other people. All the procedures about feeding, weaning, sleeping, toilet training, etc., are simply prescriptions for implementing this more general attempt to establish new kinds of child-rearing patterns. It is recognized also that something will change in those who must administer the new cultural practices, and that new methods of rearing children are actually a very important way of making changes in adult attitudes.

This was where the matter stood five years ago (21), and we could say, I think in all honesty, that we were making recommendations which were congruent with our research findings, neither claiming too much nor being unjustifiably cautious in putting what we believed to be true into practice for the benefit of the contemporary generation.

But during the past few years a whole new set of factors has entered the picture. These may be briefly enumerated as: 1) Exaggerated statements about the role of single procedures (27), which, although usually made by critics (28, 36, 45) rather than advocates of the procedures, have affected the climate of opinion on such matters as breast feeding. 2) Exaggerated and poorly supported claims of the importance of the mother as a single figure in the infant's life (of which Ribble's work [31] is an outstanding example; cf. Pinneau [30]) which have included drawing extreme conclusions from the type of work summarized by Bowlby (5). 3) The use of still photographs, moving pictures, and sound recordings in the study of interpersonal relationships, so that we can now make precise recordings of events which are so complex that we previously had to summarize verbally what could not be recorded (2, 3, 4, 12, 13, 32, 33, 38, 43). 4) The possibility of tackling from a new point of view—that of comparative ethnology (Lorenz [18], Tinbergin [42])—the whole question of the instinctual elements in parent-child relationships.

Taken together, they should make it possible for us to distinguish much better than we have in the past the biologically given elements in maternity and infancy and to measure the extent to which these are intractable or subject to modification. This means that it is necessary to distinguish between practices surrounding conception, pregnancy, gestation, delivery, and lactation, as far as the mother is concerned, and birth, sucking, and the subsequent set of experiences of the child in which the patterning is given during growth in the total interpersonal situation of the first two or three years of life. Put concretely, how much better and in what ways for mother and for infant are a "natural delivery," and putting the infant to the breast early and often, and how much better and in what ways is the mother's relation to the child established if she is conscious during delivery, has the child with her from birth, etc.? I have purposely phrased this as an applied problem rather than a pure research problem, because whatever research is done will immediately be subject to application. We need to know not only what part is played by consciousness or pain in establishing maternal feeling, but also what practices seem best suited to our stated child-rearing goals.

We need to know such detailed things as the effects of the infant's cry on the contraction of the uterus, whether there are definable stages during labor in which the mother shifts from positive to negative attitudes (which would have serious implications for the point at which an anesthetic is administered, etc.). We need to know whether there is something in the early days of sucking behavior which is precursor behavior for thumb-sucking, as is suggested by the specific absence of reported thumb-sucking among even very oral primitive people. We need to know whether specific accession to pregnancy cravings has any effect on maternal feelings. We need to define and specify situations like these and distinguish them sharply from the generalized needs of the child for interpersonal interaction with other human beings.

At present, the specific biological situation of the continuing relationship of the child to its biological mother and its need for care by human beings are being hopelessly confused in the growing insistence that child and biological mother, or mother surrogate, must never be separated, that all separation even for a few days is inevitably damaging, and that if long enough it does irreversible damage. This, as Hilde Bruch (6) has cogently pointed out, is a new and subtle form of antifeminism in which men—under the guise of exalting the importance of maternity—are tying women more tightly to their children than has been thought necessary since the invention of bottle feeding and baby carriages. Actually, anthropological evidence gives no support at present to the value of such an accentuation of the tie between mother and child (20). On the contrary, cross-cultural studies suggest that adjustment is most facilitated if the child is cared for by many warm, friendly people. Clinical studies and anthropological studies support the relationship between strong attachments to single individuals in childhood and capacity for a limited number of intense, exclusive relationships in adulthood. It may well be, of course, that limiting a child's contacts to its biological mother may be the most efficient way to produce a character suited to lifelong monogamous marriage, but if so then we should be clear that that is what we are doing, that the biological mother is necessary for a sort of "imprinting" strong enough for monogamy, and that that is the reason we insist that mothers alone care for their children without help from fathers, grandparents, servants, or siblings.

Present anthropological studies give us little help when we approach the questions of specificity in the mother-child tie. All peoples have introduced various types of artificiality into the birth process. They have patterned posture, decreed whether birth is to be viewed as painful or easy, set up some sort of rules about when and by whom the neonate is to be first suckled. It may well be that there are a large number of instinctual elements in this relationship, like those found in the behavior of birds, and that one item in the child's behavior is the cue for the next item in the mother's as the shadow of the parent bird makes the nestlings open their mouths which in turn cues the parent to push food into the nestlings' mouths. Spitz's work on the smile (38) and reported work on responses to snakes in Vienna by institutionalized children who had never seen snakes (41) suggest that there may well be in human beings hereditary structures for which there are specific releasing elements in the behavior of parent, child or mate. On the other hand, man is a domestic animal, and so is comparable not with wild birds but with domesticated animals, among whom these hereditary structured mechanisms are found in a much more irregular and less highly patterned form, any detail of which is likely to be present or absent in any given individual. Survival may have depended upon man's developing socially patterned behavior which lacked a precise fit to any given hereditary pattern, because such precisely fitted behavior might contain lethal elements. For example, if some mothers' expulsion of the afterbirth were triggered by the child's cry, and no other means of expulsion were provided for in a given culture for any mother, mothers who did not have this particular mechanism would suffer. Some infants may depend on the beginning of breathing on one type of situation, some on another. As far as nutritive behavior is concerned we know that, although human beings probably have a high capacity for correct nutritional choices, a balanced diet with suitable devices for teaching all children to eat it seems to allow a wider margin of safety than relying on idiosyncratic elements of choice (19).

But whichever turns out to be the case, whether there are certain elements of maternal and infant behavior which are human and include all individuals (and here Spitz's findings on the cues for a smile—an oval shape with two eyeholes, nodding—are very suggestive), or whether there are a large number of specific elements distributed in a variety of ways through the population, it is most essential that they be identified. Those which are common to all human beings could then be built into our cultural practices to give additional protection to mother and child. Consider, for example, three possibilities for infant feeding—cues given by the state of the mother's breasts (as among Russian peasants), cues given by the child's expressed hunger, or cues given by some impersonal standard such as a feeding schedule implemented by a clock. If it is demonstrated that building the *child's* cues into an individualized schedule results in a different order of adjustment between mother and child than either of the other two, then self-regulatory schedules ("self-demand") could be established as universal practice. (It is important to point out that self-regulatory scheduling is not a return to a primitive style of child feeding, but a method of conscious, disciplined, recorded adjustment of the feeding schedule for which a clock and pencil and paper—all absent at the primitive level—are essential; without them it is not possible to identify the personal schedule the infant gradually establishes.) Or, if it were found that the capacity for self-regulation is associated, for example, with some particular strength of the sucking reflex or with some identifiable peculiarity of that reflex, and that infants capable of establishing a viable demand schedule could be identified at birth, then this method of feeding could be institutionalized as *one* formal alternative in the culture. Similarly, sufficiently detailed research might indicate that there are identifying characteristics in women who lose their milk unless they give their infants a night feeding which are not present in other women. Some women might be found to establish a relationship to the child immediately if they see it within five minutes of its birth but to take days to establish the same relationship if the child is not seen for two hours after birth, and so forth.

From the research side, these new questions are made possible by the theoretical framework of ethology and also by our new techniques of recording. Specificity of instinctual manifestations was abandoned in our working theories of psychology, partly under the tremendous impetus given to understanding personality by Freud, modern anthropology, and learning theory, all of which stressed the importance of learning and experience, and partly because instinct theory was so gross and undifferentiated, and concepts like the sex instinct, the maternal instinct, the instinct of self-preservation were found to be unworkable. The concept of drives which succeeded it (cf. 10, for example) stressed the enormous capacity for modification of drives and the importance of learned cues, but it neglected the possibility of much finer, more precise mechanisms, such as "imprinting" and "internal releasing mechanisms." This neglect was probably due in part to our lack of tools for sufficiently precise recording, but that lack has now been overcome, and we can begin to work with moving pictures and sound recordings, preserving details which formerly had to be organized by single clinical observers. It is notable that it is the "impressionistic" and "intuitive" clinicians and anthropologists who have welcomed these finer tools which permit behavior to be analyzed without changing its internal organization by intervening operations (45).

Very possibly we may find that the kind of negative results which David Levy (17) got for most of the criteria which he used in his study of maternal feeling will be reduced to order when we look for patterned sets of constitutionally determined mechanisms which differ in pattern rather than along a continuum. Thus we may find that sets of internally consistent patterns would emerge, all of them differentially responsive to experience, if any one of Levy's factors (such as the size of the areola, baby carriage peeking, or the copiousness and duration of menstrual flow) is examined in the light of other factors—age at menarche, uterus size as determined by X ray rather than simply by pelvic measurements, shape of breasts, copiousness and type of lactation, etc. The circumstance that some cultures regard prepubertal, and others pubertal, girls as most subject to maternal impulses is suggestive.

The discovery of much more precise patterns of interrelationship might also throw light on the frequent baffling cases in which it is possible to predict backwards but not forward. We find, for instance, that a large number of children who have asthma had whooping cough at a time when they were having feeding conflicts with their mothers (23), but we also find that we have no criteria for explaining the children who have whooping cough and feeding problems at the same time but do not develop asthma. Here Arthur Mirksy's type of research, in which he attempts to make such predictions with the help of specific physiological measures, is relevant.[2]

Anthropologists have contributed to the tendency to emphasize the learned nature and flexibility of human responses and the importance of such learning, no doubt because they work specifically with those human inventions constructed so that they *can* be learned. A "natural language" is precisely a language every nondefective human child of whatever race or constitution can learn to speak and understand; an artificial language differs in that the economy produced by a reduction in redundancy lowers the margin of safety. All cultures that survive have to contain sufficient leeway for the gamut of human potentialities. The increases in crime, alcoholism, drug addiction, and mental disease which occur in periods of culture breakdown are negative illustrations of this aspect of culture. But it is exceedingly probable that when we have done enough detailed research we may find that no culture that has ever existed is as well adapted to the actual range of human needs as a culture could be, even when such an adaptation is culture-wide—i.e., fixed-time feeding schedules adjusted to weight and weight gain alone, with a fixed habitual pattern to which radio schedules, commuter trains, and Fuller Brush men can adapt. It may be possible to make a new cultural invention, on the other hand, to enable us to discriminate and cater to widely varying individual needs, which may themselves be systematic and recurrent from culture to culture and period to period or unsystematic and nonrecurrent.

## NOTES

1. For general discussion of anthropological method and for bibliography, see Mead (22), Métraux (26), Gorer (14). For general discussion of interdisciplinary research on problems of infancy, see Senn (35, 36).
2. Ongoing research at the University of Pittsburgh, as described in a personal communication by Arthur Mirsky.

## REFERENCES

1. BAKWIN, H. *Psychogenic Fever in Infants.* Am J. Dis. Child., 67: 176–181, 1944.
2. BATESON, G., and M. MEAD. *Balinese Character: A Photographic Analysis.* New York Academy of Sciences, New York, 1942.
3. ———, *Character Formation in Different Cultures* (6 Films). New York University Film Library, New York, 1951–53.
4. BATESON, G., J. RUESCH, and W. KEES. *Communication and Interaction in Three Families.* Kinesis Films, San Francisco, n.d.
5. BOWLBY, J. *Maternal Care and Mental Health.* WHO Monogr. 2. World Health Organization, Geneva, 1951.
6. BRUCH, H. *Don't Be Afraid of Your Child.* Farrar, Straus & Young, New York, 1952.
7. BURLINGHAM, D. T., and A. FREUD. *Young Children in Wartime: A Year's Work in a War Nursery.* Allen & Unwin, London, 1942.
8. DENNIS, W. *The Hopi Child.* Appleton-Century, New York, 1940.
9. DEUTSCH, F. *The Choice of Organ in Organ Neuroses.* Internat. J. Psa., 20: 3 and 4, 1939.

10. DOLLARD, J., and N. E. MILLER. *Personality and Psychotherapy: An Analysis in Terms of Learning, Thinking, and Culture.* McGraw-Hill, New York, 1950.
11. ERIKSON, E. *Childhood and Society.* Norton, New York, 1950.
12. ESCALONA, S., and M. LEITCH. *Eight Infants: Tension Manifestations in Response to Perceptual Stimuli.* New York University Film Library, New York, n.d.
13. FRIES, M., and P. J. WOOLF. *Series of Studies on Integrated Environment: The Interaction Between Child and Environment* (5 Films). New York University Film Library, New York, n.d.
14. GORER, G. "The Concept of National Character," in *Science News,* 18. Penguin Books, England, 1950.
15. HENRY, J., and J. W. BOGGS. *Child Rearing, Culture, and the Natural World.* Psychiatry, 15: 261–271, 1952.
16. JACKSON, E., and E. H. KLATSKIN. "Rooming-in Research Project: Development of Methodology of Parent-Child Relationship in a Clinical Setting," in *The Psychoanalytic Study of the Child,* Vol. 5. Internat. Univ. Press, New York, 1950.
17. LEVY, D. *A Method of Integrating Physical and Psychiatric Examination.* Am. J. Psychiatry, 9: 121–194, 1929.
18. LORENZ, K. *King Solomon's Ring.* Methuen, London, 1952.
19. MEAD, M. "Cultural Context of Nutritional Patterns," in *Centennial.* American Association for the Advancement of Science, Washington, 1950.
20. ——. "Cultural Patterning of Sexual Behavior," in *Sex and Internal Secretions* (E. Dempsey, Ed.). In press.
21. ——. *Male and Female.* Morrow, New York, 1949.
22. ——. "National Character," in *Anthropology Today* (A. L. Kroeber, Ed.). University of Chicago Press, Chicago, 1953.
23. ——. "The Primitive Child," in *Handbook of Child Psychology* (C. Murchison, Ed.). Clark University Press, Worcester, Mass., 1931.
24. ——. *Sharing Child Development Insights Around the Globe.* Understanding the Child, 21: 98, 1952.
25. MEAD, M., and F. C. MACGREGOR. *Growth and Culture: A Photographic Study of Balinese Childhood.* Putnam, New York, 1951.
26. MEAD, M., and R. MÉTRAUX (Eds.). *The Study of Culture at a Distance.* University of Chicago Press, Chicago, 1953.
27. MOLONEY, J. C. *Child Rearing on Okinawa* (a Film), n.d.
28. ORLANSKY, H. *Infant Care and Personality.* Psychol. Bull., 46: 1–48, 1949.
29. PETERSON, C. H., and F. L. SPANO. *Breast Feeding, Maternal Rejection and Child Personality.* Character and Personality, 10: 62–66, 1941.
30. PINNEAU, S. R. *A Critique on the Articles by Margaret Ribble.* Child Develpm., 21: 203–228, 1950.
31. RIBBLE, M. *The Rights of Infants.* Columbia University Press, New York, 1943.
32. ROBERTSON, J. *A Two-Year-Old Goes to the Hospital* (Film). World Federation for Mental Health, London, 1953.
33. ROUDINESCO, J. *Severe Maternal Deprivation and Personality Development in Early Childhood.* Understanding the Child, 21: 104–108, 1952.
34. ROUDINESCO, J., and G. APPELL. *Maternal Deprivation in Young Children* (Film). Association pour la Santé Mentale de l'Enfance, Paris, n.d.
35. SENN, M. J. E. (Ed.). *Symposium on the Healthy Personality.* Macy Foundation, New York, 1950.

36. ——. *Transactions: Problems of Infancy and Childhood.* Macy Foundation, New York, 1947, 1948, 1949, 1950.
37. SEWELL, W. H. *Infant Training and the Personality of the Child.* Am J. Sociol., 58: 150–159, 1952.
38. SPITZ, R. A. *The Smiling Response.* Film: New York University Film Library; article; Genet. Psychol. Monogr., 34: 47–125, 1946.
39. ——. "Hospitalism," in *The Psychoanalytic Study of the Child,* Vol. 1. Internat. Univ. Press, New York, 1945.
40. SPITZ, R. A., and K. M. WOLF. "Anaclitic Depression," in *The Psychoanalytic Study of the Child,* Vol. 2, 1946.
41. TANNER, J. (Ed.). *Proceedings of the Study Group on the Psychobiological Development of the Child, 1952.* World Health Organization, Geneva (in preparation).
42. TINBERGEN, N. *The Study of Instinct.* Oxford, London, 1951.
43. Vassar College, Department of Child Study. *Studies in Normal Personality Development* (10 Films with explanatory notes by L. J. Stone). New York University Film Library, New York, n.d.
44. WEAVER, W. *Science and Complexity.* Am. Scientist, 36: 1948.
45. WHITING, J. W., and I. L. CHILD. *Child Training and Personality.* Yale University Press, New Haven, 1953.

# CHAPTER 8 Childrearing

## 8.1 E. E. LeMASTERS

# *Parenthood as Crisis*

In the developmental model of the family, a man and a woman marry and subsequently give birth to a child. In reality, the timing, the frequency, and under what circumstances couples become parents varies. For example, parents who divorce and remarry bring children immediately to the marriage, while single parents do not marry at all before becoming parents. Same-gender couples might rely on artificial insemination or adoption to obtain children, and grandparents sometimes inherit their own children's children. Whether parenthood is planned or unplanned, whether it is biological or technological, children change the family system. Even when parenthood is an expected change, it can constitute a crisis. Any new mom or dad who stays up late to feed a crying baby and then tries to work the next day would attest to the fact that parenting can be stressful on the mind and the body and that it can be a financial and emotional strain.

E. E. LeMasters was one of the first family professionals to look at parenthood as a crisis event. In doing so, he opened the door to studies on transition to parenthood and parent education. LeMasters wrote "Parenthood as Crisis," *Marriage and Family Living* (November 1957), from which this selection has been taken, while at Beloit College. He went on to describe different types of parents in his book *Parents in Modern America* (Dorsey Press, 1974).

**Key Concept:** parenting

# INTRODUCTION

In recent decades the impact of various crises on the American family has been subjected to intensive analysis. Eliot,[1] Waller,[2] Angell,[3] Komarovsky,[4] Cavan and Ranck,[5] Koos,[6] Hill,[7] and Goode[8] have published what is perhaps the most solid block of empirical research in the field of family sociology.

In all of these studies of how the modern family reacts to crisis, it appears that the shock is related to the fact that the crisis event forces a reorganization of the family as a social system. Roles have to be reassigned, status positions shifted, values reoriented, and needs met through new channels.

These studies have shown that crises may originate either from within the family itself or from the outside. It has also been demonstrated that the total impact of the crisis will depend upon a number of variables: (1) the nature of the crisis event; (2) the state of organization or disorganization of the family at the point of impact; (3) the resources of the family; and (4) its previous experience with crisis.[9]

These studies report a sequence of events somewhat as follows: level of organization before the crisis, point of impact, period of disorganization, recovery, and subsequent level of reorganization.

This study was conceived and designed within the conceptual framework of the above research.

# THE PRESENT STUDY

In the study being described in this report, the main hypothesis was derived through the following line of analysis:

A. If the family is conceptualized as a small social system, would it not follow that the *adding* of a new member to the system could force a reorganization of the system as drastic (or nearly so) as does the *removal* of a member?

B. If the above were correct, would it not follow that the arrival of the *first* child could be construed as a "crisis" or critical event?[10]

To test this hypothesis, a group of young parents were interviewed, using a relatively unstructured interviewing technique. In order to control socioeconomic variables, couples had to possess the following characteristics to be included in the study: (1) unbroken marriage; (2) urban or suburban residence; (3) between twenty-five and thirty-five years of age at the time of the study; (4) husband college graduate: (5) husband's occupation middle class; (6) wife not employed after birth of first child; (7) must have had their first child within five years of the date interviewed. Race and religion were not controlled.

Using these criteria, forty-eight couples were located by the device of asking various persons in the community for names. As a precaution, the exact nature of the study was not stated in soliciting names for the sample—the project was described as a study of "modern young parents."

Once a name was obtained that met the specifications, every effort was made to secure an interview. No refusals were encountered, but two couples left the community before they could participate, leaving forty-six couples for the final study group. The couples, then, were not volunteers. All of the interviewing was done by the writer during the years 1953–1956. Both the husband and wife were interviewed.

Typical occupations represented include minister, social worker, high school teacher, college professor, bank teller, accountant, athletic coach, and small business owner.

Various definitions of "crisis" are available to the worker in this area. Webster, for example, states that the term means a "decisive" or "crucial" period, a "turning point."[11] Koos specifies that crises are situations "which block the usual patterns of action and call for new ones."[12] Hill defines as a crisis "any sharp or decisive change for which old patterns are inadequate."[13] This is the definition used in this analysis.

A five point scale was used in coding the interview data: (1) no crisis; (2) slight crisis; (3) moderate crisis; (4) extensive crisis; (5) severe crisis.

## THE FINDINGS

The essential findings of this exploratory study are as follows:

1. Thirty-eight of the forty-six couples (83 per cent) reported "extensive" or "severe" crisis in adjusting to the first child. This rating was arrived at jointly by the interviewer and the parents.

In several cases there was some difference of opinion between the husband and wife as to what their response should be. In all but two cases, however, the difference was reconciled by further discussion between the interviewer and the couple. In the two cases, the wife's rating was recorded, on the theory that the mother makes the major adjustment to children in our culture.

For this sample, therefore, the evidence is quite strong in support of the hypothesis. The eight couples (17 per cent) who reported relatively mild crisis (values 1–2–3 in the ... scale) must be considered the deviants in this sample.

Stated theoretically, this study supports the idea that adding the first child to the urban middle class married couple constitutes a crisis event.

2. In this study there was strong evidence that this crisis reaction was *not* the result of not wanting children. On the contrary, thirty-five of the thirty-eight pregnancies in the crisis group were either "planned" or "desired."

3. The data support the belief that the crisis pattern occurs whether the marriage is "good" or "poor"—for example: thirty-four of the thirty-eight in the crisis group (89 per cent) rated their marriages as "good" or better. With only three exceptions, these ratings were confirmed by close friends. By any reasonable standards, these marriages must be considered adequate.

4. There is considerable evidence that the crisis pattern in the thirty-eight cases was not the result of "neurosis" or other psychiatric disability on the part of these parents. Judging by their personal histories, their marriages, and the ratings of friends, it seemed clear that the vast bulk of the husbands and wives in the crisis group were average or above in personality adjustment.

5. The thirty-eight couples in the crisis group appear to have almost completely romanticized parenthood. They felt that they had had very little, if any,

effective preparation for parental roles. As one mother said: "We knew where babies came from, but we didn't know *what they were like.*"

The mothers reported the following feelings or experiences in adjusting to the first child: loss of sleep (especially during the early months); chronic "tiredness" or exhaustion; extensive confinement to the home and the resulting curtailment of their social contacts; giving up the satisfactions and the income of outside employment; additional washing and ironing; guilt at not being a "better" mother; the long hours and seven day (and night) week necessary in caring for an infant; decline in their housekeeping standards; worry over their appearance (increased weight after pregnancy, et cetera).

The fathers echoed most of the above adjustments but also added a few of their own: decline in sexual response of wife; economic pressure resulting from wife's retirement plus additional expenditures necessary for child; interference with social life; worry about a second pregnancy in the near future; and a general disenchantment with the parental role.

6. The mothers with professional training and extensive professional work experience (eight cases) suffered "extensive" or "severe" crisis in every case.

In analyzing these cases, it was apparent that these women were really involved in two major adjustments simultaneously: (1) they were giving up an occupation which had deep significance for them; and (2) they were assuming the role of mother for the first time.

## INTERPRETATION OF THE FINDINGS

There are, of course, various ways of interpreting the findings in this study. It may be, for example, that the couples obtained for the sample are not typical of urban middle class parents. It might also be true that the interviewing, the design of the study, or both, may have been inadequate. If we assume, for the present, that the findings are reliable and valid for this social group, how are we to interpret such reactions to parenthood? It is suggested that the following conceptual tools may be helpful.

1. That parenthood (and not marriage) is the real "romantic complex" in our culture. This view, as a matter of fact, was expressed by many of the couples in the study.

In a brilliant article some years ago, Arnold Green [14] suggested as much —that urban middle class couples often find their parental roles in conflict with their other socio-economic commitments. If this is true, one would expect to find the reconciliation of these conflicts most acute at the point of entering parenthood, with the first child. Our findings support this expectation.

2. Ruth Benedict has pointed out that young people in our society are often the victims of "discontinuity in cultural conditioning."[15] By this she means that we often have to "unlearn" previous training before we can move on to the next set of roles. Sex conditioning is perhaps the clearest illustration of this.

Using this concept, one can see that these couples were not trained for parenthood, that practically nothing in school, or out of school, got them ready to be fathers and mothers—*husbands* and *wives*, yes, but not *parents*. This helps explain why some of the mothers interviewed were actually "bitter" about their high school and college training.

3. One can also interpret these findings by resorting to what is known about small groups. Wilson and Ryland, for example, in their standard text on group work make this comment about the two-person group: "This combination seems to be the most satisfactory of human relationships."[16] They then proceed to pass this judgment on the three-person group: "Upon analysis this pattern falls into a combination of a pair and an isolate.... This plurality pattern is the most volatile of all human relationships."[17] This, of course, supports an earlier analysis by von Wiese and Becker.[18]

Viewed in this conceptual system, married couples find the transition to parenthood painful because the arrival of the first child destroys the two-person or pair pattern of group interaction and forces a rapid reorganization of their life into a three-person or triangle group system. Due to the fact that their courtship and pre-parenthood pair relationship has persisted over a period of years, they find it difficult to give it up as a way of life.

In addition, however, they find that living as a trio is more complicated than living as a pair. The husband, for example, no longer ranks first in claims upon his wife but must accept the child's right to priority. In some cases, the husband may feel that he is the semi-isolate, the third party in the trio. In other cases, the wife may feel that her husband is more interested in the baby than in her. If they preserve their pair relationship and continue their previous way of life, relatives and friends may regard them as poor parents. In any event, their pattern of living has to be radically altered.

Since babies do not usually appear to married couples completely by surprise, it might be argued that this event is not really a crisis—"well adjusted" couples should be "prepared for it." The answer seems to be that children and parenthood have been so romanticized in our society that most middle class couples are caught unprepared, even though they have planned and waited for this event for years. The fact that parenthood is "normal" does not eliminate crisis. Death is also "normal" but continues to be a crisis event for most families.

4. One can also interpret the findings of this study by postulating that parenthood (not marriage) marks the final transition to maturity and adult responsibility in our culture.[19] Thus the arrival of the first child forces young married couples to take the last painful step into the adult world. This point, as a matter of fact, was stated or implied by most of the couples in the crisis group.

5. Finally, the cases in this sample confirm what the previous studies in this area have shown: that the event itself is only one factor determining the extent and severity of the crisis on any given family. Their resources, their previous experience with crisis, the pattern of role organization before the crisis —these factors are equally important in determining the total reaction to the event.

# CONCLUSION

In this study, it was hypothesized that the addition of the first child would constitute a crisis event, forcing the married couple to move from an adult-centered pair type of organization into child-centered triad group system. Of the forty-six middle class couples located for this study, thirty-eight (83 per cent) confirmed the hypothesis.

In all fairness to this group of parents, it should be reported that all but a few of them eventually made what seems to be a successful adjustment to parenthood. This does not alter the fact, however, that most of them found the transition difficult. Listening to them describe their experiences, it seemed that one could compare these young parents to veterans of military service—they had been through a rough experience, but it was worth it. As one father said: "I wouldn't have missed it for the world."

It is unfortunate that the number of parents in this sample who did not report crisis is so small (eight couples) that no general statements can be made about them. Somehow, however, they seem to have been better prepared for parenthood than was the crisis group. It is felt that future work on this problem might well include a more extensive analysis of couples who have made the transition to parenthood with relative ease.

If the basic findings of this study are confirmed by other workers, it would appear that family life educators could make a significant contribution by helping young people prepare more adequately for parenthood.

# NOTES

1. See Thomas D. Eliot, "Bereavement: Inevitable but Not Insurmountable," in *Family, Marriage, and Parenthood,* edited by Howard Becker and Reuben Hill, Boston: D.C. Heath and Company, Second Edition, 1955.
2. Willard Waller, *The Old Love and the New,* New York: Liveright, 1930.
3. Robert C. Angell, *The Family Encounters the Depression,* New York: Charles Scribner's Sons, 1936.
4. Mirra Komarovsky, *The Unemployed Man and His Family,* New York: Dryden Press, 1940.
5. Ruth Cavan and Katherine Ranck, *The Family and the Depression,* Chicago: University of Chicago Press, 1938.
6. E. L. Koos, *Families in Trouble,* New York: King's Crown Press, 1946.
7. Reuben Hill, *Families Under Stress,* New York: Harper and Brothers, 1949.
8. William J. Goode, *After Divorce,* Glencoe: The Free Press, 1956.
9. See Hill, *op. cit.,* for an excellent review of this research.
10. To some extent, the original idea for this study was derived from Hill's discussion. See *op cit.,* ch. 2.
11. *Webster's Collegiate Dictionary,* Springfield: G. and C. Merriam Co., Second Edition, 1944, p. 240.
12. Koos, *op. cit.,* p. 9.

13. Hill, *op. cit.,* p. 51. See also his review of definitions ch. 2.
14. Arnold W. Green, "The Middle-Class Male Child and Neurosis," *American Sociological Review,* 11 (February, 1946), pp. 31–41.
15. Ruth Benedict, "Continuities and Discontinuities in Cultural Conditioning," *Psychiatry,* 1 (May, 1939), pp. 161–67.
16. Gertrude Wilson and Gladys Ryland, *Social Group Work Practice,* Boston: Houghton Mifflin Company, 1949, p. 49.
17. *Ibid.*
18. Leopold von Wiese, *Systematic Sociology,* adapted and amplified by Howard Becker, New York: Wiley, 1932.
19. This is essentially the point of view in Robert J. Flavighurst's analysis, *Human Development and Education,* New York: Longmans, Green, 1953.

# 8.2 DIANA BAUMRIND

# Child Care Practices Anteceding Three Patterns of Preschool Behavior

One of the goals of parent education is to teach parents how to raise their children to be responsible, caring adults who contribute to society. Research such as Diana Baumrind's provides empirical data to support such education. Baumrind has identified three parenting styles: authoritarian, authoritative, and permissive. Authoritarian parents value obedience and produce children who follow the rules at home and are passive in authority situations outside the home. Authoritative parents set specific standards but listen to their children; they produce responsible, self-reliant children. Permissive parents provide few rules for their children and produce children who are not self-reliant and are unsure of themselves.

Baumrind believes that parents have a powerful influence over the way their children's personalities develop. For over 20 years she studied preschool children's behavior with their parents and in a school setting. Baumrind's article "Child Care Practices Anteceding Three Patterns of Preschool Behavior," *Genetic Psychology Monographs* (1967), from which this selection has been taken, was followed by other publications that supported and extended her previous findings.

Baumrind (b. 1927) studied at Hunter College and the University of California, Berkeley. Her work has been published in such journals as *Youth and Society, Developmental Psychology Monographs,* and *Psychology Bulletin*. Her work also appears in most child development and family life textbooks.

**Key Concept:** parenting styles

# INTRODUCTION

The major objective of the present investigation is to study systematically child-rearing practices associated with competence in the young child. In order to do this a group of preschool children were identified who were self-reliant, self-controlled, explorative, and content (Pattern I in this investigation). The childrearing practices of their parents were contrasted with those of parents whose children were discontent, withdrawn, and distrustful (Pattern II), and those of parents whose children had little self-control or self-reliance and tended to retreat from novel experiences (Pattern III). Multiple assessment procedures were used to measure parental control, maturity demands, clarity of communication, and warmth. Observations were made in natural and structured settings and data obtained on parents and children independently.

The conceptual approach to parent-child relations from which the study proceeds starts with the assumption that the physical, cognitive, and social development of middle-class preschool children in America is largely a function of parental childrearing practices. With varying degrees of consciousness and conscientiousness, parents create their children psychologically as well as physically. The child's energy level, his willingness to explore and will to master his environment, and his self-control, sociability, and buoyancy are set not only by genetic structure but by the regimen, stimulation, and kind of contact provided by his parents. The child's inherent cognitive potential can be fully developed by a rich, complex environment or inhibited by inadequate and poorly timed stimulation. The young child learns from his parents how to think as well as how to talk, how to interpret and use his experience, how to control his reactions, and how to influence other people. Children learn from their parents how to relate to others, whom to like and emulate, whom to avoid and derogate, how to express affiliation and animosity, and when to withhold response. The parents' use of reinforcement, whether punishment or reward, alters the child's behavior and affects his future likes and dislikes. Parents differ in the degree to which they wish to influence their children, and they differ in their effectiveness as teachers and models. Some parents attempt to maximize and others to minimize the direct influence that they have upon their children. Some parents enjoy prolonged and intense contact and others are discomforted by such contact. Parents differ in their ability to communicate clearly with their children and in their desire to reason with and listen to the ideas and objections of their offspring. They vary in the frequency and kinds of demands that they make of their children. Some parents require of their preschool children that they participate in household chores, or that they care for themselves and their rooms, or that they control their feelings, while others seek to prolong the early period of dependency, immaturity, and spontaneous expression of feelings.

The parent variables assess the childrearing practices described above, and were selected for their theoretical importance as predictors of competence in preschool children. A great deal of attention has been given in the past to the negative effects on children of too much control. The disciplinary variables selected for study reflected this particular bias. An effort was made in this investigation to define the control variables separately from the restrictive variables and then to study the interaction of control with nurturance rather than restrictiveness with nurturance.

# SUBJECTS

### Selection of Subjects

Subjects were 32 three- and four-year-olds chosen from among children enrolled at the Child Study Center, Institute of Human Development, University of California, Berkeley during the Fall semester of 1961.

The 110 children enrolled at the Child Study Center were assessed along five dimensions: namely, self-control, approach-avoidance tendency, self-reliance, subjective mood, and peer affiliation. In conferences attended by nursery school teachers and the observer staff, each dimension of child behavior was given concrete meaning by reference to relevant time sample categories and illustrated by instances of actual observed behavior. After 14 weeks of observation, the children in the four participating nursery school groups were ranked on each dimension by their nursery school teacher and the observing psychologist. Where the nursery school teacher and psychologist disagreed about the placement of a child, the disagreement was resolved by conference or the child was disqualified. A respectful relationship existed between nursery school staff and the team of psychologists, each group of whom had the opportunity to observe the children from a different perspective and thus contribute to the discussion in important ways and on an equal footing. Fifty-two children, who received among the five highest or among the five lowest rankings on two or more dimensions, after conference, composed the first pool of potential subjects. These children were further observed in a laboratory setting where they were exposed to standardized stimuli. For example, the children were presented by a psychologist with three puzzles graded in difficulty so that each child experienced easy success, probable success, and certain failure. Their responses to success and failure were observed and rated by the testing psychologist and another psychologist who in each case had also observed and ranked the children in the nursery school setting. The psychologist responsible for initial selection of the child had the opportunity then to see the child function in a second and entirely different type of setting. In order for the child to remain in the study, the observing psychologist's ratings of the child in the two settings had to concur and to be confirmed by the psychologist who presented the children with the structured stimuli. By using multiple assessment procedures, groups of children with clear-cut, stable patterns of interpersonal attributes were obtained.

All children who were reliably rated over settings and had one of the patterns of high and low scores designated... were used as subjects. A total of 32 subjects met these criteria. The three patterns of children were selected in order that a set of hypotheses concerning the interacting effects of parental control, parental maturity demands, parent child communication, and parental nurturance could be tested. Children who were ranked high on mood, self-reliance, and approach or self-control were designated as Pattern I ($N=13$). Children who were ranked low on the peer affiliation and mood dimensions and were not ranked high on the approach dimension were designated as Pattern II ($N=$

11). Children who were ranked low on self-reliance and low on self-control or approach were designated as Pattern III ($N = 8$)....

# CHILD BEHAVIOR DIMENSIONS

The five dimensions of child behavior used in establishing pattern membership were chosen to assess aspects both of socialized behavior and independent behavior.

### Self-Control

Self-control is defined as the tendency, in a consistent and reliable fashion, to suppress, redirect, inhibit, or in other ways control the impulse to act, in those situations where self-restraint is appropriate. In order for an instance of self-restraint to be treated as an index of self-control, the child must be motivated to engage in an act and there must be adaptive reasons for restraint in the form of an adult prohibition or a safety rule.

Aspects of self-control assessed were (*a*) obedience to school rules that conflict with an action that the child is motivated to perform, under circumstances where such prohibitions are known to the child; (*b*) ability to sustain a work effort; (*c*) capacity to wait his turn in play with other children or in use of washroom facilities; (*d*) ability to restrain those expressions of excitement or anger that would be disruptive or destructive to the peer group; and (*e*) low variability of self-control as shown by absence of explosive emotional expression or swings between high and low control.

### Approach-Avoidance Tendency

Approach-Avoidance tendency measures the extent to which the child reacts to stimuli that are novel, stressful, exciting, or unexpected, by approaching these stimuli in an explorative and curious fashion (contrasted to avoiding these stimuli or becoming increasingly anxious when challenged to approach them).

Aspects of approach assessed were (*a*) vigor and involvement with which child reacts to his normal environment; (*b*) preference for stimulating activities, such as rough and tumble games or climbing and balancing; (*c*) interest in exploring the potentialities of a new environment (noted in particular when the child is invited to come to the laboratory to participate in the structured observation); (*d*) tendency to seek out experiences with challenge (e.g., tasks which are new for him, or cognitive problems at the upper limits of his ability); and (*e*) tendency to attack an obstacle to a goal rather than retreat from the goal.

### Subjective Mood (Buoyant-Dysphoric)

This dimension refers to the predominant affect expressed by the child with regard to the degree of pleasure and zest shown. A buoyant mood is demonstrated behaviorally by happy involvement in nursery school activities. If the child is outgoing, he may appear lively and perhaps aggressively good-humored. If less outgoing, the child may appear contemplative and privately engrossed, in a contented, secure manner. A dysphoric mood is expressed by anxious, hostile, and unhappy peer relations and low involvement in nursery school activities. If the child is outgoing he may appear angry, punishing, and obstructive, when dysphoric. If less outgoing, the child may appear fearful, bored, or subdued.

### Self-Reliance

Self-reliance refers to the ability of the child to handle his affairs in an independent fashion relative to other children his age. As this variable is defined, realistic help-seeking may be regarded as an aspect of self-reliance rather than dependency when the child actively searches for help in order to perform a task too difficult for him to accomplish alone. The child rated high in self-reliance, however, does not seek help as a way of relating to others or of avoiding effort, but as a means of achieving a goal or learning a new technique.

Aspects of self-reliance assessed were (*a*) ease of separation from parents; (*b*) matter-of-fact rather than dependent manner of relating to nursery school teachers, especially when seeking help; (*c*) willingness to be alone at times; (*d*) pleasure expressed in learning how to master new tasks; (*e*) resistance to encroachment of other children; (*f*) leadership interest and ability; and (*g*) interest expressed in making decisions and choices which affect him.

### Peer Affiliation

This dimension refers to the child's ability and desire to express warmth toward others of his own age.

Aspects assessed were (*a*) expressions of trust in peers and expectation of being treated by them in an affiliative manner; (*b*) expressions of affection congruent with the particular peer relationship; (*c*) cooperative engagement in group activities; and (*d*) absence of sadistic, hostile, or unprovoked aggressive behavior toward playmates.

## PARENT BEHAVIOR DIMENSIONS

... The dimensions studied are parental control, parental maturity demands, parent-child communication, and parental nurturance. The dimensions of parent-child interaction were assessed during home visits, structured observation, and interviews. The individual variables that defined the dimensions operationally are described. The operational definitions of each dimension appear beneath the conceptual definition and consist of the component variables listed under Home Visit Sequence Analysis (HVSA) and Summary Ratings for the Structured Observation (SRSO)....

### Parental Control

The term parental control refers to the socializing functions of the parent: that is, to those parental acts that are intended to shape the child's goal-oriented activity, modify his expression of dependent, aggressive, and playful behavior, and promote internalization of parental standards. Parental control as defined here is not a measure of restrictiveness, punitive attitudes, or intrusiveness. Parental control included such variables as consistency in enforcing directives, ability to resist pressure from the child, and willingness to exert influence upon the child....

### Parental Maturity Demands

Maturity demands refer both to the pressures put upon the child to perform at least up to ability in intellectual, social, and emotional spheres (independence-training) and leeway given the child to make his own decisions (independence-granting)....

### Parent-Child Communication

By clarity of parent-child communication is meant the extent to which the parent uses reason to obtain compliance, solicits the child's opinions and feelings, and uses open rather than manipulative techniques of control....

### Parental Nurturance

The term nurturance is used to refer to the caretaking functions of the parent: that is, to those parent acts and attitudes that express love and are directed at guaranteeing the child's physical and emotional well-being. Nurturance is expressed by warmth and involvement. By warmth is meant the parent's personal love and compassion for the child expressed by means of sensory stimulation, verbal approval, and tenderness of expression and touch. By involvement is meant pride and pleasure in the child's accomplishments, manifested by words of praise and interest, and conscientious protection of the child's welfare. (We speak of the child's welfare from the parent's perspective.)...

## CONCEPTUAL APPROACH

The propositions upon which the study hypotheses are based will be presented in this section. A general statement of the expected related effects of parental control, parental maturity demands, parent-child communication, and parental nurturance is as follows: parents who are both controlling and demanding (referred to as nonpermissive), but also nurturant and communicative, should generate in their children self-reliant, self-assertive, and self-controlled (Pattern I) behavior; parents who are nonpermissive and non-nurturant should generate moderately self-reliant and self-controlled, but also dysphoric and disaffiliative (Pattern II), behavior; and parents who are noncontrolling and nondemanding (permissive) should promote dependence, avoidance of stress, and low self-control (Pattern III) behavior....

**Proposition A:** Nonpermissive, nurturant parents are more effective reinforcing agents for their children than are nonpermissive, nonnurturant or permissive, nurturant parents....

**Proposition B:** Nonpermissive, nurturant parents will effectively model behavior that is self-assertive (approach-oriented and self-reliant) and affiliative....

**Proposition C:** Low maturity demands will result in low self-reliance, especially if the parent is nurturant....

**Proposition D:** High maturity demands will result in higher aspirations, greater self-reliance, and a more buoyant attitude when the parents are nurturant than when they are nonnurturant....

**Proposition E:** Clarity of communication accompanying high parental control will promote the development of conformity without loss of self-assertiveness....

## PROCEDURES

To permit internal validation of results, multiple measures were used. Each measure was devised to perform a slightly different function. The structured observation was devised to maximize the crucial group differences by presenting, to each mother-child pair, standard stimuli designed to elicit influence attempts by the parent and resistance from the child. A rating instrument, the Parent Behavior Rating Scales (PBRS), was devised to provide the latitude needed for clinical inference, and as a convenient way of summarizing information gathered during the home visit. The Home Visit Sequence Analysis (HVSA) measured parent-child interactions directly and discretely. Data obtained from this source are minimally affected by halo, since each variable from the HVSA is associated with a theoretical dimension of parent-child interaction via an inferential chain unknowable to the coder. Additional information about childrearing practices and attributes was obtained by interviewing each parent separately.

Although the data obtained on child training practices from the several sources were not collected independently, the data obtained from these sources were defined so differently that they could reasonably be used as corroborative.... In no case did results obtained by the different methods contradict one another.

All parents and children selected for study agreed to participate. They were promised feedback about results which they received in the form of a report, describing the hypotheses and general results. In approaching the family to participate, we acknowledged gratefully the extent of our debt to the subjects and the initial discomfort that subjects and observers alike might be expected to experience during the home visit....

## RESULTS AND DISCUSSION....

### Summary of Results

In order that the reader might have a visual picture of the total results the variables measuring each dimension were composited for the HVSA and SRSO and are presented in Figure 1.... The two measures, very different in unit and setting, give nearly identical pictures of between-group differences. Parents of Pattern I children are uniformly high on all dimensions by comparison with other parents. Pattern II and Pattern III show reverse relationships on the control and nurturance scores. Parents of the disaffiliated and dysphoric children were more controlling and less nurturant, while the opposite is true for parents of immature children. This relationship between the control and nurturance composites is more striking than the between-group difference on either dimension. Of particular interest is the similarity of parents of both contrast groups on communication scores, when compared to the parents of Pattern I children whose scores are very much higher....

### Discussion

*Childrearing Practices Associated With Pattern I Child Behavior.* Pattern I children were both socialized and independent. They were self-controlled and affiliative on the one hand and self-reliant, explorative, and self-assertive on the other hand. They were realistic, competent, and content by comparison with Pattern II and Pattern III children. Boys and girls were equally represented, as were children of different birth orders. The differences between Pattern I children and children in the other patterns were far more pronounced than were the differences between children in Patterns II and III.

The magnitudes of group differences for their parents were similarly discrepant. In the home setting, parents of Pattern I children were markedly consistent, loving, conscientious, and secure in handling their children. They respected the child's independent decisions but demonstrated remarkable ability to hold to a position once they took a stand. They tended to accompany a directive with a reason. On the SRSO, mothers of Pattern I children demonstrated firm control and demanded a good deal of their children. They also were more supportive and communicated more clearly with their children than did parents of children in Patterns II and III. Despite vigorous and at times

**FIGURE 1**

*Profile of Composited Parent Dimension Scores from the Summary Ratings for the Structured Observation (SRSO) and the Home Visit Sequence Analysis (HVSA) for Each Pattern*

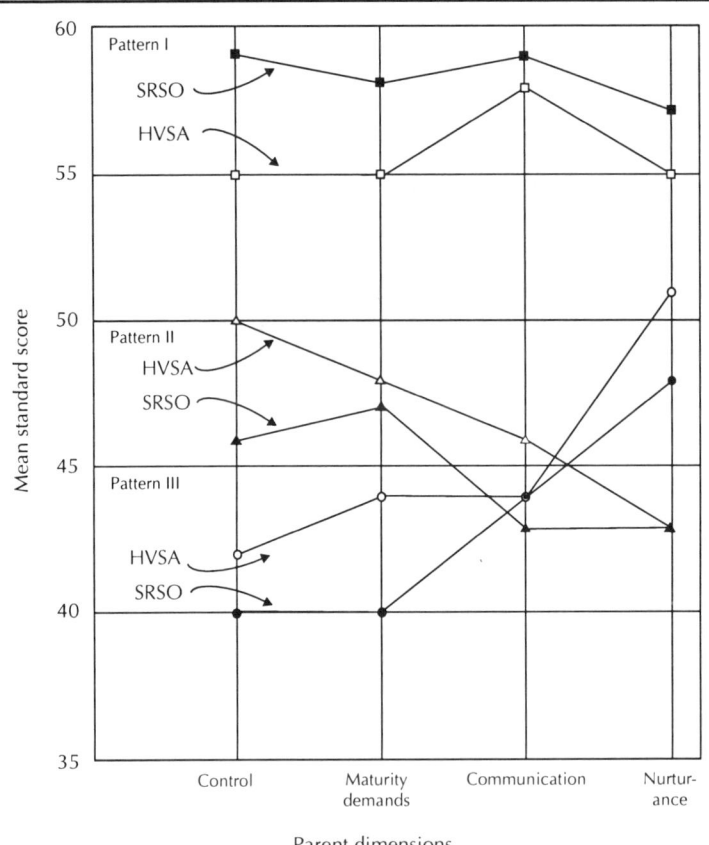

conflictful interactions, their homes were not marked by discord or dissensions. The above findings were true when parents of Pattern I children were compared with parents of children in either Pattern II or Pattern III. Parents of Pattern I children balanced high nurturance with high control and high demands with clear communication about what was required of the child. Under the conditions pertaining in their homes, Pattern I children were not adversely affected by their parents' socialization and maturity demands and, indeed, seemed to thrive under the pressure imposed. We are inclined to think that by using reason to accompany a directive and by encouraging verbal give and take, these parents were able to maintain control without stimulating rebellion or passivity.

By comparison with parents of Pattern III children in the home setting, parents of Pattern I children had firmer control over the actions of their children, engaged in more independence training and did not baby their children. It is clear from the PBRS that the Pattern I household by comparison with the Pattern III household was better coordinated, that there were fewer instances of disciplinary friction, and the policy of regulations was clearer and more effectively enforced. Power was used in an open and nonmanipulative fashion by parents of Pattern I children, and yet the child was more satisfied by interactions with his parents than was the Pattern III child. According to interview data, by comparison with fathers of Pattern III children, fathers of Pattern I children accepted a more important role in the disciplining of their children. Both parents of Pattern I children expressed greater feeling of control over the behavior of their children and less internal conflict about disciplinary procedures than did parents of Pattern III children.

*Childrearing Practices Associated With Pattern II Child Behavior.* Pattern II children were significantly less content, more insecure and apprehensive, less affiliative toward peers, and more likely to become hostile or regressive under stress than Pattern I children. They were more inclined to do careful work and functioned at a higher cognitive level than Pattern III children. The group was composed, by comparison with Pattern III, of (significantly) more first-born and only children of one- and two-child families, and (nonsignificantly) more girls.

Parents of Pattern II children were, by comparison with parents of the other two groups, less nurturant and involved with their children. They exerted firm control and used power freely, but offered little support or affection. They did not attempt to convince the child through use of reason to obey a directive, nor did they encourage the child to express himself when he disagreed. According to interview data, the mother was more inclined to give an absolute moral imperative as a reason for her demands than were Pattern I parents. Her expressed attitudes were less sympathetic and approving and she admitted more to frightening the child. Her expressed nonnurturant attitudes were reflected in her observed behavior on HVSA and SRSO measures.

*Childrearing Practices Associated With Pattern III Child Behavior.* Pattern III children were lacking in self-control and self-reliance by comparison with children in the other groups.

By comparison with parents of Pattern I children, the parents of Pattern III children behaved in a markedly less controlling manner and were not as well organized or effective in running their households. They were self-effacing and insecure about their ability to influence their children, lacking the qualities of a strong model. Neither parent demanded much of the child and fathers were lax reinforcing agents. They engaged in less independence training and babied their children more. There are some indications that by comparison with parents of Pattern I children these parents were less intensely involved with their children and used love manipulatively. Mothers used withdrawal of love and ridicule rather than power or reason as incentives.

The most significant difference between parents of Pattern II and Pattern III children was that the former were the more controlling. Since parents of Pattern III children were the warmer, the control-nurturance ratios are in opposite directions: parents of the dysphoric and disaffiliated children were controlling and not at all warm, while parents of the immature children were not at all controlling and comparatively warm.

The prototypic child-centered parent who is both permissive (noncontrolling and nondemanding) and warm did not appear. The most mature and competent children sampled certainly did not have child-centered parents. But neither did the least mature and self-reliant group of children.

*The Interacting Effects of Control and Warmth.* The interacting effects of control and warmth clearly differ from the interacting effects of restrictiveness and warmth. Becker (1, p. 198) summarized the interactions of restrictiveness *vs.* permissiveness with warmth *vs.* hostility. He reported that warm-restrictive parents tend to have dependent, well socialized, submissive children. In this study warm-controlling parents were not paired with submissive, dependent children, but rather with assertive, self-reliant children. Parents of Pattern I children enforced directives and resisted the child's demands, but they did not overprotect or overrestrict the child. The children were well socialized but not passive-dependent. Apparently early control, unlike restrictiveness, does not lead to "fearful, dependent, and submissive behaviors, a dulling of intellectual striving and inhibited hostility" (1, p. 197). Becker reports that children of warm-nonrestrictive parents were socially outgoing, successfully aggressive, independent, and friendly. In this study, children of warm-noncontrolling parents were immature and avoidant. They were not self-assertive and self-reliant, as were children of warm-nonrestrictive parents.

Restrictiveness and control, then, relate to quite different behaviors and have contrasting effects on self-assertiveness and self-reliance in young children. In order to understand the effects of either control or restrictiveness in child behavior, a configurational analysis that takes into account interactions with nurturance variables is necessary.

# SUMMARY

Childrearing practices of parents with self-reliant, self-controlled, approach-oriented, buoyant children were contrasted with childrearing practices of other parents whose children were drawn from the same preschool population. There were two contrast groups of children. Members of one contrast group were dysphoric and disaffiliated, while members of the other group were immature. Parent dimensions measured were parental control, parental maturity demands, parent-child communication, and parental nurturance.

Parent-child interaction data were obtained by means of focussed interviews, home visits, and structured observations. The home visits offered the opportunity to observe the family in a natural setting, while the structured observation confronted the mother and child with a standard set of arousal stimuli designed to elicit responses of theoretical interest.

Certain hypotheses were tested about the effects of childrearing practices using data obtained from independent observations of parents and children in natural and contrived situations.

The following points should be kept in mind when generalizing from the findings. It does not follow from these results that either parental control or nurturance bears a positive linear relationship to competence in preschool children. The total range is not represented. Parents of subjects with scores in the middle range on the child attributes measured may have even more extreme scores on the parent dimensions measured. Also the directions of cause-effect relationships were inferred only from the successful predictions of these relationships.

The following are conclusions about the subgroups studied. Parents of the most competent and mature boys and girls (Pattern I children) were notably firm, loving, demanding, and understanding. Parents of dysphoric and disaffiliative children (Pattern II children) were firm, punitive, and unaffectionate. Mothers of dependent, immature children (Pattern III children) lacked control and were moderately loving. Fathers of these children were ambivalent and lax. The spontaneity, warmth, and zest of Pattern I children were not affected adversely by high parental control.

# REFERENCES

Becker, W. C. Consequences of different kinds of parental discipline. In M. L. Hoffman & L. W. Hoffman (Eds.), *Review of Child Development Research (Vol. 1)*. New York: Russell Sage Foundation, 1964. Pp. 169–208.

8.3 MURRAY A. STRAUS

# Ten Myths That Perpetuate Corporal Punishment

One of the most common discussions that parents have is on the subject of how to discipline their children. Although there are many alternative ways to raise responsible children, spanking is often seen as necessary to help children learn the difference between right and wrong. To spank children or not to spank children is an emotional debate that parents wage when trying to find the best method for raising responsible children. Research is used to support both sides of the issue, and there has been little agreement between the opposing sides as to how to resolve the debate. Murray A. Straus has consistently been in the middle of this controversy, and since the 1970s he has supported the battle against spanking, which he considers to be a form of violence in the family.

Straus has spent a good deal of his professional career investigating the effects of spanking on children's development. Increasing concern about violence in families has led to increased attention being paid to how spanking children within the family environment may be related to violence in the home. This selection is from Straus's 1994 book *Beating the Devil Out of Them: Corporal Punishment in American Families and Its Effects on Children* (Lexington Books). The book is the culmination of 20-plus years of research.

Straus (b. 1926) is founder and codirector of the Family Research Laboratory at the University of New Hampshire. He is author, coauthor, or coeditor of over 150 articles and 15 books on the family, including *Intimate Violence*, with Richard J. Gelles (Simon & Schuster, 1988), and *Behind Closed Doors: Violence in the American Family*, with Richard J. Gelles and Suzanne K. Steinmetz (Anchor Books, 1981). Straus received his bachelor's, master's, and doctoral degrees from the University of Wisconsin. He has held a variety of academic positions at Washington State University, the University of Wisconsin–Madison, Cornell University, the University of Minnesota, and the University of New Hampshire.

**Key Concept:** corporal punishment

[H]itting children is legal in every state of the United States and 84 percent of a survey of Americans agreed that it is sometimes necessary to give a child a good hard spanking.... [A]lmost all parents of toddlers act on these beliefs. Study after study shows that almost 100 percent of parents with toddlers hit their children. There are many reasons for the strong support of spanking. Most of them are myths.

## MYTH 1: SPANKING WORKS BETTER

There has been a huge amount of research on the effectiveness of corporal punishment of animals, but remarkably little on the effectiveness of spanking children. That may be because almost no one, including psychologists, feels a need to study it because it is assumed that spanking is effective. In fact, what little research there is on the effectiveness of corporal punishment of children agrees with the research on animals. Studies of both animals and children show that punishment is *not* more effective than other methods of teaching and controlling behavior. Some studies show it is less effective.

Ellen Cohn and I asked 270 students at two New England colleges to tell us about the year they experienced the most corporal punishment. Their average age that year was eight, and they recalled having been hit an average of six times that year. We also asked them about the percent of the time they thought that the corporal punishment was effective. It averaged a little more than half of the times (53 percent). Of course, 53 percent also means that corporal punishment was *not* perceived as effective about half the time it was used.

LaVoie (1974) compared the use of a loud noise (in place of corporal punishment) with withdrawal of affection and verbal explanation in a study of first- and second-grade children. He wanted to find out which was more effective in getting the children to stop touching certain prohibited toys. Although the loud noise was more effective initially, there was no difference over a longer period of time. Just explaining was as effective as the other methods.

A problem with LaVoie's study is that it used a loud noise rather than actual corporal punishment. That problem does not apply to an experiment by Day and Roberts (1983). They studied three-year-old children who had been given "time out" (sitting in a corner). Half of the mothers were assigned to use spanking as the mode of correction if their child did not comply and left the corner. The other half put their non-complying child behind a low plywood barrier and physically enforced the child staying there. Keeping the child behind the barrier was just as effective as the spanking in correcting the misbehavior that led to the time out.

A study by Larzelere (in press) also found that a combination of *non-*corporal punishment and reasoning was as effective as corporal punishment and reasoning in correcting disobedience.

Crozier and Katz (1979), Patterson (1982), and Webster-Stratton et al. (1988, 1990) all studied children with serious conduct problems. Part of the treatment used in all three experiments was to get parents to stop spanking. In all three, the behavior of the children improved after spanking ended. Of course, many other things in addition to no spanking were part of the intervention. But, as you will see, parents who on their own accord do not spank also do many other things to manage their children's behavior. It is these other things, such as setting clear standards for what is expected, providing lots of love and affection, explaining things to the child, and recognizing and rewarding good behavior, that account for why children of non-spanking parents tend to be easy to manage and well-behaved. What about parents who do these things and also spank? Their children also tend to be well-behaved, but it is illogical to attribute that to spanking since the same or better results are achieved without spanking, and also without adverse side effects.

Such experiments are extremely important, but more experiments are needed to really understand what is going on when parents spank. Still, what Day and Roberts found can be observed in almost any household. Let's look at two examples.

In a typical American family there are many instances when a parent might say, "Mary! You did that again! I'm going to have to send you to your room again." This is just one example of a non-spanking method that did *not* work.

The second example is similar: A parent might say, "Mary! You did that again! I'm going to have to spank you again." This is an example of spanking that did *not* work.

The difference between these two examples is that when spanking does not work, parents tend to forget the incident because it contradicts the almost-universal American belief that spanking is something that works when all else fails. On the other hand, they tend to remember when a *non*-spanking method did not work. The reality is that nothing works all the time with a toddler. Parents think that spanking is a magic charm that will cure the child's misbehavior. It is not. There is no magic charm. It takes many interactions and many repetitions to bring up children. Some things work better with some children than with others.

Parents who favor spanking can turn this around and ask, If spanking doesn't work any better, isn't that the same as saying that it works just as well? So what's wrong with a quick slap on the wrist or bottom? There are at least three things that are wrong:

- Spanking becomes less and less effective over time and when children get bigger, it becomes difficult or impossible.
- For some children, the lessons learned through spanking include the idea that they only need to be good if Mommy or Daddy is watching or will know about it.
- ... [T]here are a number of very harmful side effects, such as a greater chance that the child will grow up to be depressed or violent. Parents don't perceive these side effects because they usually show up only in the long run.

# MYTH 2: SPANKING IS NEEDED AS A LAST RESORT

Even parents and social scientists who are opposed to spanking tend to think that it may be needed when all else fails. There is no scientific evidence supporting this belief, however. It is a myth that grows out of our cultural and psychological commitment to corporal punishment. You can prove this to yourself by a simple exercise with two other people. Each of the three should, in turn, think of the most extreme situation where spanking is necessary. The other two should try to think of alternatives. Experience has shown that it is very difficult to come up with a situation for which the alternatives are not as good as spanking. In fact, they are usually better.

Take the example of a child running out into the street. Almost everyone thinks that spanking is appropriate then because of the extreme danger. Although spanking in that situation may help *parents* relieve their own tension and anxiety, it is not necessary or appropriate for teaching the child. It is not necessary because spanking does not work better than other methods, and it is not appropriate because of the harmful side effects of spanking. The only physical force needed is to pick up the child and get him or her out of danger, and, while hugging the child, explain the danger.

Ironically, if spanking is to be done at all, the "last resort" may be the worst. The problem is that parents are usually very angry by that time and act impulsively. Because of their anger, if the child rebels and calls the parent a name or kicks the parent, the episode can escalate into physical abuse. Indeed, most episodes of physical abuse started as physical punishment and got out of hand (see Kadushin and Martin, 1981). Of course, the reverse is not true, that is, most instances of spanking do not escalate into abuse. Still, the danger of abuse is there, and so is the risk of psychological harm.

The second problem with spanking as a last resort is that, in addition to teaching that hitting is the way to correct wrongs, hitting a child impulsively teaches another incorrect lesson—that being extremely angry justifies hitting.

# MYTH 3: SPANKING IS HARMLESS

When someone says, I was spanked and I'm OK, he or she is arguing that spanking does no harm. This is contrary to almost all the available research. One reason the harmful effects are ignored is because many of us (including those of us who are social scientists) are reluctant to admit that their own parents did something wrong and even more reluctant to admit that we have been doing something wrong with our own children. But the most important reason may be that it is difficult to see the harm. Most of the harmful effects do not become visible right away, often not for years. In addition, only a relatively small percentage of spanked children experience obviously harmful effects....

Another argument in defense of spanking is that it is not harmful if the parents are loving and explain why they are spanking. The research does show that the harmful effects of spanking are reduced if it is done by loving parents who explain their actions. However,... a study by Larzelere (1986) shows that although the harmful effects are reduced, they are not eliminated. The ... harmful side effects include an increased risk of delinquency as a child and crime as an adult, wife beating, depression, masochistic sex, and lowered earnings.

In addition to having harmful psychological effects on children, hitting children also makes life more difficult for parents. Hitting a child to stop misbehavior may be the easy way in the short run, but in the slightly longer run, it makes the job of being a parent more difficult. This is because spanking reduces the ability of parents to influence their children, especially in adolescence when they are too big to control by physical force. Children are more likely to do what the parents want if there is a strong bond of affection with the parent. In short, being able to influence a child depends in considerable part on the bond between parent and child (Hirschi, 1969). An experiment by Redd, Morris, and Martin (1975) shows that children tend to avoid caretaking adults who use punishment. In the natural setting, of course, there are many things that tie children to their parents. I suggest that each spanking chips away at the bond between parent and child....

Contrary to the "spoiled child" myth, children of non-spanking parents are likely to be easier to manage and better behaved than the children of parents who spank. This is partly because they tend to control their own behavior on the basis of what their own conscience tells them is right and wrong rather than to avoid being hit. This is ironic because almost everyone thinks that spanking "when necessary" makes for better behavior.

## MYTH 4: ONE OR TWO TIMES WON'T CAUSE ANY DAMAGE

The evidence in this book indicates that the greatest risk of harmful effects occurs when spanking is very frequent. However, that does not necessarily mean that spanking just once or twice is harmless. Unfortunately, the connection between spanking once or twice and psychological damage has not been addressed by most of the available research. This is because the studies seem to be based on this myth. They generally cluster children into "low" and "high" groups in terms of the frequency they were hit. This prevents the "once or twice is harmless" myth from being tested scientifically because the low group may include parents who spank once a year or as often as once a month. The few studies that did classify children according to the number of times they were hit by their parents ... show that even one or two instances of corporal punishment are associated with a slightly higher probability of later physically abusing your own child, slightly more depressive symptoms, and a greater probability of violence and other crime later in life. The increase in these harmful side effects when parents use only moderate corporal punishment (hit only occasionally) may be small, but why run even that small risk when the evidence shows that corporal punishment is no more effective than other forms of discipline in the short run, and less effective in the long run.

# MYTH 5: PARENTS CAN'T STOP WITHOUT TRAINING

Although everyone can use additional skills in child management, there is no evidence that it takes some extraordinary training to be able to stop spanking. The most basic step in eliminating corporal punishment is for parent educators, psychologists, and pediatricians to make a simple and unambiguous statement that hitting a child is wrong and that a child *never*, ever, under any circumstances except literal physical self-defense, should be hit.

That idea has been rejected almost without exception every time I suggest it to parent educators or social scientists. They believe it would turn off parents and it could even be harmful because parents don't know what else to do. I think that belief is an unconscious defense of corporal punishment. I say that because I have never heard a parent educator say that before we can tell parents to never *verbally* attack a child, parents need training in alternatives. Some do need training, but everyone agrees that parents who use *psychological* pain as a method of discipline, such as insulting or demeaning, the child, should stop immediately. But when it comes to causing *physical* pain by spanking, all but a small minority of parent educators say that before parents are told to stop spanking, they need to learn alternative modes of discipline. I believe they should come right out, as they do for verbal attacks, and say without qualification that a child should *never* be hit....

This can be illustrated by looking at one situation that almost everyone thinks calls for spanking: when a toddler who runs out into the street. A typical parent will scream in terror, rush out and grab the child, and run to safety, telling the child, No! No! and explaining the danger—all of this accompanied by one or more slaps to the legs or behind.

The same sequence is as effective or more effective *without the spanking*. The spanking is not needed because even tiny children can sense the terror in the parent and understand, No! No! Newborn infants can tell the difference between when a mother is relaxed and when she is tense (Stern, 1977). Nevertheless, the fact that a child understands that something is wrong does not guarantee never again running into the street; just as spanking does not guarantee the child will not run into the street again....

Of course, when the child misbehaves again, most spanking parents do more than just repeat the spanking or spank harder. They usually also do things such as explain the danger to the child before letting the child go out again or warn the child that if it happens again, he or she will have to stay in the house for the afternoon, and so on. The irony is that when the child finally does learn, the parent attributes the success to the spanking, not the explanation.

# MYTH 6: IF YOU DON'T SPANK, YOUR CHILDREN WILL BE SPOILED OR RUN WILD

It is true that some non-spanked children run wild. But when that happens it is not because the parent didn't spank. It is because some parents think the alternative to spanking is to ignore a child's misbehavior or to replace spanking with verbal attacks such as, Only a dummy like you can't learn to keep your toys where I won't trip over them. The best alternative is to take firm action to correct the misbehavior without hitting. Firmly condemning what the child has done and explaining why it is wrong are usually enough. When they are not, there are a host of other things to do, such as requiring a time out or depriving the child of a privilege, neither of which involves hitting the child.

Suppose the child hits another child. Parents need to express outrage at this or the child may think it is acceptable behavior. The expression of outrage and a clear statement explaining why the child should never hit another person, except in self-defense, will do the trick in most cases. That does not mean one such warning will do the trick, any more than a single spanking will do the trick. It takes most children a while to learn such things, whatever methods the parents use.

The importance of how parents go about teaching children is clear from a classic study of American parenting—*Patterns of Child Rearing* by Sears, Maccoby, and Levin (1957). This study found two actions by parents that are linked to a high level of aggression by the child: permissiveness of the child's aggression, namely ignoring it when the child hits them or another child, and spanking to correct misbehavior. The most aggressive children... are children of parents who permitted aggression by the child and who also hit them for a variety of misbehavior. The least aggressive children are... children of parents who clearly condemned acts of aggression and who, by not spanking, acted in a way that demonstrated the principle that hitting is wrong.

There are other reasons why, on the average, the children of parents who do not spank are better behaved than children of parents who spank:

- Non-spanking parents pay more attention to their children's behavior, both good and bad, than parents who spank. Consequently, they are more likely to reward good behavior and less likely to ignore misbehavior.
- Their children have fewer opportunities to get into trouble because they are more likely to child-proof the home. For older children, they have clear rules about where they can go and who they can be with.
- Non-spanking parents tend to do more explaining and reasoning. This teaches the child how to use these essential tools to monitor his or her own behavior, whereas children who are spanked get less training in thinking things through.
- Non-spanking parents treat the child in ways that tend to bond the child to them and avoid acts that weaken the bond. They tend to use more rewards for good behavior, greater warmth and affection, and

fewer verbal assaults on the child (see Myth 9). By not spanking, they avoid anger and resentment over spanking. When there is a strong bond, children identify with the parent and want to avoid doing things the parent says are wrong. The child develops a conscience and lets that direct his or her behavior. That is exactly what Sears et al. found.

## MYTH 7: PARENTS SPANK RARELY OR ONLY FOR SERIOUS PROBLEMS

Contrary to this myth, parents who spank tend to use this method of discipline for almost any misbehavior. Many do not even give the child a warning. They spank before trying other things. Some advocates of spanking even recommend this. At any supermarket or other public place, you can see examples of a child doing something wrong, such as taking a can of food off the shelf. The parent then slaps the child's hand and puts back the can, sometimes without saying a word to the child. John Rosemond, the author of *Parent Power* (1981), says, "For me, spanking is a first resort. I seldom spank, but when I decide... I do it, and that's the end of it."

The high frequency of spanking also shows up among the parents [studied]. The typical parent of a toddler told us of about 15 instances in which he or she had hit the child during the previous 12 months. That is surely a minimum estimate because spanking a child is generally such a routine and unremarkable event that most instances are forgotten. Other studies, such as Newson and Newson (1963), report much more chronic hitting of children. My tabulations for mothers of three- to five-year-old children in the National Longitudinal Study of Youth found that almost two-thirds hit their children during the week of the interview, and they did it more then three times in just that one week. As high as that figure may seem, I think that daily spanking is not at all uncommon. It has not been documented because the parents who do it usually don't realize how often they are hitting their children.

## MYTH 8: BY THE TIME A CHILD IS A TEENAGER, PARENTS HAVE STOPPED

As we have seen, parents of children in their early teens are also heavy users of corporal punishment, although at that age it is more likely to be a slap on the face than on the behind.... [M]ore than half of the parents of 13- to 14-year-old children in our two national surveys hit their children in the previous 12 months. The percentage drops each year as children get older, but even at age 17, one out of five parents is still hitting. To make matters worse, these are minimum estimates.

Of the parents of teenagers who told us about using corporal punishment, 84 percent did it more than once in the previous 12 months. For boys, the average was seven times and for girls, five times. These are minimum figures because we interviewed the mother in half the families and the father in the other half. The number of times would be greater if we had information on what the parent who was not interviewed did.

## MYTH 9: IF PARENTS DON'T SPANK, THEY WILL VERBALLY ABUSE THEIR CHILD

The scientific evidence is exactly the opposite. Among the nationally representative samples of parents [surveyed], those who did the least spanking also engaged in the least verbal aggression.

It must be pointed out that non-spanking parents are an exceptional minority. They are defying the cultural prescription that says a good parent should spank if necessary. The depth of their involvement with their children probably results from the same underlying characteristics that led them to reject spanking. There is a danger that if more ordinary parents are told to never spank, they might replace spanking by ignoring misbehavior or by verbal attacks. Consequently, a campaign to end spanking must also stress the importance of avoiding verbal attacks as well as physical attacks, and also the importance of paying attention to misbehavior.

## MYTH 10: IT IS UNREALISTIC TO EXPECT PARENTS TO NEVER SPANK

It is no more unrealistic to expect parents to never hit a child than to expect that husbands should never hit their wives, or that no one should go through a stop sign, or that a supervisor should never hit an employee. Despite the legal prohibition, some husbands hit their wives, just as some drivers go through stop signs, and a supervisor occasionally may hit an employee.

If we were to prohibit spanking, as is the law in Sweden (see Deley, 1988; and Haeuser, 1990), there still would be parents who would continue to spank. But that is not a reason to avoid passing such a law here. Some people kill even though murder has been a crime since the dawn of history. Some husbands continue to hit their wives even though it has been more than a century since the courts stopped recognizing the common law right of a husband to "physically chastise an errant wife" (Calvert, 1974).

A law prohibiting spanking is unrealistic only because spanking is such an accepted part of American culture. That also was true of smoking. Yet in less than a generation we have made tremendous progress toward eliminating smoking. We can make similar progress toward eliminating spanking by showing parents that spanking is dangerous, that their children will be easier to bring up if they do not spank, and by clearly saying that a child should *never*, under any circumstances, be spanked.

## 8.4 LAWRENCE KOHLBERG

# *The Child as a Moral Philosopher*

Lawrence Kohlberg developed a theory of moral development that has been widely adopted by child and family professionals. He used the work of Swiss psychologist Jean Piaget in developing his theory, which explains how children perceive right and wrong based on their cognitive development. His theory includes three levels of moral thinking: preconventional, conventional, and postconventional. Children at the preconventional level define right and wrong in terms of how they are punished. At the conventional level, children feel a need to be good, and at the postconventional level, children become aware that a variety of values drive one's moral orientation. These levels are described in greater detail in this selection from "The Child as a Moral Philosopher," *Psychology Today* (1968).

Kohlberg (1927–1987) began his career as a clinical psychology trainee with the Veteran's Administration in 1952 after completing his doctoral degree at the University of Chicago. He worked in a variety of schools across the United States, and he was serving as a professor of education and social psychology at Harvard University, a post he had held since 1968, when he died from drowning at the age of 60. Kohlberg authored many publications related to his theory of moral development, including *Essays on Moral Development, vol. 1: The Philosophy of Moral Development* (Harper & Row, 1981) and *Child Psychology and Childhood Education: A Cognitive-Developmental View* (Longman, 1987).

**Key Concept:** moral development

How can one study morality? Current trends in the fields of ethics, linguistics, anthropology and cognitive psychology have suggested a new approach which seems to avoid the morass of semantical confusions, value-bias and cultural relativity in which the psychoanalytic and semantic approaches to morality have foundered. New scholarship in all these fields is now focusing upon structures, forms and relationships that seem to be common to all societies and all languages rather than upon the features that make particular languages or cultures different.

For 12 years, my colleagues and I studied the same group of 75 boys, following their development at three-year intervals from early adolescence through young manhood. At the start of the study, the boys were aged 10 to 16. We have now followed them through to ages 22 to 28. In addition, I have explored moral development in other cultures—Great Britain, Canada, Taiwan, Mexico and Turkey.

Inspired by Jean Piaget's pioneering effort to apply a structural approach to moral development, I have gradually elaborated over the years of my study a typological scheme describing general structures and forms of moral thought which can be defined independently of the specific content of particular moral decisions or actions.

The typology contains three distinct levels of moral thinking, and within each of these levels distinguishes two related stages. These levels and stages may be considered separate moral philosophies, distinct views of the sociomoral world.

We can speak of the child as having his own morality or series of moralities. Adults seldom listen to children's moralizing. If a child throws back a few adult cliches and behaves himself, most parents—and many anthropologists and psychologists as well—think that the child has adopted or internalized the appropriate parental standards.

Actually, as soon as we talk with children about morality, we find that they have many ways of making judgments which are not "internalized" from the outside, and which do not come in any direct and obvious way from parents, teachers or even peers.

# MORAL LEVELS

The *preconventional* level is the first of three levels of moral thinking, the second level is *conventional,* and the third *postconventional* or autonomous. While the preconventional child is often "well-behaved" and is responsive to cultural labels of good and bad, he interprets these labels in terms of their physical consequences (punishment, reward, exchange of favors) or in terms of the physical power of those who enunciate the rules and labels of good and bad.

This level is usually occupied by children aged four to 10, a fact long known to sensitive observers of children. The capacity of "properly behaved" children of this age to engage in cruel behavior when there are holes in the power structure is sometimes noted as tragic (*Lord of the Flies, High Wind in Jamaica*), sometimes as comic (Lucy in *Peanuts*).

The second or *conventional* level also can be described as conformist, but that is perhaps too smug a term. Maintaining the expectations and rules of the individual's family, group or nation is perceived as valuable in its own right. There is a concern not only with *conforming* to the individual's social order but in *maintaining,* supporting and justifying this order.

The *postconventional* level is characterized by a major thrust toward autonomous moral principles which have validity and application apart from authority of the groups or persons who hold them and apart from the individual's identification with those persons or groups.

## MORAL STAGES

Within each of these three levels there are two discernible stages. At the preconventional level we have:

Stage 1: Orientation toward punishment and unquestioning deference to superior power. The physical consequences of action regardless of their human meaning or value determine its goodness or badness.

Stage 2: Right action consists of that which instrumentally satisfies one's own needs and occasionally the needs of others. Human relations are viewed in terms like those of the marketplace. Elements of fairness, of reciprocity and equal sharing are present, but they are always interpreted in a physical, pragmatic way. Reciprocity is a matter of "you scratch my back and I'll scratch yours" not of loyalty, gratitude or justice.

And at the conventional level we have:

Stage 3: Good-boy–good-girl orientation. Good behavior is that which pleases or helps others and is approved by them. There is much conformity to stereotypical images of what is majority or "natural" behavior. Behavior is often judged by intention—"he means well" becomes important for the first time, and is overused, as by Charlie Brown in *Peanuts*. One seeks approval by being "nice."

Stage 4: Orientation toward authority, fixed rules and the maintenance of the social order. Right behavior consists of doing one's duty, showing respect for authority and maintaining the given social order for its own sake. One earns respect by performing dutifully.

At the postconventional level, we have:

Stage 5: A social-contract orientation, generally with legalistic and utilitarian overtones. Right action tends to be defined in terms of general rights and in terms of standards which have been critically examined and agreed upon by the whole society. There is a clear awareness of the relativism of personal values and opinions and a corresponding emphasis upon procedural rules for reaching consensus. Aside from what is constitutionally and democratically agreed upon, right or wrong is a matter of personal "values" and "opinion." The result is an emphasis upon the "legal point of view," but with an emphasis upon the possibility of *changing* law in terms of rational considerations of social utility, rather than freezing it in the terms of Stage 4 "law and order." Outside the legal realm, free agreement and contract are the binding elements of obligation. This is the "official" morality of American government, and finds its ground in the thought of the writers of the Constitution.

Stage 6: Orientation toward the decisions of conscience and toward self-chosen *ethical principles* appealing to logical comprehensiveness, universality and consistency. These principles are abstract and ethical (the Golden Rule, the categorical imperative); they are not concrete moral rules like the Ten Commandments. Instead, they are universal principles of *justice,* of the *reciprocity* and *equality* of human rights, and of respect for the dignity of human beings as *individual persons.* ...

## MORAL REASONS

In our research, we have found definite and universal levels of development in moral thought. In our study of 75 American boys from early adolescence on, these youths were presented hypothetical moral dilemmas, all deliberately philosophical, some of them found in medieval works of casuistry.

On the basis of their reasoning about these dilemmas at a given age, each boy's stage of thought could be determined for each of 25 basic moral concepts or aspects. One such aspect, for instance, is "Motive Given for Rule Obedience or Moral Action." In this instance, the six stages look like this:

1. Obey rules to avoid punishment.
2. Conform to obtain rewards, have favors returned, and so on.
3. Conform to avoid disapproval, dislike by others.
4. Conform to avoid censure by legitimate authorities and resultant guilt.
5. Conform to maintain the respect of the impartial spectator judging in terms of community welfare.
6. Conform to avoid self-condemnation.

In another of these 25 moral aspects, the value of human life, the six stages can be defined thus:

1. The value of a human life is confused with the value of physical objects and is based on the social status or physical attributes of its possessor.
2. The value of a human life is seen as instrumental to the satisfaction of the needs of its possessor or of other persons.
3. The value of a human life is based on the empathy and affection of family members and others toward its possessor.
4. Life is conceived as sacred in terms of its place in a categorical moral or religious order of rights and duties.
5. Life is valued both in terms of its relation to community welfare and in terms of life being a universal human right.
6. Belief in the sacredness of human life as representing a universal human value of respect for the individual.

I have called this scheme a typology. This is because about 50 per cent of most people's thinking will be at a single stage, regardless of the moral dilemma involved. We call our types *stages* because they seem to represent an *invariant developmental sequence.* "True" stages come one at a time and always in the same order.

All movement is forward in sequence, and does not skip steps. Children may move through these stages at varying speeds, of course, and may be found half in and half out of a particular stage. An individual may stop at any give stage and at any age, but if he continues to move, he must move in accord with these steps. Moral reasoning of the conventional or Stage 3–4 kind never occurs before the preconventional Stage-1 and Stage-2 thought has taken place. No adult in Stage 4 has gone through Stage 6, but all Stage-6 adults have gone at least through 4.

While the evidence is not complete, my study strongly suggests that moral change fits the stage pattern just described. (The major uncertainty is whether all Stage 6s go through Stage 5 or whether these are two alternate mature orientations.) . . .

## ACROSS CULTURES

When I first decided to explore moral development in other cultures, I was told by anthropologist friends that I would have to throw away my culture-bound moral concepts and stories and start from scratch learning a whole new set of values for each new culture. My first try consisted of a brace of villages, one Atayal (Malaysian aboriginal) and the other Taiwanese.

My guide was a young Chinese ethnographer who had written an account of the moral and religious patterns of the Atayal and Taiwanese villages. Taiwanese boys in the 10–13 age group were asked about a story involving theft of food. A man's wife is starving to death but the store owner won't give the man any food unless he can pay, which he can't. Should he break in and steal some food? Why? Many of the boys said, "He should steal the food for his wife because if she dies he'll have to pay for her funeral and that costs a lot."

My guide was amused by these responses, but I was relieved: they were of course "classic" Stage-2 responses. In the Atayal village, funerals weren't such a big thing, so the Stage-2 boys would say, "He should steal the food because he needs his wife to cook for him."

This means that we need to consult our anthropologists to know what content a Stage-2 child will include in his instrumental exchange calculations, or what a Stage-4 adult will identify as the proper social order. But one certainly doesn't have to start from scratch. What made my guide laugh was the difference in form between the children's Stage-2 thought and his own, a difference definable independently of particular cultures. . . .

# TRADING UP

In summary, the nature of our sequence is not significantly affected by widely varying social, cultural or religious conditions. The only thing that is affected is the *rate* at which individuals progress through this sequence.

Why should there be such a universal invariant sequence of development? In answering this question, we need first to analyze these developing social concepts in terms of their internal logical structure. At each stage, the same basic moral concept or aspect is defined, but at each higher stage this definition is more differentiated, more integrated and more general or universal. When one's concept of human life moves from Stage 1 to Stage 2 the value of life becomes more differentiated from the value of property, more integrated (the value of life enters an organizational hierarchy where it is "higher" than property so that one steals property in order to save life) and more universalized (the life of any sentient being is valuable regardless of status or property). The same advance is true at each stage in the hierarchy. Each step of development then is a better cognitive organization than the one before it, one which takes account of everything present in the previous stage, but making new distinctions and organizing them into a more comprehensive or more equilibrated structure. The fact that this is the case has been demonstrated by a series of studies indicating that children and adolescents comprehend all stages up to their own, but not more than one stage beyond their own. And importantly, *they prefer this next stage.*

We have conducted experimental moral discussion classes which show that the child at an earlier stage of development tends to move forward when confronted by the views of a child one stage further along. In an argument between a Stage-3 and Stage-4 child, the child in the third stage tends to move toward or into Stage 4, while the Stage-4 child understands but does not accept the arguments of the Stage-3 child.

Moral thought, then, seems to behave like all other kinds of thought. Progress through the moral levels and stages is characterized by increasing differentiation and increasing integration, and hence is the same kind of progress that scientific theory represents. Like acceptable scientific theory—or like *any* theory or structure of knowledge—moral thought may be considered partially to generate its own data as it goes along, or at least to expand so as to contain in a balanced, self-consistent way a wider and wider experiential field. The raw data in the case of our ethical philosophies may be considered as conflicts between roles, or values, or as the social order in which men live.

# PART FOUR

# Societal Influences on the Family

Chapter 9   Family Subcultures   215

Chapter 10   Work and the Family   235

Chapter 11   Violence and Abuse   256

Chapter 12   Stress and the Family   279

Chapter 13   Divorce and Remarriage   303

# On the Internet . . .

## Sites appropriate to Part Four

This site offers divorce statistics and articles on divorce and divorce reform.

```
http://www.divorcereform.org/econ.html
```

This is the home page of the Gay and Lesbian Alliance Against Defamation (GLAAD). It seeks to improve public attitudes toward homosexuality and to put an end to violence and discrimination against lesbians and gay men.

```
http://www.glaad.org/glaad/
```

CHAPTER 9 Family Subcultures

## 9.1 ROBERT STAPLES

# Changes in Black Family Structure

Robert Staples is a professor in the Department of Sociology at the University of California in San Francisco. He is among the most insightful and prolific writers about African American families. Staples has worked hard to refute many of the myths and stereotypes that tended to shroud earlier writings about African Americans in general and African American families in particular.

This selection is from "Changes in Black Family Structure: The Conflict Between Family Ideology and Structural Conditions," *Journal of Marriage and the Family* (November 1985). In it, Staples offers thought-provoking insights into the societal conditions that impede the fulfillment of typical family roles by African American men. He uses the theoretical framework of exchange theory as the basis for his arguments.

**Key Concept:** African American families

Historically, family theorists have argued that family structure and achievement interact with one another (Goode, 1963; Parsons and Bales, 1955). While that may have some validity for certain ethnic groups in America, none of those groups share the history and current social conditions of the black population in the United States. The peculiar history of black Americans, combined with structural conditions inimical to family formation and maintenance, have precipitated a crisis in the black family.

The basic theoretical perspective that informs the present analysis of black family life is that of exchange theory. This theory focuses on the reinforcement patterns, the history of rewards and costs, that lead people to do what they do. Essentially it argues that people will continue to do what they have found rewarding in the past. The basic premise here is that certain kinds of family structures exist when there is an exchange of rewards; on the other hand, family arrangements that are costly to one or both parties are much less likely to continue (Blau, 1964; Homans, 1961).

We assume, first, that being married is important to the majority of blacks, especially women. The fact that a near majority of black Americans are not married and living in traditional nuclear family units is not a result of any devaluation of marriage qua institution but rather a function of limited choices to find individuals in a restricted and small pool of potential partners who can successfully fulfill the normatively prescribed familial roles. While many blacks fail to marry, the history of black marriages shows only a minority surviving a lifetime with the same people. Exchange theory suggests that a person will not remain in a relationship where the services provided seem relatively meager compared with what the person knows about other relationships. It appears, then, that blacks do not marry because the perceived outcome, derived from knowledge of past rewards and costs, is one where alternative sources of goal mediation are preferred risks (Thibaut and Kelley, 1959). This cost-benefit analysis is mediated by structural conditions among the black male population that give rise to dissonance between black family ideology and actual family arrangements.

## BLACK FAMILY IDEOLOGY

The popular image of blacks as a group pressing for change in the area of race relations and economic opportunities often is translated into the image of a radical group in the forefront of social change. Other than being opposed to unfair discrimination against any group and favoring liberal social and economic policies, blacks often hold very traditional, even conservative, attitudes on other social issues—attitudes that place them in the mainstream of American mores and folkways. Some years ago Robert Hill (1972) noted that blacks have a strong work, achievement, and religious orientation. In particular, they believe strongly in the institution of the family. Gary and his associates (1983) found that the greatest source of life satisfaction among their black subjects was family life.

Their unconventional family arrangements and lifestyles easily can mislead outsiders to assume that blacks are strongly in accord with newly emerging alternative family lifestyles. While they are tolerant of people—especially blacks—who live in other than nuclear families, the family ideology of most blacks is in the direction of traditional family forms. Several studies, for instance, show that black women wish to marry and maintain traditional roles in the conjugal relationship (Broderick, 1965; Kulesky and Obordo, 1972). One indication of the black value of marriage is the fact that in the past more black women entered into a marital union than their white counterparts. In 1973, among black women 65 years and over, only 3.5% had never married, compared with 6.9% of white women (U.S. Bureau of the Census, 1978).

Among the most traditional of values is that of motherhood and childrearing. Except for college-educated black women, almost all black women bear children unless infertile. The role of mother is regarded as more important than any other role, including that of wife (Bell, 1971). While respectful of a woman's right to control her body, blacks tend to have a more negative attitude towards abortion. The Zelnik and Kantner (1974) study revealed that 35% of white teenagers terminated their first pregnancy by abortion compared with only 4% of black teenagers. However, some of this racial variation may reflect differential access to abortion rather than differential inclination. The black mother's childbearing techniques are also more traditional. She is more likely than the white mother to use physical, rather than verbal, punishment to enforce child discipline. Threatening the child with withdrawal of the mother's love, used by some white mothers, is uncommon among black women, which is one reason that the black mother-child bond remains strong throughout adult life (Nolle, 1972; Scanzoni, 1971).

Although there has been a noticeable increase in feminist ideology among women in the last 20 years, black women are greatly underrepresented in the women's liberation movement. Many black women continue to perceive racism —not sexism—as the biggest obstacle to their career and family goals. They are relatively uninvolved in such prominent feminist issues as pornography, sexual harassment, abortion, comparable pay, rape, etc. Moreover, they are more traditional in their definition of the roles that men and women should play in society and the family (Hershey, 1978). While their attitudes remain very traditional, the family lifestyles and arrangements of blacks are definitely unconventional. After examining the contemporary forms of black families, I explain it as a conflict between family ideology and structural conditions.

## CHANGES IN BLACK FAMILY STRUCTURE

Probably the most significant change in the black family during the last 30 years has been the proliferative growth of female-headed households. When the Moynihan Report (1965) was first issued in 1965, more than three-fourths of all black families with children were headed by a husband and wife. In 1982 barely one-half of all such families included parents of both sexes. Those households headed by black women had a median income of $7,458 in comparison with the median income of $20,586 for black married couples and $26,443 for white married couples (U.S. Bureau of the Census, 1983).

One of the most visible reasons for the dramatic increase in households headed by women has been a corresponding increase in out-of-wedlock births as a proportion of all births to black women. Approximately 52% of all children born to black women in 1982 were conceived out-of-wedlock. This high percentage of out-of-wedlock births is attributed largely to teenage pregnancies. Among women who turned 20 during the second half of the 1970s, 41% of blacks but only 19% of whites had already given birth. Within that same group of young black women, about 75% of all births were out-of-wedlock, compared with only 25% of births to young white women (U.S. Bureau of the Census, 1984). Although black women were twice as likely to have had nonmarital sexual intercourse as whites by the age of 19, their rate of sexual activity was remaining constant, while such activity was rapidly increasing among white teenagers (Zelnik and Kantner, 1977).

Not only has the number and proportion of black female-headed households grown rapidly, but the majority of adult black women are not married and living with spouses. In 1982 approximately 56% of all black women over the age of 14 were separated, divorced, widowed, or never married. Under the age of 30, the majority of them fall into the never-married category; past age 30 most of them are listed as divorced or separated, with a small percentage counted among the widowed. The high divorce rate creates a number of female-headed households among black women over age 30. While one out of two white marriages will end in divorce, two out of three black marriages will eventually dissolve; moreover, black women who divorce are less likely than their white counterparts to remarry. Currently, one in four adult black women are divorced (U.S. Bureau of the Census, 1983).

Some 20 years since the publication of the Moynihan Report (1965), the figures he cited as evidence that the black family was deteriorating have doubled, almost tripled in some areas. How is it that a group that regards family life as its most important source of satisfaction finds a majority of its women unmarried? Why does a group with more traditional sexual values than its white peers have a majority of its children born out-of-wedlock? Finally, we must ask how a group that places such importance on the traditional nuclear family finds a near majority of its members living in single-parent households. While a number of reasons have been cited by theorists, I suggest that the dominant force can be found in structural conditions of the black population.

# FAMILY IDEOLOGY VS. STRUCTURAL CONDITIONS

The basis of a stable family rests on the willingness, and ability, of men and women to marry, bear and rear children, and fulfill socially prescribed familial roles. In the case of women, those roles have been defined traditionally as the carrying out of domestic functions such as cooking and cleaning; giving birth to children and socializing them; providing sexual gratification, companionship, and emotional support to their husbands. There is abundant evidence that black women are willing and able to fulfill those roles (Staples, 1973). Conversely, the roles of men in the family are more narrowly confined to economic provider and family leader, but there are indications that a majority of black American males cannot implement those roles. When it comes to a choice between remaining single or getting married, individuals often do a cost-benefit analysis. Marriage is frequently a quid pro quo arrangement. The desire to enter and maintain a conjugal relationship is contingent on their perception of the benefits that can be acquired and, conversely, of the anticipated costs (Blau, 1964).

When selecting a mate, black women must consider the nature of the pool from which they will draw. In 98% of marriages with a black female bride, the groom will be a black male. Hence, her pool consists of unmarried black males with a variety of attributes. The most distinguishing characteristics of that pool is the shortage of men relative to the number of women during the marriageable years. According to the U.S. Bureau of the Census (1983), there are almost 1,500,000 more black women than men over the age of 14. By the Census Bureau's own account, the undercount of black males means that about 925,000 black males exist that were not added to the black population total. It should be noted that the uncounted black male is likely to be transient and unemployed (Joe and Yu, 1984). Since there is an excess number of black males at birth, the subsequent shortage of black males over the age of 14 must be attributed to their higher infant mortality rate and the considerably greater mortality rate of young black males through such causes as homicide, accidents, suicide, drug overdose, and war casualty (Staples, 1982; Stewart and Scott, 1978).

The major problem for black women, however, is not the quantity in the available supply of potential mates, but the quality. Whereas black women may select a mate on the basis of a number of attributes, a minimum prerequisite is that he be gainfully and regularly employed. According to a study by Joe and Yu (1984), almost a majority of working-age black males fail to meet those minimum prerequisites. After an analysis of the economic and census data, they concluded that 46% of the 8.8 million black men of working age were not in the labor force. Based on 1982 statistics, they found that 1.2 million black men were unemployed, 1.8 million had dropped out of the labor force, 186,000 were in prison, and 925,000 were classified as "missing" because the Census Bureau said it could not locate them.

Furthermore, their study overstates the number of "desirable" and available black males in the marriage pool. Even with the census undercount, there are still a half million more black women over the age of 14 than black men. Also, we must subtract from the marriage pool black men with certain characteristics by which they substantially outnumber black women. Among those characteristics would be blacks serving in the Armed Forces. Approximately 90% of them will be male. The U.S. Bureau of the Census (1983) reports that there were 415,000 blacks under arms in 1982, representing 20% of all United States military personnel. It can be stated reliably that a large number of those black males had poor prospects for employment in the civilian labor force (Stewart and Scott, 1978). While the salaries and other benefits of military personnel have improved in recent years and a number of black soldiers are currently married, the military does take out of circulation a number of marriage-age black males by stationing them in foreign posts and isolated military stations. Furthermore, once their period of enlistment ends, black veterans experience a higher rate of unemployment, even in relation to black civilian males with no military service (Stewart and Scott, 1978). Hence, military service only postpones the entry of black males into the ranks of the unemployed, one reason black males have a higher rate of re-enlistment than their white counterparts.

Included in the factors that reduce the number of desirable black males in the marriage pool is the high rate of underemployed black males. The U.S. Civil Rights Commission (1982) reported that black men are overeducated for their jobs and have greater difficulty translating education into suitable occupations. Even college-educated black males have an unemployment rate four times greater than their white peers. Among black males employed in the labor force, one out of three will suffer from unemployment in a given year (Staples, 1982). However, these facts serve to explain why black marriages dissolve, not why they never take place. In Hampton's (1980) study, the respondents who reported the highest number of employment problems had a marital disruption rate three times higher than the overall rate for the sample.

Another group of black males regarded as undesirable or unavailable are those confined to mental institutions or who are otherwise mentally unstable. While their exact number is unknown, black males are more likely to be committed to mental institutions than are black women, and the strictures of racism are such that blacks are more likely to suffer from mental distress. In 1970, 240 nonwhites per 100,000 population were confined to mental institutions, compared with 162 whites per 100,000 population. Blacks also used community mental health centers at a rate almost twice their proportion in the general population. The rate of drug and alcohol abuse is much greater among the black population—especially males—based on their overrepresentation among patients receiving treatment services (U.S. Dept. of Health, Education and Welfare, 1979: 163–183). It is estimated that as many as one-third of the young black males in the inner city have serious drug problems (Staples, 1982). Many of the mentally unstable, drug and alcohol abusers will have been included in the figures on black males who have dropped out of the labor force or are incarcerated in prison. The magnitude of the problem simply reinforces the fact that black women are seriously disadvantaged in choosing from the eligible and desirable males in the marriage pool.

A large category of black males who fit into the desirable group must also be considered not available. By all reliable estimates, the black male homosexual population is considerably larger than the black female homosexual population (Bell and Weinberg, 1978). Based on the often-quoted Kinsey estimate (Kinsey et al., 1948) that 10% of the adult male population is homosexual, that would mean about 800,000 black men are not available to heterosexual black women. Of course, many of these gay males do marry, for a variety of reasons, and serve well in the roles of husband and father; but, due to the increasing public tolerance of overt male homosexuality, it is reasonable to expect that fewer gay males will choose to enter into heterosexual marriages in the future. Finally, it should be noted that black men marry outside their race at a rate twice as great as that of black women (Heer, 1974; Staples, 1982).

Although the shortage and desirability of black males in the marriage pool largely affects the non-college-educated black woman's marriage chances, the college-educated black female is not spared the problem if she desires to marry within her race and socioeconomic level. In 1980 there were 133,000 more black women enrolled in college than black men—about 57% of all black college students. Moreover, black male students have a much higher attrition rate than their female peers. In the University of California system, for instance, only 12 of every 100 black male students graduate within four years. Thus, in 1981, 36,200 of 60,700 bachelor's degrees awarded to blacks went to women (60%); and between the years 1976 and 1981, black women receiving bachelor's degrees increased by 9%, and comparable black males declined by 9%. These same trends existed for graduate degrees during the years 1976–1981: black women declined by 12% and black men by 21% in the receipt of the master's degree; in the receipt of the first professional degree, black women increased by 71% while black men declined by 21%; and at the doctoral level, black men declined by 10%, while black women increased at a rate of 29% (National Center for Education Statistics, 1983).

College-educated black women do have the option of marrying men with less education and making a viable choice. In the past as many as 50% of college-educated black women married men of a lower socioeconomic level (Noble, 1956), but increasingly there is resistance among these women to marrying down. Almost one-third of college-educated black women remain unmarried past the age of 30 (Bayer, 1972; Staples, 1981). Of course, they face a similar shortage in the marriage pool of male high school graduates and must compete with lesser educated black women for these same men. Also, such middle-level men tend to marry early and have the most stable marriages in the black community (Glick and Mills, 1974). The marriage patterns of college-educated black males tend to put college-educated black women at a disadvantage. Many of these men marry women of a lower educational level, and the interracial marriage rate is highest in this group of black men (Heer, 1974; Staples, 1981).

## STRUCTURAL CONDITIONS AND THE CHANGING BLACK FAMILY

There is no great mystery as to what has happened to the black family in the last 20 years: it is an acceleration of trends set in motion during the 1960s. A highly sexualized culture—via media, clothing and example—has conveyed to American youth the notion that nonmarital sexual relations are not only acceptable but required for individual fulfillment. Women are reaching puberty earlier and emotional maturity later. Furthermore, the consequences of teenage sexual behavior are counteracted somewhat by easier access to effective contraceptives and abortion; and the number of pregnant teenagers has not really increased—only the proportion of births to that group of women as a result of the rapid decline in births to older married women.

While the nonmarital sexual activity rate of black and white teenage women is converging, the black female is more likely to be engaged in unprotected intercourse and less likely to marry or have an abortion if she becomes pregnant. According to Zelnik and Kantner (1974) only 8.5% of their black sample (15–19 years) entered into marriage as an outcome of premarital pregnancy, compared with 50.8% of comparable white women. In addition, 35.5% of white women had their premarital pregnancies terminated by abortion, in contrast to 4.9% of similar black women.

While it is reasonable to question the wisdom of young black women attaining motherhood at such an early age, their decision to bear the children and raise them alone reflects their traditional values and limited options in life. Among black males their age, the official unemployment rate is 52%, and as many as 75% of young black men remain outside the work force (Malabre, 1980). While employment may be easier for black women to obtain, it often will be in dead-end jobs that pay only half the wages earned by white males. Rather than remain childless and husbandless, these women choose to have the children and raise them alone. A good explanation of these life choices is given by Hortense Canady, President of Delta Sigma Theta Sorority (1984:40): "Having a child is probably the best thing that's ever going to happen to them in their whole lifetime and the only thing they can contribute—this is not true in most other countries in the world. But if you belong to a class or a group of people who have no educational opportunities stretching out before them, no other goals, that's probably the single, best thing that's ever going to happen to you in your life."

Having limited educational and career options to set against bearing a child is not the only reason for the increase in female-headed households. A welfare system that often requires men to be absent from the home is part of the problem; and black women realize that the meager welfare payments are more reliable than a class of men who may never know gainful employment in their entire lives. In general, unemployed men do not make good husbands and fathers. Since employment and income are the measure of a man's masculinity in this society, men who have neither do not tend to feel good about themselves or act very positively toward their wives and children. In the Hampton (1980) study, for example, husbands who were not satisfied with themselves had a fairly high level of marital disruption.

However, the major reason for the increase in black female-headed households is the lack of "desirable" men with whom to form monogamous marriages. According to Joe and Yu (1984), between 1976 and 1983 the number of black families headed by women rose by 700,000, and the ranks of black men out of the labor force or unemployed increased by the same number. The same trend has existed for the last 25 years: almost 75% of black men were working in 1960, and black families headed by women accounted for 21% of all black families in the same year; but by 1982 only 54% of all black men were in the labor force, and 42% of all black families were headed by women (Joe and Yu, 1984).

Having a child out-of-wedlock and failing to marry accounts for 41% of all black households headed by women. Another 51% are divorced or separated from their spouses (U.S. Bureau of the Census, 1983). These marriage disruptions are generally susceptible to the same structural conditions that plague never-married black women. Unemployment and underemployment, the public assistance complex, the educational system, and the health care system all produce economic and psychological alienation in the black male. As Hampton (1980) found, the pressures that push many black males out of other social institutions within society also work to push them out of marital relationships. For every 1,000 black married persons with spouses present, the number of divorces increased from 92 in 1971 to 233 in 1981; the comparable increase for whites was from 48 to 100. Black separations increased from 172 to 225 per 1,000 married persons in the same period; white separations rose from 21 to 29 (U.S. Bureau of the Census, 1983).

A number of social characteristics place blacks at risk for divorce. They have a higher rate of urbanization, greater independence of women, earlier age at marriage, earlier fertility, a higher education and income levels for the wife and lower income status for the husband (Cherlin, 1981). Most black marriages involve a wife who is more highly educated than her husband (Spanier and Glick, 1980). In one out of five black marriages, the wife earns a higher income than her husband (U.S. Bureau of the Census, 1983). This incongruity between the socially assigned roles of the male as the primary provider and the wife as a subordinate member of the marital dyad may undermine the husband's self-esteem, frustrate the wife, and create marital dissatisfaction for both partners. In Hampton's (1980) study, the highest percentage of disrupted marriages (27.4%) was observed among wives with incomes accounting for 40% or more of the family's income. His explanation is that, when women have other means of support in the form of welfare or their own earnings, they may be less constrained to remain in a personally unsatisfying relationship. Alternatively, the wife may be satisfied with the husband's role; but her high income may threaten the husband's authority and status, undermining his self-concept so that *he* becomes unhappy.

These problems of the black family are only variations of the general problems of American families. The direction of change in the family structure is basically the same for all racial groups in the United States and for the same reasons. Guttentag and Secord (1983) demonstrated that unbalanced sex ratios have certain predictable consequences for relationships between men and women. They give rise to higher rates of singlehood, divorce, out-of-wedlock births, and female-headed households in different historical epochs and across different societies. According to Ehrenreich (1983) the breakdown of the family began in the 1950s when men began a flight from commitment to the husband and father role. In the case of the black family, it stems from the institutional decimation of black males.

# REFERENCES

Bayer, A. 1972. "College impact on marriage." Journal of Marriage and the Family 34 (November): 600–610.
Bell, A. and Weinberg, M. 1978. Homosexualities. New York: Simon and Schuster.
Bell, R. 1971. "The related importance of mother and wife roles among black lower class women." Pp. 248–255 in R. Staples (Ed.), The Black Family: Essays and Studies (2nd ed.). Belmont, CA: Wadsworth.
Blau, P. 1964. Exchange and Power in Social Life. New York: John Wiley.

Broderick, C. 1965. "Social heterosexual development among urban Negroes and whites." Journal of Marriage and the Family 27 (May): 200–203.

Canady, H. 1984. Quoted in "Words of the week." Jet Magazine (March 19): 40.

Cherlin, H. 1981. Marriage, Divorce, Remarriage. Cambridge, MA: Harvard University Press.

Ehrenreich, B. 1983. The Hearts of Men: American Dreams and the Flight from Commitment. Garden City, NY: Doubleday.

Gary, L., Beatty, L., Berry, G. and Price, M. 1983. Stable Black Families. Final Report. Institute for Urban Affairs and Research, Howard University, Washington, DC.

Glick, P. and Mills, K. 1974. Black Families: Marriage Patterns and Living Arrangements. Atlanta: Atlanta University, 9.

Goode, W. 1963. World Revolution and Changing Family Patterns. Glencoe, IL: The Free Press.

Guttentag, M. and Secord, P. 1983. Too Many Women: The Sex Ratio Question. Beverly Hills, CA: Sage.

Hampton, R. 1980. "Institutional decimation, marital exchange and disruption in black families." Western Journal of Black Studies 4 (Summer): 132–139.

Heer, D. 1974. "The prevalence of black-white marriages in the United States 1960 and 1970." Journal of Marriage and the Family 35 (February): 246–258.

Hershey, M. 1978. "Racial differences in sex role identities and sex stereotyping: evidence against a common assumption." Social Science Quarterly 58 (March): 583–596.

Hill, R. 1972. The Strengths of Black Families. New York: Emerson Hall.

Homans, G. 1961. Social Behavior: Its Elementary Forms. New York: Harcourt, Brace and World.

Joe, T. and Yu, P. 1984. The "Flip-Side" of Black Families Headed by Women: The Economic Status of Black Men. Washington, DC: The Center for the Study of Social Policy.

Kinsey, A., Pomeroy, W. and Martin, C. 1948. Sexual Behavior in the Human Male. Philadelphia: W. B. Saunders.

Kulesky, W. and Obordo, A. 1972. "A racial comparison of teenage girls projections for marriage and procreation." Journal of Marriage and the Family 34 (February): 75–84.

Malabre, A., Jr. 1980. "Recession hits blacks harder than whites." The Wall Street Journal (August 21): 1.

Moynihan, D. P. 1965. The Negro Family: The Case for National Action. Washington, DC: U.S. Government Printing Office.

National Center for Education Statistics. 1983. Participation of Black Students in Higher Education: A Statistical Profile from 1970–71 to 1980–81. Washington, DC: U.S. Department of Education.

Noble, J. 1956. The Negro Woman College Graduate. New York: Columbia University Press.

Nolle, D. 1972. "Changes in black sons and daughters: a panel analysis of black adolescents' orientation toward their parents." Journal of Marriage and the Family 34 (August): 443–447.

Parson, R. and Bales, R. 1955. Family, Socialization and Interaction Process. Glencoe, IL: The Free Press.

Scanzoni, J. 1971. The Black Family in Modern Society. Boston: Allyn and Bacon.

Spanier, G. and Glick, P. 1980. "Mate selection differentials between blacks and whites in the United States." Social Forces 58 (March): 707–725.

Staples, R. 1973. The Black Woman in America: Sex, Marriage and the Family. Chicago: Nelson-Hall.

Staples, R. 1981. The World of Black Singles: Changing Patterns of Male-Female Relations. Westport, CT: Greenwood Press.

Staples, R. 1982. Black Masculinity: The Black Male's Role in American Society. San Francisco: The Black Scholar Press.

Stewart, J. and Scott, J. 1978. "The institutional decimation of black males." Western Journal of Black Studies 2 (Summer): 82–92.

Thibaut, J. W. and Kelley, H. W. 1959. The Social Psychology of Groups. New York: John Wiley.

U.S. Bureau of the Census. 1974. Marital Status and Living Arrangements: March 1973, Series P-20. Washington, DC: Government Printing Office.

U. S. Bureau of the Census. 1978. Current Population Reports. March 1977, Series P-20, No. 314. Washington, DC: Government Printing Office.

U. S. Bureau of the Census. 1983. America's Black Population, 1970 to 1982: A Statistical View, July 1983, Series P10/POP83. Washington, DC: Government Printing Office.

U. S. Bureau of the Census. 1984. Fertility of American Women: June 1983, Series P-20, No. 386. Washington, DC: Government Printing Office.

U.S. Civil Rights Commission. 1982. Unemployment and Underemployment Among Blacks, Hispanics and Women (November). Washington, DC: Government Printing Office.

U.S. Dept. of Health, Education and Welfare. 1979. Health Status of Minorities and Low-Income Groups. Washington, DC: Government Printing Office.

Zelnik, M. and Kantner, J. F. 1974. "The resolution of teenage first pregnancies." Family Planning Perspectives (Spring): 74–80.

Zelnick, M. and Kantner, J. F. 1977. "Sexual and contraceptive experience of young unmarried women in the United States, 1976 and 1971." Family Planning Perspectives 9 (May/June): 55–59.

9.2 JUDSON T. LANDIS

# Religiousness, Family Relationships, and Family Values in Protestant, Catholic, and Jewish Families

This selection is from "Religiousness, Family Relationships, and Family Values in Protestant, Catholic, and Jewish Families," by Judson T. Landis, *Marriage and Family Living* (November 1960). It was originally presented at the 1959 annual meeting of the National Council on Family Relations. (This professional organization continues to be one of the foremost promoters of research on marriage and the family in the world.) Landis's paper was based upon data collected in the early 1950s. The main focus of this research was to examine whether or not characteristics of religious and nonreligious families affect the attitudes of the children in these homes. It is one of the earliest research studies dealing with religion and the family.

Landis is currently chair of the Department of Sociology at California State University at Sacramento. Landis coauthored with his wife, Mary G. Landis, *Building a Successful Marriage* (Prentice Hall, 1948), which became one of the more popular textbooks on marriage and the family. One of his major areas of research and publication in marriage and the family was religiosity as it impacts family life.

**Key Concept:** religion and the family

$A$ series of sociological studies have found an association between marital success and the religious background of married couples. One or more studies of married couples found Sunday school attendance in childhood, church membership and attendance, participation in church activities, and having been married in a religious rather than a civil ceremony to be associated with success in marriage.[1] Burgess and Cottrell, and Burgess and Wallin gave some weight to these background situations in constructing their marital prediction schedules.[2]

Is the association between religious background and marital success explainable primarily in terms of the socially active, conventional characteristics of families who are likely to be religion oriented? Or are certain kinds of relationships, value patterns, or interactional patterns found in religious families, which in themselves tend to be predictive of marriage success?

The present study was initiated to examine in more detail some of the characteristics of religiously and nonreligiously oriented homes as they seem to be revealed through parent-child relationships and attitudes held by the children. Our hypothesis is that in any culture those who tend to be among the more stable and conventional in the society not only subscribe to a religious faith and have more stability in marriage, but further that: (1) parents who subscribe to religion pass on to their children religious and social values closely related to values of the parents, which values in themselves may be predictive of success in marriage for the children; (2) that closeness to parents and a higher conception of self are more characteristic of children from religiously oriented families than from the non-religiously oriented; (3) that a positive association between religiousness and (a) marriage stability, and (b) the transmission of family and social values would be found within each of the major faith groups in a society.

In order to test these hypotheses we analyzed data provided by college students concerning the religiousness of their parental family, the parental happiness as the children assessed it, their own religious and social values, their relationship with parents, their assessment of the pattern of father or mother dominance in the home, and their conception of self.

From a sample composed of 3,000 students in family sociology courses, we use in this study responses of single students and those who specified their religious preference as Protestant, Catholic, Jew, and none.[3] Students of other faiths and married students were eliminated from the sample. For our sample we have 2,654 subjects, 904 males and 1,750 females. The students in the sample are of middle class or upper middle class background; slightly over half of the fathers of the students were professional men or were engaged in business, and about 40 per cent of both the fathers and the mothers had had some college education.

Each respondent stated his own religious preference and rated his family on religiousness at the time that he was growing up. Ratings on religiousness were: very devout, devout, slightly religious, indifferent, antagonistic. In the analysis we combined very devout and devout, and indifferent and antagonistic. When this was done 34.4 per cent of the families were rated as devout by the children, 48.1 per cent were rated as religious and 17.5 per cent as indifferent. *No significant differences were found in religiousness when the data were analyzed by the occupation of the father.*

Sixty-nine per cent of the respondents gave Protestant as their religious preference, 15.2 per cent Catholic, 9.3 per cent Jewish, and 6.4 per cent gave none.

# FINDINGS OF THE STUDY

*Marital happiness, divorce and religiousness.* The findings support previous sociological studies which have found a positive association between religiousness and success in marriage. In our sample there is a close association between parents' marital happiness and the religiousness of the parents as assessed by their children. There is also a close association between separation and divorce of parents and parental religiousness as assessed by the children. Percentages of divorced and separated parents were: 5.5 per cent of the devout, 8.9 per cent of the religious, 19.8 per cent of the indifferent. The information as given here does not tell us whether religious people who divorce then become indifferent to religion or whether religiously indifferent people are more likely to divorce.

The association between parents' marital success and religiousness held for Protestants, Catholics, and those of no faith, and as reported by male and female students within each of these faith groups. Jewish female respondents reported the same pattern as other female students although the percentage differences were not significant. The responses of the Jewish male students showed a slight negative association between parents' marital happiness and religiousness.

There were great differences in parental marital happiness as reported by the children in the four faith groups. Approximately 80 per cent of the Jewish students, 70 per cent of the Protestants, 70 per cent of the Catholics, and 47 per cent of those with no religious preference reported their parents to be happy or very happy. The occurrence of divorce and separation also differed widely as reported by the faith groups. The percentages of divorced and separated parents were: Protestant, 10.0 per cent; Catholic, 7.7 per cent; Jewish, 3.3 per cent; no faith, 18.2 per cent.

It will be observed that the Jewish group in our study stands out as different from the other groups. The Jews in the study rated low in religiousness but high in marital happiness when compared with the other faith groups.

Little relationship between religiousness and parents' marital happiness appeared for the Jews in this study. Throughout the remainder of the study we will observe this same tendency among Jews; a low positive association between family religiousness, and (1) values held by children and (2) family relationships.

*Closeness to mother and father and religiousness of parents.* Religiousness of parents is positively associated with the child's reported feeling of closeness to mother and father. Females report a closer relationship to both parents than do males. For both sexes the feeling of closeness to the father is positively associated with parental religiousness more than is closeness to the mother. In looking at the four faith groups by devoutness of the parents we found that the positive association between religiousness and closeness to parents held for all groups except for Jewish males and those of no religious preference (both sexes). Closeness of the children to their parents differed widely by faith. Jews were the closest to their parents, Catholics next, then Protestants. Those of no specific faith were the most distant from their parents. Distance of children from parents appears to be in part dependent upon success or failure of the parents' marriage. Jewish parents in our sample had the happiest marriages and the fewest divorces while the parents of those children reporting no specific faith had the fewest happy marriages and the highest percentage of divorces.

Since distance from parents was found to be associated with success of the parents' marriages we thought it might be that marital happiness rather than religiousness was the controlling factor in children's feeling close to or distant from their parents. We examined our data by looking at the separate marital happiness groups—the happy, the average, and the unhappy. These three happiness groups were then sorted by the three devoutness groups—the devout, the slightly religious, and the indifferent—and related to the variable of closeness of children to parents. The analyses showed devoutness to be positively associated with closeness of children to parents in marriages classified as happy (at the .01 level of confidence) and marriages classified as average (percentages in the direction of positive association but not significant), but showed no relationship between devoutness and closeness of children to parents in marriages classified as unhappy. In happy marriages both the happiness of parents and the devoutness of parents are important factors leading to the closeness of children to parents; but stronger as a determining factor is the happiness of parents' marriage. In unhappy marriages religiousness is not associated with closeness of children to parents.

*Conception of self and family religiousness.* Several items relative to the individual's conception of self were tested to see whether family religiousness might be associated with a higher conception of self in the children. Respondents reported upon their wishes to be of the opposite sex. Desire to be of the other sex would seem to indicate at least some dissatisfaction with the self. We found no association at all between frequency of desire to be of the other sex and family religiousness.

The respondents rated their own physical appearance in early adolescence (before 15) on a five-point scale. Although percentages were consistently in the direction of high family religiousness being associated with a self-rating of above average in physical appearance, and family religious indifference being associated with a rating of below average in physical appearance, the differences were not significant at the 5 per cent level.

Respondents gave an evaluation of their own personalities and personal attractiveness as they felt it to have been in early adolescence. For both sexes a high evaluation of one's own personality was found to be associated with high family religiousness, and a low evaluation of one's own personality with family religious indifference. However, the relationship for males was not significant at the 5 per cent level of confidence.

Difficulty or ease that females have in making friends with the other sex in early adolescence is positively associated with family religiousness. Percentages are consistently in the direction of significance for males, also, but they are not significant at the 5 per cent level. The association between difficulty or ease in making friends with the other sex and family religiousness was generally consistent for faith groups and for both sexes. Males and females reporting no religious preference reported the largest percentages having great difficulty in making friends with the other sex.

Of all the items relating conception of self and family religiousness the most significant relationship found was on doubtfulness of one's ability to have a successful marriage. Both males and females who reported no doubt about having a successful marriage were more likely to be from devout homes; those who reported frequent doubts were more likely to be from indifferent homes. The association was found to be consistent for both sexes in all faith groups. Those of no religious faith have by far the largest percentages of males (83 per cent) and females (92 per cent) expressing doubts about their chances for successful marriages. Approximately 75 per cent of males and females indicating religious affiliation reported such doubts. A difference found within the religious faiths was that Catholics from devout or slightly religious families expressed more doubts of having a successful marriage than Jews and Protestants from devout or slightly religious families.

To summarize here: the total picture is that a higher conception of self is associated with growing up in a devout religious home, especially for females. Differences not found to be significant for males were in the same direction.

*Mother or father dominance in the home and family religiousness.* Because of the Protestant and Catholic emphasis upon the teachings of the Apostle Paul it might seem that devout families of these faiths would be husband dominated. However, our data showed devoutness to be associated with the 50-50 pattern of dominance in the home as reported by these students, while indifference to religion is associated with the extremes of a father- *or* mother-dominated home. Differences were significant at the 1 per cent level of confidence. The four faith groups were similar in their reports upon patterns of dominance in the home; that is, about the same percentages in all faith groups and in the non-faith group reported the 50-50 pattern of dominance and the same percentages reported mother- or father-dominated homes.

The association between patterns of dominance and family religiousness held for Protestants and Catholics, but it did not hold for Jews and those of no faith preference.

*Family religiousness and the children's religiousness.* A close association exists between religiousness of children and religiousness of parents. Children of devout parents tend to report themselves as devout and children of religiously indifferent families tend to report themselves as indifferent to religion. The association between religiousness of children and religiousness of parents held for all faith groups and for both sexes.

Two interesting faith differences appeared. One difference is that Protestant and Catholic women rated themselves as more devout than their parents. In contrast, Jewish children and children of no specific faith rated themselves as less devout than their parents. Another difference was that a larger proportion of Catholic children rated their parents' religiousness as being high than did either of the other groups. Jews were at the opposite extreme; Protestants were in between.

*Social values and family religiousness.* Willingness or unwillingness to marry a person of a different religious faith is closely associated with family religiousness. Of devout, slightly religious, and indifferent females, 48, 57, and 67 per cent, respectively, reported they would be willing to marry outside their faith. The percentages for the respective groups of males are 43, 57, and 71. The relationship holds for all faith groups and for both sexes. Jews are the least willing to marry outside their faith, and among Jewish females willingness to marry outside the Jewish faith has a very close association to family religiousness. Only 12 per cent of Jewish females from devout families would marry outside the faith while 60 per cent of Jewish females from indifferent families would marry outside the faith. Family religiousness of Catholics, especially Catholic females, is not highly related to willingness to marry outside the faith. Of Catholic females 69 per cent of those from devout families would marry outside the faith and 77 per cent of those from indifferent families. Little difference was found between males and females of a faith in their expressed willingness to marry outside the faith, excepting that Jewish males were more willing to marry outside the faith than Jewish females.

Willingness or unwillingness to adopt the faith of the spouse is associated with religiousness of the family among females but not among males. Willingness or unwillingness to change faith to that of the spouse is associated with religiousness among females of all faiths, but the relationship is not high. Among all faiths the percentage of women who say they would change faith is higher than the percentage of men who say they would change faith. The willingness or unwillingness of the male to change faith seems to have nothing to do with his religiousness.

Although Catholics express the most willingness to marry outside the faith (72 per cent), they express the least willingness to change faiths. Only 13 per cent of the Catholic females who report they would marry outside their faith would change to the faith of the spouse and only 7 per cent of the Catholic males. Jewish males show a similar pattern; 41 per cent reported they would be willing to marry outside their faith, but only 13 per cent said they would change to the faith of the spouse. Those reporting no religious faith were most willing to marry across faith lines (85 per cent of the females and 77 per cent of the males), but they were not willing to take up a religious faith; only 38 per cent of the females and 20 per cent of the males said they would take the spouse's religious faith.

Studies of mixed religious marriages have found a higher divorce rate in mixed religious marriages than in marriages within a faith.[4] Our data here show that it is those who were reared in homes indifferent or antagonistic to a faith who express most willingness to make a mixed marriage. In other words, those from nonreligious homes are more willing to make marriages which have been found to have above average hazards to success.

Willingness or unwillingness to marry a divorced person is associated with religiousness in the family home. Of devout, slightly religious, and indifferent females, 39, 52, and 58 per cent, respectively, reported they would be willing to marry a divorced person. The percentages for the respective groups of males are 44, 63, and 56. These differences are significant at the .01 level of confidence. The relationship holds for all faith groups and for both sexes. Males of all faith groups are more willing to marry a divorced person than are females. Of the faith groups Catholics are the least willing to marry a divorced person while those of no faith preference are the most willing.

Those who have failed in one marriage are more likely to fail a second time according to analyses of marriage and divorce statistics.[5] Our data suggest here, again, that children reared in the least religious homes are those the most willing to make a marriage which has greater hazards.

*Sex behavior, sex values and family religiousness.* The respondents reported on their virginity at the time of the study. According to our data, family religiousness is not significantly associated with virginity in females although the percentages are in the direction of a positive association. A difference appeared with males in that more of the males from devout Protestant families are virgins than males from families classified as slightly religious or indifferent. Males from Catholic, Jewish, or families of no religious preference show little association between family religiousness and reported virginity. Women from families with no religious preference have the largest percentage who are not virgins (21 per cent); and Jewish men (55 per cent) and men from families of no specific faith (50 per cent) have the largest percentage who report not being virgins. As a group there was little difference in the reported virginity of Protestant, Catholic and Jewish females, and of Protestant and Catholic males.

Family religiousness is positively associated with reporting that "religious belief" is a reason for refraining from having premarital sexual relations. However, when we examine faith differences we observe that this does not hold true for Jews, only for Catholics and Protestants. Only 8 per cent of Jewish females and 3 per cent of Jewish males report religious teachings as an influencing factor against having premarital sexual relations, while approximately 70 per cent of Catholic and 30 per cent of Protestant males and females reported religious belief as a factor in their premarital sexual behavior.

Family religiousness is positively associated with children reporting that "family training" was a factor in their refraining from having had premarital sexual relations. This association held for Protestants, Catholics and Jews. The percentages of females and males reporting "family training" as a reason for refraining did not differ greatly among Protestants, Catholics, and Jews. A much smaller percentage of those reporting no specific faith than of the three faith groups gave family training as a reason for refraining.

A stated willingness to marry a person who has had premarital sexual relations is associated with the devoutness of the family of origin. In all faith groups, the less devout the family the more willingness the child, male or female, expresses to marry a person with premarital experience. The largest percentage here was among Jewish females, 92 per cent of whom said they would marry one who had premarital experience. The percentage for females of no religious preference is 85, for Catholics 74, and for Protestants 71. Of the males, 83 per cent of those of no religious preference, 78 per cent of the Jews, and 71 per cent of the Catholics and Protestants reported they would be willing to marry one who had premarital sexual experience.

*Family religiousness and sex education of children in the home.* Students were asked to report upon the source of most of their sex information by checking from a list of specific items on sex information those which they had or had not received from their parents, and to state their conclusions about the place of sex in life from what they had been taught by their parents.

A significantly larger percentage of girls from devout than from indifferent homes had received sex information from their mothers, had formed desirable attitudes toward the place of sex in life, and had received more items of information from their mothers. Although the percentages were in the same direction for boys as for girls on the above items the only significant association was on the number of items of sex information received from the parents. There were no significant differences between devoutness and having received sex information from siblings, other children, school classes, reading and "other" sources.

The analyses did not show any significant faith differences in sex education in the home. The mothers were given credit for giving almost all the information to girls and slightly more information to boys than did the fathers. By far the most common source of information for males and the second most common source for females had been "other children." This held for all faith groups. There were no significant differences between faith groups in the type or amount of sex information given in the home. Although differences were not significant, percentagewise, Catholic parents and parents with no religious preference had given their children the least sex information, and more respondents from Catholic than from Protestant and Jewish homes reported undesirable attitudes, and fewer reported desirable attitudes toward the place of sex in life from what they had learned about sex from parents.

Since major organized churches have been vocal in advocating that sex education of children should be given in the home, it might seem that there would be more significant association between religious devoutness in the home and the sex training of children. Significant faith differences might be expected also since the Catholic church takes a stronger position than any other faith in advocating sex education in the home. However, in all the different areas of life which we have investigated in this study the lowest association appears between family religiousness and sex education and sex behavior of children.

## SUMMARY OF FINDINGS

The study was initiated as an attempt to determine: (1) What, if any, differences in family success exist between religious and nonreligious families, (2) whether any existing differences tend to develop in children's attitudes, feelings, and values which may perpetuate successful or unsuccessful marriages, and (3) whether there are significant differences on these points between families of four faith groups—Protestants, Catholics, Jews, and those of no specific faith.

When most of the items denoting family success were related to family religiousness, a positive association was found. Children from more religious homes, in contrast to the less religious, tended to hold attitudes and values which may tend to perpetuate successful marriages. In general the positive association between family religiousness and success in family living held when analyzed by faiths—Protestant, Catholic, Jewish, and no faith. The exceptions most often occurred among Jews, especially Jewish men, and next most often among those of no faith.

## NOTES

1. Ernest W. Burgess and Leonard S. Cottrell, Jr., *Predicting Success or Failure in Marriage*, New York: Prentice-Hall, 1939; Ernest W. Burgess and Paul Wallin, *Engagement and Marriage*, Chicago: J. B. Lippincott Company, 1953; Charles E. King, "The Burgess-Cottrell Method of Measuring Marital Adjustment Applied to a Non-White Southern Urban Population," *Marriage and Family Living*, 14 (November, 1952), pp. 280–285; Harvey J. Locke, *Predicting Adjustment in Marriage: A Comparison of a Divorced and a Happily Married Group*, New York: Henry Holt and Company, 1951; Lewis M. Terman, *Psychological Factors in Marital Happiness*, New York: McGraw-Hill Book Company, 1938; Lewis M. Terman and M. H. Oden, *The Gifted Child Grows Up: Twenty-Five Years Follow-Up of a Superior Group*, Palo Alto: Stanford University Press, 1947.

2. Ernest W. Burgess and Leonard S. Cottrell, Jr., *Predicting Success or Failure in Marriage*, New York: Prentice-Hall, 1939. See Chapter XIV; Ernest W. Burgess and Paul Wallin, *Engagement and Marriage*, Chicago: J. B. Lippincott Company, 1953. Chapter XVI.

3. The data were collected between 1952–1955 in the following schools: Universities of Illinois, Nebraska, Louisiana, Minnesota (Duluth Branch), Kansas, Stanford, Dubuque, California, New York (New Paltz); and from Whittier College and Fullerton Junior College.

4. Loren E. Chancellor and Thomas P. Monahan, "Religious Preference and Interreligious Mixtures in Marriage and Divorce in Iowa," *The American Journal of Sociology*, 61:3 (November, 1955), pp. 233–239; Judson T. Landis, "Marriages of Mixed and Non-Mixed Religious Faith," *American Sociological Review*, 14:3 (June, 1949), pp. 401–407; H. Ashley Weeks, "Differential Divorce Rates by Occupations," *Social Forces*, 21:3 (March, 1943), p. 336.

5. Thomas P. Monahan, "How Stable Are Remarriages?" *The American Journal of Sociology*, 58:3 (November, 1952), pp. 280–288.

CHAPTER 10 Work and the Family

## 10.1 LOIS WLADIS HOFFMAN

# The Decision to Work

Lois Wladis Hoffman was one of the premier scholars on issues related to work and family during the middle of the twentieth century. This selection is an excerpt from chapter 2, "The Decision to Work," of the classic book that she coedited with F. Ivan Nye in 1963, *The Employed Mother in America* (Rand McNally). In this selection, Hoffman describes women's motivation to work. The article, written just prior to the emergence of the women's movement of the late 1960s, is among the classics in the field of work and family. Because it was written before the women's movement, one might expect the article to contain many traditional and stereotypical descriptions about women and their aspirations to gain employment outside of the family. However, the reader will readily see that this article is groundbreaking in its insights into how and why women make the decision to work.

**Key Concept:** work and family

### Kinds of Data Available on Maternal Employment Motives

Despite the importance of understanding the factors involved in the decision to seek employment, there is little research which has focused on this problem. Most of the existing data are of two kinds: those showing demographic differences between working and non-working women and those reporting women's responses to direct questions about why they did or did not go to work. The former data exist almost in abundance. It is known, for example, that whether or not a woman works is related to her marital status, husband's income, education, the number of children she has, the age of her children, her place of residence, race, and ethnic background (6). Occasionally two of these variables have been considered simultaneously in relation to maternal employment. For example, the negative relationship between the husband's income and maternal employment is strongest for mothers of small children. For mothers of older children, the relationship is not linear, and the figures suggest that financial need is a less salient reason for employment.[1] Such analyses in which the relationship between maternal employment and another demographic variable is examined, with a third controlled, are unusual, although they are much more useful for theory development than simple two-variable correlations.

An example of a finding that could be theoretically suggestive if examined this way is the relationship between female employment rates and ethnic background. In certain areas, Japanese-American women are the most highly represented in the working force, followed by Negro women, Puerto Rican, "white" women, Chinese, Indian, and Mexican, respectively (6, p. 78). This order does not follow the economic position of these groups in society, nor does it seem to reflect directly such factors as family size. The Puerto Rican group has a relatively high female employment rate and the Mexican group, a low one, although both are predominantly Catholic, Spanish-speaking, and economically underprivileged. This is an interesting finding in itself, but one might gain considerable insight by examining the order of these groups within each of several categories. Is this order the same, for example, for single women, married women without children, and married women with children? If so, we would know that it was not merely the reflection of marital status and family size and, further, if the order reflected group attitudes, that these attitudes applied to women in general rather than to mothers only.

The demographic data, then, by showing certain correlates of maternal employment, suggest variables that need to be controlled, but as yet they have not been sufficiently exploited for theoretical purposes.

Data of the second kind—those based on women's responses to direct questions about motivation for employment—often suffer from superficiality. The questions have been simple, and only the first responses given are usually reported. Measuring motivation by the response to a single, direct question is inadequate at best. Motives in general, and certainly motives for maternal employment, are not that simple.

An additional complication is that respondents often feel there is considerable social censure of maternal employment. The direct question is, therefore, apt to put a respondent on the defensive, and as a result she may not readily give her most personal reasons. She would most likely hold back entirely an answer which suggested that she was rejecting her child or working for personal pleasure.

Another reason for the inadequacy of this approach is that the question has an answer that borders on the cliché: "Why do you work?" "For money." Indeed, this is the response overwhelmingly given by women (3, 8, 9, 10, Chapter Three).[2] Somewhere between 55 and 90 per cent of the answers will be in terms of money, depending on the particular sample of women being interviewed, the phrasing of the question, whether it is part of a questionnaire or personal interview, etc. The answer may be worded sometimes as simply "the money," sometimes as monetary need, sometimes as money to repay debts, "money for the children," money for some specific purchase such as a home, extra money, personal money, or the high pay. If the respondent is encouraged to elaborate on her answer, she will usually come forth with additional reasons. At this point, she will often talk about boredom, having insufficient work in the home, being "nervous" at home, and about the positive aspects of the job. Sometimes more specific concerns are added like: "The plant was near enough that I could get home before the kids get back from school."

But such answers as these are still insufficient. What is needed is a focussed interview designed to obtain data on the complexities of the decision.[3] The simpler questions may be useful for specific research purposes, but until more intensive interview procedures are employed, we can only speculate about the factors involved in the decision to work.

## THE MOTIVATIONS

The decision to be a working mother may be made thoughtfully and deliberately or so subtly that the actors involved—the decision-makers—do not know a decision has been made. Whichever is the case, the decision may be thought of as having two components—motivations and facilitators. The first are the needs and desires both conscious and unconscious that make maternal employment attractive. The second... are those factors which make it possible.

### Money

We have already noted that women give "money" as their major reason for working and, cliché though it may be, it is undoubtedly a major motivation. A bulletin put out by the Women's Bureau of the Department of Labor (8) demonstrates, by calling on the results of many other studies, that working women are often supporting dependents and, in fact, are frequently the sole support of their families. The relationship between father's income and mother's employment has already been mentioned. In addition to the actual size of the income, income satisfaction and *perceived* financial need are important. Sobol found that wives were more likely to enter the working force when their family incomes dropped from their former level than when they remained stable or increased. This finding was statistically significant for each socio-economic level.[4] Just as wives will go to work to maintain their standard of living, they will also take employment to achieve the level of those around them. Thus, if working does not detract from one's social status, families which strive for upward mobility and take as their reference group families with incomes higher than their own, may augment their income through maternal employment. In certain occupational groups such as teaching, the actual income is considerably below the desired style of life—not so much because of mobility strivings as because of education. A school teacher usually hopes that his children can go to college, but he may not be able to afford this unless his wife works. In each of these situations, where there is financial deprivation relative to a particular standard, the mother may enter the labor force out of what she may perceive as financial need.

Sometimes the mother works to pay debts. These debts may have been incurred by necessity—such as when there is prolonged illness—or by credit buying. These situations are like the above except that here the spending precedes the employment, so employment becomes a very real as well as a perceived necessity. The particular order—spending and then working—may be a function of greater resistance to employment, poor financial planning, or even good financial planning (i.e., when the family engages in deficit spending knowing that the mother will go to work at a later and more convenient date). Consideration of how the family managed to get into debt is important in determining the significance of this motive. The distinction between expensive illness and blatant extravagance is, of course, an extreme one. Further, if extravagance is the reason, which parent was the lavish one might be crucial in determining the impact of the employment on the family.

Financial *desires* are also important. Maternal employment has brought an unprecedented level of living to many working-class families. American advertising has succeeded in keeping people's desires for material goods beyond their ability to obtain them. Furthermore, the coveted purchase is often expensive enough to require an extra income, yet inexpensive enough to be obtainable without a permanent commitment by the supplementary wage-earner, and durable enough to make a sustained effort worth while. It is a washing machine, a drier, a car, a down payment on a house, carpeting, or possibly even a mink coat. Among the eighty-nine working mothers of Detroit elementary school children... the down-payment on a house was mentioned most frequently. Financial desires also may be non-specific: sometimes the mother works for "pin money." "Pin money" seems to mean money that can be used for incidental luxuries that can be spent without family consultation. It is closely akin to "personal money"—i.e., money which the wife controls and can spend independently.

Any of these monetary motivations can also be tied in with other attitudes that are important to consider. For example, is the financial motivation related to a feeling that the father is a failure? If so, the mother's employment could symbolize his failure for the whole family. On the other hand, the mother's employment could be part of cooperative planning and perceived as a symbol of family unity. Perhaps the working mother is paying penance for her poor management and extravagance. Or, she might want an independent income because of marital difficulties or simply out of a desire for autonomy in an otherwise close and congenial relationship. Clearly, the possible underlying motives are many, and the family climate surrounding employment cannot be automatically inferred from the monetary motive alone.

Money also operates as a motivation for employment in less concrete ways. Because of the availability of jobs, because so many women are working, and because so many have worked at some time in their lives, a woman's time has come to have monetary meaning. A modern woman who bakes her own bread must figure into its cost not only the cost of the ingredients but the cost of her labor. A mother whose children are all in school could spend her day diligently trying to save money by sewing the family's clothes, doing all of her own cooking, canning, cleaning, repair work, and redecorating and still not save enough money to compensate her for her time. It is more economical for her to obtain outside work and use commercial facilities for the needed household services. Goods are produced at less cost by mass production than they can be produced at home. Thus, if her household activities are not intrinsically satisfying, the woman may choose outside employment; and even if they are, she may choose employment because these household activities then become akin to leisure in that she must acknowledge that she does them for pleasure. The mother who does not work may feel that she is actually "spending" money for the privilege of not working, and therefore, particularly where all her children are of school age, she may feel guilty about *not* working. This seems to be a switch from the usual view, but as employment becomes increasingly common and increasingly possible, it may become more fruitful to ask "Why don't mothers work?" than "Why do they work?" The former is also becoming, in some cases, the question that the disapproving neighbors ask. The working mother of adolescent children who does not seem to be neglecting her roles as wife and mother is often admired for "working so hard." The mother of adolescent children who does not work and who can be seen sunning herself in her back yard or visiting with the neighbors, is often the object of disapproval. The Protestant Ethic is still very much with us,[5] and if the mother and wife roles do not fill the working day, it is increasing felt that this time should be spent in gainful employment.

The notion that a woman's time represents potential wages has led some young wives to consider their salaries in estimating the cost of having a baby. Although it was said partly as a jest, this point was brought home when a young professional woman said to her secretary, "It's all right for you to have a baby; it only costs you $4,000 to quit your job. But it would cost me $9,500, so I can't afford it."

Money operates as a motive for employment in still another way. The role of housewife and mother, however important it may be to society, carries with it little opportunity for a sense of achievement, competence, and contribution. The educational system and cultural values have tied feelings of achievement to success in the intellectual or business world. These have been intimately linked to money and the increasing size of the pay check, whether it increases because of inflation, union demands, or promotion. The housewife has none of these rewards.... Because of the lack of significance attached to her work, the housewife feels she is incompetent and that her contribution is a small one. No one expresses this more clearly than housewives themselves when they answer the inquiry about their occupation with the poignant phrase, "just a housewife." Bringing home a pay check, whether it is added to the family budget, saved for a rainy day, or used only as pin money, seems, in contrast, to be a sign of competence and a tangible contribution to the family.

## The Housewife and Mother Roles

Although the absence of wages may contribute to the housewife's feeling that her contribution is not great, this is not the whole story. Part of it lies in certain intrinsic aspects of the housekeeping role. Leaving aside temporarily the role of mother, and examining only that of housekeeper, one cannot fail to note the lack of creativity it affords. There is very little skill demanded and very little room for excellence. Take cooking, perhaps the most creative of the household tasks. A woman married about the time of World War I came to marriage well schooled in the art of cooking. Since this art was usually passed on from mother to daughter and developed through trial and error in private kitchens, each woman usually had certain dishes that were hers individually. It was a mysterious art which some could perform well and some could not. In a small community a woman could become famous for her cherry pie, and since the recipe was not written down and the quantity of the ingredients depended on the size of her hand, and the firmness of her "pinch," she usually remained the only person in the community who made pie just like that. Betty Crocker (2) does not depend on the size of a hand but says "seven-eights of a cup of sifted flour." If a guest admires a dish, the generous hostess can say, "page 42 in Betty Crocker." With this message the guest has all of the skill needed to reproduce the dish exactly. With the introduction of package mixes, even the skill of literacy is no longer required, and many a housewife is *saddened* to learn that with a package mix she can make an angle food cake two inches higher than the one she had previously made from one cookbook and twelve left-over egg whites.

If cooking is no longer creative, what is dusting, vacuuming, turning on the washing machine, running the drier, ironing, making beds, and doing 3,500 dishes every month?[6] Furthermore, the repetitive nature of these tasks makes the housewife wonder if it is necessary to do them as often as she does, and indeed, there is some evidence that it is not necessary. A frequent remark by the Detroit mothers in discussing the changes that occurred when they started or quit work was that when they were home all day, they were busy doing housework every minute, but when they were working, they could not see what they were leaving undone....

Of the 178 mothers interviewed in the Detroit study, 108 had started or returned to work after a period of not working. This figure of 108 excludes all situations which were unusual in that the husbands were in the armed services, ill, or unemployed, but includes situations where there were as yet no children. Asked to report changes in their household, 25 per cent reported that they became more efficient in accomplishing household tasks; 46 per cent, that they cleaned less often or less thoroughly; 17 per cent, that they stopped ironing certain items which could be simply folded and put away; 22 per cent, that they spent less time on meal preparation; and 50 per cent, that they baked less. This does not mean that the reduced activities were not missed, but it does suggest that much of the work that is done by the full-time housewife is at least not *essential*....

This is not to say that work on an assembly line is a mad, gay lark, but it does have certain advantages. It takes place outside the home. However unattractive the place of work may be, the fact that there is a change of scenery —in traveling between work and home as well as in actually doing the work —adds a variety to the day. In addition, outside work usually starts and stops at a specified time and the job is "done" when the worker leaves the shop. It usually involves interaction with other adults, not only at coffee breaks, which the housewife may also have, but also during the working hours. In addition, outside work often does offer opportunities for creativity and feelings of contribution and competence. This is clearly true for the professional and social service occupations such as teacher, nurse, and social worker; but it is also true for many white-collar jobs. Being judged as satisfactory on the basis of one's performance and by persons outside the family who are considered to be more objective and who usually have higher social status, add considerably to one's sense of competence. Occupying a particular niche in a large-scale organization, such as that of receptionist or secretary, often makes one feel an essential part of something important. Having contact with important people and distant places (the switchboard operator who places calls to foreign countries) often adds significance to a job. But for all jobs, even the dullest and most routine, there is at least the pay check which says, "You have done work which someone considers worth money" and "You are helping to buy a house by your employment."

Weiss and Samelson (7) asked a national sample of women what activities made them feel useful and important. They found that employed mothers were more likely to mention some aspect of their job than they were to mention either housework or their role in the family as wife and mother. They also found that although about 55 per cent of the mothers who were not employed mentioned housework as one response, only 36 per cent of the employed mothers did.[7] The percentage who mentioned the wife and mother roles, incidentally, was not affected by whether or not the wife worked. These data support the notion that the outside job is indeed an important source of feelings of usefulness and importance. They also suggest that whether or not housework is named as a source of these feelings depends in part on whether there are alternative sources.

But what about the mother role? Isn't this the most creative of all? Very likely it is, and, viewed from the perspective of a lifetime, most mothers would probably say and really feel that here was their most creative endeavor. But in the day-to-day experience of the mother, it is easy to lose sight of this long-range creativity. Changing and washing diapers, picking up toys, putting on snowsuits, and wiping up footprints do not feel creative when they are being done. However, especially when there is a preschool child in the family, there are highly creative moments, there are feelings of being irreplaceable, and there is enough work to easily fill the working day. But when the youngest child enters school, the mother is again left with a day full of housework rather than mothering. The Weiss-Samelson data mentioned above also show that satisfactions from "family inter-relationships," which include the mother role, diminish when the child enters school. While 58 per cent of the non-working mothers of preschool children mention this source of satisfaction, only 41 per cent of the non-working mothers of school children do so.

It is possible that the greater the joys of mothering for a woman, the more empty the days when the children are all in school. Even women who were satisfied with the housewife role before there were children may not be content to return to it. They have been used to a fuller and, in many ways, a richer day, and the house-cleaning tasks may seem less important and more boring than ever.

The period when the youngest child enters school can be very difficult for many mothers. Not only is the child physically absent from the home, but he is less dependent on the mother, and for some women this is a great loss. Just as many women themselves wish to remain dependent, some also wish to have others remain dependent on them. This is a time when mothers often feel they are no longer needed and their major role is over. They may feel, too, that they are growing old or at least that they have lost the vigor of youth. Thus, the mothers who return to work when their youngest child enters school may be motivated not only by practical reasons—i.e., they are now more dispensable to the household—but also by psychological reasons, namely, the dissatisfactions that emerge at this time.

There is yet another reason why this time would be psychologically appropriate for women to return to work. The period when there are preschool children at home can have many frustrating moments for the mother. In addition to the unrewarding work activities mentioned above, the mother's freedom is often considerably restricted. In fact, in one part of the Detroit study, 217 mothers were asked, "How is a woman's life changed by having children?" By far the most common response was that children meant less freedom, particularly that they restricted the mother's freedom of movement. Forty women gave as their first response that children "tie you to the house," "tie you down," or some *very similar* wording. Most of the answers to this question were negative—four times as many gave totally negative responses as gave totally positive. Only half the respondents gave answers that could, *in any part,* be considered positive.[8] Thus, the period when the mother has preschool children may be an extremely frustrating time—a time when she must hold back impulses, defer gratification, and above all, remain physically in the home. For perhaps twelve years, she has had at least one preschool child in the house and been unable to express these frustrations. She did not express them because her role demanded certain behaviors, because she felt that to do a good job she should not, and perhaps because she was not able to acknowledge them to herself. Whatever the reasons, the youngest child's entering school can provide a release for many of the frustrations of the preceding years, and outside employment may be one expression of this release. This motivation is, in a sense, the opposite of the one discussed earlier and would characterize a different group of women. The former involves the notion that the early years of mothering are gratifying and the later years represent a relative dissatisfaction. This one, on the other hand, suggests that the early years are frustrating and the later years allow for the release of these suppressed tensions.

For some women, of course, these tensions are not suppressed. For some the loss of freedom that the preschool child brings to the mother is itself a motivation for employment. For some, the gratifying aspects of these years are outweighed by the dull day-to-day routines, loneliness and the longing for adult company, boredom with the same physical surroundings, frustration because of the constant requirement that the child's needs have priority over the mother's, the ever presence of the child's needs, the noise level, and the overwhelming sense of personal responsibility. Thus, even in the preschool years, the intrinsically negative aspects of the housewife and mother roles can provide motivations for outside employment....

## SUMMARY

... [We] have pointed to the importance of studying the factors involved in the mother's decision to work. These factors are important methodologically because differences between working and non-working mothers may be due to their operation rather than to employment itself. They are important theoretically because they may operate as variables which interact with the employment situation and influence its effects on the family.

The monetary motive was given special attention as one which is frequently articulated. It may be based on actual financial need, perceived need, desire, and also on other motives not truly monetary in origin but which become focussed and expressed in monetary terms.

The significance of the housewife and mother roles for employment motivations was considered. Technological advances have made the housewife role less time-consuming and less satisfying. Particularly when the youngest child has entered school, the mother may look to outside employment to fill her day. In addition, certain frustrating aspects of the maternal role itself might motivate some women to seek employment.

## NOTES

1. For mothers of older children there is little difference in employment rates according to husband's income if his income is under $5,000. These rates fall sharply in the $5,000 to $10,000 range but rise somewhat in the group where the husband earns over $10,000 (6, p. 72).
2. Industrial sociologists have noted that inarticulate and unacceptable frustrations and desires on the part of workers often find expression in the form of wage demands. The tendency for women to say they work for money may be a similar phenomenon. Money may seem to be a more acceptable reason for employment than the satisfaction of a vaguely felt need.
3. The focussed interview is discussed in detail by Merton, Fiske, and Kendall (4).
4. This unpublished finding is reported by Marion G. Sobol in personal communication. It is based on a panel study of urban families carried out by the Economic Behavior Program, Institute for Social Research, University of Michigan, 1954–1957.
5. The existence of the Protestant Ethic in the present day has been brought out in a study by Morse and Weiss (5).
6. The 3,500 dishes per month was estimated for a family of four and reported in an advertisement in *Better Homes and Gardens* (1, p. 160).
7. Respondents gave more than one response.

8. There was essentially no difference between working mothers and non-working mothers in the number of positive or negative responses given.

## REFERENCES

1. *Better Homes and Gardens,* October, 1956.
2. General Mills, Inc. *Betty Crocker's Picture Cook Book.* New York: McGraw-Hill, 1956.
3. LaFollette, Cecile Tipton. *A Study of the Problems of 652 Gainfully Employed Married Women Homemakers.* New York: Teachers College, Columbia University Press, 1934.
4. Merton, Robert, Fiske, M., and Kendall, Patricia L. *The Focussed Interview.* Glencoe, Ill.: Free Press, 1956.
5. Morse, Nancy C., and Weiss, R. S. "The Function and Meaning of Work and the Job," *American Sociological Review,* XX (April, 1955), 191–98.
6. National Manpower Council. *Womanpower.* New York: Columbia University Press, 1957.
7. Weiss, R. S., and Samelson, Nancy M. "Social Roles of American Women: Their Contribution to a Sense of Usefulness and Importance," *Marriage and Family Living,* XX (November, 1958), 358–66.
8. *Women Workers and their Dependents.* United States Department of Labor, Women's Bureau, Bulletin No. 239. Washington, D.C.: Government Printing Office, 1951.
9. *Women Workers in Ten War Production Areas and their Postwar Employment Plans.* United States Department of Labor, Women's Bureau, Bulletin No. 209. Washington, D.C.: Government Printing Office, 1946.
10. Zweig, F. *Women's Life and Labour.* London: Gollancz, 1952.

## 10.2 PATRICIA VOYDANOFF AND ROBERT F. KELLY

# Determinants of Work-Related Family Problems Among Employed Parents

Patricia Voydanoff is director of the Center for the Study of Family Development at the University of Dayton in Ohio. She is among the most prolific contemporary scholars with regard to researching and writing about the issue of work and family. Her coauthor on this selection, Robert F. Kelly, was a sociologist at Wayne State University when they wrote "Determinants of Work-Related Family Problems Among Employed Parents," *Journal of Marriage and the Family* (November 1984). Originally, this paper was presented at the 1983 meeting of the American Sociological Association. The article is based on data collected from working parents in 1979. The purpose of the research was to examine the relationships between the individual, work and family demands and resources, and work-related family problems. The research focused on work and family role strain and family economic well-being. This selection is important because it is one of the early research projects in the field of work and family among contemporary family scholars. Many of the ideas presented in this piece offered others insights to further their own research on the complex and challenging issue of how work and family interface.

**Key Concept:** work and family

*T*his paper examines the relative importance of several individual, work, and family characteristics in relation to work-related family problems as perceived by employed parents. Two problem areas are considered: work/family role strain and family economic well-being.

Previous research (Bohen and Viveros-Long, 1981; Keith and Schafer, 1980; Pleck, 1979) suggests that work-related family problems may be more severe among employed parents. Being a working parent involves the performance of multiple roles: worker, parent and, in most cases, spouse. These three roles are interdependent in terms of the time, energy, and commitment required for adequate performance. This interdependence can result in asynchrony or role strain of two types, overload and interference (Voydanoff, 1980). Overload occurs when the total prescribed activities of one or more roles are greater than an individual can handle adequately or comfortably. Interference exists when responsibilities conflict—that is, the expectations are contradictory or an individual is required to do two things at the same time. Thus, time shortage is an important type of work/family role strain among employed parents.

In addition, problems of family economic well-being also tend to be relatively serious among families with children. The literature indicates that life-cycle squeezes occur among childbearing families and families with teens (Oppenheimer, 1982). Families with young children and teenagers are differentially vulnerable to unemployment and income loss during recessions (Moen, Kain and Elder, 1983).

Within this context we need to understand more about the conditions under which these potential imbalances between demands and resources become translated into work-related family problems among employed parents. We attempt to do this in the present study by asking three questions:

1. Which individual, family, and work characteristics are more strongly associated with perceived time shortage and income inadequacy, the two work-related family problems that we examine?
2. What is the relative importance of the various individual, work, and family characteristics in relation to time shortage and income inadequacy?
3. What is the significance of the pattern of results for the understanding of factors in a parent's work and family life that influence work-related family problems?

These questions are addressed through an analytic strategy that is both inductive and deductive in nature....

The model suggests that work-related family problems can result from characteristics of the individual, the family, and the work role. Within each of these categories, we include stressors and resources that may be expected to influence work-related family problems. Stressors are situations and demands to which an individual or family must respond or adapt. They include life strains associated with work and family roles and other life events having potential impact on these roles. The presence of these stressors is expected to increase the likelihood that employed parents will experience work-related family problems. Resources refer to what is available to an individual or family to cope with stressors. We include Pearlin and Schooler's (1978) social resources and psychological resources and add a third type, human capital resources. Although we do not measure coping responses, we hypothesize that the availability of resources useful for coping will be associated with less severe work-related family problems....

## METHODS

### Data

The analysis is based on a sample of 468 working parents drawn from a medium-sized southeastern metropolitan area of approximately 160,000 people. Data were collected in the spring of 1979 through a self-administered, mail-back questionnaire. The questionnaires were distributed to parents at their place of employment. Forty-five randomly selected employers with over 100 employees were asked to assist in the distribution of the questionnaires; 12 agreed.[1] Usable questionnaires were returned by 20%–25% of the working parents who received them. Since the response rate is low, subsequent findings should be considered as exploratory and suggestive in nature.

The basic demographic characteristics include the following: 88% white; 60% female; 88% currently married; and 70% with more than a high school education. The average age of respondents is 36 years. For women the average is 35.6, and for men the comparable figure is 37.8.

To determine possible sources of bias due to the low response rate, sample frequencies were compared with county-level statistics.[2] Black men are seriously underrepresented, while white women are overrepresented. The per capita income of the sample, $7,850, was comparable to the figure for the population. White-collar workers (professionals, technical workers, managers, administrators, clerical workers) are overrepresented; sales workers, craftsmen, service workers, operatives, and laborers are seriously underrepresented. The sample overrepresents the public administration and service sectors of the economy. In terms of workplace size, the sample's representation of sites with more or less than 500 workers closely mirrors the general distribution of workplaces in the country. Finally, the sample was compared with the general population along the pivotal dimension of the proportion of women in the labor force with children under 6. In the general population 40% of all employed women had children under 6; in the sample the comparable figure was 34.2%—a relatively close match.

### Dependent Variables

Respondents were presented with a list of 17 work-related problems which they and their families might face or experience in their everyday lives. They were asked to indicate how much of a problem each of these situations represented to them on a scale of 1 (not at all) to 3 (a lot). Working parents in the sample experienced work-related family problems at levels comparable to those reported in national surveys (Pleck et al., 1979). On average, approximately 20% of the respondents answered that they had experienced these problems a lot.

Factor analysis was used to identify underlying dimensions in the structure of responses. Preliminary analysis of the 17 items indicated that 6 items could be disregarded as uninterpretable, redundant, or singular measures.... The solution is orthogonal—i.e., the four factors are forced to be statistically independent of each other.[3] Four interpretable dimensions resulted from the analysis. They have been named Job Tension ($F_1$), Time Shortage ($F_2$), Income Inadequacy ($F_3$) and Job Insecurity ($F_4$).

These four variables represent two types of work-related family problems. Time shortage and income inadequacy are problems resulting from the combined effects of individual, family, and work demands and needs. Job tension and job insecurity reflect the "spillover" of work demands on family life....

**Independent Variables**

... *Ascribed characteristics* (I) includes stressors and sources of coping resources at the *individual* level. For example, because working women may have high and often conflicting role expectations in the workplace and the home, the ascribed status of woman may be translated into a social circumstance that is highly susceptible to work-related family problems. A similar argument can be made with respect to the ascribed status, race, and its socially based economic consequences.

*Age/life-cycle characteristics* (II) should be significant sources of stressors and coping resources. This group of variables is located at the *family* level. Early marriage and childbearing have negative effects on family economic well-being. Young children, especially preschool children, consume large amounts of parental time and emotional energy. Teenagers, while more financially demanding than younger children, may be able to provide assistance with housework and other tasks (Kelly, 1983). Thus, it is suggested that life-cycle family variables provide a way to map the impact of the supply and demand of both stressors and coping resources in the family. The respondent's age is included either as a measure of the *individual's* stage in the life cycle or as an indicant of the individual's cohort.

*Family structure/composition and employment-related characteristics* (III) measure not only family-related sources of stressors and coping resources but also sources related to ways in which *employment intersects with the family environment*. Included in this category are indicators of whether a single female parent is the sole earner in the family and whether, in a two-parent family, both parents are employed. It is hypothesized that both of these family-earner types will be more likely to experience time shortage and that single-parent earners will encounter income inadequacy. Also included in this category are several measures that gauge the availability of help from other adults in the household. The availability of such assistance may attenuate the degree of work-related family problems (Angel and Tienda, 1982; Kelly, 1983; Stack, 1974). Measures of status inconsistency also are placed within this category. Although status inconsistency has not been used in previous analyses of work-related family problems, it is reasonable to suggest that significant degrees of inconsistency may influence these problems either because they themselves may be a source of stress between spouses or because they may deplete the resources available to cope with other stress, due to an increase in the likelihood of conflict between spouses (Hiller and Philliber, 1982; Hornung and McCullough, 1981). The last measure in this category is a count of significant life events that occurred in the family during the last year, such as a birth, a death, or someone leaving home. In addition to economic consequences, health-based stress research has provided some evidence that such events constitute stressors that increase generalized susceptibility to illness (Antonovsky, 1981; Catalano and Dooley, 1983; Rabkin and Struening, 1976).

The availability of *human/family capital* (IV) should be related both to an *individual's* and a *family's* ability to cope with work-related problems in much the same manner, labor economists have suggested, as human capital is related to achievement in the labor market (Becker, 1964, 1981). Thus, the respondent's health or the health of other members of the household may be viewed as a positive coping resource or as a stressor, depending on whether health is good or bad. Similarly, education may be conceptualized as a generalized resource for dealing with work-related family problems. It can be argued that more highly educated persons have developed management and resource allocation and location skills, to name only a few, which would assist in problem avoidance or reduction.

*Income* (V) variables are included to examine the role of financial resources and demands in relation to work-related family problems. It is suggested that persons with higher incomes should, on average, be better able to handle problems because they are marginally advantaged in their ability to buy the goods and services with which to cope with their own or their family's problems. On the other hand, a low income, or an income derived from public assistance or unemployment benefits, would be indicative of a generalized stressor contributing to work-related family problems. Measures of these dimensions are total household income, respondent's income, and a dummy variable indicating whether or not anyone in the household received AFDC or unemployment benefits in the past year. Also included is the proportion of household income contributed by adults other than the respondent. This measure of the structure of household income contributed by adults other than the respondent. This measure of the structure of household income is included to explore the possibility that diversity of income sources (versus one family member being the major earner) may represent either a resource or a stressor with respect to work-related family problems. At this point available research provides no clear suggestion as to the expected direction for this relationship.

The income category variables do not fit unambiguously into the individual, family, or work clusters of independent variables [here]. For example, respondent's income is a function both of his/her *individual* characteristics and of his/her *work* condition. Similarly household income is a function of *family* conditions and *work* conditions.

*Work environment and satisfaction characteristics* (VI) assess the impact of work-related factors on time shortage and income inadequacy. Several measures are used to gauge the temporal demands imposed by work on the parents in the sample—for example, number of hours worked per week, overtime, moonlighting, a nontraditional work schedule, and amount of time in overnight travel. Various occupational prestige measures (Duncan scores, blue collar/white collar distinction) are included in the analysis for reasons similar to those for income and education, namely, that high prestige and its correlated social benefits may serve as resources in problem management and coping. Two measures of job satisfaction (with one's self as a worker and with one's job) are used to assess the degree to which employment as a source of personal gratification may serve as a resource to cope with work-related problems. Specific characteristics of the workplace also are examined as possible sources of stressors or coping resources. Workplace size (number of workers) and industry type (construction/manufacturing, service, etc.) are analyzed to specify problem-related or problem-immune workplaces.

The final group of variables examined is referred to as *family involvement/satisfaction and self-satisfaction* (VII). Included in this category are measures of gratification derived from the roles of parent or spouse and from one's overall assessment of self. The final variable is one that measures the degree to which the respondent, and his or her family, commit time to family activities. This variable is used as an indicant of commitment to the family as a unit and as a valued source of gratification. Each of these measures is used to ascertain the impact of subjective environments and perceptions on work-related family problems. Antonovsky (1981) has suggested that internal dispositions of this type—locus of control, for example—are related both to susceptibility and to ability to cope.

### Strategy of Analysis

An inductive and staged model-fitting strategy was used to arrive at the final models of time shortage and income inadequacy. The seven categories of independent variables form a continuum from immediate, objective, and behavioral characteristics (e.g., ascribed, life-cycle, and family-structure characteristics) to more distant, attributed, and attitudinal measures (e.g., work environment, self-satisfaction). This continuum was used to determine the priority by which the categories of variables were entered in the stages of the analysis. Thus, ascribed characteristics were examined first, then life-cycle characteristics, and so on. Each stage built upon the previous stage in that relationships found to be significant in Stage 1 were retained in Stage 2. Inclusion in the model was determined by the level of statistical significance, with the .05 level used as an approximate cutoff. As the models progressed to their final form, all variables that had been eliminated previously from the models were repeatedly entered to determine whether spurious relationships existed or whether previous variable exclusion might be a source of misspecifications. In the final models, all of the independent variables are significant at the .01 level.... The ordinary least squares regression procedure was used to estimate the models....

# RESULTS

### Time Shortage

... The final model includes all types of independent variables except human/family capital. These variables explain a relatively low 18.7% of the variance in time shortage. About half of the variance is explained by family-related variables, i.e., age/life-cycle characteristics, family structure/composition and employment-related characteristics, and family involvement/satisfaction. Several work environment and satisfaction characteristics explain another 4.4% of variance, with the rest accounted for by sex and respondent's income. These results suggest that a wide range of individual, family, and work characteristics influence perceived time shortage among working parents. The low percentage of explained variance indicates that other significant characteristics are not included in the model.

Sex, the only ascribed characteristic in the final model, is a major variable in relation to time shortage. Women are significantly more likely to report time shortage than are men, reflecting the combined demands of outside employment and a high level of family responsibilities. This variable has the highest zero-order correlation with time shortage and the highest standardized beta coefficient, indicating its importance when the effects of the other characteristics are controlled..

Life-cycle characteristics are a second source of relatively important variables in relation to time shortage. The presence of preschool or school-age children is significantly related to time shortage. Children in these age groups place different, yet extensive, time demands on their parents. Pre-school children require close supervision and a high level of energy from adults; the timing of school and outside activities of school-age children often conflicts with the work schedules of parents. Individuals who married relatively early report more time shortage than those marrying later. Perhaps these parents have assumed heavy work and family responsibilities at an earlier age with fewer resources in terms of human capital and planning and time management skills.

Two characteristics associated with family structure/composition and employment-related characteristics appear in the model. Individuals experiencing three or more important changes in their families during the past year—such as divorce, death, new relationships, or increased expenses—have higher levels of time shortage. Changes such as these are often stressors associated with additional demands within families. These demands involve time-consuming activities and the need for coping resources. Secondly, among families in which the wife's occupation has higher prestige than her husband's, both husbands and wives report high time shortage.[4] Although this is not a major variable in the model, it has interesting implications. The fact that both husbands and wives report time shortage suggests that the husband perceives more demands on his time compared with other husbands; however, apparently husbands are not responding to this time shortage in ways that affect the time shortage of wives, and wives are not reducing the shortage experienced by their husbands by performing all family duties.

Respondents with higher incomes experience significantly less time shortage. This variable may indicate resources associated with high income such as other human capital assets and the flexibility and skills needed to meet time demands.

Of the work environment and satisfaction characteristics, three time-related variables and job satisfaction are in the final model. Long work hours, overtime, and moonlighting are related to time shortage. Despite the significance of these variables in previous research, they are among the least important in the current study, perhaps due to the extensive controls contained in our models. Moonlighting is more important than the total number of hours worked or overtime on one job. Moonlighting may exacerbate the effects of long hours by adding the conflicting demands of two jobs. Job satisfaction also is a significant factor in relation to time shortage. Individuals who are satisfied with their jobs may be less likely to bring work-related problems and stress into their home lives, thereby preventing a negative generalization from work to family life. This may not create additional time at home; however, it may lead to a greater psychological availability of the worker to the demands of family life (Piotrkowski, 1979).

From the last group of variables, family involvement/satisfaction and self-satisfaction, the amount of time spent in family activities is included in the final model. Individuals spending relatively more time in family activities are able to manage their time so that work does not limit their family activities to the extent that they say they spend little time in family activities.

### Income Inadequacy

... All types of independent variables appear in the final model, which explains 26.9% of the variance in income inadequacy. Family-related variables explain 14.4%, 54% of the total variance explained. Ascribed characteristics, human/family capital, income, and work environment and satisfaction characteristics account for the remaining 12.5%. Thus, perceived income inadequacy is about equally dependent on family-related characteristics and income and work-related variables.

Race is the only ascribed characteristic in the final model. Blacks are more likely to perceive their incomes as inadequate than are whites, although the relationship is not strong. In general, blacks earn less than whites with similar educational and occupational backgrounds.

Two life-cycle characteristics are included in the model: age at marriage and length of time between marriage and birth of the first child. Those who married late, i.e., later than the average age represented in the sample, have slightly higher levels of perceived income inadequacy. It is possible that economic difficulties contributed to the late timing of the marriage (Furstenberg, 1974). The length of time between marriage and the birth of the first child shows a strong negative relationship to income inadequacy, suggesting that a lengthier establishment period contributes to economic well-being.

The model incorporates several components of family structure/composition and employment-related characteristics. As might be expected, having an unemployed spouse is associated with income inadequacy. Experiencing at least three important life or family events in the past year is strongly related to income inadequacy, indicating the financial consequences of events such as divorce, birth of a child, and major expenses such as college tuition. Female single-parent earners have high levels of income inadequacy, reflecting the financial demands on single-parent families. Wives reporting that their husbands have higher occupational status than themselves have low levels of income inadequacy; however, a husband's report that his wife has higher occupational status is related to income inadequacy. Thus, husband's relatively higher occupational status is associated with income adequacy, although the relationships are not strong.

Two human capital variables, respondent's education and number of months on present job, are negatively related to income inadequacy. Generally, education and job tenure show consistent relationships with income. Household income, as expected, is strongly related to income adequacy.

Of the work environment and satisfaction characteristics, being in the service sector is most strongly related to income inadequacy. This is not surprising since service sector occupations tend to be poorly paid. Satisfaction with job duties shows a weak negative relationship to income inadequacy, supporting other findings that jobs that are intrinsically satisfying also are generally well paying.

Family satisfaction and self-satisfaction are represented in the model by family activity time. Family activity is weakly but negatively related to income inadequacy. It may be that those with inadequate incomes are unable to spend time in family activities because of income-producing activities or lack of financial resources.

# CONCLUSION

The models reveal similarities and differences in the composition and pattern of individual, work, and family demands and resources related to time shortage and income inadequacy. Factors important in relation to time shortage suggest a pattern of role strain in which time-related demands exceed time management resources. Demands associated with time shortage include being a female working parent, the presence of preschool and school-age children, experiencing three or more important family changes, a wife with higher occupational status than her husband, and work hours and scheduling. Characteristics providing resources for coping with time demands include high income, job satisfaction, not marrying early, and an apparent ability to arrange time for family activities.

The model for income inadequacy suggests the relative significance of family-related economic demands and family timing, income-producing resources or barriers, and a lack of economic supports. Family-related demands associated with income inadequacy include experiencing three important life/family events, having an unemployed spouse, and being a female single-parent earner. It is interesting that children's ages did not appear in the model despite their significance in research on the life-cycle squeeze. For this sample children's ages were significant for time shortage but not for income inadequacy. A relatively long time period between marriage and the birth of the first child contributed to lower levels of income inadequacy. Income-producing resources and barriers include education, job tenure, husband's relative occupational status, race, and being in the service sector. Variables indicating economic supports, such as being a two-earner family or number of earners, do not appear in the model; however, this factor may be accounted for partially by the inclusion of total household income.

The two models support the basic model—i.e., that a combination of individual, family, and work characteristics will determine the levels of work-related family problems among employed parents. In addition, both demands and resources are important. The time shortage model emphasizes time demands, the income inadequacy model focuses on family-related economic demands, and both models include other life and family events. Both models also incorporate resources useful for dealing with demands, including human capital, the timing of marriage, and job satisfaction.

The results document the value of examining work-related family problems in the context of several life strains or stressors and the availability of resources useful for coping with these stressors. A wide range of individual, family, and work demands and resources are examined in relation to time shortage and income inadequacy. The limited nature of previous work in this area required a relatively inductive approach in the selection of variables expected to be related to time shortage and income inadequacy. This study has ascertained several specific individual, family, and work demands and resources of significance to time shortage and income inadequacy. It provides an empirical base for future research and policy analysis in this emerging area.

## NOTES

1. This implies that the sample is biased in the direction of employers who, for various reasons, would be unapprehensive about research that might reflect upon their employment practices.
2. These comparisons can only be approximate because labor force county-level data are not available in a form that distinguishes between parents and non-parents. Also note that the comparisons are based on 1970 Census figures.
3. The orthogonal solution was chosen in order to isolate unique dimensions of work-related problems and to thereby facilitate the development of unambiguous predictive models of each dimension. Initially, factor analyses were run for men and women separately; however, the separate solutions were nearly identical to that for the unified sample. Thus, the total sample was used for the multivariate analysis.
4. This relationship was equally robust regardless of whether the husband or the wife was the source of occupational information, i.e., the respondent.

# REFERENCES

Angel, R. and Tienda, M. 1982 "Determinants of extended household structure: cultural pattern or economic need?" American Journal of Sociology 87:1360–1383.

Antonovsky, A. 1981 Health, Stress and Coping. San Francisco: Jossey-Bass.

Becker, G. S. 1964 Human Capital. New York:National Bureau of Economic Research.

Becker, G. S. 1981 A Treatise on the Family. Cambridge, MA: Harvard University Press.

Bohen, H. H. and Viveros-Long, A. 1981 Balancing Jobs and Family Life. Philadelphia: Temple University Press.

Catalano, R. and Dooley, D. 1983 "Health effects of economic instability: a test of economic stress hypotheses." Journal of Health and Social Behavior 24:46–60.

Furstenberg, F., Jr. 1974 "Work experience and family life." Pp. 341–360 in J. O'Toole (Ed.), Work and the Quality of Life. Cambridge, MA:MIT.

Hiller, D. V. and Philliber, W. W. 1982 "Predicting marital and career success among dual-worker couples." Journal of Marriage and the Family 44 (February):53–61.

Hornung, C. A. and McCullough, B. C. 1981 "Status relationships in dual-employment marriages: consequence for psychological well-being." Journal of Marriage and the Family 43 (February):125–141.

Keith, P. M. and Schafer, R. B. 1980 "Role strain and depression in two-job families." Family Relations 29 (October):438–488.

Kelly, R. F. 1983 "Welfare dependency under depressed labor market conditions: lessons from the 1970's for the 1980's." Journal of Urban Affairs 5 (Fall):331–348.

Langer, E. 1972 "Inside the New York Telephone Company." Pp. 307–360 in W. L. O'Neill (Ed.), Women at Work: Two Studies. Chicago: Quadrangle.

Moen, P., Kain, E. L. and Elder, G. H., Jr. 1983 "Economic conditions and family life: contemporary and historical perspectives." Pp. 213–259 in R. R. Nelson and F. Skidmore (Eds.), American Families and the Economy: The High Costs of Living. Washington, DC:National Academy Press.

Oppenheimer, V. K. 1982 Work and the Family: A Study in Social Demography. New York: Academic Press.

Pearlin, L. I. and Schooler, C. 1978 "The structure of coping." Journal of Health and Social Behavior 19 (March):2–21.

Piotrkowski, C. 1979 Work and the Family System. New York:Free Press.

Pleck, J. H. 1979 "Work-family conflict: a national assessment." Paper presented at the annual meeting of the Society for the Study of Social Problems.

Pleck, J., Staines G. L. and Lang, L. 1979 "Conflicts between work and family life." Monthly Labor Review (March):29–31.

Rabkin, J. G. and Struening, E. L. 1976 "Life events, stress and illness." Science 194:1013–1020.

Stack, C. B. 1974 All Our Kin: Strategies for Survival in a Black Community. New York:Harper & Row.

Voydanoff, P. 1980 "Work-family life cycles." Paper presented at the Workshop on Theory Construction and Research Methodology, National Council on Family Relations.

CHAPTER 11 **Violence and Abuse**

11.1 RICHARD J. GELLES

# Abused Wives: Why Do They Stay?

Spousal abuse and the larger topic of family abuse have become popular issues of discussion among politicians and policymakers in the 1990s. Because abuse is not only a societal issue but an economic issue, the public is asking for a quick fix to the devastating problem. Richard J. Gelles and his colleagues have studied family violence for years, and their diligent attempts to understand the problem and to outline some intervention strategies have yielded significant information and possible solutions. Gelles offers some insights into abused wives in the following selection from "Abused Wives: Why Do They Stay?" *Journal of Marriage and the Family* (November 1976).

Gelles (b. 1946) earned his doctorate at the University of New Hampshire in 1970. In 1973 he became director of the Family Violence Research Program at the University of Rhode Island, where he wrote *The Violent Home: A Study of Physical Aggression Between Husbands and Wives* (Sage Publications, 1974). Gelles has presented more than 75 papers on family issues. He has authored, coauthored, or coedited many books, contributed to numerous professional journals, and contributed chapters to other edited books. Among his more recent publications are *Current Controversies on Family Violence*, coedited with Donileen Loseke, (Sage Publications, 1993), and *Sociology: An Introduction*, coauthored with Ann Levine (McGraw-Hill College, 1999).

**Key Concept:** spousal abuse

Why would a woman who has been physically abused by her husband remain with him? This question is one of the most frequently asked by both professionals and the lay public in the course of discussions of family violence, and one of the more difficult to adequately answer. The question itself derives from the elementary assumption that any reasonable individual, having been beaten and battered by another person, would avoid being victimized again (or at least avoid the attacker). Unfortunately, the answer to why women remain with their abusive husbands is not nearly as simple as the assumption that underlies the question. In the first place, the decision to either stay with an assaultive spouse or to seek intervention or dissolution of a marriage is not related solely to the extent or severity of the physical assault. Some spouses will suffer repeated severe beatings or even stabbings without so much as calling a neighbor, while others call the police after a coercive gesture from their husband. Secondly, the assumption that the victim would flee from a conjugal attacker overlooks the complex subjective meaning of intrafamilial violence, the nature of commitment and entrapment to the family as a social group, and the external constraint which limits a woman's ability to seek outside help. As has been reported elsewhere (Parnas, 1967; Gelles, 1974; Straus, 1974, 1975), violence between spouses is often viewed as normative and, in fact, mandated in family relations. Wives have reported that they believe that it is acceptable for a husband to beat his wife "every once and a while" (Parnas, 1967:952; Gelles, 1974:59–61).

This paper attempts to provide an answer to the question of why victims of conjugal violence stay with their husbands by focusing on various aspects of the family and family experience which distinguish between women who seek intervention or dissolution of a marriage as a response to violence and those women who suffer repeated beatings without seeking outside intervention. We shall specifically analyze how previous experience with family violence affects the decision to seek intervention, and how the extent of violence, educational status, occupational status, number of children, and age of oldest child influence the wife's actions in responding to assaults from her husband. Finally, we shall discuss how external constraints lessen the likelihood of a woman seeking intervention in conjugal assaults.

*Richard J. Gelles*

## VICTIMS OF FAMILY VIOLENCE

Although no one has systematically attempted to answer the question of why an abused wife would stay with her husband, there has been some attention focused on women who attempt to seek intervention after being beaten by their husbands. Snell, Rosenwald, and Robey (1964) examined 12 clinical cases to determine why a wife takes her abusive husband to court. They begin by stating that the question answers itself (because he beats her!), but they go on to explain that the decision to seek legal assistance is the result of a change in the wife's behavior, not the husband's, since many wives report a history of marital violence when they did not seek assistance.

Truninger (1971) found that women attempt to dissolve a violent marriage only after a history of conflict and reconciliation. According to this analysis, a wife makes a decision to obtain a divorce from her abusive husband when she can no longer believe her husband's promises of no more violence nor forgive past episodes of violence. Truninger postulates that some of the reasons women *do not* break off relationships with abusive husbands are that: (1) they have negative self-concepts; (2) they believe their husbands will reform; (3) economic hardship; (4) they have children who need a father's economic support; (5) they doubt they can get along alone; (6) they believe divorcees are stigmatized; and (7) it is difficult for women with children to get work. Although this analysis attempts to explain why women remain with abusive husbands, the list does not specify which factors are the most salient in the wife's decision to either stay or seek help.

There are a number of other factors which help explain the wife's decision to stay or get help in cases of violence. Straus (1973) states that self-concept and role expectations of others often influence what is considered to be an intolerable level of violence by family members. Scanzoni's (1972) exchange model of family relations postulates that the ratio of rewards to punishments is defined subjectively by spouses and is the determining factor in deciding whether to stay married or not. The decision of whether or not to seek intervention or dissolution of a marriage may be partly based on the subjective definitions attached to the violence (punishment) and partly on the ratio of this punishment to other marital rewards (security, companionship, etc.).

Additional research on violence between husbands and wives suggests that severity of violence has an influence on the wife's actions (see O'Brien, 1971 and Levinger, 1966, for discussion of petitioners for divorce and their experience with violence). Research on victims of violence sheds little additional light on the actions of abused wives (Straus, 1975).

# METHODOLOGY

Data for this study were derived from interviews with members of 80 families. An unstructured informal interview procedure was employed to facilitate data collection on the sensitive topic of intrafamilial violence. Twenty families suspected of using violence were chosen from the files of a private social service agency. Another 20 families were selected by examining a police "blotter" to locate families in which the police had been summoned to break-up violent disputes. An additional 40 families were interviewed by selecting one neighboring family for each "agency" or "police" family.

### Strengths and Limitations of the Sample

The interviews were carried out in two cities in New Hampshire. The sampling procedure employed enhanced the likelihood of locating families in which violence had occurred, but it also meant that this sample was not representative of any larger population.

Major limitations of this study are that it is exploratory in nature, the sample is small, and the representativeness of the sample is unknown. The small sample, the unknown representativeness, and the possible biases that enter into the study as a result of the sampling procedure all impinge on the generalizability of the findings presented in this paper.

There are, however, strengths in the study which tend to offset the limitations of sample design and sample size. First, this is a unique study. The area of spousal violence has long suffered from "selective inattention" (Dexter, 1958) on the part of both society and the research community. While some data has been gathered on the topic of family violence, most of the studies focus on one type of population—either petitioners for divorce (O'Brien, 1971; Levinger, 1966), patients of psychiatrists (Snell, Rosenwald, and Robey, 1964), or college students (Straus, 1974; Steinmetz, 1974). This study is one of the few which examines not only those in special circumstances (agency clients or those calling police), but also an equal number of families who had no contact with agencies of social service or control. While the sample is obviously not representative, it is one of the closest yet to a study of violence in a cross-section of families.

A second strength of the methodology is that it yielded a population without a working class, lower class, or middle class bias. The sample ranged from families at the lowest regions of socioeconomic status, to middle class families in which one or both spouses had graduated from college and had a combined family income exceeding $25,000. (For a complete discussion of the social characteristics of the respondents and their families, see Gelles, 1974:205–215.)

Although the methodology was not designed specifically to address the issue posed in this paper, it turned out to be particularly well suited for the proposed analysis. The sampling technique yielded wives who were divorced from violent husbands, wives who called the police, wives who were clients of a social service agency, and wives who had never sought any outside intervention.

The interviews with the 80 family members yielded 41 women who had been physically struck by their husbands during their marriage. Of these, nine women had been divorced or separated from their husbands; 13 had called on the police and were still married; eight sought counseling from a private social service agency (because of violence and other family problems); and 11 had sought no outside intervention.

## FINDINGS

We derived some ideas and predictions concerning factors which distinguished between beaten wives who obtained outside intervention and those who did not attempt to bring in outside resources or file for a divorce. These ideas are based on the interviews with the 41 members of violent families and on previous research on family violence. We utilized both quantitative and qualitative data obtained from the interviews to assess the effect of: (1) severity and frequency of violence; (2) experience and exposure to violence in one's family of

**TABLE 1**

*Violence Severity by Intervention Mode*

| Intervention | Mean Violence Severity |
| --- | --- |
| No Intervention | 2.1 |
| Divorced or Separated | 5.1 |
| Called Police | 4.0 |
| Went to Agency | 4.6 |
| Total for all who sought intervention | 4.6 |

$F = 5.2$  Statistically significant at the .01 level

orientation; (3) education and occupation of the wife, number of children, and age of oldest child; and (4) external constraint on the actions of the victimized wife.

### Severity and Frequency of Violence

Common sense suggests that if violence is severe enough or frequent enough, a wife will eventually attempt to either flee from her abusive husband or to bring in some mediator to protect her from violence.

In order to analyze whether severity of violence influenced the reactions of the wife, we constructed a 10 point scale of violence severity (0 = no violence; 1 = pushed or shoved; 2 = threw object; 3 = slapped or bit; 4 = punched or kicked; 5 = pushed down; 6 = hit with hard object; 7 = choked; 8 = stabbed; 9 = shot). This scale measured the most severe violence the wife had ever experienced as a victim.

Table 1 indicates that the more severe the violence, the more likely the wife is to seek outside assistance. An examination of wives' reactions to particular instances of violence reveals even more about the impact of violence severity on the actions of abused wives. Of the eight women who were either shot at (one), choked (six), or hit with a hard object (one), five had obtained divorces, two had called the police, and one had sought counseling from a social service agency. At the other extreme, of the nine women who had been pushed or shoved (eight), or had objects thrown at them (one), one had gotten a divorce, one had called the police, and seven had sought no assistance at all.

How frequently a wife is hit also influences her decision whether to remain with her husband, call the police, go to a social worker, or seek dissolution of the marriage. Only 42 percent of the women who had been struck once in the marriage had sought some type of intervention, while 100 percent of the women who had been hit at least once a month and 83 percent of the women who had been struck at least once a week had either obtained a divorce or separation, called the police, or [gone] to a social service agency. Frequency of violence is also related to what type of intervention a wife seeks. Women hit weekly to daily are most likely to call the police, while women hit less often (at least once a month) are more inclined to get a divorce or legal separation.

There are a number of plausible explanations as to why frequency of violence influences mode of intervention. Perhaps the more frequent the violence, the more a wife wants immediate protection, whereas victims of monthly violence gradually see less value in staying married to a husband who explodes occasionally. A possible explanation of the findings might be that women who were divorced or separated were ashamed to admit they tolerated violence as long as they did (for fear of being labeled "sado-masochists"). Also, it may be that victims of frequent violence are afraid of seeking a temporary or permanent separation. Victims of weekly violence may be terrorized by their violent husbands and view police intervention as more tolerable to their husbands than a divorce or separation. Finally, women who are struck frequently might feel that a separation or divorce might produce a radical or possible lethal reaction from an already violent husband.

### Experience With and Exposure to Violence as a Child

Studies of murderers (Gillen, 1946; Guttmacher, 1960; Leon, 1969; Palmer, 1962; Tanay, 1969), child abusers (Bakan, 1971; Gelles, 1973; Gil, 1971; Kempe *et al.*, 1962; Steele and Pollock, 1974), and violent spouses (Gelles, 1974; Owens and Straus, 1975) support the assumption that the more an individual is exposed to violence as a child (both as an observer and a victim), the more he or she is violent as an adult. The explanation offered for this relationship is that the experience with violence as a victim and observer teaches the individual how to be violent and also to approve of the use of violence. In other words, exposure to violence provides a "role model" for violence (Singer, 1971). If experience with violence can provide a role model for the offender, then perhaps it can also provide a role model for the victim.

Women who observed spousal violence in their family of orientation were more likely to be victims of conjugal violence in their family of procreation. Of the 54 women who never saw their parents fight physically, 46 percent were victims of spousal violence, while 66 percent of the 12 women who observed their parents exchange blows were later victims of violent attacks. In addition, the more frequently a woman was struck by her parents, the more likely she was to grow up and be struck by her husband.

There are two interrelated reasons why women who were exposed to or were victims of intrafamilial violence would be prone to be the victims of family violence as adults. It is possible that the more experience with violence a woman has, the more she is inclined to approve of the use of violence in the family. She may grow up with the expectation that husbands are "supposed" to hit wives, and this role expectation may in turn become the motivator for her husband to use violence on her. Another explanation of these findings integrates the subculture theory of violence (Wolfgang and Ferracuti, 1967) with the homogamy theory of mate selection (Centers, 1949; Ecklund, 1968; Hollingshead, 1950). Thus, it could be argued that women who grew up in surroundings which included and approved of family violence, are more likely to marry a person who is prone to use violence.

**TABLE 2**

*Intervention Mode by Wife's Experience With Violence as a Child*

| | Type of Intervention | | | |
|---|---|---|---|---|
| Type of Experience as Child | Divorced or Separated | Called Police | Went to Agency | Total Seeking Intervention |
| A. *Parents Violent to Respondent:* | | | | |
| None (N = 3) | 33% | 0% | 66% | 100% |
| Infrequent[a] (N = 13) | 23% | 38% | 15% | 76% |
| Frequent[b] (N = 17) | 24% | 35% | 18% | 77% |
| B. *Parents Violent to Each Other:* | | | | |
| None observed (N = 25) | 28% | 28% | 20% | 76% |
| Observed (N = 8) | 63% | 13% | 13% | 89% |

[a] less than 6 times a year
[b] from monthly to daily

Given the fact that being a victim of violence as a child or seeing one's parents physically fight makes a woman more vulnerable to becoming the victim of conjugal violence, does exposure and experience with violence as a child affect *the actions* of a beaten wife? There are two alternative predictions that could be made. First, the less a woman experienced violence in her family of orientation, the more likely she is to view intrafamilial violence as deviant, and thus, the more she is willing to seek intervention or a divorce when hit by her husband. On the other hand, exposure to violence may provide a role model for the woman as to what to do when attacked. Thus, the *more* violence she was exposed to, the more she will know about how to get outside help, and the more she will seek this help.

Being a victim of parental violence and frequency of victimization appear to have no bearing on the beaten wife's decision whether or not to seek outside intervention (Table 2). Those women who observed their parents engaged in physical fights were slightly more likely to obtain outside intervention after being hit by their husbands. For those women who did see their parents engage in conjugal violence, the predominant mode of intervention in their own family of procreation was a divorce or separation. There is no predominant mode of intervention chosen by those women who did not witness violence in their families of orientation.

Thus, neither of the alternative predictions is strongly supported by the data on experience and exposure to violence. There is the suggestion that exposure to conjugal violence makes women *less tolerant* of family violence and more desirous of ending a violent marriage. Along these lines, some of the women we interviewed stated that after they saw their parents fight they vowed that they would never stand for their own husbands hitting them. However, the data do not support the claim that this position is widespread among wives who witnessed violence as they grew up.

### Education, Occupation, Number of Children, Age of Children

Truninger (1971) has proposed that the stronger the commitment to marriage, the less a wife will seek legal action against a violent husband. We have modified this hypothesis by proposing that the fewer resources a wife has in a marriage, the fewer alternatives she has to her marriage; and the more "entrapped" she is in the marriage, the more reluctant she will be to seek outside intervention. Thus, we hypothesize that unemployed wives with low education will not do anything when beaten. It is difficult to predict what influence number of children and age of children have on the actions of the wife. Snell, Rosenwald and Robey (1964) state that the presence of an older child motivates women to take their husbands to court.

Looking at the relationship between each variable and intervention, we see that the variable which best distinguishes wives who obtain assistance from those who remain with their husbands is holding a job. While only 25 percent of those wives who sought no help worked, 50 percent of the wives who called the police, went to a social service agency, or were separated or divorced from their husbands held jobs. This confirms our hypothesis that the more resources a wife has, the more she is able to support herself and her children, the more she will have a low threshold of violence and call outside agents or agencies to help her. Thus, the less dependent a wife is on her husband, the more likely she is to call for help in instances of violence. In addition to this resource dimension, wives reported that holding a job gave them a view of another world or culture. This new perspective made their own family problems seem less "normal" and more serious than they had felt when they were at home. This point is illustrated in the following excerpt from one of our interviews with a women who was the client of a social service agency and who had been beaten by her husband when they were first married:

> Until I started being out in the public, to realize what was going on around me, I was so darned stupid and ignorant. I didn't know how the other half of the world lived. And when I started being a waitress I used to love to sit there—when I wasn't busy—and watch the people—the mother and the father with their children—and see how they acted. And I started to feel like I was cheated... and it started to trouble me and I started to envy those people. So I said, "you know... am I supposed to live the way I'm living?"

Women who called the police or went to an agency often had teenage children. The data confirm the Snell, Rosenwald, and Robey (1964) finding that women who brought their husbands to court had teenage children. In some of our interviews, wives reported that they started calling the police when their son or daughter was old enough to get embroiled in the physical conflicts. In these cases, the wives wanted help to protect their children rather than themselves.

Neither education (measured by mean years of school completed and completed high school) nor number of children distinguishes between abused women seeking help and those staying with their husbands.

*Richard J. Gelles*

**TABLE 3**

*Education, Occupation, Number of Children, Age of Oldest Child by Intervention Mode*

|  | Mean Education | Percentage Completed High School | Percentage Employed | Mean Number of Children | Mean Age of Oldest Child |
|---|---|---|---|---|---|
| No Intervention (N = 11) | 11.9 | 63% | 25% | 2.5 | 9.3 |
| Divorced or Separated (N = 9) | 11.7 | 66% | 44%* | 3.3 | 9.3 |
| Called Police (N = 13) | 11.0 | 69% | 38% | 3.0 | 13.0 |
| Went to Agency (N = 8) | 11.1 | 62% | 75% | 2.6 | 13.7 |
| All Intervention | 11.3 | 67% | 50% | 3.0 | 12.0 |

*For those wives who are divorced or separated, some may have found employment *after* the divorce or separation. The data did not allow us to determine *when* the wife found employment.

**Combined Effects of Variables on Intervention**

Up to this point we have examined the effects of the variables which we believed would be likely determinants of whether or not a wife sought intervention. This analysis, however, does not allow us to assess the effects of all these variables in explaining whether or not a wife would seek outside help in cases of conjugal violence. In order to examine the impact of all the variables together, we employed a step-wise multiple regression procedure which allowed us to see what proportion of the variance of intervention or particular intervention modalities is explained by combinations of the independent variables.

*Intervention.* Table 4 reveals that the best predictor of whether or not a wife seeks intervention is violence severity in her family of procreation. Thus, women who seek intervention are strongly influenced by the level of violence in their family. The five variables entered into the regression analysis explain 32 percent of the variance in seeking intervention or not.

*Divorced or Separated.* The best predictor of whether or not a wife obtains a divorce or separation is the level of violence in her family of procreation. The combined effect of all the variables entered into the equation is the explanation of 14 percent of the variance in the dependent variable; however, the multiple $R$'s are not statistically significant at the .05 level.

*Called Police.* We are able to explain 11 percent of the variance in this variable, but again, multiple $R$'s are not statistically significant at the .05 level. Unlike separation or divorce, in which cases severity and extent of violence in her family of procreation played major roles in the wife's actions, the calling of police is associated with the wife's occupational status and her education. Women with less occupational status and lower education are likely to call the police for help. This finding is consistent with the popular assumption that the poor man's social worker is the police officer.

## TABLE 4
*Step-Wise Regression of Independent Variables and Intervention and Intervention Modalities*

|  | Multiple R | $R^2$ | Beta |
|---|---|---|---|
| A. Regression of Intervention on: | | | |
| Violence Severity | .434[a] | .189 | .365 |
| Completed High School | .488[a] | .238 | .331 |
| Parental Violence to Respondent | .530[a] | .280 | −.260 |
| Frequency of Violence | .559[a] | .312 | .221 |
| Wife's Occupational Status[c] | .570[a] | .324 | −.136 |
| B. Regression of Divorced or Separated on: | | | |
| Violence Severity | .281 | .080 | .211 |
| Wife's Education | .314 | .099 | .298 |
| Frequency of Violence | .324 | .105 | .154 |
| Completed High School | .340 | .115 | −.136 |
| Wife's Occupational Status[c] | .347 | .120 | .089 |
| Violence Between Parents | .352 | .124 | −.027 |
| Number of Children | .355 | .126 | .261 |
| Age of Oldest Child | .373 | .140 | .231 |
| C. Regression of Called Police on: | | | |
| Wife's Occupational Status[c] | .195 | .038 | −.231 |
| Completed High School | .256 | .065 | .423 |
| Wife's Education | .314 | .099 | −.245 |
| Parental Violence to Respondent | .319 | .101 | −.016 |
| Age of Oldest Child | .324 | .105 | −.233 |
| Number of Children | .340 | .115 | .233 |
| D. Regression of Went to Agency on: | | | |
| Parental Violence to Respondent | .326[b] | .106 | −.191 |
| Age of Oldest Child | .350 | .122 | .480 |
| Number of Children | .425[b] | .180 | −.496 |
| Violence Severity | .442 | .196 | .144 |

[a] statistically significant at the .01 level
[b] statistically significant at the .05 level
[c] Occupational Status measured using Bureau of Census status score (see Robinson, Athanasiou, and Head, 1969: 357).

*Went to Agency.* The best predictor of going to a social service agency is how much violence the wife experienced as a child. The less violence, the more likely she is to seek a social worker's help. In contrast to the previous dependent variables, age and number of children play a greater part in influencing a wife's decision to go to a social service agency. Almost 20 percent of the variance in seeking agency assistance is explained by the four variables included in the regression.

*Chapter 11
Violence
and Abuse*

The fact that a woman would call the police or seek agency assistance after repeated incidents of conjugal violence does not necessarily mean that she will call the police again or continue going to an agency. One fact remained quite clear at the end of the eighty interviews: most agencies and most legal organizations are quite unprepared and unable to provide meaningful assistance to women who have been beaten by their husbands. With minor exceptions, such as the work done by Bard and his colleagues (1969; 1969; 1971), little formal training has been given to police in how to intercede in conjugal disputes. Truninger (1971) reports that the courts are often mired in mythology about family violence (e.g., "violence fulfills the masochistic need of women victims") and consequently the justice system is ineffective in dealing with marital violence. Field and Field (1973:225) echo these sentiments and state that unless the victim dies, the chances that the court system will deal seriously with the offender are slight. Women who are abused by their husbands must suffer grave injury in order to press legal charges. The California Penal Code states that a wife must be more injured than commonly allowed for battery to press charges against her husband (Calvert, 1974:89). As Field and Field (1973) state, there is an official acceptance of violence between "consenting" adults and the belief that this violence is a private affair. This attitude, held by police, the courts, and the citizenry, constrains many wives from either seeking initial help, or once obtaining help, continuing to use it.

Although social work agencies are not as "indifferent" about marital violence as the courts and police are (Field and Field, 1973:236), they are often unable to provide realistic answers for victims of violence because of the rather limited amount of knowledge in this area. The data on marital violence are so scanty that few policy or intervention strategies have been worked out for the use of social workers. Without a good knowledge of the causes and patterns of marital violence, many social workers have had to rely on stop-gap measures which never address the real problem of marital violence.

A final source of external constraint is the wife's fear that the myth of her peaceful family life will be exploded. Many women we spoke to would never think of calling the police, going to a social work agency, or filing for a divorce because those actions would rupture the carefully nurtured myth of their fine family life. One woman, who had been struck often and hard over a 30 year marriage said she would never call the police because she was afraid it would appear in the papers. Truninger (1971:264) supports these findings by stating that part of the reason why the courts are ineffective in dealing with marital violence is the strong social pressure on individuals to keep marital altercations private.

In summary, even if a woman want to get help and protection from her husband, she all too frequently finds out that the agents and agencies she calls are ineffective or incapable of providing real assistance. During the course of the interviews, many wives who had sought intervention complained about the futility of such actions. One woman in particular had sought agency help, called the police, and finally filed for a divorce. However, none of these actions actually protected her, and her estranged husband almost strangled her one weekend morning.

The deficiencies of these external agencies and the pressure to cover-up family altercations are two powerful forces which keep women with their abusive husbands.

## CONCLUSION

The purpose of this paper has been to address the important question of why victims of conjugal violence stay with their husbands. Our analysis of the variables which affect the decision to either stay with an abusive husband or to seek intervention, uncovered three major factors which influence the actions of abused women. First, the less severe and the less frequent the violence, the more a woman will remain with her spouse and not seek outside aid. This finding is almost self-evident in that it posits that women seek intervention when they are severely abused. However, the problem is more complex, since severity and frequency of violence explain only part of the variance in abused wives' behavior. A second factor is how much violence a wife experienced as a child. The more she was struck by her parents, the more inclined she is to stay with her abusive husband. It appears that victimization as a child raises the wife's tolerance for violence as an adult. Lastly, educational and occupational factors are associated with staying with an abusive husband. Wives who do not seek intervention are less likely to have completed high school and more likely to be unemployed. We conclude that the fewer resources a woman has, the less power she has, and the more "entrapped" she is in her marriage, the more she suffers at the hands of her husband without calling for help outside the family.

Another factor which appears to influence the actions of a wife is external constraint in the form of police, agency, and court lack of understanding about marital violence.

Although we have presented some factors which partly explain why abused wives remain with their husbands, we have not provided a complete answer to the question this paper raises. The reason for this is that the factors influencing the reactions of an abused wife are tremendously complex. It is not simply how hard or how often a wife is hit, nor is it how much education or income she has. The decision of whether or not to seek intervention is the result of a complex interrelationship of factors, some of which have been identified in this paper.

Although we have provided tentative answers to the central question of this paper, a main underlying issue of this topic has not been addressed. Even though more than 75 percent of the women who had been struck had tried to get outside help, the end result of this intervention was not totally satisfactory. The outlook for women who are physically beaten and injured by their husbands is not good. For those who have few resources, no job, and no idea of how to get help, the picture is grim. But even the women who have the resources and desire to seek outside help often find this help of little benefit.

# REFERENCES

*Chapter 11
Violence
and Abuse*

Bakan, David 1971 Slaughter of the Innocents: A Study of the Battered Child Phenomenon. Boston:Beacon Press.

Bard, Morton 1969 "Family intervention police teams as a community mental health resource." The Journal of Criminal Law, Criminology, and Police Science 60 (June): 24–250.

Bard, Morton, and Bernard Berkowitz 1969 "Family disturbances as a police function." In S. Cohen (Ed.), Law Enforcement Science and Technology II. Chicago:I.I.T. Research Institute.

Bard, Morton, and Joseph Zacher 1971 "The prevention of family violence: Dilemmas of community intervention." Journal of Marriage and the Family 33 (November):677–682.

Calvert, Robert 1974 "Criminal and civil liability in husband-wife assaults." Pp. 88–90 in Suzzanne K. Steinmetz and Murray A. Straus (Eds.), Violence in the Family. New York:Harper and Row.

Centers, Richard 1949 "Marital selection and occupational strata." American Journal of Sociology 54 (May):530–535.

Dexter, Louis A. 1958 "A note on selective inattention in social science." Social Problems 6 (Fall):176–182.

Ecklund, Bruce K. 1968 "Theories of mate selection." Eugenics Quarterly 15 (June):71–84.

Field, Martha H., and Henry F. Field 1973 "Martial violence and the criminal process: Neither justice nor peace." Social Service Review: 47 (June):221–240.

Gelles, Richard J. 1973 "Child abuse as psychopathology: A sociological critique and reformulation." American Journal of Orthopsychiatry 43 (July):611–621.

1974 The Violent Home: A Study of Physical Aggression Between Husbands and Wives. Beverly Hills:Sage Publications, Inc.

Gil, David G. 1971 "Violence against children." Journal of Marriage and the Family 33 (November):637–648.

Gillen, John Lewis 1946 The Wisconsin Prisoner: Studies in Crimogenesis. Madison:University of Wisconsin Press.

Guttmacher, Manfred 1960 The Mind of the Murderer. New York:Farrar, Straus, and Cudahy.

Hollingshead, August B. 1950 "Cultural factors in the selection of mates." American Sociological Review 15 (October):619–627.

Kempe, C. Henry, Frederic N. Silverman, Brandt F. Steele, William Droegemueller, and Henry K. Silver 1962 "The battered child syndrome." Journal of the American Medical Association 181 (July 7):17–24.

Leon, C. A. 1969 "Unusual patterns of crime during 'la Violencia' in Columbia." American Journal of Psychiatry 125 (May):1564–1575.

Levinger, George 1966 "Sources of marital dissatisfaction among applicants for divorce." American Journal of Orthopsychiatry 26 (October):803–897. Pp. 126–132 in Paul H. Glasser and Louis N. Glasser (Eds.), Families in Crisis. New York:Harper and Row.

O'Brien, John E. 1971 "Violence in divorce prone families." Journal of Marriage and the Family 33 (November):692–698.

Owens, David J., and Murray A. Straus 1975 "Childhood violence and adult approval of violence." Aggressive Behavior 1 (2):193–211.

Palmer, Stuart 1962 The Psychology of Murder. New York:Thomas Y. Crowell Company.

Parnas, Raymond I. 1967 "The police response to domestic disturbance." Wisconsin Law Review 914 (Fall):914–960.

Robinson, J. P., R. Athanasiou, and K. Head 1969 Measures of Occupational Attitudes and Occupational Characteristics. Ann Arbor, Michigan:Survey Research Center.

Scanzoni, John H. 1972 Sexual Bargaining. Englewood Cliffs, New Jersey:Prentice-Hall.

Singer, Jerome 1971 The Control of Aggression and Violence. New York:Academic Press.

Snell, John E., Richard J. Rosenwald and Ames Robey 1964 "The wifebeater's wife: A study of family interaction." Archives of General Psychiatry 11 (August):107–113.

Steele, Brandt F., and Carl B. Pollock 1974 "A psychiatric study of parents who abuse infants and small children." Pp. 89–134 in Ray E. Helfer and C. Henry Kempe (Eds.), The Battered Child. Chicago:University of Chicago Press.

Steinmetz, Suzanne K. 1974 "Occupational environment in relation to physical punishment and dogmatism." Pp. 166–172 in Suzanne K. Steinmetz and Murray A. Straus (Eds.). Violence in the Family. New York:Harper and Row.

Straus, Murray A. 1973 "A general systems theory approach to the development of a theory of violence between family members." Social Science Information 12 (June):105–125.

Straus, Murray A. 1974 "Leveling, civility, and violence in the family." Journal of Marriage and the Family 36 (February):13–30.

Straus, Murray A. 1975 "Cultural approval and structural necessity or intrafamily assaults in sexist societies." Paper presented at the International Institute of Victimology, Bellagio, Italy, July.

Tanay, E. 1969 "Psychiatric study of homicide." American Journal of Psychiatry 125 (March):1252–1258.

Truninger, Elizabeth 1971 "Marital violence: The legal solutions." The Hastings Law Journal 23 (November):259–276.

Wolfgang, Marvin E., and F. Ferracuti 1967 The Subculture of Violence. London:Tavistock Publications.

## 11.2 JOHN SCANZONI

# Family Organization and the Probability of Disorganization

In the 1960s married couples were bombarded with changes that new roles for women were producing. More women were not only working outside the home but, in some cases, they were getting jobs that were better paying than their husbands' jobs. These changes had a profound effect on the family system, and couples were striving to adapt to these changes by developing ways to relate to one another besides the traditional roles of breadwinner and homemaker. The family disorganization that resulted from these societal role changes were evident in the rising divorce rate as well as the changing roles of husbands and wives.

John Scanzoni (b. 1935) received his doctorate in 1964 from the University of Oregon. Soon after he published his first book, *Readings in Social Problems* (Allyn & Bacon, 1967). He has published more than a dozen other books, and he has contributed to numerous professional journals and anthologies. He has been a professor of sociology at the University of Florida since 1987.

Scanzoni delineates his model for predicting family dissolution in this selection from "Family Organization and the Probability of Disorganization," *Journal of Marriage and the Family* (November 1966).

**Key Concept:** family violence

The construct of family disorganization[1] is associated with a good deal of confusion both at the formal and empirical levels. One of the root causes of this has been that the generic term "social disorganization" tends to take on evaluative overtones. For example, such phenomena as slums, school dropouts, crime, delinquency, prostitution, mental illness, illegitimacy, as well as divorce have often been described as instances of social disorganization. In the absence of any consistent conceptual framework or empirical procedures to link these substantive areas, there has arisen the vague notion of "social problems." Thus, the usual place where these phenomena are dealt with as a unit is in a social problems text. By definition, "social problem" implies some sort of value-judgment. Therefore, by linking examples of social disorganization through an evaluated framework of "undesirable" elements, social disorganization becomes the product of its definitions, i.e., something undesirable.

At the same time, what is often lacking is any rigorous attempt at an operational definition of the term either in its broad sense or in its application to a particular substantive area. This approach to social disorganization reflects the upper middle-class, liberal, reformist Judaeo-Christian heritage in which sociology was nurtured. One of the consequences of this viewpoint for research has been to try to discover ways in which "better" (i.e., from this standpoint) social conditions can be developed.

For example, the terms "marital adjustment" and "marital success" imply inherently that some marriages are "better" than others, so that the task of research becomes that of identifying the elements that contribute to adjustment or success. In some present-day work, there are attempts to establish criteria for the "efficient family" or "functional family." One great danger of an evaluative approach is that it tends to put blinders on the investigator. He tends automatically to exclude a large range of variables which might otherwise play an important role in the problem at hand.[2]

Likewise, it tends to magnify certain other variables out of proportion. For example, associated with the "marital adjustment" notion has been great stress on the role of expressive gratifications. Yet some have carried this so far as to suggest that the basic explanation for marital dissolution is "affectional failure."[3] The argument is made that, since the modern nuclear family is stripped of its traditional functions (another notion which is in conceptual chaos), all that remains to bind it together is its "affectional function."

In order to escape the joint pitfalls of exclusion and over-magnification, we need to discard the evaluative approach, i.e., what is a "good," "functional," "successful," or "efficient" family. This does not imply the absurd notion that one must divest himself of values regarding the family, nor does it mean that one is not interested in the eventual practical application of knowledge. Instead, it means that in terms of long-range scientific and practical benefits, the largest good will be best served by taking a *theoretical* approach, viz., by asking significant theoretical questions.

For instance, a classic question in sociology is the conditions which contribute to the order-disorder of a social system.[4] Order can be defined as organization or maintenance of a system. This does not imply a static state, for the system itself may undergo change and still remain qua system. Disorder can be defined as the dissolution or disorganization of a system, i.e., it ceases to maintain itself as a system.

# CONDITIONS OF ORDER-DISORDER WITHIN THE CONJUGAL FAMILY

When one asks this classic question of the conjugal family, he not only avoids value-judgments about "adequate" or "inadequate" families; he also links this substantive area more closely to a larger body of social theory. To be sure, Parsons defines disorder of any system (including the family) as pathological not only for the system per se, but also for the larger society.[5] However, Parsons' biases along with those of "functionalism" in general have been criticized elsewhere, and there is no need to repeat them here.[6] The point is that as it relates to the family, Parsons notion that disorder is per se pathological must be rejected in the same way that all such evaluative notions must.

The issue then becomes how one can define and make operational the janus-like and inseparable concepts of *organization* (including its differential states of system-maintenance) and *disorganization* (system-dissolution) of the conjugal family. First it seems imperative to narrow the scope to a consideration of husband-wife roles only. While some formal schemes in the past have raised the question of the significance of child roles in connection with disorganization, at this point it seems premature. Before introducing the complexities attendant upon these kinds of variables, it appears that one needs research demonstrating actual husband-wife linkages.

Sociologists have lone realized that divorce itself is not an adequate indicator of the structure and processes that make up the social system of marriage. The absence of divorce in no way, for example, reveals how close that particular system may or may not be to actual dissolution. However, since marriage as a social system is bound by legal constraints, a divorce decree is an exceedingly useful tool to indicate the *total* dissolution of a particular system. Therefore, as compared to indices of system dissolution in other substantive areas, e.g., political parties, voluntary organization, business enterprises, etc., dissolution of marriage is somewhat easier to identify. This gives the present study at least one advantage in an area otherwise beset by numerous difficulties.

Thus, marital disorganization or disorder can be defined as system dissolution indicated by divorce and perhaps legal separation and permanent desertion as well. While so far nothing has been said as to *why* disorganization should occur, at least a clear and simple definition of marital disorganization has been established. To try to understand why it occurs, one needs to shift his focus to the phenomenon of the social organization of marriage. This seems imperative for one major reason, viz., how can one possibly understand the disorder of a system until he first understands the conditions of its order? Disorganization of X must first be preceded by a description of what X is.

This is not to imply a bipolar model in which some marriages are dissolved and others remain intact. It is suggested that, in a modern society, organization implies inherent differentiation. In other words, one needs to explore differences in the structure and processes of organized marriages. These differential structures and processes should be operationally distinguished from one another through the use of theoretically significant variables. This should enable one to identify differential patterns of organized marriages, i.e., differential patterns of structure and process.

Furthermore, one should then be able to compare these patterns in terms of their relative probability of system dissolution. These probabilities should be based on already existing knowledge as well as on predictions derived from the particular ways in which the key variables are combined. Through this approach one accounts for disorganization as well as for differences among organized marriages, while at the same time avoiding any assessments of one pattern vis-à-vis another.

The next question, of course, pertains to the kinds of variables which can be marshalled for such a demanding objective; even more difficult is a discussion of the ways in which they can be combined to describe the differential patterns. What follows is merely an initial effort in this direction. After this model is tested, it will undoubtedly be modified considerably both in terms of relevant variables and their interrelationships. (One important feature of these variables is that they cover the range of different levels of analysis: structural-cultural, social psychological, interpersonal, and individual.)

## SIGNIFICANT VARIABLES

First, therefore, the place of economic variables should be considered. Murdock argues that there are two bases to the nuclear family, the economic and the sexual (or the expressive). Without patterned husband-wife relationships in both spheres, marriage cannot be said to exist.[7] The cohesive nature of joint agricultural interaction between husbands and wives is quite apparent. Not so apparent are the kinds of elements that may serve an analogous or equivalent function in a modern society. Recent research has indicated that husband-wife congruence or conflict over (1) husband's occupational achievement and (2) life-style aspirations may be equivalent variables.[8] It seems unfortunate that such notions as "loss of traditional family functions" have diverted attention from Murdock's conclusion as well as from the compelling logic that economic factors cannot be dismissed as lightly as they have been. One of the core dimensions of a modern society is stress on achievement and success. Does it not seem reasonable to assume that these pervasive factors would in some way affect the organization-disorganization of the conjugal family?

Second, there is some evidence that social class background may also be related to the problem at hand.[9] Goode, for example, found a strong relationship between wife hypogamy (downward, measured by father's occupation and respondent's education) and divorce.[10] Hypergamy (wife upward) and homogamy were less related to divorce. He explained these relationships by arguing that it is easier for the wife to learn the occupational roles of a stratum higher than her own than it is for the husband. The relationship of homogamy to marital stability has been shown by numerous studies but never adequately explained. However, Goode's attempt at explanation provides some linkage between economic and stratification factors.

Third, there is the important variable of self-esteem. This is some evidence that in a modern society male self-esteem is dependent on occupational achievement and success.[11] Female self-esteem may be a function of her husband's occupational attainments, the resultant life-style, companionate and/or expressive relations with husband and/or children, or certain extra-familial achievements of her own.

Fourth, one cannot overlook the important realm of husband-wife companionship; but if it is to be theoretically fruitful, it must be generalized beyond this common-sense notion to the concept of nonwork interaction. This then becomes the complement of economic factors. There are certain norms and behaviors that are characteristic of the economic realm, others that are characteristic of the nonwork or leisure area. But these realms are interdependent: the Puritan view of work was inseparable from the Puritan view of leisure.[12] Goode found that husband-wife conflict over economic behavior was transferred to and resulted in "negative marital adjustment."[13] As noted earlier, some sociologists have made expressive relations between partners the major independent variable to account for dissolution. From the discussion thus far and from what shall follow, the attempt to reduce dissolution to this kind of simplistic X-Y relationship must be reckoned inadequate.

Finally, there is the variable of perceived situational satisfaction. As used by Blood and Wolfe, it refers to the actor's evaluation of the global situation in which he is involved.[14] If Farber is correct when he argues that actors tend to evaluate marriage in an individualistic sense, viz., how it meets individual interests, then this becomes a crucial variable indeed.

## PATTERNS OF HUSBAND-WIFE INTERACTION

Let us turn now to different patterns which might emerge when these variables interrelate and the probability of disorganzation inherent in these combinations. First, one should consider a pattern in which there is congruence between husband and wife over his present occupational achievement and the resultant family life-style. The partners tend to be homogamous with regard to social background and education. If the husband has a nonmanual or upper-manual occupation, chances are good that his self-esteem is reinforced or at least not threatened by the occupational structure. He defines his present level of achievement as satisfactory, as does his wife. Consequently, she does not pose a threat to his self-esteem through conflict over his "underachievement." Her self-esteem insofar as it is a function of the life-style he provides is likewise free from threat.

Structural consensus and social psychological reinforcement tend to promote! husband-wife expressive conjunctiveness during nonwork time. Companionship with each other, the children, and the same friends tend to become institutionalized, and the initial affect of the marriage is preserved. Furthermore, both actors are quite likely to define this type of marital situation as highly satisfactory. As a result, the probability that this pattern of organized marriage will dissolve is quite low. In terms of this combination of five variables, the signs point to continued maintenance of the system.

Second, a situation is posited in which there is conflict between husband and wife over his levels of achievement. The wife defines her husband as "overachieving," i.e., she believes that he gives so much time and energy to his occupational roles, that he does not adequately fulfill his conjugal expressive roles. (One would expect him to have a nonmanual occupation and the marriage to be wife-hypergamous.) It may be that his self-esteem is so low or weak that no matter what the extent of his "objective" occupational success, e.g., first vice-president of corporation X, he feels he must continually strive for more success in order to maintain any self-esteem at all. His inability and/or unwillingness to "turn off his occupational roles," makes the fulfillment of conjugal roles quite difficult.

The probabilities that this situation will eventuate in disorganization differ in terms of the wife's self-esteem. To the extent that it is a function of the life-style provided by the husband (which we would expect to be affluent at the least) or of the wife's own extra-familial activities (occupational, community), one would expect less of a tendency toward disorganization when compared to the other alternative. If the wife's self-esteem is more a function of expressive or primary relations, then one would expect the tendency toward disorganization to be higher. This is because in the former case the wife is more apt to define the total marital situation as satisfactory. In spite of the husband's minimal performance of expressive roles, the wife's self-esteem is bolstered through other elements. On the other hand in the latter case, since the wife lacks alternative sources by which to bolster self-esteem, her situational satisfaction is apt to be less. An additional element in this latter situation is that the wife is more apt to conflict with her husband in an attempt to get him to change his behavior. Thus, not only is extensive and intensive conflict introduced into the situation, but it is very likely that her demands may be perceived as a further threat to his self-esteem.

Nonetheless, while one would predict differences in the probability of disorganization between the two subpatterns, overall he would expect greater tendencies toward disorganization in this general pattern than in the first pattern discussed above. Comparatively there is less structural congruence and social psychological reinforcement; thus the potential for disorganization is greater.

For the third major pattern, no conflict between husbands and wives over achievement and life-style is posited, nor is the impact of either hypogamy or hypergamy certain. It is suggested that the husband has a manual or lower-level nonmanual job. He perceives his success goals to be frustrated or unattainable, i.e., he defines himself as achieving at a lower level than he would like to. He may define certain significant others as feeling the same way, e.g., wife, children, though in fact they may not. Consequently his self-esteem is quite low, and since he cannot raise it through greater "occupational success," he attempts to bolster it through nonwork activities which, like the occupation, are external to the marriage. Thus, for instance, Komarovsky describes the familiar working-class pattern in which adult, married males obtain mutual reinforcement for self-esteem through behaviors that are primarily significant to other males and not to family members.[15] This results in minimal fulfillment of conjugal, expressive roles.

Once again the question as to whether or not the wife will actively conflict with her husband over his minimal conjugal behavior depends on the sources of her self-esteem. May it be the kind of life-style he provides? It is probably at a lower level than that described in pattern two. Equally problematical in terms of support for self-esteem are the kinds of extra-familial activities in which the wives might engage. Compared to pattern two, the occupations open to these women are probably of a lower status level, and the community activities largely restricted to the lower-level tasks of groups such as the church and scouting.

Thus as sources of self-esteem, life-style, husband-expressive interaction, occupation, and community activities are all problematical. The one firm alternative source for the wife in this situation is the circle of female significant others whose husbands also behave in this fashion in addition to her relatives. These individuals support her self-esteem by reinforcing the universality and legitimacy of her situation.

The uncertainty of these several factors when compared to pattern two suggest[s] the probability of higher levels of conflict and lower levels of satisfaction for both partners. In other words, given even lower structural congruence and social psychological reinforcement than in pattern two, one would expect a higher probability of disorganization.

In the fourth pattern, one expects the wife to have married hypogamously in terms of background and/or present education and thus to have higher levels of achievement and life-style than her husband. (He would probably be a manual worker.) Her self-esteem appears threatened by his "underachievement" and if she conflicts with him to get him to raise his achievement levels, his self-esteem, which is presumably already low due to his lower occupational level, is severely threatened. Even more threatening to male self-esteem is the wife who in this situation goes to work in order to attain the family life-style she desires and whose role becomes defined as breadwinner or provider, as her husband's is.[16] The conflict which ensues from both sides in this situation is particularly severe[17] and probably undermines meaningful expressive relations, thus reducing total situational satisfaction. As compared to the third pattern, this contains even fewer problematic elements which might maintain the system. There appear to be almost no alternative forms of behavior for either the husband or wife other than a radical reorientation, viz., the husband increases his achievement levels markedly, or the wife relinquishes her demands in this regard.

Therefore, it appears that this pattern more than any of the others contains the greatest inherent probability of disorganization. The well-known inverse relationship between occupation and dissolution lends support to this observation.

Finally, one must consider a residual pattern. In the first instance husbands and wives shared the same high achievement levels; in the second the husband exceeded the wife; third, the husband perceived himself as underachieving; fourth, the wife perceived the husband in this fashion; and fifth, *neither* partner defines occupational achievement as a meaningful form of behavior. Recent poverty studies have suggested that a certain proportion of the population simply have no meaningful integration into the opportunity structure and, what is more, they do not desire it.[18] Thus, from Murdock's standpoint that the conjugal family requires an economic dimension, in these cases there is none. (Survival of individual is guaranteed by the larger society, but relief checks are hardly able to supply even the minimal life-style valued in American society.) When one considers the expressive dimension, the high rates of illegitimacy and sexual promiscuity within these strata suggest that norms operative in the larger society are generally inoperative here.[19]

The absence of either dimension makes discussion of the disorganization of the conjugal family somewhat of a reductio ad absurdum, since the question can be raised as to whether any "organization" existed in the first place. Nevertheless, to be consistent with the development of the model thus far, the inability of large numbers of males and females to maintain systemic relationships suggests that it is here that one will find the highest rates of marital disorganization.

## SUMMARY

It has been suggested that conjugal family organization-disorganization be treated as a janus-like construct. Organization is defined as system-maintenance and disorganization as system-dissolution. Since in a modern society organization implies differentiation, five different patterns of organized marriages were suggested, each differing from one another in terms of combinations of five key variables and, most important, in terms of the probability of their dissolution. It is stressed that this model is only an initial effort and will undoubtedly be modified after an empirical test in the city of Indianapolis in the early part of 1967.

## NOTES

1. A thorough review of the literature on family disorganization is contained in Jetse Sprey. "Family Disorganization: A Conceptual Approach," a paper presented at the April, 1966, meetings of the Ohio Valley Sociological Society.
2. For example, see Lewis A. Coser, *The Functions of Social Conflict*, New York: The Free Press, 1956, p. 83, where he points out that "marriage prediction analysis" has assumed that any conflict within marriage is per se dysfunctional, whereas, in fact, certain kinds of conflicts could be described as functional for the marriage.
3. For example, see Robert F. Winch, *The Modern Family,* New York: Holt, Rinehart, Winston, rev. ed., 1963, p. 702 ff.
4. Alex Inkeles, *What is Sociology?* Englewood Cliffs, N.J.: Prentice-Hall, 1964, p. 25.
5. Talcott Parsons, *The Social System,* New York: The Free Press, 1951, chaps. 7 and 11.
6. Coser, *op. cit.*
7. George P. Murdock, *Social Structure,* New York: The Macmillan Co., 1949, pp. 6–9.
8. John Scanzoni, "Structure and Process in Marital Organization-Disorganization," (in press).

9. *Ibid.*

10. William J. Goode, *After Divorce,* New York: The Free Press, 1956, p. 97 ff.

11. Ephraim Mizruchi, *Success and Opportunity,* New York: The Free Press, 1964, p. 150.

12. See Bennett M. Berger, "The Sociology of Leisure: Some Suggestions," *Industrial Relations,* 1 (February 1962), pp. 31–45.

13. *Op. Cit.,* p. 63.

14. Robert O. Blood and Donald M. Wolfe, *Husbands and Wives,* New York: The Free Press, 1960, p. 101, *passim.*

15. Mirra Komarovsky, *Blue-Collar Marriage,* New York: Random House, 1962, chap. 9.

16. See Goode, *op. cit.,* p. 62.

17. Conflict that Coser, *op. cit.,* labels as that which "threatens the very bonds of system-cohesion."

18. For example, see Michael Schwartz, "The Northern United States Negro Matriarchy: Status vs. Authority," *Phylon,* 26:1 (1965), pp. 18–24.

19. In 1963 the illegitimacy ratio of white births was 63.3; for nonwhite births it was 235.9. *Natality Statistic Analysis: United States-1963,* Washington, D.C.: U.S. Public Health Service, Series 21, Number 8, pp. 25–26.

# CHAPTER 12 Stress and the Family

## 12.1 REUBEN HILL AND ELISE BOULDING

# *Crisis Situations Experienced by All Families*

Reuben Hill published his book *Families Under Stress: Adjustment to the Crises of War Separation and Reunion* (Harper & Brothers) in 1949. By that time, World War II had ended, but its effects on families were still evident. The family system that had adapted to the separation of family members due to the war and the sacrifices of a prewar way of life had to readapt once again. Families had to reform with all family members who had been gone because they were fighting the war. This selection from *Families Under Stress*, written in collaboration with Elise Boulding, now a professor emerita of sociology at Dartmouth College, details problems associated with family composition changes and outlines some solutions to these problems.

Hill has received many awards for his extensive work in the family field. He was the first recipient of the Ernest W. Burgess Award for continuous and meritorious contributions to family theory and research; he was given the Helen DeRoy Award for research on social problems; and he was appointed Regents' Professor of Family Sociology in the Department of Sociology and the Family Study Center at the University of Minnesota. Among his publications are *Family Development in Three Generations* (Schenkman,

1970) and a revision of Willard Waller's *The Family: A Dynamic Interpretation* (Dryden Press, 1951).

**Key Concept:** family crisis

*T*his [selection] was written by Elise Boulding from our case study materials. It provides an understanding of the variety of crises and reactions to crisis which the statistical analysis misses. Depth of family living and processes of adjustment are also caught by this method, supplementing nicely the generalizations reached from the statics of statistical analysis....

# CONTENT OF THE CRISIS SITUATION

### Hardships and Definitions of Hardships

The external realities of a situation as seen by other people and the conception of that same situation by the person who is participating in it, may be two very different things. Thomas and Znaniecki, in the *Polish Peasant*, have pointed out the importance of the definition of the situation in determining its effect on the person who is experiencing it. The materials gathered in this study [of 135 Iowa families] illustrate this point extremely well. Time and time again we find families faced with circumstances that would be termed hardships by any observer, and, yet, because the circumstances are regarded differently by the family, they may not only fail to produce hardship reactions but they may serve as a stimulus to better adjustment. On the other hand, a family may be faced with a situation that would not seem to other people to involve any hardships, and yet the family itself considers that it had trouble: Because our study offers such a unique opportunity for validating this concept of the definition of the situation, a distinction will be made, as we discuss each, between the trouble itself and the family's conception of it. This will be done by using two or three cases to illustrate each hardship; the first case will be one in which the family faces what would be considered by the general public to be a hardship, and feels itself that the situation is a hardship; and the second case will reveal a situation where trouble, as defined by the outside world, is present but is not defined as such by the family. Where an example is available of a family which considers that it has a hardship which outsides would not define as such, this will be given also.

### Missing the Husband as a Companion, Father, Handy Man, and Protector

Theoretically, all the families suffered the same hardship in the mere fact of being deprived of their men; that is, they were all deprived of companion, father, handy man, protector, and whatever other things the man of the house was to them. However, ... the men played widely different roles in their respective families, and each family missed its man in terms of his own special role in the home. In most families, the man was all of the four things mentioned above, and more, and these folks, like the B's, missed him hourly and longed for his return:

> The B's were an extremely happy, coöperative, equalitarian family who tried to make the best of a bad situation when it became evident that B was to be drafted. The B's were still romantic about each other after nine years of marriage and letters were no substitute for the frequent demonstrations of affection they were used to. The older child never got used to his father's absence, moped, and did poorly in school, and Mrs. B missed his disciplining hand with the children very much. The responsibility of keeping the home running smoothly and making decisions about family activities, expenditures, etc., seemed very heavy to her also, and she longed for the day when Mr. B could take over again.

Let us turn now to the families that missed their man in a more specific way.

> The C family, for example, missed Mr. C chiefly as a companion. The C family was an equalitarian partnership which had wanted to do its part when war broke out. Mr. C tried to enlist but was turned down, so the draft a year later came as an unexpected shock. Mrs. C had always taken a good deal of responsibility in the home, but was also very dependent on her husband emotionally—he gave her the love and security that her childhood in an orphanage had lacked. She managed the physical routines of the house well but poured out her soul in letters and lived for the day when he would return, as did the children.

In other families he was missed only as the children's father, the wife feeling completely adequate in every way except as disciplinarian.

> Mrs. J, a charming and intelligent woman, had for years submitted to a tyrannic patriarchal husband as was the custom in the Italian group of which they were a part, and found herself free to plan her own days for the first time since their marriage. Her enjoyment of the separation would have been complete if it had not been for the fact that she was so accustomed to having her husband rule the children that she did not know how to manage them alone, and always missed him when a disciplinary situation arose.

In some cases the children were still close to their father when the parents were already estranged. One wife refrained from divorcing her husband while he was overseas only because her daughter, who loved her father dearly, begged her not to.

Some women who had felt that husbands could be dispensed with discovered to their dismay that a home was a complicated physical plant, among other things, and that a man was mighty helpful in keeping it going.

> In the D matriarchy, Mrs. D had long ignored her home and concentrated on a career which was to her all-important, while her husband with the help of her grandmother attended to many domestic details and helped make their house a home for their two children. She welcomed his departure, feeling that she could get along better without him, and was considering a divorce. She felt very differently about it after the furnace went on the blink on the coldest day of winter, the

gas stove broke down and filled the house with gas, and the sewer pipes got out of order. She found that running the home was practically a full-time job and longed for the days when her husband used to look after things for her.

Twenty-three of the families did not miss their husbands at all, were glad to be free. The reason for this total inversion of the expected attitudes was chiefly, as one could guess, poor marital adjustment. However, there were also cases where the wife was so self-sufficient and emotionally self-contained and the children already so dependent on the wife, that the departure of the husband really seemed to make no difference to the family. He would, nevertheless, be welcomed back when he returned. The A family is an example of failure to miss the husband because of poor marital adjustment.

> Mr. A was a very prosperous lawyer who was able to provide well for his wife and three children, but the marriage relationship had turned from one of love to a cold business partnership. Mr. A would not divorce his wife because of the damage to his reputation that would ensue, but delighted to practice refined mental torture on her. She bore this because there was no other way of providing for the children, and her husband's departure for the service meant a blessed respite from his cruelty.

The majority of today's hardy womanhood would hardly sympathize with the hardship claimed by timid women who missed their husbands as physical protectors; they were literally afraid to be alone in their own homes. One brought a sister to live with her, the other already had a mother in the home, and added a 200-pound girl friend as extra protection whenever she went down town.

### Finances

Money trouble, which might have been expected to affect a large number of families, was more a source of challenge than a hardship. Considerable adjustment was necessary, however, in twenty-nine families. Actually, some families had a larger income while Uncle Sam was sending them allotment checks than they ever had before, and in most cases where the income was reduced the wife took pride in managing on the smaller sum. In some cases, however, the drop in income was sufficiently severe that the wife had a real struggle to make ends meet, as in the Z family.

> The Z's were a coöperative matriarchy with a comfortable income and two children. When Mr. Z was drafted, their income was cut by two-thirds and Mrs. Z tried to work to supplement it. She had no one to help her with the children, however, and found that she couldn't care for them and the home adequately and work too. She gave up her job and spent the rest of the separation turning every penny twice in an effort to manage on their inadequate income. She actually did avoid going into debt, although it meant going without many of the things they were used to and living under considerable strain.

Eight of the twenty-nine families who had money trouble did not define it as a hardship, chiefly because they had been through that difficulty before, in the depression, and knew how to handle it. To them the allotment check represented at least security, if not riches. The BD's, for example, took an income cut easily in their stride.

> Mrs. BD was a slight, hardworking woman in an equalitarian family who had helped pull her husband and two children through the long lean years of the depression. She had expected her husband to be deferred because of his health, so the induction caught them unprepared, with unpaid debts and a smaller income. When she got over the initial shock of his departure, she just started scrimping a little harder and saved her worries for more important things like having a baby in Mr. BD's absence in a tiny house in an isolated area where no help was available. Scrimping was second nature anyhow, she said, with no special hardship.

A few families were fairly secure financially but had money trouble because the wife wasn't used to handling money and didn't plan her expenditures well. No observer would think that the S family had any cause for complaint.

> Mr. S was a kindly patriarch. Mrs. S had been a lonely and neglected child who found her first real happiness in marriage, and depended on her husband for everything, never handling money or making any household decisions. She was overwhelmed with the responsibility of deciding how the money should be spent in addition to all her new responsibilities in regard to the home and her two children. However, she was living with her husband's parents, had few of the usual household expenses, and had a sufficiently good relationship with her in-laws that they were able to help her in many ways. In spite of this assistance and an adequate income, she never learned to manage her money well.

### Child Discipline

"Making the children mind" was a problem in sixty-nine cases. It might generally be considered that child discipline in the father's absence would always be a hardship, but this was not the case. In a number of families the wife had already carried most of the responsibility for the children, as in the case of the doctor's family where the father only saw his children on Sundays; and in other cases there was a male relative in the home or nearby who became a father substitute. The C family was not so fortunate.

> In the patriarchal C family, Mrs. C had never trusted her own judgment. She had never managed her two children well because she had never been sure of herself, and she always depended on backing from her husband in dealing with them. Now she found herself powerless to make them mind. Her sister was living with her and helped with the children but that only added to the trouble. Whenever Mrs. C tried to assert her authority, her daughter would threaten her with "I'll tell daddy on you!"

In rare cases the children actually were behavior problems but their mothers did not admit it, even to themselves, because they wanted to feel themselves completely adequate to the situation. The F family is a case in point.

Mrs. F was all mother and no wife, considered herself and her daughter the complete family unit, and had for some years left her husband "out in the cold." She had always felt that she could run the home just as well, if not a little better, without a husband around to clutter up the place. His departure was no great sorrow to her, but her daughter did not share her attitude and moped constantly for daddy. She brooded alone for hours and became unresponsive and uncoöperative, in spite of mother's insistence that they got along fine.

It is well known that all mothers at times have mixed feelings about their "little darlings." In one interesting case little Johnny took his daddy's role in the home in a way that gave him the fond admiration of the community but drove his mother wild. The hardship in this case was not obvious to the observer but very real to the mother.

The DS couple had gradually built up a coöperative, equalitarian relationship after an estrangement early in their married life. Mr. DS wanted to enlist and do his part, but for a year his wife wouldn't let him. When she finally gave in, he had a little talk with their eleven-year-old son before he left, in which he told him to be the man of the house while daddy was away and take good care of mother. The son became transformed overnight from a carefree boy who played with the gang all the time and was never home, to a serious-minded little gentleman who stayed home and helped mother in the house. This was what the community admired, but what drove mother wild was that he considered part of his duty to be making a minute check on all mother's activities. She had to account to him for every moment spent away from the house and was scolded when she went out too much. He told her how to do things in the home and was generally bossy in the way that only self-important children can be bossy. She was helpless to assert herself, particularly as the son wrote long letters keeping his father minutely informed about mother as well as about himself.

### Prolonged Maladjustment of Children

The children were surprisingly little disturbed by the departure of their fathers. There was usually an initial upset followed by a fairly quick recovery. In only twenty-one families did we find children who remained more or less maladjusted during the entire separation period. The mothers of the children are unanimous in defining this maladjustment as a hardship, which is understandable considering that most of these maladjustments expressed themselves as behavior problems. One of the hardest-hit children was Sally H, an only child.

The H family was a contented, equalitarian one that wisely faced the possibility of induction a whole year before it happened, prepared for it by planning to move in with the in-laws and have Mrs. H go to work. The plans made little impression on Sally, though. All she knew was that the tight little family group within which all her world and her joys lay was suddenly disrupted. Father had gone off to war and might be killed. Mother went out to work every day because there wasn't enough money and it helped keep her mind occupied. They moved from the nice little apartment that had always been home to a big house in a strange neighborhood and there was no one home all day to take care of her except grandmother. All of a sudden the very bottom had dropped out of her happy, secure existence, and she was badly frightened. She began to feel that nobody loved her, and as the comfortless situation continued she lost all confidence in her mother, becoming convinced that she and the whole family hated her and wanted to get rid of her. Evenings spent by Mrs. H with Sally did nothing to dispel her fears, and it was not until father returned and the old three-way companionship was reëstablished that she regained her zest for life.

A case less fraught with emotional tension but, nevertheless, hard on the mother was in the G family.

The G family was a matriarchy only because Mr. G wanted his wife to mother him and run things; she had raised seven brothers and sisters and was tired of family responsibility. Mr. G was always willing to romp with the children, but never to assume authority with them. Mrs. G gave good care to their two children, however, and welcomed the separation as a respite from her too dependent husband. Billy, the four-year-old, didn't say much about missing his father and acted pretty normal until one day he drove a rusty nail through his foot while he was playing. The ensuing infection kept Billy off his feet for a few days but when the wound healed Billy reverted to crawling instead of walking. Despite all his mother's pleas and artful wiles, the boy remained on all fours until the day daddy came home. On that day he walked again, and there was no more trouble of that kind!

**Living With In-Laws**

A change of residence sometimes had to be made when the family was left without its furnace man. Twenty-six of the families went to live with grandparents or had grandparents move in with them. The reasons for these moves were numerous. In one or two cases the husband insisted on it before he left, so that he could feel that the family was looked after. Sometimes it was a question of saving money, sometime of easing the wife's burdens by letting the grandparents take over some of the husband's responsibilities. Sometimes it was just plain loneliness that drove the wife out of her own home. The more the move was dictated by necessity, the more it was apt to be regarded as a hardship; twenty-six families did combine with grandparents, and fourteen of them regarded it as a hardship. Mrs. I was one of these.

The I family had done well financially and had a lovely, well-ordered home. Mr. I was the leader in the family but the couple were coöperative and affectionate. They enjoyed their home and had established a pattern of family living which suited them very well. Mrs. I had always been sheltered, however, first by her parents and then by her husband, and when she was faced with the prospect of having a second baby after her husband left for the service, she did not feel up to managing it alone and asked her parents to come and live with her. The parents assumed their old protective attitude and tried to take over the rearing of the older child, but Mrs. I had learned different ways of doing things from her husband. The child became spoiled and insecure as a result of too many bosses and there were many conflicts about how things should be done.

Other families got along with the grandparents very well and were grateful for the help and security they were able to give. Perhaps no other family enjoyed the situation as much as the F's.

> The F's were a flexible, democratic family who took everything in their stride. When faced with the prospect of induction, they accepted Mr. F's departure in terms of "a job to be done" and moved in with Mrs. F's family for the duration. It seemed like the most natural thing in the world for Mrs. F to pack up and go home with her only daughter to mother. She slipped right back into her old place as the favorite child, the grandchild got a good deal of fond attention, and the family enjoyed the separation as a sort of prolonged vacation, although daddy was missed.

In one or two cases where observers would not have anticipated hardships as a result of living with grandparents, the wife felt a severe hardship. In the case below, Mrs. CT had lived with her parents ever since her marriage and a new hardship would not be expected as a result of the departure of her husband from the service.

> In the CT family, the husband was an irresponsible patriarch who made all the decisions but left the work and worry to his wife. He had never made a separate home for his wife and two children, living with them at the home of her parents when he chose, working elsewhere and making unfulfilled promises of sending for them at other times. He enlisted without consulting his wife, and her struggle to maintain her self-respect and her confidence in him against the onslaught of her increasingly critical parents created a very unpleasant situation in the home. Conflicts which had long been repressed as Mrs. CT waited and hoped for a home of her own now suddenly broke out. Since she was now handling the money for the first time since her marriage she also felt more independent than ever before, and less willing to put up with the insulting pity of her parents.

### Housing Inadequacies

Housing troubles, precipitated by the induction of the husband, in terms of overcrowding, inadequate facilities or sheer inability to locate a place to live, were felt by only seven of the families, and only three of these considered it a hardship. The J family were hit hard by this problem.

> Mr. J was an ex-army man who liked to give orders, but made a happy home for his love-starved, dependent wife and only daughter. They had been on the move when the war began, looking for a place to settle down, and accepted the husband's call to service philosophically enough but were caught without a place to live. Mrs. J and her child moved from bleak boarding house to bleak boarding house for months in an effort to find a place where they could settle down until the end of the war, and were despairing of ever finding a more permanent residence when her husband's mother invited them to share her home until Mr. J came back. Now the earlier experience is only a distant nightmare.

A situation that few wives used to the privacy of their own homes would care to put up with was forced upon Mrs. M, but she and two or three others in similar situations thought nothing of it.

> The M's were a highly individualistic but coöperative family, used to getting along without their man for fairly long periods at a time because of his long-distance trucking job. Between the time of notification by the draft board and Mr. M's actual departure, the family had done their crying, dried their tears, and moved into a larger house together with her parents and a sister with husband and two children. The M's also had two children. The house was not nearly large enough for such a tribe, and privacy was impossible. Mrs. M, instead of complaining, was grateful that they had a home at all in the face of their reduced financial circumstances and cheerfully and patiently spent the next couple of years sorting out children, possessions, and tempers.

### Managing the Home

The physical management of the home was a hardship for forty-three of the families. This problem, like child discipline, was in a sense common to all the families, but again a number of women had carried the full responsibility for the home previous to the separation, either by common consent or because the husband was lazy or irresponsible. Also, a number of families had husband-substitutes in the shape of grandparents or other relatives, who helped with odd jobs, budgeting and planning for the family. Of the forty-three families who had no such help or who had trouble in spite of help or previous experience, thirty-five defined their problem as a hardship. The KL's were among these.

> The KL's were Bohemians and followed traditional patterns of family living. The husband was rigidly patriarchal and his wife was very dependent on him in everything. She couldn't believe that he would have to go into service until he actually left, so she was unprepared and wept a great deal. She had just returned recently from the hospital with a second baby, and just didn't feel able to take on her new responsibilities. They also lived in an isolated area where help was hard to get. Never during the whole separation period did she make an independent decision. She either wrote to her husband, or, if there wasn't time for that, she asked her parents who lived in a nearby town what to do. She barely kept the daily routine moving, and the parents handled any exigencies.

The M's in their crowded home, mentioned above, had a more difficult situation but were better equipped to meet it. Mrs. M considered her job as manager of their home as a challenge rather than a hardship. It was her job to clean and keep orderly the overcrowded quarters. It was she who called in the plumber, did the shopping and cooking, supervised all the children while her sister worked, and kept everyone from getting in each other's hair. She succeeded to an astonishing degree, too!

In other cases the wife thought she was having a pretty hard time of it when the community thought she was well cushioned from hardships. Mrs. K was one of these fretters.

The K family was happy but turbulent, equalitarian but with plenty of bickering, especially over how the only son should be handled. Another source of quarrels was that Mr. K thought, with some justification, that his wife was a poor manager. After he left for the service, Mrs. K went to live with his parents, and in spite of their sympathetic help she was as disorganized and impractical as ever. The mother-in-law was glad to take care of the housework and cooking because whenever Mrs. K tried, the house never looked right and the meals were never on time. Just caring for her new baby seemed more than she could handle, and she managed to run through all the family savings in spite of help from the in-laws.

### Illness of a Wife

When the man of the family is gone, illness of the mother can create a very difficult problem, and all fifteen of the families who faced this difficulty felt that it had been a hardship. The women on the whole were a hardy group, and there seems to have been no feigning of illness in order to avoid assuming unpleasant responsibilities. The situation in the A family was nearly desperate.

The A's had traditional patriarchal patterns of family living, but the general standard of role-fulfillment was low because husband and wife were in poor health and keeping their five children fed and clothed seemed to be almost more than they could manage. Mrs. A was tubercular, and feared that she would not be strong enough to look after the family alone if her husband was drafted. Her fears were realized, because she was soon so weak and ill that she could scarcely move around the house. She could not cook, so the children lived on bread and milk, and had not a brother come to live with Mrs. A and taken care of the food shopping and some chores, the family would not have managed to keep going. As it was, they barely managed to survive until the husband returned, and the latter would certainly have been eligible for a dependency discharge had the wife applied to the Red Cross for aid.

A number of wives worried constantly while their husbands were away. They worried about their husbands' safety, and even more about their own responsibilities and the welfare of their children. Several women suffered from insomnia and two from nervous breakdowns as a result of extreme nervous tension, while a fourth who was already a migraine sufferer found that her attacks increased in intensity and frequency. The women who had nervous breakdowns were the only ones who were incapacitated as family heads. In both these cases the families just barely existed until the husbands returned, and one husband received a dependency discharge.

### Illness of a Child

Serious illness of a child hit seven families, and, as might be expected, all seven considered this a hardship. None of the families had quite such a dose of illness as the T's, however.

The T's were a highly flexible, coöperative family that had survived all sorts of ups and downs with their five children and managed to have a good time doing it. Mrs. T missed her husband very much when he left for the service but made the best of it. She usually had her hands full when all the children were well, and was even busier after she came home from the hospital, a couple of months after Mr. T's departure, with her sixth baby. Soon after this, however, all five children fell ill one after the other, two of them with pneumonia, and for a time they were all in bed at once. Mrs. T had not yet recovered from childbirth, the allotment check was not large, and their home was small and inadequate, with only two beds for five children. Sheer grit and determination, plus some help from a parental family used to such crises, helped Mrs. T to pull her family through.

### Having a Baby

Having a baby while the father was away was the hardship that most clearly revealed the mettle of these war wives. Most of them admitted that it had been tough (ten out of twelve) but they nearly all came through with flying colors. It should be remembered that all these wives already had from one to five children at home. We have just mentioned Mrs. T, who came home from the hospital with her sixth only to have the other five fall ill all at once, and who somehow managed to nurse them back to health before she had regained her own strength. Nearly every family seemed to suffer from additional complications when the childbirth period was at hand. Mrs. G, whose family [was previously] described, barely made it to the hospital. Just as she was ready to leave to have her third child, her mother-in-law informed her over the telephone that she couldn't come to care for the other children, as she had earlier promised to do. Mrs. G had to sit down to the telephone while the taxi was waiting at the door and make a whole new series of arrangements regarding the children. Not only was she able to keep her presence of mind and make the new arrangements, but she was even able to forgive her mother-in-law for letting her down at the last moment.

### Wife Working

Thirty-one of the wives went to work after their husbands left, and only eleven of them considered this a hardship. Those who considered it a hardship were doing it for financial reasons alone, although many who started working for financial reasons ended by thoroughly enjoying their work. A great deal was demanded of these women, because they had the same problems all the other women in the study did of being father and mother both to the children, making decisions for the family, and so on, in addition to giving a major portion of each day to an entirely different and often exacting set of tasks. On the whole, those women managed best who had relatives who could help care for the children, but several women who had children of school age managed to give them everything they needed and work too. Part-time jobs were the answer for a few. Mrs. CT, [whose family was described previously,] was one of the eleven who agreed with the general public that working was a hardship in a husbandless family.... In an effort to be even more independent of her parents and save for a separate home, she tried working. She had always been a worrier, however, and spent the days on the job fretting about how her mother was handling the children. She could not bear to give up any part of her own role as a parent and finally preferred staying home with the children to working and saving for a separate home. This merely shifted the emphasis from the hardship of working to the hardship of being cooped up with her parents.

Most of the women enjoyed working. If they didn't do it for financial reasons, they usually did it in order to "keep busy," to occupy their minds, to keep from missing their husbands. To many of them it gave a feeling of independence and self-sufficiency they had never had before. This was true of Mrs. U.

> In the U family, Mr. U was the affectionate and indulgent patriarch who liked to make his wife feel important by asking her opinion on family matters. His induction caught them unprepared, and left her feeling lost, or, as she put it, "only half alive." Money was short, and she was faced with the necessity of earning additional income. She had never worked before, having lived the sheltered life of the daughter of self-respecting Italian immigrants. She left the baby with grandmother, and, with much fear and trembling, got herself a job in a bank. To her amazement, they liked her work very much. She soon discovered that she was perfectly capable of handling money and making decisions herself, and took great pride in being able to save a nice sum of money to be used when Mr. U got back.

### Husband Reported Missing

Only one family had to go through this agony, the V's. This was a cooperative patriarchy in which induction was accepted as a necessary evil and the family prepared to make the best of it. For six months after the notification that Mr. V was missing, mother and child lived in a nightmare of fear. They said little to one another because the family was not one to display emotions or be loquacious, and they performed the family routines in a mechanical manner. Another few dreary but more hopeful months set in when Mr. V was discovered to be a prisoner of war, and only his sudden return, weak but whole, brought this family back to life.

### Lack of Social Life

No social life was reported as a hardship by only one wife. The tendency of most wives was to increase their social contacts, especially with other war wives, but Mrs. W had to cut out social life entirely.

> Mr. W was a patriarch, kind to his shy and somewhat shrinking wife who had been rejected by her own parents. Induction took the family by surprise as they were starting to build a home, so they had to live in a temporary structure until he returned. Their income was cut in half, so Mrs. W felt that all her efforts were needed to keep the family above water and rejected all social life. She devoted herself more fully to her child but missed the social contacts sorely and felt that deprivation as much as her financial difficulties.

### No Hardships

Eleven families felt that they had had no hardships during the separation period. None of these families missed their men enough to be worth mentioning, although some of them had had a good marital adjustment before he left and wanted him back. In these cases the wives were unusually self-sufficient or unusually close to their parental families. In other words, the wife either ran the home quite capably alone and was adequate to all the children's needs, or she went home to mother and resumed her premarital status in the home, except that attention was now divided between her and her children. The F family, described [earlier], typifies the latter situation. The Z's, in contrast, are an excellent example of a family that not only felt no hardships, but found the going easier without Mr. Z.

*Reuben Hill and Elise Boulding*

> The Z's were a leaderless, disunited Negro family. Mr. Z preferred hanging around the YMCA and Scouting headquarters, doing things that gave him a certain amount of recognition in both colored and white communities, to going out to work to support his family. At the time of his induction he was taking no part in the family life at all. Mrs. Z was supporting the family by doing house cleaning by the hour; she handled all the family finances, looked after the children, kept her own house in reasonable order, and quarreled constantly with her husband in an effort to get him to take some responsibility whenever he was home. When he left, she felt that a great weight had been lifted from her shoulders. The allotment checks meant that she did not have to be the chief wage earner, and the house ran much more smoothly because, as she told the interviewer, "There wasn't any use nagging my husband to do the chores, because he wasn't around, so the children and I did them without any fussing!" Possibly another result of her not being able to nag at him was that he took more interest in the family while in service than he ever had before, and they reëstablished a companionship by mail that they had not known for many years.

## SUMMARY OF SEPARATION CRISES

We have seen that the induction of the husband and the father into the armed forces meant very different things to different families, and that it was by no means a crippling crisis for all of them. Keeping in mind the three variables which determine whether or not an occurrence becomes a crisis—the hardships of the event, the resources of the family to meet the event, and the family's definition of the event—we have examined a number of family situations characterized by one or more hardships. The hardships included absence of the husband as companion, father, handy man, and protector, finances, child discipline, and prolonged maladjustment of a child, living with in-laws, housing, managing the home, illness of the wife, illness of children, having a baby, wife working, lack of social life, and, in one case, having the husband reported missing. Some families ran the gamut of these hardships; others felt few of them. The resources were examined in terms of the previous role structure of the family, the wife's experience in family management and her latent abilities, and the availability of relatives outside the immediate family circle. The family was observed in action as it prepared to meet the crisis in ways ranging from ineffective worrying and hoping the induction wouldn't happen, to combining households with a relative and the wife going to work to supplement an anticipated decrease in income. Finally, the enormous range of variation in the definitions of the situations was delineated. There were families who had their full share of troubles and felt that the going was tough but made the best of it. There were other families who would be considered by the community to have just as many troubles, but because of past experiences of a deviant husband-wife relationship these families didn't feel that they were suffering any hardships. Still other families had what the community would regard as pretty easy going, and yet special circumstances made these families regard themselves as in trouble. In the last analysis, the family's definition of the event would seem to be the determining factor in deciding whether or not the separation was a crisis. If the family felt that it was having difficulty, no matter how easy the situation might seem to others, that family acted in a disorganized and ineffective manner or suffered extreme emotional upset, which is typical crisis behavior. If the family continued to function smoothly and was not in the least disturbed by the adjustments it had to make, then no matter how many hardships knocked at the door, it experienced no crisis.

## 12.2 HAMILTON I. McCUBBIN AND JOAN M. PATTERSON

# *The Family Stress Process*

This selection is based on work that was funded by a grant from the Agricultural Experiment Station at the University of Minnesota. Hamilton I. McCubbin was a professor in and head of the Department of Family Social Science at the University of Minnesota, St. Paul, where Joan M. Patterson was a research associate, when the original article was published.

McCubbin's interest in family stress began in 1975, when he was head of the Family Studies Branch for POW (prisoner of war) Studies at the Naval Health Research Center in San Diego. He later joined a task force that assisted the families of American personnel who were trapped in Iran from 1979 to 1981. McCubbin delivered the keynote address on family stress in 1980 to the Groves Conference on Marriage and the Family, which inspired him to edit a two-volume series entitled *Stress and the Family* with Charles Figley (Brunner/Mazel, 1983). This selection comes from a 1983 book of readings entitled *Social Stress and the Family: Advances and Developments in Family Stress Theory and Research* (Haworth, 1983), which McCubbin coedited with Patterson and Marvin B. Sussman.

Patterson is currently working in the Department of Health Management and Policy at the University of Minnesota. She is the author of numerous articles and the editor of several books. She has also produced an evaluative instrument, the Adolescent Coping Orientation for Problem Experiences (A-COPE), for the Center of Evaluation Research in Minneapolis.

**Key Concept:** family stress

## THE HILL ABCX MODEL REDEFINED

Family scholars have attempted to identify the variables which account for the observed differences among families in their positive adaptations to stressful situations. The earliest conceptual foundation for research to examine this variability has been the Hill (1949; 1958) ABCX family crisis model:

> A (the stressor event)—interacting with B (the family's crisis meeting resources)—interacting with C (the definition the family makes of the event)—produce X (the crisis).

### Family Demands: Stressor and Hardships (a Factor)

In an effort to render clarity to the ABCX model and to establish a link to physiological (Selye, 1974) and psychological (Lazarus, 1966; Mikhail, 1981) concepts of stress, we define a *stressor* as a life event or transition impacting upon the family unit which produces, or has the potential of producing, change in the family social system. This change may be in various areas of family life such as its boundaries, goals, patterns of interaction, roles, or values. Family *hardships* are defined as those demands on the family unit specifically associated with the stressor event. An example of hardships would be the family's need to obtain more money or to rearrange family work and recreation plans to accommodate the increased medical expenses and the demand for home care of a handicapped member. Both the stressor and its hardships place demands on the family system which need to be managed.

### Family Capabilities: Resistance Resources (b Factor)

The b factor, the family's resources for meeting the demands of a stressor and hardships, has been described as the family's ability to prevent an event of change in the family social system from creating a crisis or disruptiveness in the system (Burr, 1973). Resources, then, become part of the family's capabilities for resisting crisis. Angell (1936), one of the early theorists attempting to describe more specifically what constituted family resources, emphasized the value of family integration, that is, the thorough family life, of which common interests, affection, and a sense of economic inter-dependence are perhaps the most prominent; and family adaptability, that is, the family's capacity to meet obstacles and shift its course of action. Cavan and Ranck (1938) and Koos (1946) identified additional resources of family agreement about its role structure, subordination of personal ambitions to family goals, satisfactions within the family obtained because it is successfully meeting the physical and emotional needs of its members, and goals toward which the family is moving collectively. Hill (1958) summarized the b factor as "adequacy-inadequacy of family organization."

### Family Definition: Focus on Stressor (c Factor)

The c factor in the ABCX model is the definition the family makes of the seriousness of the experienced stressor. There are objective cultural definitions of the seriousness of life events and transitions which represent the collective judgment of the social system (see Reiss & Oliveri, Chapter 3), but the c factor is the family's subjective definition of the stressor and its hardships and how they are affected by them. This subjective meaning reflects the family's values and their previous experience in dealing with change and meeting crisis. A family's outlook can vary from seeing life changes and transitions as challenges to be met to interpreting a stressor as uncontrollable and a prelude to the family's demise.

### Family Tension: Stress and Distress

Stressor events and related hardships produce tension in the family which needs to be managed (Antonovsky, 1979). When this tension is not overcome, stress emerges. Family stress (as distinct from stressor) is defined as a state which arises from an actual or perceived demand-capability imbalance in the family's functioning and which is characterized by a multidimensional demand for adjustment or adaptive behavior. Stress, then, is not stereotypic, but rather varies depending upon the nature of the situation, the characteristics of the family unit, and the psychological and physical well-being of its members. Concomitantly, family distress is defined as an unpleasant or disorganized state which arises from an actual or perceived imbalance in family functioning and which is also characterized by a multidimensional demand for adjustment or adaptive behavior. In other words, stress becomes distress when it is subjectively defined as unpleasant or undesirable by the family unit.

### Family Crisis: Demand for Change (x Factor)

These factors taken together: (a) the stressor event and hardships; (b) the family's resources for dealing with stressors and transitions; (c) the definition the family makes of this situation; and (d) the resulting stress or distress, all influence the family's resistance, that is, its ability to prevent the stressor event or transition from creating a crisis. Crisis (the x factor) has been conceptualized as a continuous variable denoting the amount of disruptiveness, disorganization, or incapacitatedness in the family social system (Burr, 1973). As distinct from stress, which is a demand-capability imbalance, crisis is characterized by the family's inability to restore stability and by the continuous pressure to make changes in the family structure and patterns of interaction. In other words, stress may never reach crisis proportions if the family is able to use existing resources and define the situation so as to resist systemic change and maintain family stability.

## LONGITUDINAL OBSERVATIONS OF FAMILIES IN CRISIS: EMERGING CONCEPTS

... In previous publications (McCubbin, Olson, & Patterson, in press; McCubbin & Patterson, 1982; in press), we have used these observations to advance a Double ABCX model of family behavior which uses Hill's original ABCX model as its foundation and adds post-crisis variables in an effort to describe: (a) the additional life stressors and strains which shape the course of family adaptation; (b) the critical psychological, intra-familial, and social resources families acquire and employ over time in managing crisis situations; (c) the changes in definition and meaning families develop in an effort to make sense out of their predicament; (d) the coping strategies families employ; and (e) the range of outcomes of these family efforts.

[W]e will describe the components of the Double ABCX model with select observations from these 216 families which provide the inductive support for this line of theory building....

**Family Demands: Pile-up (aA Factor)**

Because family crises evolve and are resolved over a period of time, families seldom are dealing with a single stressor, but rather, our longitudinal data suggests they experience a pile-up of stressors and strains (i.e., demands), particularly in the aftermath of a major stressor, such as a death, a major role change for one member, or a natural disaster. This pile-up is referred to as the "aA" factor in the Double ABCX model. These demands or changes may emerge from (a) individual family members, (b) the family system, and/or (c) the community of which the family and its members are a part.

There appear to be at least five broad types of stressors and strains contributing to a pile-up in the family system in a crisis situation: (a) the initial stressor and its hardships, (b) normative transitions, (c) prior strains, (d) the consequences of family efforts to cope; (e) ambiguity, both intra-family and social.

*Stressor and its hardships.* Inherent in the occurrence of a stressful event such as a husband/father being reported as missing or a prisoner of war are hardships which increase and possibly intensify as the stressor situation persists or is unresolved. Wives in our longitudinal study, whose husbands were absent, were taxed with both the traditional and inherited responsibilities of the dual mother-father role (McCubbin, Hunter, & Metres, 1974) which required solo decision making, disciplining of children, handling family finances, and managing children's health problems. Many wives experienced anxieties, frustrations, and feelings of insecurity and showed emotional symptoms of strain with the extended absence and uncertainty of their spouses' returns. Hardships, such as these, often are not readily resolved (as was true for these wives) and when they persist, they become additional sources of strain contributing to family distress.

*Normative transitions.* The demands of individual members and the family system are not static but change over time. For example, these families experienced the normal growth and development of child members (e.g., increasing need for independence), of adult members (e.g., mother's desire to pursue a career), of the extended family (e.g., death of grandparent, births) and family life cycle changes (e.g., school transitions, launching young adults). Such transitions occur concomitantly, but independently, of the initial stressor. These transitions or opportunities also place demands on the family unit since they require change.

*Prior strains.* It would appear that most family systems carry with them some residue of strain which may be the result of unresolved hardships from earlier stressors or transitions or may be inherent in ongoing roles such as parent, employer, etc. (Pearlin & Schooler, 1978). When a new stressor is experienced by the family, these prior strains are exacerbated and families become aware of them as demands in and of themselves. For example, wives whose husbands were missing became much more aware of the unresolved strains in their relationships with in-laws. Parent-child conflicts, which had existed when fathers were home, were often exacerbated for mothers functioning as single parents. These prior strains are not usually discrete events which can be identified as occurring at a specific point in time but rather, emerge more insidiously in the family. They do, however, contribute to the pile-up of demands families must contend with in a crisis situation.

*Consequences of family efforts to cope.* The fourth source of pile-up includes stressors and strains which emerge from specific coping behaviors the family may use in an effort to cope with the crisis situation. For example, wives acting as head of the household in their husbands' absence appeared to become more independent and self-confident. As mother changed her role and strengthened her authority and sought out new sources of emotional support, members of the kin network, especially in-laws concerned about possible divorce, challenged and questioned this style of coping. Their disapproval caused additional strain, contributing to the pile-up.

*Intra-family and social ambiguity.* Ambiguity is inherent in every stressor since change produces uncertainty about the future. Internally, the family may experience ambiguity about its structure. Certainly, having a spouse missing is most ambiguous in light of the unpredictability of his return. On the basis of systems theory and the symbolic interactionist perspective, Boss (1977) has suggested that boundary ambiguity within the family system is a major stressor since a system needs to be sure of its components, that is, who is inside of the system boundaries physically and psychologically, and who is outside. The concept of boundary ambiguity has also been applied to describe normative transitions (Boss, 1980) such as a young adult leaving home. Is this person in or out of the family unit?

Additionally, given the expectation that society will offer guidelines or blueprints for families coping with crises, it is probable that families will face the added strain of social ambiguity in those situations where needed social prescriptions for crisis resolution are unclear or absent. Families of the missing lacked legitimate procedures for resolution and were often confronted with conflicting or unclear messages about what to do. For example, powers of attorney expired, leaving wives with no legal power to sell jointly held property. Remarriage posed the threat of a bigamy conviction since there had been no declaration of death. The family's ability to manage stress may depend upon the efficacy and/or adequacy of the solutions the culture or community provide. However, these community solutions may lag far behind the times and offer little to families struggling to manage a difficult situation. As Hansen and Hill (1964) and Mechanic (1974) have pointed out, the fit between the family and the community may well be the major determinant of successful adaptation to stress.

### Family Adaptive Resources (bB Factor)

Resources are part of the family's capabilities for meeting demands and needs and include characteristics (a) of individual members, (b) of the family unit, and (c) of the community. When viewed over time and in response to a crisis situation, the family's adaptive resources appear to be of two general types: existing resources and expanded family resources.

*Existing resources.* These resources are already part of the family's repertoire and serve to minimize the impact of the initial stressor and reduce the probability that the family will enter into crisis. Existing individual resources the wives in the longitudinal study appeared to use included the ability to nurture and meet the expressive needs of their children, manage the home, and to sublimate by engaging in hobbies, recreation, or work. They drew on the family resources of togetherness, role flexibility, shared values, and expressiveness. Community resources like friendships and religious involvement were also important.

*Expanded family resources.* The second type of resources (B of the bB factor) are those new resources (individual, family, and community) strengthened or developed in response to the additional demands emerging out of the crisis situations or as a result of pile-up. For example, wives availed themselves of educational opportunities to enhance their earning potential in anticipation of their spouse not returning. These opportunities for personal development also served to enhance their self-esteem and self-reliance. The family unit reallocated roles and responsibilities (e.g., oldest child member took a job to increase family income), involved extended kin in meeting family needs, relocated the family in a new community to gain a fresh start, and some remarried. Additionally, the family sought, and in some cases, created new community resources tailored to meet their needs. Wives joined the National League of Families, community-based counseling groups, and financial investment clubs. These groups offered various benefits such as encouragement, concrete guidance, empathic understanding, as well as a sense of membership.

One of the most important resources comprising the bB factor is social support. Social support has been defined as information that a family (a) is cared for and loved, (b) is esteemed and valued, and (c) belongs to a network of mutual obligation and understanding (Cobb, 1976). Families who have and are able to develop sources of social support (e.g., kin, friends, work associates, church, etc.) are both more resistant to major crisis and are better able to recover from crisis and restore stability to the family system.

### Family Definition and Meaning (cC Factor)

In the Double ABCX model, the cC factor is the meaning the family gives to the total crisis situation which includes the stressor believed to have caused the crisis, as well as the added stressors and strains, old and new resources, and estimates of what needs to be done to bring the family back into balance.

While families with a husband/father missing struggled, they also appeared to reach a level of adaptive or functional stability—an outcome which could be attributed in part to wives' redefining the situation. For example, wives differentiated father's role (boundaries) in terms of his instrumental contributions versus his expressive contributions (Boss, 1977). Wives appeared to redefine the situation by endowing father's role with some value and meaning (i.e., as financial provider) and at the same time legitimate their personal efforts and the family's efforts to establish a new life for themselves (e.g., by developing new ways to meet expressive needs).

When families are able to successfully redefine the crisis situation and give it new meaning, it involves efforts to (a) clarify the issues, hardships, and tasks so as to render them more manageable and responsive to problem solving efforts; (b) decrease the intensity of the emotional burdens associated with the crisis situation; and (c) encourage the family unit to carry on with its fundamental tasks of promoting member social and emotional development. Generally speaking, family efforts to redefine a situation as a "challenge," as an "opportunity for growth," or to endow the crisis with meaning such as "believing it is the Lord's will" appear to play a useful role in facilitating family coping and, eventually, adaptation. Viewed in this way, the family's definition and meaning, or the cC factor, becomes a critical component of family coping.

### Family Adaptive Coping: Interaction of Resources, Perceptions, and Behavior

Although family resources and perceptions have been studied independently and offer investigators a gauge of family capabilities used to meet demands, these same observations suggest that we could improve upon our understanding of family adaptation to crises by looking at these two variables simultaneously along with what families do to cope with the situation. Coping, then, becomes a bridging concept which has both cognitive and behavioral components wherein resources, perception, and behavioral responses interact as families try to achieve a balance in family functioning. Family coping efforts may be directed at (a) eliminating and/or avoiding stressors and strains; (b) managing the hardships of the situation; (c) maintaining the family system's integrity and morale; (d) acquiring and developing resources to meet demands; and (e) implementing structural changes in the family system to accommodate the new demands (McCubbin, 1979; McCubbin & Patterson, 1982).

What became apparent from observations of these families is that coping efforts following a crisis are directed at multiple stressors and strains (the pileup) simultaneously. In other words, coping is not stressor specific, but involves efforts to manage various dimensions of family life at the same time, realizing that a "perfect" solution is never possible. Families learn to compromise, accepting the best possible outcome given their circumstances.

### Family Adaptation Balancing (xX Factor)

Hill's x factor (1958), the amount of crisis in the family system, generally has been adopted as the major outcome variable describing disruptions in family routines in response to a stressor. Burr (1973) conceived of a crisis as a continuous variable, denoting variation in the amount of disruptiveness, incapacitatedness, or disorganization of the family. Given this definition, it might be concluded that the purpose of post-crisis adjustment or the goal of regenerative power (Hansen, 1965) is primarily to reduce or eliminate the disruptiveness in the family system and restore homeostasis. It might be argued, however, that family disruptions potentially help to maintain family relationships and even stimulate desirable changes in family life. Hansen and Johnson (1979) called attention to the restrictive focus of crisis and noted that "families are often observed 'accepting' disruptions of habit and tradition not so much as unwelcome problems; but more as opportunities to renegotiate their relationships" (p. 584). Systems theorists (Hill, 1971; von Bertalanffy, 1968) point out that it is characteristic of living systems to evolve toward greater complexity, and consequently, families may actively initiate changes to facilitate such growth. It is questionable then, whether "reduction of crisis" alone is an adequate index of a family's post-crisis adjustment.

Observations reviewed [here] suggest that family adaptation would be a useful concept for describing the outcome of family post-crisis adjustment. There are three elements to be considered in family adaptation: (a) the individual family member; (b) the family system; and (c) the community of which family members and the family unit are a part. Each of these elements is characterized by both demands and capabilities. Family adaptation is achieved through reciprocal relationships where the demands of one of these units are met by the capabilities at another so as to achieve a "balance" simultaneously at two primary levels of interaction.

*Balance: Member to family fit.* At the first level, a balance is sought between individual family members and the family system (e.g., family encouraging and supporting adolescent needs for independence and adolescent family member completing family maintenance tasks or participating in shared family activities). Based on the Double ABCX model, it could be hypothesized that family stress emerges when there is a demand-capability imbalance at this level of family functioning. Specifically, the demands an individual member may place on the family may exceed the family's capabilities for meeting these demands, thus resulting in an imbalance. For example, the stressor of a member entering adolescence may precipitate an imbalance by virtue of the family's demand for member adherence to rigid rules and their inability to alter expectations which would allow for the independence an adolescent needs for personal development. The family is therefore called upon to reconcile this matter and work to achieve a new "balance" between the individual member and the family unit.

*Balance: Family to community fit.* At the second level, a balance is sought between the family unit and the community of which this family is a part (e.g., family support of parental involvement in work and community activities and the employer's demand for extensive work time and commitment). It has frequently been observed that two social institutions, the family and the work community, compete for the involvement and commitment of family members which often results in stress—a demand-capability imbalance at this second level of family functioning. For example, the stressor of a wife-mother entering or returning to work may precipitate an imbalance if the family demands she make a priority commitment to family life and the children. Additionally, the family may be reluctant to modify its rules and behaviors (e.g., towards shared tasks, shared responsibilities) to permit the transitioning parent to invest in work-for-pay without the added burden of emotional guilt and the felt need to fulfill home and work responsibilities with equal competence. The family is called upon to reestablish and achieve a balance between family and work-community demands and capabilities.

*Family coherence: A critical factor in adaptation.* Even as families try to achieve bonadaptation by minimizing the discrepancy between family resources and demands, they are faced with the reality that there is no "perfect" fit where demands and resources are absolutely balanced. Successful adaptation in a less than perfect world calls for a general orientation by the family which reflects a sense of acceptance and understanding that this is the best they can do under the circumstances. Antonovsky (1979) describes this orientation as "coherence," that is, the pervasive, enduring, though dynamic feeling of confidence that internal and external environments are predictable and there is a high probability that things will work out as well as can reasonably be expected.

A family's sense of coherence is based primarily on its ability to balance two dimensions relative to its life circumstances: control and trust. For some life events and circumstances, a family can influence and shape the occurrence and/or the outcome. On the other hand, many life experiences of families cannot be directly controlled by them and they must trust that things will work out okay because other controlling factors—persons, institutions, a higher power—will act with their best interests in mind. Coherence is being able to differentiate when the family should take charge from when they should trust and believe in and support legitimate authority and/or power of other sources.

In the case of the families of the missing in action, many were able to trust the efforts of the United States to do what was best under the circumstances in terms of ending the war, finding and/or returning their spouses and establishing policies to help families. Many trusted God and their spiritual beliefs that somehow this was going to be okay for them. At the same time, these same families, wives in particular, were able to move ahead, get jobs, make decisions about child rearing and shape an acceptable, desirable (even though not perfect) future for themselves and their families. This realistic balance between trust and control leads to coherence and moves a family towards bonadaptation even when all demands are not absolutely met with available resources.

Therefore, family adaptation becomes the central concept in the Double ABCX model used to describe the outcome of family efforts to achieve a new level of balance in family functioning which was upset by a family crisis. In crisis situations the family unit struggles to achieve a balance at both the individual-family and the family-community levels of family functioning. Since the family is a social system and a change in one level affects the other, family efforts at adaptation always involve an attentiveness and responsiveness to both levels of family functioning simultaneously.

*Outcome: Bonadaptation and maladaptation.* The concept of family adaptation is used to describe a continuum of outcomes which reflect family efforts to achieve a balanced "fit" at the member-to-family and the family-to-community levels. The positive end of the continuum of family adaptation, called bonadaptation, is characterized by a balance at both levels of functioning which results in (a) the maintenance or strengthening of family integrity; (b) the continued promotion of both member development and family unit development; and (c) the maintenance of family independence and its sense of control over environmental influences. Family maladaptation, at the negative end of the continuum, is characterized by a continued imbalance at either level of family functioning or the achievement of a balance at both levels but at a price in terms of (a) deterioration in family integrity; (b) a curtailment or deterioration in the personal health and development of a member or the well-being of the family unit; or (c) a loss or decline in family independence and autonomy.

At the present time, family adaptation is but a descriptive criterion of family post-crisis outcomes rather than a clearly defined and operationalized set of measures. One obvious and complicating factor is that any form of adaptation may be viewed as having both long and short run consequences. What may be functional in meeting a family's or member's immediate needs, such as accepting a member who is abusing alcohol, may be maladaptive in light of the long-range, adverse consequences on family stability and the psychological well-being of its members.

CHAPTER 13 **Divorce and Remarriage**

## 13.1 FRANK F. FURSTENBERG, JR.

# *Divorce and the American Family*

Divorce can be viewed in several ways. Divorce can be considered a problem in that it dissolves a marriage and creates a strain on the family unit. Divorce can also be devastating to children who need an intact family unit for security and comfort. On the other hand, divorce can be seen as a solution to a problem. Without the possibility of divorce, how could abused spouses leave their abusers to find more healthy relationships? And how could couples who realize they made a mistake by getting married resolve that problem? When the rise in divorce rates became evident in the 1960s, much of the literature focused on divorce as a problem to be resolved. Today family scientists are more likely to approach divorce as a societal issue as opposed to a problem that needs to be resolved.

Frank F. Furstenberg, Jr., is the Zellerbach Family Professor of Sociology at the University of Pennsylvania in Philadelphia. He received his Ph.D. from Columbia University in New York. He has written many articles concerning the family, including "Divorce and the American Family," *Annual Review of Sociology* (1990), from which this selection has been excerpted, and "The Future of Marriage," *American Demographics* (1996). Furstenberg's other research interests are reflected in a 1997 article evaluating Philadelphia Health Resource Centers published in *Family Planning Perspectives* and a 1997 article published in the journal *Childhood* entitled "State-Family Alliances and Children's Welfare: A Research Agenda."

**Key Concept:** divorce

# INTRODUCTION: SOURCES OF MARITAL INSTABILITY

Americans have always had a higher propensity to divorce than do Europeans and people of North Atlantic countries. A century ago, when voluntary dissolution was still uncommon, divorce rates in the country were unusually high by European standards (Good 1963). This trend has continued throughout the twentieth century. In the 1930s, the incidence of divorce was ten times higher in the United States than in Britain or Canada and four to five times the rate in Scandinavia (Carter & Glick 1976). These relative differences have narrowed during the past 50 years, but the United States still has the highest rate of marital instability among developed nations, by a considerable margin, (Davis 1985, Lye 1988).

It is not obvious why divorce is a more popular solution to marital discontent in this country than elsewhere. Many scholars who have studied the matter believe that divorce is an inevitable byproduct of a marriage system that puts a high premium on voluntary choice and that values emotional satisfaction above all (Goode 1956, Bohannon 1970). Even before the industrial revolution, Americans were unusually willing to give young people a high amount of discretion in mate selection. Broader kinship concerns figured little into marriage decisions, and parents exercised minimal control either in the timing of marriage or in children's choice of a partner (Rothman 1987). Partly for these reasons, Americans married much earlier than Europeans, a fact which may have contributed to the instability of unions.

Apart from the limited degree of control exercised by the kinship network on married couples, Americans have long regarded marriage as a central locus for emotional gratification (Degler 1980). From the 1930s and onward, a central focus of family sociology was the study and measurement of marital compatibility (Lasch 1977). This professional preoccupation seemed to capture the growing concern of Americans with the personal benefits of marriage, companionship and intimacy. The historical movement from a "contractual marriage," founded on instrumental exchange, to a "companionate marriage," supported by mutual interests and emotional exchange, was first noted by Ernest Burgess (1948) and heralded by a host of family scholars, who believed that the institution of marriage was evolving into a more personally rewarding arrangement.

The more that marriage was touted for its personal benefits, the less stability was valued for its own sake (Swidler 1980). As emotional gratification became the sine qua non of marriage, divorce became an indispensable element in the institution of matrimony, permitting couples to rectify poor choices (Goode 1956). Gradually, the standard shifted from one which required couples to remain married even if they were not in love to one which virtually demanded divorce unless they remained in love.

These shifting cultural standards, no doubt, also reflected a change in the economic basis of marriage (Huber & Spitze 1988). The gender-based division of labor that created a strong interdependency between men and women began to disintegrate in the latter half of the twentieth century. Married women steadily increased their participation in the labor force (Ross & Sawhill 1975, Bianchi &

Spain 1986). The increase has been most spectacular among those with younger children, who previously were totally reliant on the economic support of their spouses. The quest for a better standard of living partially brought about these changes. More recently, women have insisted on a large role in the market place as a source of power and independence (Sorensen & McLanahan 1987). Though difficult to demonstrate empirically, it is probably the case that women have also entered and remained in the labor force as an insurance policy against the increasingly likely prospect of having to support themselves and their children (Cherlin 1988, Huber & Spitze 1988).

This shift in cultural norms and social roles has been described in economic terms by Becker (1981) as the reduction of gender-specific capital within marriage. In the past, specialization of tasks within the family fostered exchange, encouraging women to trade domestic labor, principally childcare, for men's greater earning capacity outside the home. During the second half of the twentieth century, this bartering system has disintegrated as women entered the job market and domestic services could be more easily purchased outside the home. Declining fertility rates and the diminished value of domestic labor have depreciated the value of full-time motherhood. At the same time, the growth of a service-based economy has expanded the opportunities for women in the labor force, further eroding the claim of male superiority in the work force (Fuchs 1983).

While women have indisputably increased their involvement in the labor market, it is not as clear whether men have responded by expanding their involvement in domestic activities (Bernard 1981, Huber & Spitze 1988, Goode 1982, Lamb 1987). Evidence suggests that men are more actively involved in parenthood, but it is still an open question whether they are assuming a larger share of household tasks (Presser 1990, Thompson & Walker 1989). Egalitarian marriage—in which partners more or less equally share economic and domestic tasks—may be more difficult to achieve, or it may take time to modify long-standing patterns of behavior (Ross & Sawhill 1975). Undoubtedly, the current high rates of divorce reflect the present state of role conflict and ambiguity within our marriage system—the unwillingness of women to settle for an unfair share of family tasks and the reluctance of men to give up the advantages that they traditionally enjoyed when they contributed most or all of the household income (Becker et al 1977).

In a very real sense, then, the causes of the high rate of marital instability are "over determined" by a confluence of cultural, economic, and political change, any one of which might have brought about a significant revision of the institution of marriage. In combination, they have profoundly shaken the commitment to lifelong marriage. These trends have occurred in all Western nations (Davis 1985), but they have been most dramatic in the United States because of a preexisting tendency toward a voluntaristic form of marriage. There seems little reason to predict that the currently high levels of divorce in the United States or the growing rates of divorce in other Western nations will subside in the near future (Lesthaege & Meekers 1986). Divorce has become an intrinsic part of the family system.

For the past hundred years, the rate of divorce (divorces per 1000 *marriages* until 1920; after 1920, divorces per 1000 *married women*) has risen more than ten-fold (Cherlin 1981). As an indicator of marital instability, it must be said that divorce rates have certain limitations. A century ago, formal divorce was difficult to obtain and undoubtedly dissolution resulting from desertion was undercounted. Today, divorce rates have leveled off but the rising numbers of informal marriages formed by cohabitation go unrecorded. Moreover, when the incidence of marriage drops, as it has in the past decade, the divorce rate necessarily will probably fall at least temporarily. This happens because fewer couples in the early stages of marriage (those at highest risk of divorce) are in the pool of married persons. Divorce rates also can be affected by changes in the age composition of the marriage population or the duration of marriages.

Recently, demographers have calculated a more precise measure of marital stability—the proportion of a given marriage cohort that voluntarily ends their union by a fixed time interval. A century ago, fewer than one in ten marriages were ended by divorce (after 40 years). By mid-century, slightly under a third of all marriages contracted would end in divorce (Preston & McDonald 1979, Cherlin 1981). Today, if projections prove to be correct, at least half of all those marrying will divorce. Many experts think that the rate of voluntary dissolution is actually much higher than that because a number of couples who separate may never bother to obtain a divorce. Disputing the claims of some demographers that divorce is leveling off, if not declining (Norton & Moorman 1986), Castro-Martin and Bumpass (1989) estimate that close to two thirds of all first marriages contracted in the 1980s will end in separation or divorce.

Marital disruption, of course, is not randomly distributed. The risk of dissolution in first marriages is far higher for younger couples than those marrying after their early twenties. Similarly high school dropouts have twice the rate of marital breakup as those with at least some college. And the rate of disruption is about 50% higher among blacks (net of socio-economic status) (Carter & Glick 1976, Sweet & Bumpass 1987, Castro-Martin & Bumpass 1989).

Second marriages have a higher risk of divorce than do first marriages (McCarthy 1978, Weed 1980). Cherlin (1978), among others, has argued that this risk can be traced to the strains on remarriage involving children (cf Bohannon 1985). The ambiguity of stepfamily roles jeopardizes the formation of strong marital bonds (White & Booth 1985). Cherlin's hypothesis of "incomplete institutionalization" has been the subject of some debate as researchers have begun to probe the link between stepfamily life and divorce. Some researchers have argued that second marriages are more prone to divorce principally because those who enter second marriages include individuals who are willing to leave an unhappy relationship or who are more vulnerable to marital instability (Halliday 1980, Furstenberg & Spanier 1984). Castro-Martin & Bumpass (1989) discovered that virtually all the risk associated with second marriages could be explained by compositional differences. In other words, remarriers constitute a different risk pool than first marriages because of lack of education and because they married prematurely the first time.

# Children and Divorce

*Frank F. Furstenberg, Jr.*

The growing instability of marriages has altered the course of childhood during the past century; the change has been most sharply experienced in the past several decades as divorce has become a common event in children's lives. At the turn of the century, general mortality rates were still quite high. Even though voluntary disruption was rare, children had a substantial risk of losing a parent through death. Uhlenberg (1983) has estimated that about a quarter of all children lost one or both parents by age 15. The added risk of divorce and desertion is difficult to estimate, but perhaps as many as a third of all children spent time in a single parent family by their mid-teens.

The overall rate of marital instability due to death and divorce probably declined by mid-century. Less than a tenth of all children witnessed the death of a parent by their mid-teens. The incidence of separation and divorce was correspondingly greater, but it still had not reached epidemic proportions. While it is difficult to arrive at a precise estimate, it seems unlikely that more than a quarter of all children born in the 1940s and 1950s spent time in a single-parent family —a decline in the numbers of those experiencing disruption, compared to numbers from the beginning of the century. The world of childhood changed after the mid-1960s when both the incidence of divorce and out-of-wedlock childbearing soared. Several demographers have attempted to calculate the odds of a child born today spending time in a single parent family by their mid-teens. Their estimates range widely depending on their projections of the future and the data source. Hofferth (1985), for example, figured that close to three fourths of all children either would be born to a single parent or would lose a parent to divorce. Bumpass (1984) and Glick (1984) in separate estimates arrive at a lower figure—about three out of five. Recently Bumpass & Sweet (1989) calculated that 44% of children will live in a single parent household by age 16.

The odds of growing up in a single-parent family or, at least spending some time in one, are significantly greater for blacks. Three fifths of all black children are born to single mothers, most of whom will remain unmarried for at least a few years (US Bureau of the Census 1989b, Furstenberg 1987). Rates of marital instability are also much higher for blacks (Sweet & Bumpass 1987). Extrapolating from current figures, fewer than one black child in five born in the 1980s will spend their entire childhood living with both of their biological parents.

For most children, black and white alike, living in a single-parent household is a transitional status. Marriages dissolve, but most unmarried and formerly married parents enter or re-enter marriage. This means that most children of single parents in time acquire a stepparent. The average length of time in a single-parent household is about six years, but it is likely to be much shorter for children who encounter divorce at an early age (Bumpass 1984). About a quarter of all children born in the late 1960s could be expected to acquire a stepparent before reaching the age of 18 (Furstenberg et al 1983). That figure might be slightly higher for children born today. Many children who enter stepfamilies in early life will see the breakup of those unions before they reach the age of 18. The National Survey of Children disclosed that more than a third of all children whose parents remarried had already witnessed a second divorce by the early teens. Overall, it seems likely that close to 15% of *all* children will go through at least two family disruptions by late adolescence. This estimate includes only recorded marriages. If cohabitational unions were included, the figure would be significantly larger.

Since the middle of this century, then, family life has become considerably less stable and predictable. Half or more of all children will spend some time living in a single-parent family. At least a quarter will enter a stepfamily, and about half of these children will see the breakup of this new family unit before the end of their teens. Rates of family flux are particularly high for black children. The following section traces some of the consequences of marital instability for adults, children, and society at large.

### Divorce Consequences

The most obvious effect of divorce is that it typically brings about a sudden reconfiguration of the family. The transition from a two-parent household to a single-parent household disrupts the parenting system and usually reduces the economic support available to children. Custody and economic support legally are separate issues, but in fact they are inextricably related.

### Custody Practices

Until the end of the nineteenth century, men were generally awarded custody of their children following a divorce (Halem 1980, Weitzman 1981). But as divorce became more common, children generally remained with their mothers. Specialized roles within the family led courts to favor maternal custody. Possibly, too, as children became less of an economic asset and more of a responsibility, men were less eager to maintain their rights. Recently, custody dispositions have been reconsidered in light of the changing roles of women and the recognition that bonds between noncustodial fathers and their children have become extremely tenuous. In the late 1960s and 1970s, the "divorce revolution" brought about a demand for joint custody (Weitzman 1985)—the sharing of parental responsibility for the child.

Even in states such as California, which promoted joint custody, most women continued to maintain principal responsibility for childcare. In the most systematic investigation of how joint custody actually operates, Albiston, Mnookin & Maccoby (1990) have followed a sample of California families from the time of separation for several years. They show that even among couples who are awarded joint custody of their children, women assume a greater measure of childcare over time while men often diminish their contact. Their study confirms the impression of many previous studies that custody arrangements frequently are revised following divorce (Spanier & Furstenberg 1984, Furstenberg 1987). Joint physical custody is an especially unstable arrangement, but sole custody is often informally renegotiated as well. Older children are especially likely to shift residence, often going to live with their fathers for a time during adolescence. About twice as many children in one-parent families lived with their fathers at 15 to 17 as children under the age of two (13.1 vs. 6.5%) in 1980 (Sweet & Bumpass 1987).

The enthusiasm over joint physical custody waned during the 1980s. For a brief time, it was viewed as a panacea for maintaining parental responsibilities in the wake of divorce. Most studies have shown that only a small minority of formerly married parents are willing and able to adopt this arrangement (Emery 1988). It is still an open question whether children benefit if they divide their time between two households. It also remains to be seen whether joint legal custody (as opposed to joint physical custody) is a useful device for maintaining parental collaboration and reenforcing the role of the parent who does not have physical custody.

### The Economic Consequences of Marital Instability

Divorce typically is a transitional family status. Eventually, nearly three fourths of all men and about three fifths of all women reenter marriage (Spanier & Furstenberg, 1987). But the interval between unions has been growing as remarriage rates have slowed during the past decade (Cherlin forthcoming). Men remarry more quickly than women in large measure due to the greater availability of marriage partners. Males typically marry women of younger ages whereas women generally face a more restricted marriage pool. This differential rate of remarriage contributes to the significant economic disadvantage that formerly married women experience, especially those with children.

Abundant evidence shows that the economic effects of marriage are quite divergent for men and women. Males generally leave marriage with much greater earning capacity (Kahn & Kamerman 1988, Duncan & Hoffman 1985). Moreover, they typically do not bear a fair share of child support when children remain in the mother's custody. Since almost 90% of women retain physical custody of the children, most females are severely disadvantaged by divorce.

Varying estimates of the size of this disadvantage have been calculated (Weitzman 1985, Weiss 1979, Duncan & Hoffman 1985, Peterson 1989). Using longitudinal data from the Panel on Income Dynamics, Duncan & Hoffman (1985) show that men actually improve their economic status following a divorce, doing about as well as men in intact families. In contrast, women experience a significant drop in income, which lasts for several years. Gradually, most women recover, that is, return to the income level prior to divorce, though they do much less well than women in stably married families. Most of the recovery occurs as a result of remarriage. Women who remain unmarried continue to experience a sizable economic loss despite the fact that they greatly increase their participation in the labor market. One present study suggests that over time, women who remain divorced improve their position in the labor market substantially (Peterson 1989).

Alimony and child support are potentially important mechanisms for redressing the imbalances created by divorce. The changing economic status of women and the movement to no-fault divorce may have reduced the claim for alimony (Weitzman 1985). Data collected by the Census Bureau shows a sharp decline in the past decade in alimony payments. More surprising is the persistent pattern of low child support provided by noncustodial fathers to their children. In 1985, 61% of single women living with children under 21 had child support agreements; the remainder had no award. Of those who had a legal award and were entitled to support, just half were receiving their full payments (US Bureau of the Census 1989a). In other words, fewer than one custodial mother in four was receiving regular and full child support. The prevalence of child support agreements has remained relatively stable over the past seven years despite strenuous efforts to increase compliance. Moreover, the actual amount of payments, adjusted for inflation, has declined.

Interpretation of these trends is complicated by changes in the composition of the pool of custodial mothers. More women today are never married, lowering, evidently, the level of support awards (because paternity was not established) and the compliance. Moreover, more separated and divorced women are working now than in the late 1970s; this fact may lead courts to reduce court-ordered child support. Still, nearly half of all separated and divorced women were unable to obtain awards despite a desire to do so. Many of these women are not earning sufficient incomes to provide adequate support to their children. In 1985, 26% of divorced mothers, 47% of separated mothers, and 58% of never married mothers were living in poverty. Women who received child support payments had substantially lower rates of poverty though it is not clear whether or how much income transfers per se accounted for the reduction of poverty (US Bureau of the Census 1989a). Nevertheless, lack of adequate child support places great economic strain on women who often suffer the twin disadvantages of low earnings capacity and poor marriage prospects (Ellwood 1988).

Formerly married black women and their children are especially vulnerable to all these sources of poverty. They have limited earnings capacity, face bleak prospects of remarriage, and receive less help from noncustodial fathers than do previously married white women. In 1986, black separated women between the ages of 15 and 44 were 28% more likely to be living below the poverty line than were white separated women (52 vs. 40.5%), and black divorced women were more than twice as likely to be poor—61.3 vs 25.2% (US Bureau of the Census 1988).

The income figures cited above provide only a rough measure of the economic consequences of divorce. Studies of the process of divorce reveal that downward mobility has many far-reaching effects on family life (Newman 1988). Divorce often requires the sale of the family home and unsettling residential changes. Mothers may be forced to increase work hours, change childcare arrangements, and rely more heavily on the domestic contributions of children (Weiss 1979). These changes are not always unwelcome or wholly negative, but they usually are stressful for parents and children. McLanahan (1988) has speculated that the indirect effects of rapid economic decline frequently contribute to the adverse consequences of divorce for children. Several studies have examined the economic ramifications of divorce for the adjustment of women and children in single-parent households (Brandwein et al 1974, Weiss 1975,

Arendell 1986, Peterson 1989). In an excellent summary of the economic effects of divorce, Garfinkel & McLanahan conclude:

> According to official government data, about half of all children and mothers in families headed by women suffer from the most extreme form of economic insecurity—poverty. No other major demographic group is so poor, and none stays poor longer.... Even mother-only families who are not poor are subject to economic insecurity and other forms of instability.... In view of the instabilities confronting such families, it is not surprising that family members suffer disproportionately from mental health problems and use a disproportionate share of community mental health services. (1986:167–68)

### The Declining Involvement of Fathers

One reason why noncustodial fathers contribute so little child support is that most sharply reduce their involvement in childrearing after divorce. Whether they discontinue child support because they reduce contact or vice versa is the subject of some debate (Seltzer et al 1989). The sources of disengagement are not well understood. Some fathers are pushed out of the family, but most seem to retreat from paternal responsibility when they no longer reside with their children. Elsewhere Cherlin and I have argued that many men view marriage and childcare as an inseparable role-set (Furstenberg & Cherlin, forthcoming). Accordingly, men often sever ties with their children in the course of establishing distance from their former wives. Remarriage by either former partner usually hastens this process of disengagement. Geographical mobility, increased economic demands, and new family responsibilities, which often accompany remarriage, may erode the tenuous bonds between noncustodial fathers and their children.

# 13.2 JUDITH S. WALLERSTEIN AND JOAN B. KELLY

# Children and Divorce: A Review

Many people have great concern for children who live through a divorce and who, as a result of the divorce, live in single-parent homes. These children are considered at risk for a variety of problems, such as drug use, premature pregnancy, and child abuse. As a result, these children have been studied as a population with potential problems, and much of the research has verified that these children do indeed have challenges to growing up healthy.

Judith S. Wallerstein (b. 1921) attended Hunter College in New York and received her master's degree in social work from Columbia University. She began her career at the Community Service Society in New York as assistant director of the Residential Treatment Center. She made a significant contribution to the literature when she published *Surviving the Breakup: How Children and Parents Cope With Divorce* with Joan B. Kelly (Basic Books, 1980).

Kelly (b. 1939) received her doctorate from Yale University in 1965. Kelly is cofounder and director of the Northern California Mediation Center and of the Northern California Mediation Service. She began her study of divorce in 1970 because little was known at that time about the impact of divorce on children and parents. Both Wallerstein and Kelly have contributed chapters and articles on the effects of divorce on children to numerous books and professional journals. This selection is from "Children and Divorce: A Review," *Social Work* (November 1979).

**Key Concept:** children and divorce

Divorcing couples and their children constitute a rapidly increasing population whose special needs have been insufficiently recognized, infrequently studied, and poorly served. Thus far, only a fraction of the proliferating studies focusing on divorce (Sell, 1977), have examined its impact on children, and interventions specifically addressing the needs of children whose parents are divorcing have been developed slowly. As a consequence, too little is known of the child's experience during divorce, of the extent to which children of divorced parents are at risk of developing emotional or psychological difficulties, or whether the effects of a marital split that are not immediately visible in children are likely to appear at a later developmental stage.

In their clinical work with children of divorce, practitioners have tended to rely on existing knowledge regarding separation, loss, and mourning. However, although similar in certain aspects to other experiences of loss, divorce departs from these experiences significantly in both its course and outcome. The divorce-induced changes in the child's relationship with his or her parents are clearly distinguishable from changes taking place in families following a death or instances of abandonment (Neubauer, 1960; Tessman, 1977).

For the family containing children, divorce is a multifaceted, extended process that alters but does not end the relationships existing among family members (Despert, 1953; Bohannan, 1970; Weiss, 1975; Westman et al., 1970). Furthermore, the disruption caused by divorce is often accompanied by primitive angers and impulsive acts on the part of a couple that may not have been part of their behavior or manner of interacting before their breakup. The intrapsychic distress and intrafamilial disequilibrium attendant on a divorce frequently extend over two years or more (Hetherington, Cox, and Cox, 1976). In a study that was conducted by the present authors and that will be described in this article, the average length of time required by women to reestablish a sense of stability in their lives after being divorced was $3\frac{1}{2}$ years; $2\frac{1}{2}$ years was the average time required by men (Wallerstein and Kelly, in press).

Thus, for many children, the process of divorce is characterized by initial loss and turmoil, followed by several years of relative instability in which the attention received by them from their parents fluctuates. The decreasing availability of supportive social structures, the weakening of extended-family ties, and the geographic relocation that often follows in the wake of divorce all contribute to the stress that is experienced by the child.

Children are participants affected by at least four related stages or situations in the process of divorce. These are the following: (1) the predivorce family, (2) the disruptive process of divorce itself, including the events leading up to and surrounding the parents' decision to separate, and the transition period immediately following, (3) the changed social, economic, and psychological realities of being reared in a family in which divorce has occurred, and (4) the alterations in the parent-child relationship that take place after the marital breakup. A fifth situation for many children is the remarriage of one or both parents, not infrequently to a partner with children of his or her own. Living through each of these situations and experiences may have short-term or enduring consequences. Each has the potential to interfere with the child's development, just as each represents an opportunity for growth for the child. The duration of stress over time, as well as the rhythm and degree of change, will vary for each child and within each family.

# OVERALL PERSPECTIVE

Between 1966 and 1976, the rate of divorce in the United States increased by 113 percent. Whereas in 1966 one divorce was granted for every four marriages performed, by 1976 the ratio had changed to one divorce for every two marriages. Indications exist that this spiraling increase in the divorce rate has recently begun to slow down. Nevertheless, nearly one million divorces per year may be expected to be a continuing social phenomenon over the next few years.

Divorce can occur in response to stress that is not initially related to marital incompatibility. Kaplan, Grobstein, and Smith (1976) found an increased tendency toward separation in families following the diagnosis of leukemia in a child as well as in families in which a serious accident or death had taken place. Such divorces may serve the psychodynamic function of warding off depressions in the parent, but they can be particularly stressful for the child (Wallerstein and Kelly, 1977).

Divorce and mental illness may also occur in conjunction (Blumenthal, 1967; Briscoe et al., 1973). Available data suggest that suicide, accidental death, and psychological illnesses such as serious depression are considerably higher among divorced adults (Carter and Glick, 1976). A review of eleven studies (Gove, 1972a, 1972b) reported that the rate of mental illness among divorced men was over five times as high as that for married men and that this rate was nearly three times as high for divorced women as for married women. Although these data are correlational and do not establish causal links, a higher incidence of psychological illness among divorced parents will place children of divorce at greater risk of developing psychiatric and social problems than children whose families are intact.

Whatever the causal factors involved in marital breakups, approximately 65 percent of all divorces and annulments taking place in the United States occur in families with children under 18 years of age. Since 1972, each year more than one million children under 18 years of age have been affected by their parents' divorce (Carter and Glick, 1976). It has been estimated (Bane, 1976) that between 32 and 46 percent of the children who have grown up in this country during the 1970s will experience either the separation or actual divorce of their parents.

Not surprisingly, therefore, the proportion of children who live with only one parent has almost doubled since 1960. In 1974, 15.6 percent of all children under 18 were reported to be living with one parent, and of these, nearly one-third were under the age of 6 (U.S. Bureau of the Census, 1975). Significant racial differences exist in this area. Proportionately, more than three times as many black children as white children live with one parent. More than two-thirds of the parents of the six million children who lived with one parent in 1974 were reported to be separated or divorced. The remainder were widowed or abandoned or had never married. (Carter and Glick, 1976). Overall, the vast majority of children in single-parent families live with their mothers.

Many families in which divorce has occurred face problems involving diminished financial resources, unemployment, child care arrangements, and social isolation; these difficulties are similar to those encountered by all single-parent families. One major problem that relates to divorce and has been approached uneasily and with mixed success in different legal jurisdictions is how to enforce the collection of child support payments from resistant, unreliable, or absent parents. Delinquency in the regular payment of child support is widespread. In a careful summary of available research, Weitzman (in press) reports that "after one year, less than half of the men [studied] are still paying support at all for their children." Moreover, Weitzman and Dixon (1979) found that the average amount paid for child support in a sample studied in California in 1972 and 1977 provided significantly less than one-half the cost of raising children during those years.

Levels of income and education are much higher among parents in two-parent families than they are among parents in families with only the mother present. In 1974, 51.5 percent of the children under 18 living in families headed by women were found to be below the poverty level (U.S. Bureau of the Census, 1975). Even in middle-class families, the decline in the standard of living for divorced mothers and their children is striking and occurs within a brief time span following the marital breakup.

## INITIAL IMPACT

Divorce becomes real for most children when one parent moves out of the home. However, the full acceptance of this event into the inner world of the child often requires considerable time. In preschool and latency-age children, fantasies of parents' reconciliation can persist even after the remarriage of one or both of the divorced parents has taken place. Prior to adolescence, children rarely perceive their parents' divorce as a welcome relief or a reasonable solution except when they have witnessed frequent physical violence between the parents. Of the 131 children whom the present authors studied over a five-year period, less than 10 percent experienced relief at the time of their parents' marital separation, although 30 percent had witnessed scenes of physical violence between their parents.

Initially, almost all children and many adolescents experience divorce as painful and as disruptive of their lives, and their suffering is compounded by both realistic and unrealistic fears. These fears are related to the following factors: a heightened sense of vulnerability, sadness at the loss of the protective structure of the family and of the parent who does not retain custody, guilt over fantasized or actual misdeeds that may have contributed to parents' quarrels (although such fantasies are not found in all children), worry over distressed parents, anger at the parent or parents who have disrupted the child's world, shame regarding parents' behavior, a sense of being alone, and concern about being different from peers. For many children and adolescents, the overall initial response to divorce can properly be considered a reactive depression. There is no evidence that these initial reactions are muted or are experienced as less painful because of the high incidence of divorce taking place in the surrounding community. (Wallerstein and Kelly, 1974, 1975, 1976).

Despite a wide range of individual differences in the reactions of children to divorce, certain common concerns emerge at the time of parental separation that can be related to developmental considerations and cognitive capacity. Children of preschool and kindergarten age fear disruption of nurturance and possible abandonment by both parents, and their anxieties are enhanced by their cognitive confusion. Youngsters in latency characteristically struggle with painful conflicts regarding loyalty to both parents. Younger latency-age children are often preoccupied with a longing for the father who has left the household, and this longing is often unrelated to the nature of the relationship that existed between father and child before the advent of divorce. In addition to experiencing sorrow and increased worry about themselves and their parents, older latency-age children are often intensely angry at one or both parents. In contrast, the sense of loss experienced by adolescents is heightened by their anxious perception of their parents' sexuality, loneliness, and not infrequent regression.

A child's sex and order of birth in the family can affect the intensity of his or her early response to divorce, particularly since children experience pressure from their parents to provide support or enter into an emotional alliance. Research indicates that the only child feels considerably more threatened than the child who shares the impact of divorce with siblings (Wallerstein and Kelly, in press). Children who are members of interracial or ethnically mixed families may also experience greater strain at the time of their parents' divorce. This is intensified if extended families in the situation exert additional emotional pressure that exacerbates the child's conflicts of loyalty (McDermott, 1968; Esman, 1971; Kelly and Wallerstein, 1976; Wallerstein and Kelly, 1974, 1975, 1976; Weiss, 1975).

## LONG-TERM OUTCOME

Little is known of the longer-range effects of divorce on children. Early sociological investigations (Nye, 1957; Landis, 1960, 1962, 1963; Anderson, 1968) attempted to link the behavior and attitudes displayed by adolescents and young adults in later years with the experience of being raised in a family in which divorce had taken place. The work done supported the idea that living in the environment of a strife-filled marriage may place children at greater risk than living in a family in which divorce has occurred. However, in a psychological study that was experimental in nature and provided a different perspective, Hetherington (1972) found intensified seductive and maladroit behaviors in adolescent girls whose fathers had left the household as a result of divorce. This finding emerged when the girls were compared with others whose fathers had died and with another group whose families were intact. The differences found were especially significant regarding those girls whose parents had divorced when the girls themselves were below the age of 6.

A five-year study conducted by the authors that focused on sixty families in northern California in which divorce had occurred was brought to a close in 1977. The families studied were predominantly white and middle-class, and they contained a total of 131 children, who ranged in age from 3 to 18 at the time of their parents' separation. At the end of the first eighteen months following their families' breakup, the preschool children appeared to be the most vulnerable and susceptible to developing emotional and psychological problems of those studied. Although most were initially considered psychologically intact, nearly one-half showed deterioration. Children in latency were found to be somewhat more resistant to stress related to their parents' divorce. Nevertheless, eighteen months after their parents' breakup it was found in the case of nearly one-quarter of them that their psychological condition seemed to have become worse or that difficulties they had been experiencing before the divorce had become more firmly entrenched. A surprising amount of vulnerability was found among the adolescents.

Eighteen months after their parents' separation, deterioration among the children studied correlated most highly with continued disorganization in the family, undiminished anger or psychological illness in the parent retaining custody, and insufficient contact with the parent who did not retain custody. In general, boys seemed to be faring significantly worse than girls were at this time. However, this was not true for the adolescents among whom sex differences were not discerned. Full-time employment among mothers was not per se a significant variable in the outcomes for their children if they were emotionally available to the children when not working. For children who were relatively intact, the resumption of growth and development seems to have been primarily related to the reestablishment of stability and nurturance within the family after the divorce and to the continuity of contact with the parent not retaining custody. Support systems outside the immediate family, whose unavailability was often striking, played a less significant role than expected in the outcomes for the children (Wallerstein and Kelly, 1974, 1975, 1976; Kelly and Wallerstein, 1976).

Five years after the beginning of the research, fifty-eight of the original sixty families were again studied. At that time, 34 percent of the youngsters seemed to be doing very well indeed, having regained or recently acquired a sense of well-being and self-confidence. Moreover, these children displayed good adjustment as measured in school, at play, in relationships with peers, and in relationships within the family. Unfortunately, another 37 percent of the youngsters were judged to be suffering from a moderate to severe depression that was manifested in a wide variety of feelings and behaviors, including chronic and pronounced unhappiness; sexual promiscuity; delinquency in the form of drug abuse, petty stealing, alcoholism, and acts of breaking and entering; poor learning; intense anger; apathy; restlessness; and a sense of intense, unremitting neediness. In addition, one of these youngsters suffered from a preoccupation with suicide. The remaining 29 percent of the children had resumed appropriate developmental progress but continued to experience intermittently a sense of deprivation and feelings of sadness and resentment toward one or both parents.

# PARENTS AND CHILDREN

Divorce brings about significant, complex, and sometimes surprising changes in the relationship between parents and children. This is true of children's relationships with both parents. These changes occur in part as the parent-child relationship breaks free of the context of the marital bond and acquires new meaning within the context of the needs of the separated couple after the divorce. A close tie between a parent and child before the advent of divorce may have reflected the parent's need to maintain distance from a frustrating spouse or a turning to the child for the intimacy that was not available within the marriage itself. Both parents of one-quarter of the children in the authors' study were consistently loving to their children despite the conflicts they were experiencing within their marriage. However, parental needs for closeness with a child may terminate abruptly as the marriage ends, leaving the child feeling bewildered and rejected.

Alternatively, the needs of the parent and child may bring them closer together following a divorce. Some children perceive the distress and loneliness of their divorced parents with maturity and compassion and take increasing responsibility for providing comfort, companionship, and practical help in the household. Others, particularly older latency-age and adolescent youngsters, may be caught up in aligning themselves emotionally with one parent or the other. In such instances, the anger shared by parent and child becomes the basis for malevolent, complex, and organized strategies aimed at hurting or harassing the other parent. Often, the children who participate in these strategies had warm and loving relationships prior to the divorce with the parent who becomes the target of their anger. Nevertheless, these strategic alignments may become consolidated and last for many years (Wallerstein and Kelly, 1976.)

At the time of separation, many parents are heavily burdened by their own needs and are temporarily unable to perceive or respond to their children's increased needs for parenting and understanding. The authors were startled to discover that 80 percent of the preschool children in their study had not been prepared for the marital breakup taking place in the family. This left them almost entirely alone in coping with the confusing and terrifying departure of one parent (Wallerstein and Kelly, 1975).

Hetherington, Cox, and Cox (1978) followed forty-eight recently divorced, white, middle-class couples and compared their households, their relationships with their children, and the functioning of their families with those found among a control group of intact families. The households in which divorce had occurred were characterized by greatly increased disorganization and by marked changes in the management of the children, including reduced consistency of discipline, diminished communication and nurturance, and the holding of fewer expectations of mature behavior from the children. Significant attitudinal differences were also found between mothers and fathers in the divorced families, which increased the prevailing inconsistency and confusion. Many of these changes were most pronounced after a period of one year, at the time of follow-up, with some diminution in the more disorganizing stresses noted two years after the time of divorce.

The continuation of contact between the child and the parent who has not retained custody is a crucial issue. Mounting evidence indicates that the maintenance of this relationship between parent and child is of central importance in the psychological adjustment of children within the postdivorce family. Jacobson (1978) found that children who spent little time with their fathers during the year after the marital breakup were more likely to develop psychiatric symptomatology than those youngsters who enjoyed more frequent contacts. The findings of the present authors' study point to a significant link between depression in younger children and adolescents and diminished visiting by the children's fathers. Conversely, high self-esteem in all children, especially in older boys, was tied to a good father-child relationship that had been sustained within the structure of visitation (Wallerstein and Kelly, in press).

Contrary to popular expectations, the relationship maintained between father and child through regular visits does not necessarily reflect the predivorce relationship between them. Eighteen months after divorce had taken place, no correlation was found in the authors' study between the relationship that existed while a family was still intact and the pattern or frequency of visits made by the father to his children after divorce. The extent of a father's visiting was greatly influenced by his feelings about the divorce itself, by the age of the children, and by the children's responsiveness; the mother's attitude toward visits made by her ex-spouse was less significant than expected. Overall, fathers are likely to visit younger children more frequently and more regularly than they are to visit older youngsters. In their study the authors found a decided reduction in the visits made by fathers to older children, especially to children who were full of anger and between 9 and 12 years of age at the time of their parents' separation (Kelly and Wallerstein, 1977b).

## CUSTODY ISSUES

The most tragic and clinically vulnerable children of divorce are those who become the objects of continued acrimonious legal battles between their divorcing parents. Court cases regarding these "children of Armageddon," as Watson (1969) has called them, account for a significant amount of litigation in the area of domestic relations (Bodenheimer, 1974–75; Westman et al., 1970). Although no definite statistics are available, the authors estimate that 10 to 15 percent of the divorces of couples with children under 18 are litigated over a variety of child-related issues, primarily custody and visitation rights.

The causes of extended legal contests between divorcing spouses are complex. Legally, these battles can continue indefinitely because a decision regarding custody or visitation is always modifiable by the courts. Psychologically, an individual's rage against an ex-spouse, often expressed in litigation in which the child is the pawn, can apparently remain undiminished by the passage of time or by distance. The fight for a child may serve profound psychological needs in a parent, including the warding off of severe depression and other forms of pathological disorganization.

Although the concept of the "best interests of the child" has become the standard for decisions regarding custody, the explication of this phrase, both in law and in practice, has proved extraordinarily difficult. In general, judges have tended to avoid serving on the domestic relations bench. Similarly, many mental health professionals have regarded the courts as an area outside their professional interest. Even when specialized psychological services are attached to the court and are available, they are usually characterized by inadequate staffing or are provided by staff who are not specifically trained to work with children and adolescents.

The no-man's-land between the mental health professions and the courts changed with the publication of *Beyond the Best Interests of the Child* (Goldstein, Freud, and Solnit, 1973.) Asserting forthrightly that the principles of developmental psychology bear directly on the legal processes involving children, the authors offered specific guides to judicial procedures and decision-making. They recommended that decisions regarding child custody be resolved in accelerated proceedings instead of in long, drawn-out procedures, have final effect and not be reversible, and award full control to the one "psychological parent," or the adult psychologically viewed by the child as his or her parent. Their thinking has had wide influence on the judiciary and has evoked vigorous controversy (Benedek and Benedek, 1977), but a strong countermovement in favor of joint custody and asserting the continuing significance of both parents to the child has recently developed (Roman and Haddad, 1978).

The emerging trend concerning issues of divorce is toward formal cooperation between the courts and the mental health professions (Derdeyn, 1975, 1976a, 1976b; Lewis, 1974; Littner, 1971). Diagnostic and counseling services set up or mandated by the courts have developed in widely separated legal jurisdictions (Sheffner and Suarez, 1975). Furthermore, the network of conciliation courts throughout the United States and Canada has increasingly entered into work with families in which divorce is taking place.

In addition, many social changes have affected custody decisions, and some of these changes may impel the courts to make greater use of the expertise of social workers. Among the changes are the following: (1) an increasing social and legal acceptance of the granting of custody to fathers (Keshet and Rosenthal, 1978), (2) a growing interest in awarding joint custody to parents, and increased experimentation with different postdivorce living arrangements, (3) an increased willingness among women to yield custody of their children to their ex-husbands (Schlesinger and Todres, 1976), and (4) the emergence of the declared homosexual or lesbian parent who seeks custody. Many of these changes are linked to the changing status of men and women in modern society, to changing roles within the family, and to the women's movement.

## IN THE SCHOOLS

Few studies that include observations of children in school have been done concerning the behavioral and affective changes in preschool children at the time of their parents' separation. However, the findings that do exist are consistent.

McDermott (1968) and the present authors found the great majority of children that they studied to be angry, sad, or forlorn; only in exceptional cases did no change in behavior take place. Angry and distressed responses disappeared in these children within the year following their parents' divorce, except in those youngsters whose overall level of functioning had deteriorated. In regard to these more vulnerable children, nursery school teachers reported a driven need for physical contact, inability to function in a group, and diminished self-esteem (Wallerstein and Kelly, 1975).

However, in contrast to these findings regarding preschool children, the present authors (1976) found that no straightforward relationship emerged between the intensity of the suffering experienced by children in latency over their parents' divorce and the demeanor of these children at school. About half the children displayed acute behavioral changes visible in a precipitous decline in school performance, newly troubled peer relationships, and moody, irritable behavior. Most children recovered within the first year after their parents' separation, although some developed chronic learning difficulties.

Finally, the response to divorce seemed to be bimodal among adolescents. Some teenagers moved into a coping pattern of highly accelerated social and academic activity to school. Other adolescents began to perceive school as an intolerable burden and as a place where academic and social pressures overtaxed their limited resources. They displayed unaccustomed failing grades, fantasies of dropping out, and intense anger and depression. Burchinal (1964) compared adolescents from "broken" homes with those from families who were intact and found that the first group was characterized by a greater incidence of anxiety, absence from school, proneness to illness, and fright reactions.

## IMPLICATIONS

A central and persuasive tenet in psychological and social theory has been the paradigm of the two-parent family, which has been held to provide the average expectable environment for the healthy child. With reference to the new realities represented by families in which divorce has occurred, it is important to rethink many traditional concepts of child development, psychopathology, and intervention theory and develop theoretical formulations appropriate to newly emerging family structures.

A significant portion of the patients seen by practitioners in clinics and private practice during the next decades will be children of divorced families (Gardner, 1976; Kalter, 1977; Tooley, 1976). Some of these children will present familiar clinical syndromes that are only tangentially related to their experience of their parents' divorce. Others will present an array of acute, divorce-engendered reactions occurring at different stressful points during the process of divorce and its aftermath. Still others seem severely troubled and disorganized, if they resemble those children with chronic difficulties whose parents have been divorced for some years and who are currently being referred for treatment (Tessman, 1977). Dealing with these different groups of patients will require the practitioner to be alert to the many varied psychological sequelae of divorce as well as sensitive to divorce-related responses, whether pathological or normative in character.

Particular hazards are attached to clinical work with the children just described and with their parents as well. The high levels of distress, jealousy, neediness, depression, and anger frequently experienced by divorcing parents place great pressure on the practitioner, and the potential for violent behavior between divorcing spouses is great. In addition, because the high incidence of divorce in the surrounding society can cause the clinician to feel vulnerable and unprotected, the possibility of anxiety and inappropriate interventions related to countertransference are thus magnified (Wallerstein and Kelly, 1977; Whitaker and Miller, 1969).

In addition to implications for practice, implications for research in the area of divorce should be considered. The hypotheses and incipient norms that have been derived regarding the predictable responses of children and the predictable changes in the parent-child relationship during and after divorce have been based predominantly on white, middle-class populations in Virginia (Hetherington, 1972; Hetherington, Cox, and Cox, 1976, 1978) and northern California (Wallerstein and Kelly, 1974, 1975, 1976, 1977). It is therefore important that divorcing parents and their children be studied at related points in time, in different socioeconomic groups, and with reference to diverse ethnic backgrounds.

Special groups within the general population affected by separation and divorce, such as children and adolescents within one narrow age range, only children, children having particular vulnerabilities or competences, children whose parents never married, and children whose parents are involved in litigation, should also be examined carefully. Studies dealing with such groups would reveal similarities and differences among different populations and would call attention as well to the universality or commonality of certain responses and sequelae. Also illuminated would be the ways in which initial responses and long-range outcomes are affected by individual, family, and social factors that include the following: the age of the child at the time of the marital breakup, sex, birth order, psychological competence and vulnerability, relationship between parent and child at different times during the process of divorce, and socioeconomic and structural differences in families before and after divorce.

Finally, in regard to policy implications, the development of social policy that is concerned with the children of divorce involves issues that are delicate, complex, and perhaps uncomfortable to contemplate. A central issue is the divergence of the wishes and interests of the children from those of their parents in many families in which divorce has occurred. The conventional wisdom of yesteryear was that unhappily married people should remain married "for the good of the children." The conventional wisdom of today holds, with equal vigor, that the marriage in which the adults are unhappy is also unhappy for the children and, furthermore, that the divorce promoting the happiness of the adults will, inevitably, benefit the children as well.

This presumed commonality of perceptions among adults and children and the notion that the experience of the children can be subsumed under the experience of the adults is called sharply into question by the findings of the authors. Five years after the study began, 56 percent of the children surveyed did not consider their postdivorce family to be an improvement over their predivorce household. Despite the unhappiness of their parents, many of these children had been relatively happy and had considered their situation neither better nor worse than that of other families around them. Although most of the parents surveyed felt that their lot had considerably improved despite the stresses they were undergoing, the children and adolescents studied did not as a group experience a comparable improvement in psychological health in the years following parents' separation. These differences in experience cannot be resolved by denying their presence, by blurring the separate perceptions and feelings of each of the family members, by insisting that what benefits the adults inevitably benefits the children, or by asserting that the only problems involved in divorce are economic in nature. Unfortunately, neither an unhappy marriage nor a divorce is especially congenial for children. Each imposes its own set of stresses on the children and parents involved.

Within this framework, the time has come to introduce pilot programs rather than broad changes in social and family policy. The social work profession has both the opportunity and the responsibility to develop preventive or early intervention programs directed at particular and immediate times of stress in the divorce process (Kliman, 1968; Kelly and Wallerstein, 1977a; Wallerstein and Kelly, 1977). The goal of such intervention would be to avert psychological deterioration in children not previously considered at risk but rendered vulnerable by their parents' divorce. The programs involved might include the following features: (1) broad educational efforts that inform divorcing adults about the needs of their children, (2) counseling and clinical intervention designed to help parents and children at critical junctures during divorce and remarriage, (3) mediation services (Haynes, 1978), (4) training and consultation to schools, including nursery schools and day care centers, and (5) new and improved court-related services aimed at helping couples avoid acrimonious litigation.

Furthermore, in order to fulfill the responsibilities of child rearing, divorced parents are in need of a network of supportive services that are not now available in the community. These include vocational, financial, and psychological counseling; training and employment opportunities for the newly divorced parents; competent child care; quality afterschool programs; and weekend recreational facilities appropriate to the needs of the parent who is visiting his or her children.

It is fair to say that some major building blocks for the development of informed social policy are lacking. Nevertheless, various conclusions clearly emerge from the work of the authors. The outcome of divorce after several years reflects the success or failure of parents *and* children to master the ensuing disruption, successfully negotiate the necessary transition from predivorce to postdivorce life, and create a more gratifying family life to replace the family that failed. Unfortunately, the authors found that a significant number of parents and a greater number of children are failing at different points along the way.

The life cycle of a significant proportion of families in this country is likely to include divorce and remarriage during the next decade. Yet it is a curious phenomenon that family policy in the United States, which has recognized the state's responsibility to offer services in the area of family planning, has left parents to fend for themselves in regard to most of the issues and problems arising after children's actual arrival into the family. Perhaps the time has come to develop a realistic policy that addresses the metamorphoses taking place in the American family and the stressful points of change, for this is essential to ameliorative support and intervention as well as to the overall prevention of problems.

## REFERENCES

Anderson, Robert E. "Paternal Deprivation and Delinquency," *Archives of General Psychiatry*, 18 (June 1968), pp. 641–649.

Bane, Mary Jo. "Marital Disruption and the Lives of Children," *Journal of Social Issues*, 32 (1976), pp. 103–117.

Benedek, Richard S., and Benedek, Elissa P. "Postdivorce Visitation: A Child's Right," *Journal of the American Academy of Child Psychiatry*, 16 (1977), pp. 256–271.

Blumenthal, Monica D. "Mental Health Among the Divorced," *Archives of General Psychiatry*, 16 (May 1967), pp. 603–608.

Bodenheimer, Brigette M. "The Rights of Children and the Crises in Custody Litigation: Modification of Custody In and Out of State," *University of Colorado Law Review*, 46 (1974–75), pp. 495–508.

Bohannan, Paul. "The Six Stations of Divorce," in Paul Bohannan, ed., *Divorce and After*. Garden City, N.Y.: Doubleday & Co., 1970, p. 29.

Briscoe, C. William et al. "Divorce and Psychiatric Disease," *Archives of General Psychiatry*, 29 (July 1973), pp. 119–125.

Burchinal, Lee G. "Characteristics of Adolescents from Unbroken, Broken, and Reconstituted Families," *Marriage and Family Living*, 26 (February 1964), pp. 44–51.

Carter, Hugh, and Glick, Paul C. *Marriage and Divorce: A Social and Economic Study*. Cambridge, Mass.: Harvard University Press, 1976.

Derdeyn, Andre P. "A Consideration of Legal Issues in Child Custody Contests," *Archives of General Psychiatry*, 33 (February 1976a), pp. 165–171.

———. "Child Custody Consultation," *American Journal of Orthopsychiatry*, 45 (October 1975), pp. 791–801.

———. "Child Custody Contests in Historical Perspective," *American Journal of Psychiatry*, 133 (December 1976b), pp. 1369–1376.

Despert, J. Louise. *Children of Divorce*, Garden City, N.Y.: Doubleday & Co., 1953.

Esman, Aaron H. "Unhappy Marriage and its Effects on Children," *Medical Aspects of Human Sexuality*, 5 (1971), pp. 37, 40–41, and 90–97.

Gardner, Richard A. *Psychotherapy with Children of Divorce*. New York: Jason Aronson, 1976.

Goldstein, Joseph; Freud, Anna; and Solnit, A. *Beyond the Best Interests of the Child*. New York: Free Press, 1973.

Gove, Walter R. "Sex, Marital Status, and Suicide," *Journal of Health and Social Behavior*, 13 (June 1972a), pp. 204–213.

———. "The Relationship Between Sex Roles, Marital Status, and Mental Illness," *Social Forces*, 51 (September 1972b), pp. 34–44.

Haynes, John M. "Divorce Mediator: A New Role," *Social Work*, 23 (January 1978), pp. 5–9.

Hetherington, E. Mavis. "Effects of Father Absence on Personality Development in Adolescent Daughters," *Developmental Psychology*, 7 (November 1972), pp. 313–326.

Hetherington, E. Mavis; Cox, Martha; and Cox, Roger. "The Aftermath of Divorce," in Joseph H. Stevens, Jr. and Marilyn Mathews, eds., *Mother-Child/Father-Child Relationships*. Washington, D.C.: National Association for the Education of Young Children, 1978.

———. "Divorced Fathers," *Family Coordinator*, 2 (October 1976), pp. 417–428.

Jacobson, Doris. "The Impact of Marital Separation/Divorce on Children: Parent-Child Separation and Child Adjustment," *Journal of Divorce*, 4 (1978), p. 341.

Kalter, Neil, "Children of Divorce in an Outpatient Psychiatric Population," *American Journal of Orthopsychiatry*, 47 (January 1977), pp. 40–51.

Kaplan, David M.; Grobstein, Rose; and Smith, Aaron. "Predicting the Impact of Severe Illness in Families," *Health and Social Work*, 1 (August 1976), pp. 71–82.

Kelly, Joan, B., and Wallerstein, Judith S. "Brief Interventions with Children in Divorcing Families," *American Journal of Orthopsychiatry*, 47 (1977a), pp. 23–39.

———. "Part-time Parent. Part-time Child: Visiting After Divorce," *Journal of Clinical Child Psychology*, 6 (1977b), pp. 51–54.

———. "The Effects of Parental Divorce: Experiences of the Child in Early Latency," *American Journal of Orthopsychiatry*, 46 (1976), pp. 20–32.

Keshet, Harry Finkelstein, and Rosenthal, Kristine M. "Fathering After Marital Separation," *Social Work*, 23 (January 1978), pp. 11–18.

Kliman, Gilbert. *Psychological Emergencies of Childhood*. New York: Grune & Stratton, 1968.

Landis, Judson T. "A Comparison of Children From Divorced and Nondivorced Unhappy Marriages," *Family Life Coordinator*, 11 (July 1962), pp. 61–66.

———. "Social Correlates of Divorce or Nondivorce Among the Unhappily Married," *Marriage and Family Living*, 25 (May 1963), pp. 178–180.

———. "Trauma of Children When Parents Divorce," *Marriage and Family Living*, 22 (February 1960), pp. 7–13.

Lewis, Melvin. "The Latency Child in a Child Custody Conflict," *Journal of the American Academy of Child Psychiatry*, 13 (1974), pp. 635–647.

Littner, Ner. "The Doctor's Role in Contested Child Custody Matters," *Conciliation Court Review*, 9 (1971), pp. 34–36.

McDermott, John J. "Parental Divorce in Early Childhood," *American Journal of Psychiatry*, 124 (April 1968), pp. 1424–1431.

Neubauer, Peter. "The One-Parent Child and His Oedipal Development," *Psychoanalytic Study of the Child*, 15 (1960), pp. 286–309.

Nye, Ivan F. "Child Adjustment in Broken and in Unhappy Unbroken Homes," *Marriage and Family Living*, 19 (November 1957), pp. 356–361.

Roman, Mel, and Haddad, William. *The Disposable Parent: The Case for Joint Custody*. New York: Holt, Rinehart & Winston, 1978.

Schlesinger, Benjamin, and Todres, Rubin. "Motherless Families: An Increasing Societal Pattern," *Child Welfare*, 55 (September–October 1976), pp. 553–558.

Sell, Kenneth D. *Divorce in the 1970's: A Subject Guide to Books, Articles, Dissertations, Government Documents, and Film on Divorce in the United States*. Published annually; Salisbury, N.C.: Department of Sociology, Catawba College, 1977.

Sheffner, David J., and Suarez, John M. "The Postdivorce Clinic," *American Journal of Psychiatry,* 132 (April 1975), pp. 442–444.

Tessman, Lora Heims. *Children of Parting Parents.* New York: Jason Aronson, 1977.

Tooley, Kay. "Antisocial Behavior and Social Alienation Post-Divorce: The Man of the House and His Myth," *American Journal of Orthopsychiatry,* 46 (1976), pp. 33–42.

U.S. Bureau of the Census. "Money Income and Poverty Status of Families and Persons in the United States: 1974," *Current Population Reports,* Series P-60, No. 99, Washington, D.C.: U.S. Government Printing Office, 1975.

Wallerstein, Judith S., and Kelly, Joan B. "Divorce Counseling: A Community Service for Families in the Midst of Divorce," *American Journal of Orthopsychiatry,* 47 (1977), pp. 4–22.

_____. *Surviving the Breakup: How Children and Parents Cope with Divorce.* New York: Basic Books, in press.

_____. "The Effects of Parental Divorce: Experiences of the Child in Later Latency," *American Journal of Orthopsychiatry,* 46 (1976), pp. 256–269.

_____. "The Effects of Parental Divorce: Experiences of the Preschool Child," *Journal of the American Academy of Child Psychiatry,* 14 (Autumn 1975), pp. 600–616.

_____. "The Effects of Parental Divorce: The Adolescent Experience," in E. James Anthony and Cyrille Koupernik, eds., *The Child in His Family,* Vol 3. New York: John Wiley & Sons, 1974, pp. 479–505.

Watson, Andrew. "The Children of Armageddon: Problems of Children Following Divorce," *Syracuse Law Review,* 21 (1969), pp. 231–239.

Weitzman, Lenore. *The Marriage Contract: Couples, Lovers and The Law.* Englewood Cliffs, N.J.: Prentice-Hall, in press.

Weitzman, Lenore, and Dixon, Ruth. "Child Custody Awards, Legal Standards, and Empirical Patterns for Child Custody, Support and Visitation After Divorce," *University of California, Davis Law Review,* 12 (Summer 1979).

Westman, Jack C. et al. "The Role of Child Psychiatry in Divorce," *Archives of General Psychiatry,* 23 (November 1970), pp. 416–421.

Weiss, Robert S. *Marital Separation.* New York: Basic Books, 1975.

Whitaker, Carl A., and Miller, Milton H. "A Reevaluation of 'Psychiatric Help' When Divorce Impends," *American Journal of Psychiatry,* 125 (November 1969), pp. 611–618.

## 13.3 E. MAVIS HETHERINGTON, MARTHA COX, AND ROGER COX

# Effects of Divorce on Parents and Children

Research on divorce and its effects on children and the family dominated the literature in the 1970s and the 1980s. During that time, the divorce rate was climbing, and family scientists were concerned with how divorce was permanently changing the family. No longer was the traditional family form the primary focus of education and study. Now research looked at stepfamilies, the effects of divorce, and single-parent families. Family life was much more complex because there were so many types of relationships possible: custodial parents, noncustodial parents, stepparents, stepbrothers and stepsisters, biological grandparents, grandparents from remarriages, and so on. E. Mavis Hetherington, along with a variety of associates, conducted studies and published articles related to divorce, families, and schools throughout the 1970s and 1980s.

Hetherington (b. 1926) received two of her degrees from the University of British Columbia, and she earned her Ph.D. from the University of California, Berkeley, in 1958. She began her career as a clinical psychologist then taught psychology at various institutions of higher learning. Hetherington has held positions at the University of Virginia since 1970, including the James Page Professor of Psychology and department chair. She is on the board of directors of Child Trends, Inc., and on the President's Commission on Mental Health. She is coauthor, editor, or coeditor of a number of books, including *Coping With Divorce, Single Parenting, and Remarriage: A Risk and Resiliency Perspective* (Lawrence Erlbaum, 1999), and she has published over 40 articles in professional journals.

Martha Cox, a professor of psychology at the University of North Carolina at Chapel Hill and a senior scientist at the Frank Porter Graham Child Development Center, and Roger Cox wrote several articles with Hetherington in the late 1970s while at the University of Virginia. Their work focused on children, families, and divorce. This selection is from Hetherington, Cox, and Cox, "Effects of Divorce on Parents and Children," which was published in Michael E. Lamb, ed., *Nontraditional Families: Parenting and Child Development* (Lawrence Erlbaum, 1982).

**Key Concept:** divorce

Chapter 13
Divorce and
Remarriage

The divorce rate in the United States has shown a marked increase over the past 20 years, with a notable acceleration in the past decade. The country's divorce rate has more than doubled since 1965. It is estimated that more than 40% of the current marriages of young adults will terminate in divorce. In addition, parents are no longer staying together for the sake of the children; over 60% of divorcing couples have children. After a divorce most children live with a custodial mother and see their fathers intermittently or not at all. Although the proportion of children living with a divorced father has tripled since 1960, only one tenth of children reside with their fathers following divorce, and this is more likely to be found with school-aged than with preschool children (Glick & Norton, 1978). Marital disruptions and rearrangements in nuclear family ties are increasingly common experiences in the lives of many parents and their children.

It has been noted by Bane (1977) that: "a high rate of divorce per se is not a matter for concern in a society that values individual choice, even though some of the consequences of divorce may warrant societal attention. A divorce rate of zero might, in fact, be very worrisome, if it meant that unhappy, destructive marriages could not be dissolved [p. 14]."

In spite of the fact that divorce may be a positive solution to destructive family functioning and the eventual outcome may be a constructive one, for many family members the transition period following separation and divorce is stressful (Hetherington, 1981; Wallerstein & Kelly, 1980; Weiss, 1975, 1976). Divorce can be viewed as a critical experience that affects the entire family system, and the functioning and interactions of the members within that system.

Two things must be kept in mind in attempting to appraise the effects of divorce on families.

The first is that the outcomes of divorce will differ for different members of the family. Stresses, support systems, and successful coping strategies associated with divorce vary for husbands and wives, parents and children, and even among children in the same family. The means and ability for solving problems will diverge greatly in parents and children and in children of different ages. In addition, the needs and adaptive strategies of children and parents are not always compatible. The pathway to well-being for one family member may lead to a disastrous outcome for another.

The second important consideration is that divorce cannot be viewed as an event occurring at a single point in time; it represents an extended transition in the lives of parents and children. The point at which we tap into the course of divorce will to a large extent determine our evaluation of the effects of divorce. Some sequelae of divorce emerge rapidly following separation, some increase over the first year following divorce and then abate, and still others show a delayed emergence (Hetherington, 1981; Wallerstein & Kelly, 1980).

In conceptualizing the short-term effects of divorce, a crisis model of divorce may be most appropriate. In the period during and immediately following divorce, family members may be resounding to changes in their life experiences. In this period, stresses associated with conflict, loss, change, and uncertainty may be the salient factors. Research findings suggest that most family members can adapt to the crisis of divorce within a few years if it is not compounded by multiple stresses and continued adversity. The longer term adjustment of family members is related to the more sustained or concurrent economic, environmental, social, and emotional conditions that persist or are concomitants of life in a one-parent household....

## THE CHILD IN SCHOOL[1]

It might be expected that the impact of divorce will be manifested not only in interpersonal relations within the family system but also in relations external to the family. Patterns of play and relations with peers have been found to be areas in which stress and difficulties in coping are often reflected. Age-inappropriate play, disruptions in play, and unpopularity with peers consistently have been found to be related to anxiety and emotional disturbance in children (Hartup, 1976; Roff, Sells, & Golden, 1972; Singer, 1977). In addition, children's play and interactions with peers not only provide critical opportunities to acquire certain social competencies but also play an important role for children in working through or modifying their problem behavior (Hartup, 1976, 1977a, 1977b; Singer & Singer, 1976; Sutton-Smith, 1971).

Over the course of the preschool years, children's play becomes more social and cooperative and involves more fantasy, dramatic play, and games (Parten, 1932; Piaget, 1962; Smilansky, 1968).

Disruptions and rigidity in the fantasy-play patterns of emotionally disturbed children have frequently been noted (Singer, 1977; Singer & Singer, 1976). Processes in imaginative play seem to be particularly vulnerable to the effects of psychological stress. It has been suggested that the failure to develop imaginative play is indicative of serious pathology, particularly of an acting out, impulsive type in children (Gould, 1972). Imaginativeness in play has been found to be associated not only with self-control, low impulsivity, and low aggression (Singer & Singer, 1976) but also with sharing, cooperation, independence (Singer, 1977), and social maturity (Rubin et al., 1976). In addition, children who show spontaneous imaginativeness in play are likely to show a broader range of emotions and more positive affect than less imaginative children. They are more likely to smile, be curious and interested in new experiences, and express joy in making believe and in peer relations (Singer, 1977). Singer states that: "imaginative play can be viewed as a major resource by which children can cope immediately with the cognitive, affective and social demands of growing up. It is more than a reactive behavior, however, for it provides a practice ground for organizing new schema and for transforming and storing material for more effective later expression in plans, actions or verbalization [p. 10]."

Sutton-Smith (1971) has also emphasized the important role that imaginative play provides in allowing the child to experiment with and gain some sense of competence in and control over situations with which, in reality, the child would be unable to cope. Exploring a variety of possible experiences, courses of action, roles, and outcomes in fantasy play is an important aspect of cognitive and social development.

## Free-Play Behaviors

Do the play patterns of children following divorce differ from those in nuclear families? Do these patterns change over time as the children grow older and as the children in divorced families begin coping with their new status in a single-parent family? Are the patterns different for boys and girls?

As the children aged, their play behavior became more task oriented, structured and imaginative, and involved more social interchanges with peers. With increasing age there was an increase in solitary–constructive, solitary–imaginative, associative–constructive, associative–imaginative, cooperative–constructive, and cooperative–imaginative play and in games. There was a decrease in functional play (play involving simple repetitive movements with or without objects, e.g., rocking, thumping) within all of the social–play categories. Parallel–functional and parallel–constructive play declined as children were becoming more involved in associative and cooperative play. Although the frequently reported shift from lone activities to social play was occurring, within solitary play it was only functional solitary play that declined with age, whereas constructive and imaginative solitary play increased over the 2-year period. In addition, both unoccupied and onlooker behavior decreased. Very little time was spent in games by the younger child but this too increased with age.

There were few sex differences in play and most of those obtained were involved in higher order interactions with time and family status. Girls showed more solitary functional and less solitary constructive play than did boys. Boys spent less time in parallel constructive play and were more involved in imaginative associative play than were girls.

At 2 months after divorce, boys and girls from divorced families were showing more functional play and less imaginative play in all categories than were their counterparts in nondivorced families. In addition, they were showing less associative and cooperative–constructive play. Children of both sexes from divorced families also were showing more unoccupied and onlooker behavior than were children from nondivorced families. Finally, the play episodes of children from divorced families were shorter.

These patterns of differences changed over time. By 1 year following divorce, girls in divorced families differed from those in nondivorced families only in showing less associative–imaginative and cooperative–imaginative play and in more onlooker behavior. By 2 years after divorce, even these differences had disappeared. In contrast, although boys from divorced families showed the most disruption in play at 1 year after divorce and more mature play patterns at 2 years following divorce, they still differed from boys in nondivorced families in a number of ways. In all three time periods boys from divorced families showed more solitary and parallel–functional play and less cooperative, constructive, imaginative, or game play than did boys in nondivorced families. In addition, they showed more onlooker behavior and shorter duration of play episodes at all three points in time. Finally, boys from divorced families spent an increasing amount of time playing with younger children and with girls rather than showing the more characteristic developmental pattern of a marked and increasing preponderance of time in play with same-sex peers. In classes in which there were mixed age groups, boys from divorced families also were spending more time with younger peers at 1 year and 2 years after divorce.

If these differences in play patterns between children in divorced families and those in nondivorced families can be viewed as responses to stresses and to the transition in family relationships following divorce, it appears that both boys and girls experience some disruptions in play immediately following divorce but that the effects are more sustained in boys. The play patterns of children from divorced families were less socially and cognitively mature when measured shortly after divorce. This might he due either to regression following the divorce or to a conflict-laden home situation preceding the divorce that had already retarded play development. Disturbances in play were also reflected in differences in the expression of affect. Angry, hostile, threatening affect and excitement were found more frequently in boys than in girls in both divorced and nondivorced families. At 2 months after divorce, both boys and girls in divorced families showed less happy, affectionate, and task-involved affect and more depressed, anxious, guilty, and apathetic affect than did children in nondivorced families. At 1 year after divorce, girls in divorced families were still less happy and more anxious than girls in nondivorced families, but again these differences were gone by 2 years following divorce. Negative types of emotion were more frequent and long lasting in boys following divorce. Boys from divorced families showed more hostile affect in the first year following divorce and were still less happy and more anxious 2 years after the divorce.

Let us now examine the fantasy play of the children from divorced and nondivorced families. We noted earlier that there was less imaginative play by children in divorced families and that differences among children from divorced and nondivorced families in the amount of fantasy persisted for boys but not for girls. In addition, when children from divorced families became involved in fantasy play in the first year following divorce, it was more likely to have been instigated by a peer than to have been self-initiated.

What differences were there among our groups of children in the types of imaginative processes involved in play? At all ages boys were more likely than girls to use imaginative processes involving objects that were present, and girls were more likely than boys to use fantasy processes involving imaginary objects, people, or situations. With increasing age, both boys and girls were less reliant on the presence of objects in their environment in initiating fantasy play and more often utilized fantasied objects, people, and events, and role and identity transformations. At 2 months following divorce, children from divorced families spent a larger proportion of their imaginative playtime in fantasy processes involving object-related functions, functional change in objects, and object-related animation than did children from nondivorced families. In addition, in this period they spent less of their time interacting with imaginary people. There were no fantasy process differences between girls from divorced and nondivorced families at 1 year and 2 years following divorce, but some differences for boys remained. In all three periods boys from divorced families less often made transformations of the self than did boys from nondivorced families. They seemed to have great difficulty in moving from "I" to the assumption of another's role in fantasy play. Gould (1972) has remarked that the transition from the consistent use of "I" in play to play in which the child is able to assume or alternate in playing another's role occurs between the ages of $3\frac{1}{2}$ and 4. She noted that continued focusing on the "I" in fantasy play in children beyond this age tends to be associated with a preoccupation with aggression and an inability to assume the role of providing or caring for others in imaginative play. Some support for this is found in our data, as children from divorced families were more involved with themes in which they were the recipients or agents of aggressive behavior, and boys from divorced families had a smaller percentage of prosocial themes dealing with caring for others, affection, helping, sharing and, sympathy. In both divorced and nondivorced families, boys more often utilized aggressive themes and themes of aggrandizement and girls more often used prosocial caretaking or providing themes. These were the only significant thematic differences.

A certain rigidity and narrowness was also reflected in the fantasy play of both boys and girls from divorced families at 2 months after divorce and for a more sustained period for boys. At 2 months after divorce, boys and girls from divorced families had fewer different characters involved in their fantasies, less frequently made different uses of the same object in play, and showed less diversity in either themes or affect in play. Except for less variation in themes and affect, these differences had disappeared for girls by 1 year after divorce and even the variability differences were gone by 2 years after divorce. However, these indicators of thematic and affective narrowness persisted for boys from divorced families.

### Social Interactions

When we looked at the social behavior of children across a broad range of situations in the school, we again found evidence of disrupted functioning in children immediately following divorce. Again these had largely disappeared for girls by 2 years after divorce and were decreasing but still lingering in boys.

At 2 months following divorce both boys and girls showed a pattern of greater fantasy aggression, opposition, and seeking help, attention, and proximity. In schools in which there were male adults, boys from divorced families made particularly strong attempts at maintaining contact and getting attention by following, touching, and seeking praise or affection from male adults. At 2 months after divorce children from divorced families shared and helped less than children in nondivorced families. They showed less positive nonverbal behavior (such as smiling or hugging) and more negative nonverbal behavior (such as pouting, clinging, and scowling), more crying, whining, and complaining, and more inattention, activity changes, and inactivity. We found higher fantasy aggression, more seeking of attention and affection, and more positive and negative physical contact with adults for girls from divorced families, compared to those in nondivorced families at all ages. In addition, in the first year following divorce, boys from divorced families were more likely than those from nondivorced families to make negative initiation bids and negative terminations of social interactions. Immediately following divorce, these boys showed a great deal of aversive opposition and negative commands toward both peers and adults, particularly female adults. This high rate of aversive opposition and negative demands toward female adults by boys from divorced families continued over the 2 years following divorce. They were also higher than boys from nondivorced families in physical and verbal hostile and instrumental aggression toward peers at both 2 months and 1 year after divorce. However, by 2 years after divorce, boys from divorced families, in comparison to those from nondivorced families, were showing low physical aggression and high verbal aggression, a pattern more frequently found in girls. The verbal and physical aggression displayed by girls from divorced families at 2 months, and by boys at 2 months and at 1 year, tended to be immature, unprovoked, and ineffective. They were seldom successful in gaining their ends through instrumental aggression. Their aggression was often accompanied by or followed by crying, dependency bids, or appeals to the teacher. One of the observers described them as incompetent bullies. Competent bullies are sometimes popular in the preschool set but it seems incompetent bullies rarely are.

By 2 years following divorce, boys also still were showing less helping behavior and less time affiliating or playing with people. It should be emphasized that, although the boys in the divorced families were still showing more noxious behaviors than boys from nondivorced families, their social behaviors had greatly improved. They were exhibiting less coercive behavior, less physical aggression, less aversive opposition, and fewer negative demands than they had at 1 year. However, rather than becoming more accepted, they appeared to be becoming more socially isolated relative to their male peers.

**Reactions of Others**

Perhaps by examining peer and teacher responses we can gain some understanding of what processes may be associated with these changes. The high rate of aversive behaviors in boys from single-parent homes in the first year following divorce was reacted to by male peers with high ignoring, opposition, aversive opposition, negative nonverbal responses, hostile physical aggression, hostile verbal aggression, and negative termination of interactions. By 2 years following divorce, although the negative oppositional and aggressive behavior by peers had gone, there was still more ignoring of boys from divorced families, fewer positive initiations, and more positive and negative terminations of interactions by male peers. There were few differences in the behavior of female peers when they were interacting with boys from divorced versus nondivorced families except that they spent more time playing with boys from mother-headed one-parent households.

A closer examination of initiations to peers may help clarify some of these findings. In the first two observation sessions, boys from divorced families were making many initiations toward peers. They wanted to interact. However, many of these initiations were negative, and the subsequent interactions were aversive, involving a combination of negative demands, physical and verbal aggression, dependency demands, crying, whining, and complaining. By 2 years after divorce the sons from divorced families were spending less time interacting with peers and were making fewer initiations, but a larger proportion of their initiations were positive. In fact, the proportion of positive to negative initiations is equivalent to that of boys in nondivorced families. At 2 months after divorce the boys from divorced families might attempt to initiate interactions by kicking over another child's sand castle or by standing silently staring and looming over the other child. By 2 years the boys from divorced families might say "I like building sand castles too," or "What a great sand castle," or might bring a twig with a leaf on it for a flag on the castle tower. However, their peers were neither accepting these initiations nor making initiations toward them. Perhaps they had learned to avoid them. A sequence analysis showed that males gave a high rate of opposition and ignoring responses to the initiations of these boys. Consequently, a significantly larger proportion of their time was spent in watching the play of others. The attending behaviors in boys from divorced families were often accompanied by negative nonverbal behaviors such as pouting and self-manipulation. These behaviors seem very similar to the hovering behavior in unpopular children recently described by Gottman (1978). If we break down the type of peers involved in these initiations, we find that boys from divorced families were more successful in gaining entry when making initiations toward younger children and toward girls. We argue later that this may in part explain why in this study and some previous studies more feminine play patterns and sex-typed preferences in boys from mother-headed one-parent households have been found.

When teachers interacted with boys from divorced families they also showed more negative behaviors than they did with boys from nondivorced families. In the first year following divorce they showed more negative requests or commands, more opposition, more negative terminations of interactions, and fewer positive responses. These differences were gone by 2 years following divorce.

Girls in divorced families seemed to elicit very different responses from their peers than did boys. There were no differences in responses from male peers toward girls from divorced or nondivorced families. Female peers showed more hostile verbal aggression and negative terminations in interacting with girls from divorced families, but they also showed more constructive social behavior such as sympathy, helping, and sharing at 2 months and at 1 year after divorce. There were no differences at 2 years after divorce. In the first year following divorce, teachers similarly seemed to make rather ambivalent responses toward girls from nondivorced families. They not only exhibited more negative commands and more negative verbal and physical responses but also exhibited more positive verbal and physical responses. In the first year following divorce, teachers seemed to be both more supportive and more critical of these girls. There were no teacher differences in treatment of girls from divorced and nondivorced families 2 years following divorce.

Although we have noted the greater ambivalence of the responses of peers and teachers toward girls from divorced than nondivorced families, it should be pointed out that boys from both divorced and nondivorced families receive more ambivalent responses from teachers, peers, and parents than do girls. A larger proportion of responses to boys, particularly to boys from divorced families, were negative or ambivalent responses. Crying and distress in boys received less frequent and shorter periods of comforting and more ambivalent comforting than did distress signals by girls. By ambivalent comforting we refer to instances in which a positive and negative or denying response were combined in dealing with distress in boys—A hug with "There, there! Boys don't cry," or "You're all right now," as a boy gloomily observed a bloody knee. In contrast, in the few cases where physical injury was observed in girls, the response of adults, both in the home and school, was usually either commenting on the quality of the injury ("That hurt, didn't it?") or unconditional nurturance (positive reassurance that was not accompanied by a qualifying statement).

Why should adults and peers be less supportive of boys than of girls in their attempts to cope with stress or changing life situations? It may be that sex-role standards cause people to perceive girls as requiring more support in times of stress and that signs of emotional neediness are less acceptable in boys than in girls. It also should he kept in mind that acting-out behavior, combined with a high rate of dependency demands and immature behavior, as is found in preschool boys in the first year following divorce, is a particularly noxious combination. People may be responding to the more aversive coping style of boys.

**Teacher and Peer Ratings**

We have examined the actual behavior of the children in the school setting. How do peer and teachers' perceptions of the children concur with our observations? Teachers rated children as becoming more task oriented, more cooperative and more interpersonally constructive and less hostile with age. Boys were rated as more defiant and aggressive than girls. Girls from divorced families were rated by teachers as being more dependent; boys from divorced families were viewed as more aggressive, impulsive, resistant, and lacking in task orientation.

The peer nomination inventory indicated that, both at 2 months and at 1 year after divorce, boys from divorced families were viewed as more aggressive and less socially constructive than were boys from nondivorced families. They were still viewed by their peers as more aggressive at 2 years after divorce although our observations suggest that this was not the case. This may support the notion that the earlier aversive behavior of boys in the first years after divorce was still being reacted to by their peers. There is further support of this position in the finding that boys who were shifted from one school to another between the first and second year assessments were perceived and responded to more positively by both peers and teachers in the last assessment. This was especially true of boys who had been perceived extremely negatively in that first year after divorce. This finding runs counter to the notion that stability in a child's environment following divorce facilitates adjustment. When a child has been labeled by peers or teachers in a negative fashion, the value of a move and a fresh start in a new environment may far outweigh the deleterious aspects of coping with a new school situation. The only differences in ratings between girls in divorced and nondivorced families were that girls in divorced families were rated as more aggressive at 2 months and more withdrawn, anxious, and dependent at all ages. Boys from divorced families were less popular than boys from nondivorced families both at l year and at 2 years following divorce. When boys from divorced families were selected as best friends, it was most likely to be by a younger child, or a girl. There were no differences in popularity between girls from divorced and nondivorced families.

**Relation Between Home and School Behavior**

How consistent is the behavior of children in the home, laboratory, and school situations? In the first year following divorce, there is considerable stability across situations in the behavior of children from divorced families. Observed noncompliance, negative demands, dependency, ignoring, aggression, and sustained activity were all significantly correlated for the home and laboratory situation. All these variables except ignoring were significantly correlated for home and school, and all except aggression were significantly correlated for the laboratory and school observations. In addition, there was considerable congruence between parent and teacher ratings in the first year following divorce. This was true for children in divorced families but not in nondivorced families, for whom there was much less stability across situations. The behavior of the children in divorced families also showed less stability across situations at 2 years after divorce. We could speculate that in the first year following divorce, the distress, anxiety, and problems in coping with their new family situation is most intense for the children. Under such disturbed emotional conditions, the internal state of the child rather than external situational variations may control the behavior of the child. Under high stress, the child may discriminate less well between situations and may respond less appropriately to the behavior of others. An analysis was done of the appropriateness of children's responses in the home, laboratory, and school situation. The behaviors of the child and of the people with whom the child was interacting were classified as positive, negative, or neutral. Conditional probabilities were calculated for the child's contingent positive, negative, or neutral responses to the positive, negative, or neutral responses of others. In the first year following divorce, children from divorced families were more likely than children from nondivorced families to make inappropriate responses to others. For example, they were more likely to make negative responses to a positive act of another and positive responses to a negative act of another. There were no significant differences between the groups in the appropriateness of responding at 2 years after divorce.

# NOTES

1. For more details on play and social interaction in the school see Hetherington, E. M., Cox, M., & Cox, R. Play and social interaction in children following divorce, *Journal of Social Issues*, 1979, 35, 26–49.

# PART FIVE

# *Aging Families*

**Chapter 14** Postparental Families  339

**Chapter 15** Older Families and Death  360

# On the Internet . . .

### Sites appropriate to Part Five

This is the home page of Division 20, Adult Development and Aging, of the American Psychological Association.

    http://www.iog.wayne.edu/APADIV20/apadiv20.html

The Hospice Association of America (HAA) is a national organization representing hospices, caregivers, and volunteers who serve the terminally ill and their families.

    http://www.nahc.org/HAA/about.html

The Alzheimer's Association is a national, voluntary health organization dedicated to researching the causes, cure, and prevention of Alzheimer's disease and to providing education and support services to Alzheimer's patients, their families, and their caregivers.

    http://www.alz.org/

CHAPTER 14 # Postparental Families

## 14.1 MICHAEL J. SPORAKOWSKI AND GEORGE A. HUGHSTON

# *Prescriptions for Happy Marriage*

This selection is from Michael J. Sporakowski and George A. Hughston, "Prescriptions for Happy Marriage: Adjustments and Satisfactions of Couples Married for 50 or More Years," *The Family Coordinator* (October 1978). At the time this article was written, Sporakowski was a professor and Hughston was an assistant professor in the Department of Management, Housing, and Family Development at Virginia Polytechnic Institute and State University. The article was unique for its time in that there was very little literature available on families in the later years and even less on families who had been married for over 50 years.

Presently, Sporakowski is head of the Department of Child and Family at Virginia Polytechnic Institute and State University. A licensed professional counselor, he has edited books and published articles in numerous journals. He has been active in several professional organizations throughout his career, including the National Council of Family Relations and the American Association of Marriage and Family Therapy.

Hughston, who is recently deceased, was an associate professor in the Department of Family Resources and Human Development at Arizona State University. Among his publications on the family in later life are *Counseling the Elderly: A Systems Approach,* coauthored with James F. Keller (Harper &

Row, 1981), and *Independent Aging: Family and Social Systems,* coedited with William H. Quinn (Aspen Systems, 1984).

**Key Concept:** later-life family

*Couples who were married 50 or more years were interviewed about what they felt were the most important factors in happy marriage. Their marital satisfactions were assessed over the stages of the family life cycle. Indices of their marital adjustment and personality were examined using a self, perceived-other comparison technique. Positive marital adjustment was found to be related to congruence of self-other perceptions.*

The literature on marriage and marriage adjustment is abundant as one covers the courtship and early marriage years, but decreases as length of marriage increases. There has been relatively little written about the post-parental years and even less about marriages that have been in existence 40, 50 or more years. Stinnett, Collins and Montgomery (1972, p. 665) stated: "Unfortunately, research concerned with the perceptions of older husbands and wives towards their marriage relationships and their present period of life is very limited." A review of the literature over the subsequent five years offers little evidence to cause any questioning of their conclusion at the current time.

The project reported in this paper was based on the above observations and became a reality when an opportunity presented itself to combine community awareness in a classroom setting with data gathering for a research study. The authors were teaching a course entitled "Community Programs in Family Life" and one entitled "The Second Half of Life" for which they felt a "hands on" interviewing experience would have value in terms of both student experience with the community and in obtaining insights on marriage from people who had experienced it for at least half a century.

# OBJECTIVES

In addition to the objectives related to student involvement—obtaining experience in interviewing, developing greater awareness of marriage adjustments and satisfactions over the life cycle, and becoming aware of community involvement as experienced by the elderly—the following research objectives were delineated:

1. gathering data about current satisfactions and adjustments experienced by persons who were married for 50 or more years,
2. gathering data related to past satisfactions and adjustments of this marital group over the family life cycle—retrospectively,
3. gathering of recommendations (prescriptions) of persons married 50 or more years regarding happy marriage, and
4. examining sex differences as they related to satisfactions, adjustments and prescriptions.

## DATA COLLECTION

A structured interview format was developed which included: background information; questions related to the definition of marriage and prescriptions for happy marriage; a semantic differential scale on which the respondent rated how he/she viewed marriage and then how he/she thought his/her spouse did; the Locke-Wallace Short Form Marital-Adjustment instrument (1959); the Interpersonal Checklist (LaForge & Suczek, 1955); and a chart which asked the respondents to indicate, over the family life cycle, which periods were most and least satisfying, and to what they attributed the satisfactions or lack of them at each stage.

The interviewees were couples whose names appeared in the "Family" section of the Roanoke (Virginia) Times between October 1975 and January 1976 as having celebrated their "Golden Wedding Anniversary" and couples in the Reston, Virginia area whose names were provided by students in the class there. All couples interviewed had been married for a minimum of 50 years to their current spouse. Approximately 35% (N = 40) of the initial list of names cooperated and provided interviews that were usable. The initial contact was by telephone, which was then followed by an interview, if cooperation was forthcoming. A variety of reasons for noncooperation were given: spouse or spouses were in ill health; recent death of spouse; travel; respondent "didn't want to talk about marriage to someone he/she didn't know"; and fears that the interviewers would be "selling something." Thus, the initial as well as final sampling was not random, but simply a result of who was available and willing to be interviewed. No generalizations beyond this group are intended.

After an initial contact by telephone, an appointment was kept by two interviewers (usually a male and female pair) during which the structured interview proceeded and instruments were administered. Interviews typically lasted between one and three hours, variation in time being influenced by health and educational level of the interviewees, as well as the sociability of the interviewers and subjects. In many instances the interview was a social occasion during which coffee and dessert, or a meal was provided. Following an initial introduction of the interviewers and project, the interviewees were seen separately. In several instances interviewers assisted in the filling out of forms. This was necessitated due to the physical condition of the respondents or deficits in reading and/or writing. In a number of instances, short "rest breaks" were required by the respondents before continuance of the process.

## DESCRIPTION OF THE COUPLES

The average length of marriage for the couples studied was 52.7 years, with a range from 50–68 years. The ages of the males ranged from 66–93 with a mean of 77.5 years; the females, 66–86; $\bar{x} = 75.3$. In 30 of the couples the husband was older than the wife by one or more years. Four couples had both members the same age, while in six couples the wife was older by one or more years.

The couples had known each other an average of 39.3 months before they were married. They typically met through friends or church. Other sources of contact were: country club, work, school, blind date, and a matchmaker. They had been engaged an average of 11.2 months, with a range from 1 to 72 months. Only two of the 66 interviewees who responded to the question on previous engagements indicated multiple experiences.

Educationally, the males had completed an average of 10.56 years (range = 3–20) and the females 10.38 (range = 3–18). Occupationally, 26 of the wives stated they were or had been primarily housewives. Teacher and nurse were the other primary occupations. Additional occupations which were listed included: missionary, bookkeeper, storekeeper, silk worker, dental assistant, secretary, and domestic. Husbands typically listed occupations as carpenter, farmer, merchant, minister, and railroad worker.

The couples had an average of 1.81 male children and 1.78 female children. Total number of children ranged from 1 to 9.

## RESPONSES TO OPEN-ENDED ITEMS

The first task which the couple members were asked to complete after filling out the background information section was to define marriage. Instructions were as follows:

> *The word* marriage *can have a variety of meanings or definitions. Let's suppose that you were the Webster of dictionary fame, and that you had defined all the words A through L, and were now into the M's. The next word you have to define is marriage. What would your definition(s) be?*

As the reader might guess, responses were varied. For purposes of analysis, elements most frequently found in the descriptions were isolated and tallied. For wives the most frequently mentioned elements in the definition of marriage were (in order of decreasing frequency): love; "give and take" (the idea of *quid pro quo*); having children, a family, a home; the joining of two people; God and The Bible; "forever"; and being happy. For husbands the list was as follows: "forever"; companionship; and, working together to make a marriage grow. Although there are similarities in the lists, it would appear that the wives had more ideas about what marriage is (or should be?). Commitment (i.e., "forever") obviously played a major role in both listings.

The second task which the couple members were asked to perform went as follows:

> *What we would like you to do for this part of our research is to give us the benefit [of] your many years of experience. If you can, imagine that a couple has come to you as their doctor (physician). They are considering getting married and are looking for some advice. Imagine that you are sitting there in your office, garbed in white coat and stethoscope. We would like you to tell us what would go into your prescription for a happy marriage for the couple.*

Responses to this task again produced some variation between husbands and wives. Factors in the prescriptions ranked in order of frequency of mention follow:

**Wives**

1. Importance of religion
2. Love
3. Give and take/talking things through
4. Home/family/children
5. "It takes two to make a marriage work"
6. Understanding and patience

**Husbands**

1. "It takes two to make a marriage work"
2. Honesty and trust
3. Give and take
4. "Marriage is for life"
5. Religion
6. Home/family/children
7. Love

Once again there were similarities, yet order of importance, as determined by frequency of mention, varied according to sex of the respondent.

## RESPONSES TO STRUCTURED INSTRUMENTS

One of the unique aspects of this segment of the data gathering process was that we asked each respondent to comment and rate from his/her perspective and then to do the same task as though he/she was answering for his/her spouse. For example, on the Locke-Wallace Marital Adjustment Test, Short Form (1959) the interviewee was asked to respond for himself and, after that was completed, to go back and respond as he felt his spouse would.

Scores on the Locke-Wallace have a possible range from 2–158. The average scores for the couples studied were: females, 113.795; males, 123.892. In the Locke and Wallace study (1959), their "well adjusted group" had a mean score of 135.9, while their "maladjusteds" had a score of 71.7.

When the mean of the males' scores for their spouses was calculated, the result was $\bar{x} = 116.649$. This might indicate that they felt their wives saw the marriage as somewhat less positive than they did. Females' perceived Locke-Wallace score for their spouses was $\bar{x} = 114.462$; higher than scores for self, but almost ten points fewer than males self-rated scores. Overall, males rated their marriages higher on the Locke-Wallace than the females, and were rated higher by the females than the females rated themselves. The magnitude of the differences (male-self by male-of-spouse versus female-self by female-of-spouse) was considerably larger when the males were doing the rating than the females.

Further analysis of the Locke-Wallace items showed some interesting results. On the happiness rating scale (very unhappy to perfectly happy, a seven point scale), males rated themselves higher than females rated themselves, and females rated their spouses higher than males did. On specific problems some differences occurred. One indication of adjustment difficulties can be seen in a comparison of ratings for self and as perceived for spouse. For males, the largest differences between self and perceived spouse occurred on in-laws, philosophy of life and sex. The males saw the first two as more problematic than they thought their spouses did, whereas they indicated their wives were more likely to see sex as a problem than they.

For females, the largest discrepancies between self and perceived spouse were on conventionality, philosophy of life and affection. In all three cases, they saw these adjustments as more of a problem than they felt their spouses would.

It is worthy of note that when scores for males-rating-self were compared to females-rating-spouse a varied pattern of who had a higher score on the various adjustments occurred. When females-rating-self scores were compared to males-rating-spouse the direction indicated in all cases was that females'-self-ratings were higher (they saw the adjustments producing less agreement than the males did). Comparisons of males-rating-spouse versus females-rating-spouse produced greater pattern variation. The reader should also keep in mind that in no instance was the average score on these ratings more than 2.000, when the scale in reality had limits from one to six. This indicates that the average ratings on these items tended to be somewhere between "always agree" and "almost always agree," and thus a minimum of adjustment difficulty.

The subjects were also asked to rate their marriage on a semantic differential series of items. The ratings were on a seven point scale and included items like: important-unimportant; good-bad; wise-foolish; fragile-tough; deep-shallow; etc. There were 14 items and total scores could range from 14–98. The females' rating of self was $\bar{x} = 87.48$ and the males' was $\bar{x} = 83.28$. These scores correlated positively with the Locke-Wallace results from $r = 0.74$ to $0.90$. Of note is the result that although males rated their marriage on the semantic differential more positively than they felt their spouses would,... females' ratings of self were lower than of spouse—results very similar to the Locke-Wallace outcomes. Females rated their marriages slightly higher than males on the semantic differential task. The largest discrepancy, self versus spouse, was again for the males.

Satisfactions over the life cycle were assessed using Duvall's (1957) eight stage model as a base. Interviewees were asked to indicate what were the most satisfying aspects of marriage at each stage for them, and then for their spouse. Similarly, they were asked to indicate the least satisfying aspects of their marriage at each stage for both self and spouse. Overall there tended to be a great deal of agreement between spouses for each stage.

The stages seen as most satisfying were the childbearing, preschool and aging stages. Satisfactions in the first two related to children and how they added meaning to the marriage. The aging stage meant more time together, travel and activities which they did not previously have sufficient time for.

With regard to least satisfactions, the childbearing, launching and middle years stages were most often indicated. The childbearing stage was significant for both most and least satisfactions. Although childbearing brought joy to a couple, it also was disruptive to the marriage. Least satisfactions in the launching stage seemed to be related to change in roles, especially for the wives, and the impact of such changes on the marriage. This seemed to be carried on into the middle years stage, where greater reliance on spouse for support and encouragement was needed.

The total number of most satisfying aspects exceeded the total number of least satisfying aspects for both males and females. Interestingly, both males and females saw themselves as experiencing more satisfying and unsatisfying aspects as compared to their perceptions of their spouses. This appears to confirm the couples' overall positive experience with marriage. It may also indicate that when one deals with retrospective data, that which is more positive is more likely to have been reinforced and/or idealized and is thus more likely to be recalled.

Finally, when the highest scoring quartile couples (on the Locke-Wallace) were compared to the lowest quartile couples, an interesting result was evidenced in relation to Interpersonal Checklist scores. The best adjusted group ($\bar{x} = 146.41$) was much more likely to rate self and spouse similarly in terms of personality attributes than was the least well adjusted group ($\bar{x} = 95.50$). Percentage agreement across the eight scales was 86% for those well adjusted versus 52% for those reflecting a poorer adjustment. Greater congruence associated with more positive marital adjustment seems to be in agreement with results obtained in earlier studies by Luckey (1960a, 1960b). No individual scales were more likely than others to show discongruity when such existed. Males rating self and spouse had correlations which varied more than those for females rating self and spouse. This would seem to add further verification to the Locke-Wallace and semantic differential results showing females rating self and spouse more nearly alike than males. Further investigation showed that females' ratings of self and their ratings by their spouse were in much greater agreement than males' rating of self as correlated with spouses' ratings of them.

# DISCUSSION

The most significant outcomes of this research were the findings that the persons interviewed said marriage was a very positive experience and that their experiences agreed, in many ways, with findings of previous investigators about marriages at much earlier stages of the life cycle. It is obvious that the persons interviewed were a select group because of their age as well as in terms of their willingness to participate. Although there was variability in "marital adjustment scores" of the group studied, we were not able to follow up with 65% of our initial list who refused to cooperate. Perhaps they were idyllic in their happiness and just wanted privacy; perhaps they were married for 50 + years "and hated every minute of it"; or perhaps some elements of each existed.

The idea of congruence of perception of spouses appears to continue to be of major significance in relation to marital satisfaction of couples who have surpassed their golden wedding anniversaries. Not only does this apply to personality perceptions but also to ratings of marital happiness and the various aspects of marital adjustment.

Our Interpersonal Checklist data are congruent with earlier results: Luckey found that "husbands and wives who indicated that they were satisfied with their marriage were those whose perceptions were in greater agreement with each other than were the perceptions of couples who were unsatisfied" (Luckey, 1964, p. 137).

The higher scores of males, and of males as rated by spouse on the semantic differential task and the Locke-Wallace seem to be consistent with earlier findings by Stinnett, Collins and Montgomery (1970) and appear to corroborate Bernard's (1972) view of marriage as being a better deal for men. Also of significance is the "gap" between males rating self and spouse and females rating self and spouse. The women studied seem to more congruently assess what is for them in light of what their spouse perceives.

In describing prescriptions for a happy marriage our couples basically agreed with persons studied by Stinnett *et al.* (1972) even though the way of assessing "prescriptions" versus "needs" varied. Similarly, items related to values, philosophy of life and mutual interests were likely to be at the root of difficulties when they did arise for both groups.

One area of interest which could be viewed only indirectly through the satisfactions/dissatisfactions over the life cycle approach related to Ballweg's (1967) data on conjugal role adjustment after requirement. As our couples rated satisfactions, the aging stage was one of the most frequently mentioned. Comments by the couples related to this stage emphasized more sharing and time together. This seems to substantiate Ballweg's findings which indicated there was little marital disharmony when roles were shared and there was minimal threat to the wife's self-concept.

Medley (1977) has pointed out that marital adjustment needs to be viewed as a process. Our data add some insight to the latter stages of the continuum of that process, and seem to indicate, vis-à-vis life cycle ratings of satisfaction, that marriages perceived as satisfactory usually have been so from the beginning, as did Fried and Stern in 1948.

The significance of this research was found not only in the outcomes of the data collection, but also in the process which provided the information. We found that couples in the latter stages of the family life cycle could be identified, and, when cooperative, often provided many insights into their marriages as well as marriage as experienced by their cohort. As part of the process, students learned that the popular media could open doors to finding subjects to be studied. Newspapers often provide not only information about 50-year marriages, but also current engagements, weddings, divorces and births. A somewhat unique method for identifying subjects was therefore encouraged.

Another learning experience for the students involved related to the setting up and conducting of interviews. Although we had conducted brief training sessions in the classroom setting, and had developed several pages of "contacting and interviewing instructions," the actual experience of setting up and conducting sessions was most meaningful. Role-play exercises can be useful in training interviewers, but none of our role-players were 70 + years of age or had been married 50 or more years.

Initial phone contacts frequently gave an insight into later cooperation. Some couples that were contacted refused to participate because they thought that the project really was a means of "getting in the door for some kind of sales pitch." In a few instances the spouse had died, or was in very poor health. Other couples said they were in-between trips, and would find cooperation difficult, time-wise, as they were so busy. Many couples expressed interest in the project, and also volunteered names and addresses of others who might be willing to participate. Our students gained insight and sensitivity into overcoming the problems that arose and through sharing these difficulties with other students and faculty became more skilled at initiating the contacts.

Bridging "the generation gap" was another outcome/learning experience that resulted from our efforts in this research. Although the materials used in the interviews could typically be completed in about one hour of time, the sessions often ran two to three hours in length. Interviews frequently became social occasions for both the students and their subjects. Coffee, tea, dessert, and in several instances meals became an unanticipated part of a number of the sessions. We would guess that such occurrences were, in part, the result of interest shown in the couples, general sociability, and enhanced feelings of self-worth brought on by placing the couples in an "expert" role. Too, the social aspects of the interviews allowed time for breaks in the sessions which could have been viewed as tedious by the subjects, especially considering factors such as subjects' attention span, ability to read as affected by diminishing eyesight, hearing problems and fatigue. Patience was needed in assisting the couples in filling out some aspects of the printed materials or in reading through items they did not understand. On the other hand, many of the interviewers were asked their opinions about a variety of topics, and responded, within reason, sharing commonalities as well as differences with the subjects. Quite often the student interviewers came back reporting "really neat," "fantastic," or "just great" experiences with persons who were two or three generations their senior. The students also indicated a greater appreciation of the lifestyles and experiences of their subjects which had previously been, for many of them, only a textbook/lecture kind of acquaintance.

Overall, the research project provided some data on a group which has received limited study. In so doing it facilitated the development of skills in interviewing and interacting that fostered growth and understanding across generations. As a method of learning, it brought the best of the classroom and research together in a meaningful interface.

*Chapter 14
Postparental
Families*

# REFERENCES

Ballweg, J. A. Resolution of conjugal role adjustment after retirement. *Journal of Marriage and the Family,* 1967, **29,** 277–281.

Bernard, J. *The future of marriage.* New York: World, 1972.

Duvall, E. M. *Family development.* Philadelphia: Lippincott, 1957.

Fried, E. G., & Stern, K. The situation of the aged within the family. *American Journal of Orthopsychiatry,* 1948, **18,** 31–54.

LaForge, R., & Suczek, R. An interpersonal checklist. *Journal of Personality,* 1955, **24,** 94–112.

Locke, H. J., & Wallace, K. M. Short marital-adjustment and prediction tests: Their reliability and validity. *Marriage and Family Living,* 1959, **21,** 251–255.

Luckey, E. B. Marital satisfaction and its association with congruence of perception. *Marriage and Family Living,* 1960, **22,** 49–54.

Luckey, E. B. Marital satisfaction and congruent self-spouse concepts. *Social Forces,* 1960, **39,** 153–157.

Luckey, E. B. Marital satisfaction and its concomitant perceptions of spouse and self. *Journal of Counseling Psychology,* 1964, **11,** 136–145.

Medley, M. L. Marital adjustment in the post-retirement years. *The Family Coordinator,* 1977, **26,** 5–11.

Stinnett, N., Collins, J., & Montgomery, J. E. Martial need satisfaction of older husbands and wives. *Journal of Marriage and the Family,* 1970, **32,** 428–434.

Stinnett, N., Carter, L. M., & Montgomery, J. E. Older persons' perceptions of their marriages. *Journal of Marriage and the Family,* 1972, **34,** 665–670.

## 14.2 LILLIAN E. TROLL

# *Grandparents: The Family Watchdogs*

Lillian E. Troll is an adjunct professor in the Department of Epidemiology and Biostatistics at the University of California, San Francisco. Having studied the family in later life extensively, the subject of grandparenting is of interest to her. In 1979 she published the book *Families in Later Life* (Wadsworth). This selection is from Troll's article "Grandparents: The Family Watchdogs," which was published in Timothy H. Brubaker, ed., *Family Relationships in Later Life* (Sage Publications, 1983).

The grandparent role of watchdog may be seen in grandparents' trying to keep existing families together as well as in their raising the children of their own children's failed marriages. Grandparents have always maintained a mentor role in the family, but as a group, they began to demand their rights in the 1990s. Grandparents develop a relationship with their grandchildren, but when their children get divorced, they lose contact with those grandchildren and either their relationship ends or their contact with the child is severely diminished. Thus, grandparents are asking for visitation rights and, in some cases, are asking to raise their own grandchildren.

**Key Concept:** grandparenting

*F*our general conclusions can be drawn from recent reviews of the literature on grandparenting—as distinct from that on aged family members. These are:

1. Grandparents are not absent from central family dynamics, but often play an important part in them, even though they usually play a secondary role to parents.
2. Grandparental interactions and roles are diverse—much more diverse than parental ones, varying in part with social class, ethnicity, and sex, but largely, it seems, with individual feelings and preferences and life circumstances.
3. Developmental status of both grandchild and grandparent influence their interactions and their reciprocal feelings.

4. The most important role of the grandparents may be that of maintaining the family system as a whole.

This [selection] contains a review of the research literature relevant to these four points. I will then speculate a bit beyond the data about the systemic role hinted at in the title: "family watchdogs."

## GRANDPARENTING VERSUS PARENTING

From deeply and heavily involved grandparents at one extreme to apparently uninvolved ones at the other (Kornhaber & Woodward, 1981), the importance of grandparents in family functioning is beginning to be recognized. Their influence is not always seen as beneficial, however. Twenty years ago, psychoanalytically inspired thinking about family functioning included a premise that if young couples, upon their marriage, did not separate themselves effectively from their parents, they would experience disturbed relationships between themselves and also have trouble bringing up healthy children (see Bell & Vogel, 1960). This belief is still held by many of us today. Different conclusions are being drawn by recent reviews of the empirical literature (Tinsley & Parke, 1983; Troll, 1980a; Wood, 1982). This literature includes evidence that grandparents play an important role in promoting well-being of one-parent childrearing units, particularly those of teenage mothers (see review by Tinsley & Parke, 1983).

Are surrogate parenting and supportive parenting by grandparents to be found only in distressed or deviant families, though? Three years ago, when I reviewed the then even more meager literature on grandparenting than now exists, I concluded that the significance of grandparenting may lie more in the clues it provides to the strength of general family functioning than in the actual interactions with children and grandchildren (Troll, 1980a). If grandparents, as "family watchdogs," monitor the state of family functioning and step in only when they are needed, they can often appear uninvolved.

## PERSPECTIVES ON GRANDPARENTING STUDIES

Both research and theorizing about grandparents fall into several discrete categories. These include:

1. the benefits or lack of benefits grandparents themselves derive (see Neugarten & Weinstein, 1964; Robertson, 1977; Kivnick, 1981; Hill, Foote, Aldous, Carlson, & Macdonald, 1970);
2. the effect of having grandparents upon the well-being and attitudes of young children (see Tinsley & Parke, 1983; Baranowski, 1982a, 1982b; Hartshorne & Manaster, 1982; Kornhaber & Kornhaber, 1982; Kahana & Kahana, 1970; Wood & Robertson, 1976; Gilford & Black, 1972);

3. the qualities of grandparents that children of different ages like (see Kahana & Kahana, 1970);
4. the connecting linkages between grandparents and grandchildren through the middle generation (see Hill et al., 1970: "lineage bridges"; Gilford & Black, 1972);
5. the styles and meanings of grandparenting in the eyes of the grandparents (see Neugarten & Weinstein, 1964; Wood & Robertson, 1976; Kivnick, 1981); and
6. the role of grandparents in family systems (Hader, 1965; Troll, 1980a, 1980b; Wood, 1982).

Because a large part of the research from all these perspectives derives from assumptions of grandparents as aged, essentially infirm, and otherwise unoccupied individuals, whose grandchildren and other family members fill a vacuum, we can only conjecture about the full range of grandparental interactions.

[Here], little attention will be given to the literature on what grandparents do for grandchildren per se, unless this falls within the domain of larger family support. Nor are we interested in the views grandchildren—as young children or adolescents—have of their grandparents as "old" people.

Hagestad (1982) calls our attention to the increased probability of grandparental influence upon other family members because the increases in life expectancy produce greater "life overlaps" between younger and older generations in the family. In our culture, the modal age of becoming a grandparent is around 49–51 years for women and 51–53 years for men. Teenage pregnancies, furthermore, produce many grandparents in their thirties. With life expectancy now around the age of 76 years for women and 68 years for men, most Americans can get to know their grandchildren and even their great-grandchildren. Grandmothers, in particular, can see their grandchildren develop well into their adult years. Reciprocally, most young children can get to know their grandparents and even great-grandparents. The complexities of family life have shifted from the horizontal dimension: sibling constellations to the vertical dimension. Horizontal interactions are replaced by a potentially confusing array of parent-child units that Hagestad has labeled graphically the "alpha-omega chain."

When Harris and his associates (1975) surveyed Americans over the age of 65, he found that three-fourths of them had living grandchildren and three-fourths of those saw them at least once every week. Since only about 5 percent of American households include both grandparents and grandchildren, not only must this contact be voluntary but the motivation for it has to be strong enough to induce members of one generation to go out of the home to visit members of the other generation.

Not only is contact constant in most families, but reciprocity of help and services is too, as attested by Hill and his colleagues (1970) for three generations of adult couples and by Kornhaber and Woodward (1981) for a somewhat wider age range of grandchildren. The spate of recent studies on the family situations of teenage mothers (for example, Mogey, 1976–1977; Tinsley & Parke, 1983; Smith, 1975; Badger, Burns, & Vietze, 1981; Field, Widmayer, Stringer, & Ignatoff, 1980; Hardy, King, Shipp, & Welcher, 1981; Mills & Cairns,

1981; Kellam, Adams, Brown, & Ensminger, 1982) consistently report the presence of the maternal grandmother as critical to the successful functioning of the mother-child unit and to the positive development of the infant. Similarly, Hetherington's important study of divorce (Hetherington, Cox, & Cox, 1982) found that the contributions of grandparents were highly related to the quality of the mother-child relationship in that majority of cases in which mothers were the primary child rearers.

While statistics of visiting and helping suggest that grandparents are important persons in family systems, one common finding is paradoxical. There seems to be no relationship between amount of contact with children and grandchildren and older people's morale or life satisfaction (see Wood & Robertson, 1976; Troll, Miller & Atchley, 1979). In fact, some research suggests an inverse relationship: The more older people's social life is exclusively with their children, the lower their morale. Socializing with friends is much better for them (see discussion in Troll, et al., 1979).

How can we reconcile these discrepancies? Bengtson and Kuypers (1971) provide us with the heuristic concept of "generational stake." They describe the different emphasis placed by middle-aged parents and their young-adult children upon the amount of similarity in their outlook on life, or values. Youth in their late teens or early twenties tend to exaggerate the "generation gap," disclaiming similarity of values between themselves and their parents. Their parents, on the other hand, tend to exaggerate the similarities. A parallel phenomenon has been suggested by both Bengtson and Troll for the "gap" between middle-aged children and *their* parents (see Troll & Bengtson, 1979).

The intent of this differential emphasis on separation of attitudes is to stress the uniqueness and independence of the younger generation vis-à-vis its parents. This process could be present at any time of life. At the same time, the parents want to believe in the continuity of the effects of their efforts to instill their values in their children. Again, this could hold at all ages. This may not stop with one generation of offspring, furthermore. Grandparents can be as concerned that their children continue to transmit essential values to *their* children as that their children themselves hold them.

Probably few grandparents wish to return to parenting with their grandchildren (see Lopata, 1973; Cohler & Grunebaum, 1981), but they do remain alert to what goes on. If they think all is well, they prefer to remain formal and distant or indulgent grandparents, visiting their children and grandchildren as one part of their regular life activities but otherwise enjoying their own life. It is more interesting to be with their peers, who are likely to share more recreational interests, than helping out with needy children who remind them of their lack of success in parenting. It is nice to be free of worry about the adequacy of the socialization of their descendants and the "carrying on of the torch." If there is trouble, however, they have to give up much of their personal, nonfamily life to meet the needs of the family. This means double suffering for them: deprivation as well as concern (see Mogey, 1976–1977; Tinsley & Parke, 1983).

In my ongoing three-generational research, I have found that grandparents refer spontaneously to their grandchildren 27 percent of the time, but grandchildren refer to their grandparents only 10 percent of the time. One interpretation of this difference may be that grandparents monitor the status of their grandchildren more than grandchildren monitor their grandparents.

That grandparenting is not a renewal of parenting undertaken by empty and possessive elders is seen in the contingent nature of the relationship. Both Cumming and Henry (1961) and Lopata (1973) have stressed this point: Grandparents do not want to start over as parents of young children. Gilford and Black (1972), analyzing the University of Southern California's three-generation sample, found that the grandparent-grandchild interactions and feelings depended upon the attitudes of the parents toward their own parents. Hagestad and Speicher (1981) found that the middle generation of parents remain as mediators of the older and younger generations' interactions even when the grandchildren are adults. In other words, there is replication of the "lineage bridge" phenomenon seen by Hill and his colleagues in their Minneapolis study (Hill et al., 1970). This is interesting because the youngest generation in the Los Angeles study were younger than those in the Minneapolis study. Services by grandparents are rendered when, and usually only when, their children indicate that they are needed.

French, Rogers, and Cobb (1974) see a curvilinear relationship between grandparent contact and general satisfaction of the grandparents. Hess and Waring (1978) use the apt metaphor of the "Goldilocks effect"; too much grandparenting is as bad as too little. In one respect, too much may indicate lots of family trouble and thus be even worse.

# DIVERSITY

It is often assumed that grandparenting is a roleless role because there are no overtly prescribed functions. Parents of young children generally know what is expected of them in raising the children. Grandparents do not, at least not in the same way. The diffuseness of their script can be seen in the wide diversity of grandparenting styles reported by most observers since the now classic study of Neugarten and Weinstein (1964). Efforts to categorize this wide array of styles and behaviors are reflected in the five styles noted by Neugarten and Weinstein; formal, fun-seekers, surrogate parents, reservoirs of family wisdom, and distant figures. A four-part typology is used by Wood and Robertson (1976), based on the two dimensions of personal orientation toward grandparenting and conception of the social or normative meanings attached to grandparenthood. Their four resultant types are: remote, symbolic, individualized, and apportioned. More recently, Kivnick (1981) developed a third typology, using five categories: centrality, valued elder, immortality through clan, reinvolvement with personal past, and indulgence. Rather than assume that different people fall into different categories, Kivnick found it useful to rate everybody on all five dimensions; most of the grandparents she studied fit into all five to some extent. Like other researchers before her, Kivnick found no direct relationship between grandparenthood behavior or meaning and the mental health of the grandparents.

The similarity among the three typologies is noticeable. Each ranges from heavy involvement at one extreme to remoteness at the other. So far, no systematic study has been made of the relationship between amount of involvement and such external variables as social class or ethnicity. In general, of course, family studies have found that poverty or cultural deviance are associated with clumping of relatives, either under one roof or in close geographic proximity. The increase in number of independent households over the past couple of decades, which has so frequently been interpreted as evidence for the breakdown and decline of the family, is probably more a sign of economic affluence. When money is available for multiple rents or buying of houses, not to mention quick and easy transportation among these separate dwellings, family units can spread out.

Multigenerational residences may thus be considered a sign of hard times and trouble. They may also be effective solutions to many social ills. Teenage mothers are best off living in the maternal grandmother's household (Tinsley & Parke, 1983), for example. Aged parents move in with their children (usually a daughter) when they are too poor or too frail to live alone. Grandparents are not the only relatives who jump in when the skies get stormy. Capable grandparents may be the first and foremost to do so, though. The influence of the extended family was easier to overlook when our focus was on the needs of the frail aged, who today are more likely to be great-grandparents than grandparents of young children.

Recent research on working mothers of young children shows the often overwhelming burdens of these women, particularly if they are single parents. So far, there is little study of employed grandmothers and their added household and family responsibilities and burdens.

## DEVELOPMENTAL ISSUES

When we consider that the ages of grandparents may be anywhere between 30 and 120 years and of grandchildren anywhere from birth to 80 years, we realize that the respective ages of members of the two generations must be significant in their relationship. Although chronological age per se is a treacherous and inadequate index of developmental status, there can be no question but that there are wide variations in development in both generations. Some grandparents are vigorous, youthful adults, but some are feeble and badly in need of help themselves. Some seek lots of excitement and stimulation in their lives; others want a quiet, predictable routine. Conversely, some grandchildren need infinite nurturance and protection, while others are ready to move out into heady encounters with the world outside the family. Still others may be settled into the responsibilities and restrictions of raising their own young.

These gross developmental differences are reflected in wide differences in styles of grandparenting as well as the kind of grandparents grandchildren want. Neugarten and Weinstein (1964), for example, found that younger grandparents had more diverse styles than older. Some young grandparents were fun-seekers and some were distant figures. That is, some enjoyed playing with their grandchildren and some sought enjoyment in other spheres. Older grandparents, though, were almost always formal and distant, perhaps absorbed in their own failing health.

In the ongoing three-generational study I mentioned earlier, grandparents in their fifties, sixties, and seventies were more likely to say good things about their grandchildren, whereas those in their forties and eighties were more likely to be critical. It could be the 50-, 60-, and 70-year-olds were much more comfortable about being grandparents than those who felt they were too young or too old (see Neugarten, Moore, & Lowe, 1965, who found clear age designations for when it was appropriate for different life events to occur). At the other end, both Kahana and Kahana (1970) and Clark (1969) report that younger grandchildren are more appealing to older grandparents. There may be an upper limit to this effect, however, with very old grandparents finding highly active preschoolers a trial. Cumming and Henry's (1961) respondents said that they were glad to see their grandchildren come and glad to see them go.

Children change rapidly and dramatically throughout the first two decades of life. According to Kahana and Kahana (1970), in the only systematic study so far on age differences of grandchildren and their attitudes toward grandparents, children under 10 feel closer to their grandparents than do older children, their 4- and 5-year-old respondents said they liked their grandparents to be indulgent, the 8- and 9-year-olds liked them to be fun, and children older than that preferred that they keep their distance. The wish for distancing, if true, may be temporary, because several studies of young adult grandchildren (see Hagestad, 1978; Gilford & Black, 1972; Robertson, 1977) found that all these grandchildren said their grandparents were important to them.

A poignant and, I think, relevant anecdote comes to us from the cross-species research of the anthropologist Hrdy (1981). In a troop of langurs she was observing in India, the coming to power of a new dominant male was often accompanied by his killing all the infants born to his predecessor. No animal in the troop was seen to oppose him in this infanticidal action, with one exception: an old female dubbed Sol. While the younger females—the mothers of the infants but also the future mothers of the infants to be fathered by this new leader—remained passive, it was the no-longer-fertile female who had the nerve to rescue what infants she could. Perhaps they were her grandchildren. I leave the reader to draw a possible parallel to human grandparental involvement in family crises today. Do grandparents sometimes step in where parents fear to tread?

# SEX DIFFERENCES

Early research on grandparenting led investigators and theorists to conclude that it was primarily a nurturant, and thus a woman's, function—that grandfathers became "feminized" in their approach if they were highly involved with their grandchildren. This kind of conclusion parallels that about retirement. In the early 1970s, men were supposed to find retiring more stressful than women because it involved a move into the "woman's sphere"—the home and family—

and would thus be a sharp and abrupt transition for men as well as a demeaning one. Accompanying these beliefs was another, that grandfathers had once possessed relevant information to transmit to their grandchildren: skills and observations on life that would still be useful. Further, they were able to continue in "man's work" to the end of their lives. The accelerated social change of modern times, it was further believed, made the skills of the old irrelevant and not only drove them from the workplace but also gave them nothing to hand down to their grandsons.

More recent views about sex differences in job and family spheres see the situation quite differently. Instead of men finding retirement difficult, that is, it is women who do (Atchley & Corbett, 1977). In part, perhaps, this may be because it was a lack of fulfillment at home that led them to seek work outside. This is not to deny that most women seek employment in order to contribute to family income or because they are the sole support of themselves and their children—and even parents. What is not always remembered, furthermore, is that in the "golden age" of grandparenting, when grandparents were still relevant as teachers of the culture to their grandchildren, few grandfathers survived long enough to do so.

In spite of supposed changes in sex distribution of work, traditional differences do seem to be maintained in grandparenting, as they are in parenting. Hagestad (1978, 1982) found that grandmothers are more likely to have warm relationships with their grandchildren—and their children—than are grandfathers. Further, most of these warm relationships are down the maternal line, the mother-daughter tie being a particularly strong one. Influence of grandparents is not, however, restricted to grandmothers. Neugarten and Weinstein (1964) note that although grandmothers are more likely to be surrogate parents, grandfathers are more likely to be the reservoirs of family wisdom. Hagestad's (1978) respondents, on the other hand, indicated that both grandmothers and grandfathers are reservoirs of family wisdom, but operate differently and in different domains. The grandmothers were more generalized in their advice giving, making much less distinction than the grandfathers between whether they were influencing their granddaughters or their grandsons. The grandfathers usually confined their influencing to grandsons. The topics discussed were also differentiated according to sex. Grandmothers tended to discuss interpersonal and intrapersonal topics: how to relate to the family, dating, and the relative importance of family and friends. Grandfathers concentrated on areas outside the family/personality domain: work, education, money, the management of time, and wider social issues.

When she analyzed family themes in all-male and all-female three-generational lines, furthermore, Hagestad found, as shown in Table 1, that male lines (grandfathers, sons, and grandsons) talked to each other about work, education, and money more than half the time and about their views on social issues one-third of the time. All female lines talked about interpersonal relations more than half the time, while the rest was divided relatively equally among the other four areas.

The possibility of cohort or period changes in sex differences is suggested by the fact that the grandchildren said they did not restrict their influencing

**TABLE 1**

*Percentage Distribution of Family Themes in All-Male and All-Female Three-Generation Lineage Units*

|  | All Male Units | All Female Units |
|---|---|---|
| Views on social issues | 32 | 9 |
| Work, education, money | 59 | 9 |
| Health and appearance | 9 | 15 |
| Daily living | – | 14 |
| Interpersonal relations | – | 53 |
| Total | 100 | 100 |

Note: Percentage distribution of *themes*, not families. Most families had more than one theme.
Source: Reprinted from Hagestad, 1982.

attempts to their advice-seeking by either subject matter or sex of grandparent. Whether this less traditional sex stereotyping by the grandchildren will stay with them when they become parents and grandparents is yet to be seen.

# FAMILY SYSTEMS

Little by little, the concept of families as systems is filtering into mainline family theory and research. It is noteworthy that the impressive volume, *Contemporary Theories about the Family*, edited by Burr, Hill, Nye, and Reiss (1979), contains two chapters utilizing a systems point of view: "Communication in Couples and Families," by Raush, Greif, and Nugent, and "Family Process and Child Outcomes," by Broderick and Pulliam-Krager. Even these two excellent reviews restrict their focus largely to couples and young children. An early paper by Hader (1965), titled "The Importance of Grandparents in Family Life," is, from my rapid inspection, the only—or at least one of a few—treatments of the family-system domain that includes grandparents specifically.

Laboratory observations of family interactions that include grandparents are also scarce. Twenty years ago, Scott (1962) watched an interaction sequence between both parents, a teenager, and a grandmother. She reported that the grandmother was not an active participant in the interaction. Field and her colleagues (see Field et al., 1980) have been videotaping interaction sequences in participants' homes. Their subjects are black teenage mothers in Florida, their infants, and their mothers. Like Scott, Field found that the grandmothers mostly sat back and watched the young mother with her baby. Unger (1979) did not measure interaction in life, but did assess the amount of interaction between white low-income mothers and their infants. She was interested in the effect of friends' and relatives' contact with the mothers on the mother-infant interactions. The more supportive adult contacts the mothers had, she found, the greater the amount of interaction they had with their children. We might conclude that while the grandmothers observed by Scott and Field were not interacting directly with their grandchildren, they may have promoted greater or better parent-child interactions by indirect support.

A different kind of information about the involvement of grandparents comes from the ingenious research of Feldman and Nash and their colleagues at Stanford University (for example, Abrahams, Feldman, & Nash, 1978; Feldman & Nash, 1979; Feldman, Biringen, & Nash, 1981; Feldman, Nash, & Cutrona, 1977). By staging a scene in a waiting room that included the presence of an infant, they observed the attraction of the infant for various categories of people. Thus, mothers of infants were more responsive to this "stranger" infant than were pregnant women, cohabitating women, married childless women, mothers of adolescent children, "empty-nest" women, and grandmothers of infants. On the other hand, the grandmothers of infants were more responsive than the mothers of adolescent children or "empty-nest" mothers. Grandfathers of infants were more responsive than men in any category other than fathers of infants.

Tinsley and Parke (1983) are currently pursuing an even more systematic line of research that involves varying the amount of grandparental inclusion in family interactions that take place in otherwise naturally occurring settings. As they point out, it is now time to look at more specific kinds of questions and to use more controlled or at least varied situations.

## CONCLUSION

What is the present state of the art? First, I think we can conclude that grandmothers and grandfathers are definitely not removed from the family picture. On the other hand, we must also conclude that they take a back seat to parents. Unfortunately, this kind of statement is of a low order of scientific specificity. It describes average situations. We need to know a lot more about the effect of demographic factors, about developmental factors, or of family system factors on the incidence and significance of grandparental interactions. What characteristics of the grandparents, of their children, of their grandchildren, or of the family system are associated with greater contact and significance of that contact, and what characteristics are associated with less contact and significance?

Families probably vary widely in their integration: in the strength of their boundaries (see Handel, 1968; Troll, 1980b) and in the sharing of family themes or value systems. If grandparents are really family watchdogs, they would not have to work hard at their mission in highly integrated families, even though they might or might not partake of social interactions. Where family boundaries are permeable and there is little distinction between kin and nonkin, grandparents could share the task of watching that all goes well. We could predict from this premise that only when boundaries are weakening would the grandparents' task be strenuous and active, not only as watchdogs but in filling the holes in the dyke. Divorce is a case in point. Hagestad, Smyer, and Stierman (1982) and the ongoing work of Colleen Johnson (personal communication, 1982) in San Francisco find that grandparents often have greater involvement in the lives of their grandchildren after the parents divorce. Hagestad (1982) uses the term, the "family ripple effect" of divorce. While the number of grandparents who themselves divorce in later life is low, they are very much involved in the divorces of their children.

# CHAPTER 15 Older Families and Death

### 15.1 TIMOTHY H. BRUBAKER

## *Later Life Families*

Timothy H. Brubaker is a professor and Scripps Fellow in the Department of Family Studies and Social Work at Miami University in Ohio. He has served as editor for the *Family Relations* journal, and he is the editor or author of several books, including *Family Relationships in Later Life,* 2d ed. (Sage Publications, 1990). This selection is taken from his book *Later Life Families* (Sage Publications, 1985).

*Later Life Families* is one of several volumes in the Family Studies Text Series, a series of publications on the family published in the 1980s. Other topics that were of interest in this time period include work and family life, family stress, divorce, and family power.

**Key Concept:** later life families

*Family 1:* Irene and Matt are both 75 years old and have been married for 52 years. Matt retired from teaching high school ten years ago and was very active until last year, when he became ill and was hospitalized twice. Following his return home from the hospital, Irene cared for him. Irene has been a housewife throughout their marriage. Both are satisfied with their marriage and claim that it has gotten better since the children left home and Matt retired. They now have more time to focus on each other. Their two children are married and their daughter lives about ten minutes from their house. Their son lives in a town about thirty miles away. Irene and Matt enjoy their four grandchildren and two great-grandchildren whom they see quite often.

*Family 2:* Sam and Martha have been married two years. Sam is 68 years old and Martha is 56 years old. Both had been widowed (Sam for eleven months and Martha for two years) and had known each other for many years before either of their spouses passed away. Their marriage is satisfying. Sam has three children and seven grandchildren. One son lives close by, but his other son and daughter live three hours from him. Martha's daughter lives next door and she visits with her two grandchildren very day. Sam is retired from the telephone company, and Martha continues to work full time at the local library.

*Family 3:* Judith, 43, has been divorced for fifteen years and her daughter, 23, married last year after graduating from college. Judith's son, 25, has been married for five years and has two children. Judith visits her son two or three times a week and spends a great deal of time with her grandchildren. She works at a local hospital as a nurse's aide and is very happy with her job. She hopes to remarry sometime, but she is not seeing anyone at the present time.

*Family 4:* Josephine, 84, has been widowed for fifteen years and lives in an affluent retirement community where she has organized a sewing circle. Josephine taught high school home economics for forty-five years before she retired twenty years ago. She now uses her teaching skills to teach other people how to sew. Her son sees her twice a month, and about once a month her granddaughter brings her first great-grandson to visit. Her daughter lives 500 miles away and writes or telephones often but seldom visits. She infrequently sees her daughter's children and their families. Josephine is very fond of her former husband and has not wanted to remarry. Although she is having some problems getting around, she expects these difficulties because she is "old."

What do all these families have in common? They all include persons who have been married at some time within their lives and all have children. All have grandchildren and some have great-grandchildren. One family has been married more than fifty years, another for only two years. One family divorced many years ago, and one wife was widowed fifteen years ago. Some have retired and others are working full-time. The ages vary from 43 to 84 years. Since these families represent later life families, what is the common denominator between the families?

The definition and characteristics of later life families will be discussed [here]. It is important to remember that there are differences and similarities between them.

## DEFINITION OF LATER LIFE FAMILIES

Family scholars have directed their attention to the study of the family over the life cycle. The family life cycle refers to "a predictability about family development that helps us know what to expect of any given family at any given stage" (Duvall, 1977: 141). The family life cycle approach is "based on the recognition of successive phases and patterns as they occur within the continuity of family living over the years" (p. 141). Generally, this approach to the study of the family begins with the establishment of a couple's relationship through marriage and focuses on the addition of the couple's children. The couple progresses through the stages of the family life cycle as the children mature and eventually initiate their own marital relationships. Consequently, many family scholars have directed their research to the early stages of the family life cycle.

The primary focus of this [selection] is on families who have progressed to the later stages of the family life cycle and are dealing with the tasks associated with later life. Specifically, *"later life families" refers to families who are beyond the child-rearing years and have begun to launch their children* (Brubaker, 1983). At this time in the family life cycle, the nuclear unit is contracting rather than expanding (Duvall, 1977). The emphasis is on the *remaining members* of the family of orientation *after* the children have initiated their own families of procreation. As illustrated in the above cases the remaining members may include a husband and wife who have been married for many years. Or, one spouse may be the primary survivor in the family of orientation because he or she divorced or became widowed. The survivor may remarry, and the later life family may include persons who were previously not part of the family. The remarriage may combine two families of orientation in the later years.

The use of chronological age to distinguish later life families from young or middle life families is problematic (Troll et al., 1979). Since couples marry and have children at different ages, they launch their children at different ages. Consequently, a person may be 55 years of age and still have children living at home. Or, similar to Judith in family 3, another individual aged 45 years may have two adult children who have begun their own families of procreation. When children leave home, the remaining person(s) need(s) to address issues related to family life regardless of age. Thus, chronological age alone is not an appropriate indicator of later life families.

Since children leaving their families of orientation is used as the primary requisite for defining later life families, a problem occurs with the small number of couples who have no children. When do childless couples become later life families? The family life cycle approach to the study of the family has difficulty dealing with these couples. Generally, childless couples are considered to be in the later life stages if either of the members is aged 50 years or above. Most people follow similar life courses (Atchley, 1980; Neugarten et al., 1965); for example, there seems to be a range of years during which most individuals marry, have children, establish a career, and retire. Atchley (1976) suggested that age 50 may be a reasonable estimate of the chronological age by which most individuals experience the tasks typically associated with later life. Therefore, recognizing the problems with chronological age and not having a better indicator, the age of 50 will be used as crude indicator of later life families for the few couples who do not have offspring.

# THE LATER STAGES

Evelyn Duvall (1977) identified eight stages of the family life cycle demarcated by the maturation of offspring within the nuclear family. The stages included the *married couple, childbearing, preschool-age, school age, teenage, launching center, middle-aged parents,* and *aging family members.* The last two stages—middle-aged parent (empty nest to retirement) and the aging family (retirement to death of both spouses)—are related to later life families....

In the middle-aged stage, the tasks related to the children leaving home and the reorganization of the family around the remaining members. In this book, primary concern is with the latter activities. Many later life families enter an "empty nest" period in which they adjust their lifestyles around the husband and wife roles. Parental tasks are redefined because the children are no longer living at home and most have initiated their own families of procreation. For some couples, this is the first time in twenty to thirty years that they have been living together without children in the household. Household activities may be reallocated. Couples have more opportunity to enhance positive or exacerbate problematic aspects of their relationships. Men and women who have careers are approaching their peaks—their job-related responsibilities may be demanding and their incomes may be the highest they have ever experienced.

At the same time, many couples approach or consider retirement. With the children gone, some wives begin or reenter a career, and the couple has another new encounter to which they must adjust. Thus the empty nest period is the initial contraction phase, and later life families must deal with issues related to the movement of children out of the household. While the reduction in the size of the household is the primary focus, empty nest couples are also interested in the addition of new members to the family through marriage and birth. Dealing with in-laws and becoming grandparents are expansion issues of concern to later life couples.

The aging family further contracts in a number of ways. First, it is marked by retirement—Duvall (1977) suggested that the final stage in the family life cycle is begun with retirement. Working members of the marital unit need to develop lifestyles that are not centered on or do not include the jobs they held for many years. Some may retire from full-time employment and accept part-time work. Others may retire from one job and take another. Many retire, become involved in other activities, and are not employed at all. In any case, the family—spouse and children—responds to the retiree's new way of life. This event may create an opportunity for couples to spend more time together and further strengthen their marital relationships—or it may further illuminate the shadowy aspects of a marriage.

The aging family will also need to address the aging process and any health problems that may develop. As marital partners age and their health becomes problematic, the healthier spouse may become the caregiver for the less healthy person. Care may be provided in the home, or in an institution such as a nursing home; most of the care is within the home. Some couples may move to a retirement community in which care is provided. Eventually, the aging couple will need to deal with the death of one spouse. The survivor's tasks include adjustment to additional contraction of the family unit as well as maintenance of family relationships with children and grandchildren. If the survivor remarries, the task of continuing the family relationships may be compounded.

## CHANGING FAMILY LIFE CYCLE

In comparing the demographics of the family from early 1900 to the 1970, demographer Paul Glick of the U.S. Bureau of the Census (1977) concluded that because of the longer life span and other changes in the family and society, the empty nest period has increased from two to thirteen years. With the longer empty nest period, *many families spent four to five times more years as a couple in the later stages than in the early stages of the family life cycle.* Changes in the timing of the birth of the first child are also important to the family life cycle. Glick (1977) noted that the birth rate has decreased so that there are fewer children within a family. Today, the average family has one or two children instead of three or four as in the mid 1950s. Since the number of children is smaller and persons live longer, fewer years are devoted to childrearing. Consequently, the number of years spent in the empty nest period is increased. Although much family research has focused on the early phases of marriage, it is clear that families live many years in the later stages of the family life cycle.

The timing of marriage and the birth of the first child have interesting implications for later life families. Individuals who postpone the birth of the first child may preclude the possibility of having five- or six-generation families. For example, if a woman has a child at age 18, and each subsequent generation has its first child at 18, the family could include six generations if the first woman lived to be 74. However, if the same woman postponed the birth of her first child until age 30, and subsequent generations did likewise, the family could be no larger than three or four generations. Thus, the family network would be approximately twice as large for the woman who had her first child at a younger age.

## UNIQUE ASPECTS OF LATER LIFE FAMILIES

There are two unique aspects of later life families that are important to the study of these families. The first, as noted above, is that most later life families are multigenerational. When several generations exist within the family, the oldest persons may not be the only later life couples in the family network. In some family systems, the oldest members are providing care to less healthy, younger persons. The multigenerational aspect and potential for more than two generations are important factors to consider when examining the major life events (retirement, death of a spouse) and health status of later life couples.

Another unique aspect is the lengthy family history (Brubaker, 1983). Later life families have been interacting, coping, making decisions, and developing affection and hostilities for many years. *When a couple launches a child and addresses the tasks associated with the middle and later years, they have a family track record on which to interact.* Unlike recently married couples, older couples have experienced many events together, and they may be able to predict the other's behavior with some degree of accuracy. This history may contribute positively or negatively to the family. For example, marital satisfaction may be enhanced because a satisfied couple can spend more time together while an unsatisfied couple becomes less satisfied. A strong parent-child relationship may be strengthened while a weak one may deteriorate further. Since a later life family is either blessed or haunted by its family history, it is crucial for family researchers and practitioners to become familiar with the previous family interactions to understand fully later life family interactions. The continuity of family behavior cannot be underestimated.

Before research on later life families is reviewed, demographics for these families are presented. Since census data are categorized by age and not stage in the family life cycle, the demographics are presented for persons 45 years and above in most instances.

## MARITAL STATUS OF THE ELDERLY

Statistics on the marital status of older persons indicate that men are usually married and women are likely to [be] married [or] widowed. While the majority of older men are married, the proportion declines somewhat as men reach ages 75 years and over. Women under age 65 years, however, are most likely to be married and those 65 years and older are likely to be widowed. For example, two-thirds of the women aged 55 to 64 years are married, and slightly more than two-thirds aged 75 years and over are widowed. In the oldest age category, slightly more than one out of five women are married.

As might be expected, the portion of widowers increases with age. There are approximately four times as many widowers aged 75 years and over than widowers aged 55 to 64 years. Divorced and never-married persons account for a small proportion of the elderly. With the exception of the never-married women, the numbers and percentages of divorced and never-married women appear to increase slightly with age.

It is no surprise that most older men live with their spouses and many older women live alone or with a nonrelative (Brubaker, 1983; Brotman, 1981). Specifically, 52 percent of women 75 years and older live alone or with a nonrelative and 68 percent of men the same age live with a spouse. Less than one-quarter of the women aged 75 years and above live with a spouse. For women aged 65 to 74 years, less than one-half live with a spouse and nearly 40 percent live alone or with a nonrelative. Women, more than men, are likely to live with another relative (many times an adult child).

In summary, marriage is a lifestyle experienced by most older people. These data suggest that the elderly population is either married or has been married. Most likely, older men are married and living with their wives while older women are widowed and living alone or with a nonrelative. Compared to older men, older women more often live with another relative.

## THE NEVER MARRIEDS

The proportion of older bachelors and unmarried women has declined over the past twelve years. The Bureau of the Census (U.S. Department of Commerce, 1983) reported that 7.5 percent of men aged 65 years and above had never married in 1970, while in 1982, 4.4 percent had not married. A similar decline is evidenced for women aged 65 years and older. In fact, there was a 41 percent decline in the proportion of older, never-married men from 1970 to 1982 and a 27 percent decline for never-married women. For women aged 55 to 64 years, there was a 40 percent decline, and for men, a 41 percent decline in the proportion of never marrieds. These data suggest that never-married older persons are a small segment of the elderly population and the size of this group is decreasing. Marriage is an event experienced by an increasing portion of older men and women.

## ELDERLY DIVORCE

Similar to the number of younger persons who divorce, approximately twice as many older people are divorced in the 1980s than in the 1960s (U.S. Department of Commerce, 1983). For example, there were 53 divorced women aged 45 to 64 years for every 1000 married women in 1960. In 1982, there were 129 divorcees for every 1000 married women in the same age group. For women aged 65 years and above, there were 44 per 1000 in 1960 and 99 per 1000 in 1982. Divorces for older men also increased. In 1960, there were 39 divorced men aged 45 to 64 years per 1000 married men, while in 1982 there were 83. Men aged 65 years and above had 24 divorces per 1000 marriages in 1960 and 41 per 1000 marriages in 1982. The number of older persons who are divorced has increased, and in addition, there are many older men and women who have experienced divorce within their lifetimes. It should be noted that these data do not distinguish between elderly who have been divorced earlier in life and those who become divorced in the later years. There appears to be a slight decline in the percentages of older men and women who marry and later divorce.... From 1971 to 1981, the percentage of men and women aged 65 years who married and later divorced declined slightly. The older the husband and wife, the less likely they are to divorce. For instance, men and women aged 45 to 49 years are approximately six times more likely to get divorced than persons aged 65 and above.

Becoming and being divorced in later life are significant processes of family life for some older persons. While some of divorced older persons remarry, many remain unmarried. Older divorced women are particularly disadvantaged in finding a marital partner. A potential research area concerns the differences between older persons who divorce in later life compared to those who divorce earlier in life and do not remarry. Do long-term divorced elderly differ from persons who divorced in later life?

## REMARRIAGE IN LATER LIFE

The number of older people who marry for the first time or remarry is relatively small. Only 1 percent of all brides and 2 percent of all grooms were 65 years or older in 1975 (Glick, 1979). The marriage rates per 1000 eligible persons are low because out of this 1000, there are large numbers of men and women aged 65 years and over. Glick (1979) calculates the remarriage rates for older persons as 20 per 1000 for widowers and 2 per 1000 for widows. Divorced older men remarry at a rate of 23 per 1000, while divorced women remarry at a rate of 9 per 1000. Another study (Treas and VanHilst, 1976) concluded that marriage is for the young, and older people who marry are atypical. Clearly, marriage in later life is not a frequent event.

Is it more likely that never-married, divorced, or widowed older persons will marry? Similar to other ages, divorced older persons are more likely to marry than widowed. Bachelors and unmarried women are the least likely to marry.

An analysis of remarriage statistics (Hacker, 1983) suggested that nearly 75 percent of divorced men aged 65 and over remarry while approximately 25 percent of their female counterparts remarry. Regardless of previous marital status, those who marry are most likely to marry widowed persons (Treas and VanHilst, 1976). Cleveland and Gianturco (1976) analyzed remarriage probabilities of widowed persons and illustrated that widowers are more likely to remarry than widows. Although the probabilities for remarriage decrease with age for both men and women, substantial fractions of older widowers remarry while very few older widows do so. Above age 75, 4 percent of the widowers in their sample remarried and the number of remarriages for widows was negligible. The median remarriage interval for widowers aged 65 to 74 years was 1.5 years and 1.3 years for those aged 75 years and above. For widows aged 65 to 74, the median interval is 3.8 years. Comparison of these data with rates for Black widowed men and women indicates that remarriage probabilities are lower and the interval before remarriage is greater for older Blacks.

As found in other age categories, men tend to marry younger women. Six out of ten divorced men remarry younger women while two out of ten divorced women marry younger men. One-third of the women remarry older men. This trend is supported by the social expectation that men should be older than their wives.

Differences in the male and female remarriage rates are related to the fewer number of available men and the tendency for men to marry younger women. Consequently, there are substantial numbers of older women who are divorced or widowed and who have few potential marriage partners. Since the

75 years and over category is growing, this situation will not change. Women aged 75 years and older will most likely be widowed and their probability of remarrying is low.

## COHABITATION IN LATER LIFE

Within the past several years, many adults have decided to live together and not marry. The U.S. Census data indicate that the number of unmarried households has tripled in the past twelve years (U.S. Department of Commerce, 1983). Family scholars have used the term "cohabitation" to refer to these unmarried households. Although the U.S. Census definition of "unmarried household" may include individuals who are not living together "as man and wife," it is a crude indication of the number of unmarried persons who are cohabiting.

What proportion of the cohabiting households include older people? According to the U.S. Census, the proportion of cohabitating older persons has *decreased* by more than half since 1970.

In 1970, approximately 22 percent of the cohabiting households included persons aged 65 years and over, whereas in 1982, this proportion was 5.5 percent. A decrease, though not as profound, is evidenced in the 45 to 64 years of age category. While the percentage of elderly cohabitators has decreased substantially, the number has declined less dramatically. Since the number of people aged 65 years and over has increased significantly, *and* the number of elderly cohabitators has decreased slightly, the percentage of elderly cohabitators has decreased a great deal.

While cohabitation is increasing in the United States in most age groups, it appears to be declining in the elderly segment of the population. At the present time, three-fourths of the cohabitators with no children are under 45 years of age. Will the proportion of older cohabitors increase as the group under 45 years old ages? Do cohabitors marry when they get older? There is little information to answer these questions. A study (Dressel, 1980) of marriage license applicants found that 30 percent of the older applicants listed the same address on the applications. This suggests that these persons were cohabitors before they applied for a marriage license. Were they long-term cohabitors who decide to marry when they become older? Did they live together to "try out" their relationships before marriage? Research on cohabitation of older persons would provide answers to these questions. Presently, cohabitation is primarily a lifestyle of the young but it may become more frequent in future groups of elderly.

## SUMMARY

Later life families refer to couples who have launched their child and are dealing with tasks associated with a contracting nuclear unit. For childless couples, a crude indicator of entrance into the later phases is age 50 years. Later life families address tasks associated with the smaller nuclear unit, retirement, declining health and death of a spouse. These families are characterized as multigenerational with a lengthy family history.

Most of older persons are or have been married. Older men are usually married and women are either married or widowed. A small percentage of older persons have never married or divorced. For some, remarriage is a viable lifestyle in later life. A small portion of older persons cohabitate and it appears that this lifestyle has decreased over the past decade.

For the most part, the study of later life families focuses on marriage or the survivors of marriages. As the nuclear family unit becomes smaller and the typical aging processes affect a person's health, later life families seek to adapt so they can continue their family relationships. While later life families deal with many changes, they continue to value the importance of family relationships.

*Timothy H. Brubaker*

## 15.2 ELISABETH KÜBLER-ROSS

# On Death and Dying

Elisabeth Kübler-Ross was born in Switzerland in 1926. She received her medical degree at the University of Zurich, and she currently resides in Scottsdale, Arizona. She moved to the United States soon after becoming a physician and practiced medicine in New York. Her relief work in postwar Europe has been cited as her motivation to study and explain death. In the 1960s she started teaching seminars at various hospitals to discuss feelings about death with the terminally ill. She believed that this information was needed to better equip clinicians to help patients deal with the fear that accompanies the dying process. Her book *On Death and Dying* (Macmillan), from which this selection was excerpted, was published in 1969, followed by *Questions and Answers on Death and Dying* (Macmillan, 1974) and *Death: The Final Stage of Growth* (Prentice Hall, 1978). Although she has suffered a series of strokes, Kübler-Ross has expanded her interest in death and dying to the afterlife. According to newspaper accounts, she is studying Native Americans' views of what happens after death and has been given the name Standing Eagle.

Some professionals question Kübler-Ross's mystical explanations of the afterlife and extend this wariness to her accomplishments concerning death and dying. Yet many agree that her framework of the five stages of death, delineated in this selection, has provided comfort and direction for countless people. She recently published her autobiography, *The Wheel of Life: A Memoir of Living and Dying* (Scribner, 1997) in which she explains the four stages of life after death based on her interviews with over 20,000 patients.

**Key Concept:** death and dying

## FIRST STAGE: DENIAL AND ISOLATION

Among the over two hundred dying patients we have interviewed, most reacted to the awareness of a terminal illness at first with the statement, "No, not me, it cannot be true." This *initial* denial was as true for those patients who were told outright at the beginning of their illness as it was true for those who were not told explicitly and who came to this conclusion on their own a bit later on. One of our patients described a long and expensive ritual, as she called it, to support her denial. She was convinced that the X-rays were "mixed up"; she asked for reassurance that her pathology report could not possibly be back so soon and that another patient's report must have been marked with her name.

When none of this could be confirmed, she quickly asked to leave the hospital, looking for another physician in the vain hope "to get a better explanation for my troubles." This patient went "shopping around" for many doctors, some of whom gave her reassuring answers, others of whom confirmed the previous suspicion. Whether confirmed or not, she reacted in the same manner; she asked for examination and reexamination, partially knowing that the original diagnosis was correct, but also seeking further evaluations in the hope that the first conclusion was indeed an error, at the same time keeping in contact with a physician in order to have help available "at all times" as she said.

This anxious denial following the presentation of a diagnosis is more typical of the patient who is informed prematurely or abruptly by someone who does not know the patient well or does it quickly "to get it over with" without taking the patient's readiness into consideration. Denial, at least partial denial, is used by almost all patients, not only during the first stages of illness or following confrontation, but also later on from time to time. Who was it who said, "We cannot look at the sun all the time, we cannot face death all the time"? These patients can consider the possibility of their own death for a while but then have to put this consideration away in order to pursue life.

I emphasize this strongly since I regard it a healthy way of dealing with the uncomfortable and painful situation with which some of these patients have to live for a long time. Denial functions as a buffer after unexpected shocking news, allows the patient to collect himself and, with time, mobilize other, less radical defenses. This does not mean, however, that the same patient later on will not be willing or even happy and relieved if he can sit and talk with someone about his impending death. Such a dialogue will and must take place at the convenience of the patient, when he (not the listener!) is ready to face it. The dialogue also has to be terminated when the patient can no longer face the facts and resumes his previous denial. It is irrelevant when this dialogue takes place. We are often accused of talking with very sick patients about death when the doctor feels—very rightly so—that they are not dying. I favor talking about death and dying with patients long before it actually happens if the patient indicates that he wants to. A healthier, stronger individual can deal with it better and is less frightened by oncoming death when it is still "miles away" than when it "is right in front of the door," as one of our patients put it so appropriately. It is also easier for the family to discuss such matters in times of relative health and well-being and arrange for financial security for the children and others while the head of the household is still functioning. To postpone such talks is often not in the service of the patient but serves our own defensiveness.

Denial is usually a temporary defense and will soon be replaced by partial acceptance. Maintained denial does not always bring increased distress if it holds out until the end, which I still consider a rarity. Among our two hundred terminally ill patients, I have encountered only three who attempted to deny its approach to the very last. Two of these women talked about dying briefly but only referred to it as "an inevitable nuisance which hopefully comes during sleep" and said "I hope it comes without pain." After these statements they resumed their previous denial of their illness....

In summary, then, the patient's first reaction may be a temporary state of shock from which he recuperates gradually. When his initial feeling of numbness begins to disappear and he can collect himself again, man's usual response is "No, it cannot be me." Since in our unconscious mind we are all immortal, it is almost inconceivable for us to acknowledge that we too have to face death. Depending very much on how a patient is told, how much time he has to gradually acknowledge the inevitable happening, and how he has been prepared throughout life to cope with successful situations, he will gradually drop his denial and use less radical defense mechanisms.

We have also found that many of our patients have used denial when faced with hospital staff members who had to use this form of coping for their own reasons. Such patients can be quite selective in choosing different people among family members or staff with whom they discuss matters of their illness or impending death while pretending to get well with those who cannot tolerate the thought of their demise. It is possible that this is the reason for the discrepancy of opinions in regard of the patient's needs to know about a fatal illness....

## SECOND STAGE: ANGER

If our first reaction to catastrophic news is, "No it's not true, no, it cannot involve me," this has to give way to a new reaction, when it finally dawns on us: "Oh, yes, it is me, it was not a mistake." Fortunately or unfortunately very few patients are able to maintain a make-believe world in which they are healthy and well until they die.

When the first stage of denial cannot be maintained any longer, it is replaced by feelings of anger, rage, envy, and resentment. The logical next question becomes: "Why me?" As one of our patients, Dr. G., puts it, "I suppose most anybody in my position would look at somebody else and say, 'Well, why couldn't it have been him?' and this has crossed my mind several times.... An old man whom I have known ever since I was a little kid came down the street. He was eighty-two years old, and he is of no earthly use as far as we mortals can tell. He's rheumatic, he's a cripple, he's dirty, just not the type of person you would like to be. And the thought hit me strongly, now why couldn't it have been old George instead of me?" (extract from interview of Dr. G.).

In contrast to the stage of denial, this stage of anger is very difficult to cope with from the point of view of family and staff. The reason for this is the fact that this anger is displaced in all directions and projected onto the environment at times almost at random. The doctors are just no good, they don't know what tests to require and what diet to prescribe. They keep the patients too long in the hospital or don't respect their wishes in regards to special privileges. They allow a miserably sick roommate to be brought into their room when they pay so much money for some privacy and rest, etc. The nurses are even more often a target of their anger. Whatever they touch is not right. The moment they have left the room, the bell rings. The light is on the very minute they start their report for the next shift of nurses. When they do shake the pillows and straighten out the bed, they are blamed for never leaving the patients alone. When they do leave the patients alone, the light goes on with the request to have the bed arranged more comfortably. The visiting family is received with little cheerfulness and anticipation, which makes the encounter a painful event. They then either respond with grief and tears, guilt or shame, or avoid future visits, which only increases the patient's discomfort and anger.

The problem here is that few people place themselves in the patient's position and wonder where this anger might come from. Maybe we too would be angry if all our life activities were interrupted so prematurely; if all the buildings we started were to go unfinished, to be completed by someone else; if we had put some hard-earned money aside to enjoy a few years of rest and enjoyment, for travel and pursuing hobbies, only to be confronted with the fact that "this is not for me." What else would we do with our anger, but let it out on the people who are most likely to enjoy all these things? People who rush busily around only to remind us that we cannot even stand on our two feet anymore. People who order unpleasant tests and prolonged hospitalization with all its limitations, restrictions, and costs, while at the end of the day they can go home and enjoy life. People who tell us to lie still so that the infusion or transfusion does not have to be restarted, when we feel like jumping out of our skin to be doing something in order to know that we are still functioning on some level! ...

## THIRD STAGE: BARGAINING

The third stage, the stage of bargaining, is less well known but equally helpful to the patient, though only for brief periods of time. If we have been unable to face the sad facts in the first period and have been angry at people and God in the second phase, maybe we can succeed in entering into some sort of an agreement which may postpone the inevitable happening: "If God has decided to take us from this earth and he did not respond to my angry pleas, he may be more favorable if I ask nicely." We are all familiar with this reaction when we observe our children first demanding, then asking for a favor. They may not accept our "No" when they want to spend a night in a friend's house. They may be angry and stamp their foot. They may lock themselves in their bedroom and temporarily express their anger by rejecting us. But they will also have second thoughts. They may consider another approach. They will come out eventually, volunteer to do some tasks around the house, which under normal circumstances we never succeeded in getting them to do, and then tell us, "If I am very good all week and wash the dishes every evening, then will you let me go?" There is a slight chance naturally that we will accept the bargain and the child will get what was previously denied.

The terminally ill patient uses the same maneuvers. He knows, from past experiences, that there is a slim chance that he may be rewarded for good behavior and be granted a wish for special services. His wish is most always an extension of life, followed by the wish for a few days without pain or physical discomfort. A patient who was an opera singer, with a distorting malignancy of her jaw and face who could no longer perform on the stage, asked "to perform just one more time." When she became aware that this was impossible, she gave the most touching performance perhaps of her lifetime. She asked to come to the seminar and to speak in front of the audience, not behind a one-way mirror. She unfolded her life story, her success, and her tragedy in front of the class until a telephone call summoned her to return to her room. Doctor and dentist were ready to pull all her teeth in order to proceed with the radiation treatment. She had asked to sing once more—to us—before she had to hide her face forever.

Another patient was in utmost pain and discomfort, unable to go home because of her dependence on injections for pain relief. She had a son who proceeded with his plans to get married, as the patient had wished. She was very sad to think that she would be unable to attend this big day, for he was her oldest and favorite child. With combined efforts, we were able to teach her self-hypnosis which enabled her to be quite comfortable for several hours. She had made all sorts of promises if she could only live long enough to attend this marriage. The day preceding the wedding she left the hospital as an elegant lady. Nobody would have believed her real condition. She was "the happiest person in the whole world" and looked radiant. I wondered what her reaction would be when the time was up for which she had bargained.

I will never forget the moment when she returned to the hospital. She looked tired and somewhat exhausted and—before I could say hello—said, "Now don't forget I have another son!"

The bargaining is really an attempt to postpone; it has to include a prize offered "for good behavior," it also sets a self-imposed "deadline" (e.g., one more performance, the son's wedding), and it includes an implicit promise that the patient will not ask for more if this one postponement is granted. None of our patients have "kept their promise"; in other words, they are like children who say, "I will never fight my sister again if you let me go." Needless to add, the little boy will fight his sister again, just as the opera singer will try to perform once more. She could not live without further performances and left the hospital before her teeth were extracted. The patient just described was unwilling to face us again unless we acknowledged the fact that she had another son whose wedding she also wanted to witness....

## FOURTH STAGE: DEPRESSION

When the terminally ill patient can no longer deny his illness, when he is forced to undergo more surgery or hospitalization, when he begins to have more symptoms or becomes weaker and thinner, he cannot smile it off anymore. His numbness or stoicism, his anger and rage will soon be replaced with a sense of great loss. This loss may have many facets: a woman with a breast cancer may react to the loss of her figure; a woman with a cancer of the uterus may feel that she is no longer a woman. Our opera singer responded to the required surgery of her face and the removal of her teeth with shock, dismay, and the deepest depression. But this is only one of the many losses that such a patient has to endure.

With the extensive treatment and hospitalization, financial burdens are added; little luxuries at first and necessities later on may not be afforded anymore. The immense sums that such treatments and hospitalizations cost in recent years have forced many patients to sell the only possessions they had; they were unable to keep a house which they built for their old age, unable to send a child through college, and unable perhaps to make many dreams come true.

There may be the added loss of a job due to many absences or the inability to function, and mothers and wives may have to become the breadwinners, thus depriving the children of the attention they previously had. When mothers are sick, the little ones may have to be boarded out, adding to the sadness and guilt of the patient.

All these reasons for depressions are well known to everybody who deals with patients. What we often tend to forget, however, is the preparatory grief that the terminally ill patient has to undergo in order to prepare himself for his final separation from this world. If I were to attempt to differentiate these two kinds of depressions, I would regard the first one a reactive depression, the second one a preparatory depression. The first one is different in nature and should be dealt with quite differently from the latter.

An understanding person will have no difficulty in eliciting the cause of the depression and in alleviating some of the unrealistic guilt or shame which often accompanies the depression. A woman who is worried about no longer being a woman can be complimented for some especially feminine feature; she can be reassured that she is still as much a woman as she was before surgery. Breast prosthesis has added much to the breast cancer patient's self-esteem. Social worker, physician, or chaplain may discuss the patient's concerns with the husband in order to obtain his help in supporting the patient's self-esteem. Social workers and chaplains can be of great help during this time in assisting in the reorganization of a household, especially when children or lonely old people are involved for whom eventual placement has to be considered. We are always impressed by how quickly a patient's depression is lifted when these vital issues are taken care of....

The second type of depression is one which does not occur as a result of a past loss but is taking into account impending losses. Our initial reaction to sad people is usually to try to cheer them up, to tell them not to look at things so grimly or so hopelessly. We encourage them to look at the bright side of life, at all the colorful, positive things around them. This is often an expression of our own needs, our own inability to tolerate a long face over any extended period of time. This can be a useful approach when dealing with the first type of depression in terminally ill patients. It will help such a mother to know that the children play quite happily in the neighbor's garden since they stay there while their father is at work. It may help a mother to know that they continue to laugh and joke, go to parties, and bring good report cards home from school —all expressions that they function in spite of mother's absence.

When the depression is a tool to prepare for the impending loss of all the love objects, in order to facilitate the state of acceptance, then encouragements and reassurances are not as meaningful. The patient should not be encouraged to look at the sunny side of things, as this would mean he should not contemplate his impending death. It would be contraindicated to tell him not to be sad, since all of us are tremendously sad when we lose one beloved person. The patient is in the process of losing everything and everybody he loves. If he is allowed to express his sorrow he will find a final acceptance much easier, and he will be grateful to those who can sit with him during this state of depression without constantly telling him not to be sad....

## FIFTH STAGE: ACCEPTANCE

If a patient has had enough time (i.e., not a sudden, unexpected death) and has been given some help in working through the previously described stages, he will reach a stage during which he is neither depressed nor angry about his "fate." He will have been able to express his previous feelings, his envy for the living and the healthy, his anger at those who do not have to face their end so soon. He will have mourned the impending loss of so many meaningful people and places and he will contemplate his coming end with a certain degree of quiet expectation. He will be tired and, in most cases, quite weak. He will also have a need to doze off to sleep often and in brief intervals, which is different from the need to sleep during the times of depression. This is not a sleep of avoidance or a period of rest to get relief from pain, discomfort, or itching. It is a gradually increasing need to extend the hours of sleep very similar to that of the newborn child but in reverse order. It is not a resigned and hopeless "giving up," a sense of "what's the use" or "I just cannot fight it any longer," though we hear such statements too. (They also indicate the beginning of the end of the struggle, but the latter are not indications of acceptance.)

Acceptance should not be mistaken for a happy stage. It is almost void of feelings. It is as if the pain had gone, the struggle is over, and there comes a time for "the final rest before the long journey" as one patient phrased it. This is also the time during which the family needs usually more help, understanding, and support than the patient himself. While the dying patient has found some peace and acceptance, his circle of interest diminishes. He wishes to be left alone or at least not stirred up by news and problems of the outside world. Visitors are often not desired and if they come, the patient is no longer in a talkative mood. He often requests limitation on the number of people and prefers short visits. This is the time when the television is off. Our communications then become more nonverbal than verbal. The patient may just make a gesture of the hand to invite us to sit down for a while. He may just hold our hand and ask us to sit in silence. Such moments of silence may be the most meaningful communications for people who are not uncomfortable in the presence of a dying person. We may together listen to the song of a bird from the outside. Our presence may just confirm that we are going to be around until the end. We may just let him know that it is all right to say nothing when the important things are taken care of and it is only a question of time until he can close his eyes forever. It may reassure him that he is not left alone when he is no longer talking and a pressure of the hand, a look, a leaning back in the pillows may say more than many "noisy" words.

A visit in the evening may lend itself best to such an encounter as it is the end of the day both for the visitor and the patient. It is the time when the hospital's page system does not interrupt such a moment, when the nurse does not come in to take the temperature, and the cleaning woman is not mopping the floor—it is this little private moment that can complete the day at the end of the rounds for the physician, when he is not interrupted by anyone. It takes just a little time but it is comforting for the patient to know that he is not forgotten when nothing else can be done for him. It is gratifying for the visitor as well, as it will show him that dying is not such a frightening, horrible thing that so many want to avoid.

# ACKNOWLEDGMENTS

1.1 From William J. Lederer and Don D. Jackson, *The Mirages of Marriage* (W. W. Norton, 1968). Copyright © 1968 by W. W. Norton & Company, Inc. Reprinted by permission. Some notes omitted.

1.2 From Ernest W. Burgess, "The Family as a Unity of Interacting Personalities," *The Family*, vol. 7, no. 1 (March 1926). Copyright © 1926 by *The Family*. Some notes omitted.

1.3 Excerpted from Ira L. Reiss, "The Universality of the Family: A Conceptual Analysis," *Journal of Marriage and the Family*, vol. 27, no. 4 (November 1965). Copyright © 1965 by The National Council on Family Relations. Reprinted by permission of The National Council on Family Relations, 3989 Central Ave., NE, Suite 550, Minneapolis, MN 55421. Some notes omitted.

2.1 From Carlfred Broderick and James Smith, "The General Systems Approach to the Family," in Wesley R. Burr, Reuben Hill, F. Ivan Nye, and Ira L. Reiss, eds., *Contemporary Theories About the Family, vol. 2* (Free Press, 1979). Copyright © 1979 by The Free Press. Reprinted by permission of The Free Press, a division of Simon & Schuster. Notes and some references omitted.

2.2 From David H. Olson, Douglas H. Sprenkle, and Candyce S. Russell, "Circumplex Model of Marital and Family Systems: I. Cohesion and Adaptability Dimensions, Family Types, and Clinical Applications," *Family Process* (April 1979). Copyright © 1979 by Family Process, Inc. Reprinted by permission of Family Process, Inc., P.O. Box 23980, Rochester, NY 14692 via Copyright Clearance Center, Inc. Some references omitted.

2.3 From George C. Homans, "Social Behavior as Exchange," *The American Journal of Sociology*, vol. 62 (May 1958). Copyright © 1958 by The University of Chicago. Reprinted by permission of University of Chicago Press.

3.1 From Willard Waller, "The Rating and Dating Complex," *American Sociological Review*, vol. 2, nos. 1–6 (1937).

3.2 From Margaret Mead and Rhoda Metraux, *A Way of Seeing* (McCall, 1970). Copyright © 1961 ... 1970 by Margaret Mead and Rhoda Metraux. Reprinted by permission of William Morrow and Company, Inc.

3.3 From Carl A. Ridley, Dan J. Peterman, and Arthur W. Avery, "Cohabitation: Does It Make for a Better Marriage?" *The Family Coordinator* (April 1978). Copyright © 1978 by The National Council on Family Relations. Reprinted by permission of the author. Some notes omitted.

4.1 From Alan C. Kerckhoff and Keith E. Davis, "Value Consensus and Need Complementarity in Mate Selection," *American Sociological Review*, vol. 27, no. 3 (June 1962). Notes omitted.

4.2 From Robert F. Winch, "Another Look at the Theory of Complementary Needs in Mate-Selection," *Journal of Marriage and the Family* (November 1967). Copyright © 1967 by The National Council on Family Relations. Reprinted by permission of The National Council on Family Relations, 3989 Central Ave., NE, Suite 550, Minneapolis, MN 55421. Notes omitted.

4.3 From Bernard I. Murstein, "Stimulus—Value—Role: A Theory of Marital Choice," *Journal of Marriage and the Family*, vol. 32, no. 3 (August 1970). Copyright © 1970 by The National Council on Family Relations. Reprinted by permission of The National Council on Family Relations, 3989 Central Ave., NE, Suite 550, Minneapolis, MN 55421. Some notes and references omitted.

5.1 From Harvey J. Locke and Karl M. Wallace, "Short Marital-Adjustment and Prediction Tests: Their Reliability and Validity," *Marriage and Family Living*, vol. 21, no. 3 (August 1959). Copyright © 1959 by The National Council on Family Relations. Reprinted by permission of The National Council on Family Relations, 3989 Central Ave., NE, Suite 550, Minneapolis, MN 55421.

5.2 From William Stephens, "Predictors of Marital Adjustment," in William Stephens, ed., *Reflections on Marriage* (Thomas Y. Crowell, 1968). Copyright © 1968 by Thomas Y. Crowell Company. Reprinted by permission of HarperCollins Publishers, Inc.

6.1 From Robert O. Blood, Jr., and Donald M. Wolfe, *Husbands and Wives: The Dynamics of Married Living* (Free Press, 1960). Copyright © 1960 by The Free Press. Reprinted by permission of The Free Press, a Division of Simon & Schuster.

*Acknowledgments*

6.2  From John F. Cuber and Peggy B. Harroff, "The More Total View: Relationships Among Men and Women of the Upper Middle Class," *Marriage and Family Living*, vol. 25, no. 2 (May 1963). Copyright © 1963 by The National Council on Family Relations. Reprinted by permission of The National Council on Family Relations, 3989 Central Ave., NE, Suite 550, Minneapolis, MN 55421. Notes omitted.

7.1  From Mary D. Salter Ainsworth, "Infant–Mother Attachment," *American Psychologist*, vol. 34 (1979). Copyright © 1979 by Mary D. Salter Ainsworth. Adapted by permission of The American Psychological Association.

7.2  From Margaret Mead, "Some Theoretical Considerations on the Problem of Mother-Child Separation," *American Journal of Orthopsychiatry*, vol. 63, no. 1 (January 1993). Copyright © 1993 by The American Orthopsychiatric Association, Inc. Reprinted by permission. Some notes and references omitted.

8.1  From E. E. LeMasters, "Parenthood as Crisis," *Marriage and Family Living*, vol. 19, no. 4 (November 1957). Copyright © 1957 by The National Council on Family Relations. Reprinted by permission of The National Council on Family Relations, 3989 Central Ave., NE, Suite 550, Minneapolis, MN 55421.

8.2  From Diana Baumrind, "Child Care Practices Anteceding Three Patterns of Preschool Behavior," *Genetic Psychology Monographs*, vol. 75 (1967). Copyright © 1967 by Heldref Publications, 1319 Eighteenth Street, NE, Washington, DC 20036-1802. Reprinted by permission of The Helen Dwight Reid Educational Foundation. Notes omitted.

8.3  Excerpted from Murray A. Straus, *Beating the Devil Out of Them: Corporal Punishment in American Families and Its Effects on Children* (Lexington Books, 1994). Copyright © 1994 by Jossey-Bass, Inc., Publishers. Reprinted by permission. Notes and some references omitted.

8.4  From Lawrence Kohlberg, "The Child as a Moral Philosopher," *Psychology Today*, vol. 214 (September 1968). Copyright © 1968 by Sussex Publishers, Inc. Reprinted by permission of *Psychology Today*.

9.1  From Robert Staples, "Changes in Black Family Structure: The Conflict Between Family Ideology and Structural Conditions," *Journal of Marriage and the Family*, vol. 47, no. 4 (November 1985). Copyright © 1985 by The National Council on Family Relations. Reprinted by permission of The National Council on Family Relations, 3989 Central Ave., NE, Suite 550, Minneapolis, MN 55421. Some references omitted.

9.2  From Judson T. Landis, "Religiousness, Family Relationships, and Family Values in Protestant, Catholic, and Jewish Families," *Marriage and Family Living*, vol. 22, no. 4 (November 1960). Copyright © 1960 by The National Council on Family Relations. Reprinted by permission of The National Council on Family Relations, 3989 Central Ave., NE, Suite 550, Minneapolis, MN 55421. Some notes omitted.

10.1  From Lois Wladis Hoffman, "The Decision to Work," in F. Ivan Nye and Lois Wladis Hoffman, eds., *The Employed Mother in America* (Rand McNally, 1963). Some references omitted.

10.2  From Patricia Voydanoff and Robert F. Kelly, "Determinants of Work-Related Family Problems Among Employed Parents," *Journal of Marriage and the Family*, vol. 46, no. 4 (November 1984). Copyright © 1984 by The National Council on Family Relations. Reprinted by permission of The National Council on Family Relations, 3989 Central Ave., NE, Suite 550, Minneapolis, MN 55421.

11.1  From Richard J. Gelles, "Abused Wives: Why Do They Stay?" *Journal of Marriage and the Family*, vol. 38, no. 4 (November 1976). Copyright © 1976 by The National Council on Family Relations. Reprinted by permission of The National Council on Family Relations, 3989 Central Ave., NE, Suite 550, Minneapolis, MN 55421. Notes and some references omitted.

11.2  From John Scanzoni, "Family Organization and the Probability of Disorganization," *Journal of Marriage and the Family*, vol. 28, no. 4 (November 1966). Copyright © 1966 by The National Council on Family Relations. Reprinted by permission of The National Council on Family Relations, 3989 Central Ave., NE, Suite 550, Minneapolis, MN 55421.

12.1  From Reuben Hill, *Families Under Stress: Adjustment to the Crises of War Separation and Reunion* (Harper & Brothers, 1949).

12.2  From Hamilton I. McCubbin and Joan M. Patterson, "The Family Stress Process: The Double ABCX Model of Adjustment and Adaptation," in Hamilton I. McCubbin, Marvin B. Sussman, and Joan M. Patterson, eds., *Social Stress and the Family: Advances and Developments in*

*Family Stress Theory and Research* (Haworth Press, 1983). Copyright © 1983 by The Haworth Press, Inc., New York, NY 10001. Reprinted by permission. References omitted.

13.1 From Frank F. Furstenberg, Jr., "Divorce and the American Family," *Annual Review of Sociology*, vol. 16 (1990). Copyright © 1990 by Annual Review, Inc. Reprinted by permission of the author. References omitted.

13.2 From Judith S. Wallerstein and Joan B. Kelly, "Children and Divorce: A Review," *Social Work*, vol. 24, no. 6 (November 1979). Copyright © 1979 by The National Association of Social Workers, Inc. Reprinted by permission.

13.3 From E. Mavis Hetherington, Martha Cox, and Roger Cox, "Effects of Divorce on Parents and Children," in Michael E. Lamb, ed., *Nontraditional Families: Parenting and Child Development* (Lawrence Erlbaum, 1982). Copyright © 1982 by Lawrence Erlbaum Associates, Inc. Reprinted by permission. References omitted.

14.1 From Michael J. Sporakowski and George A. Hughston, "Prescriptions for Happy Marriage: Adjustments and Satisfactions of Couples Married for 50 or More Years," *The Family Coordinator*, vol. 27, no. 4 (October 1978). Copyright © 1978 by The National Council on Family Relations. Reprinted by permission of The National Council on Family Relations, 3989 Central Ave., NE, Suite 550, Minneapolis, MN 55421.

14.2 From Lillian E. Troll, "Grandparents: The Family Watchdogs," in Timothy H. Brubaker, ed., *Family Relationships in Later Life* (Sage Publications, 1983). Copyright © 1983 by Sage Publications, Inc. Reprinted by permission. References omitted.

15.1 From Timothy H. Brubaker, *Later Life Families* (Sage Publications, 1985). Copyright © 1985 by Sage Publications, Inc. Reprinted by permission. References omitted.

15.2 From Elisabeth Kübler-Ross, *On Death and Dying* (Macmillan, 1969). Copyright © 1969 by Elisabeth Kübler-Ross. Reprinted by permission of Simon & Schuster.

# Index

ABCX family crisis model, 293–302
Aberle, David, 23, 24
abortion, 217, 222
acceptance, as stage of dying, 376–377
achievement, family structure and, 215–216
achievement-vicariousness, as complementary needs, 104
adaptability, role of, in the circumplex model of family systems theory, 42–51
adaptive resources, family stress and, 297–298, 299–302
adoption, 79, 177
African Americans, changes in family structure of, 215–225
age: marital adjustment and, 130–139; mate selection and, 98–107
aggression, in children: divorce and, 332–333; spanking and, 202
Aid to Families with Dependent Children (AFDC), 249
Ainsworth, Mary D. Salter, on infant-mother attachment, 157–165
alimony, 309–310
ambiguity, social, family stress and, 297
anger, as stage of dying, 372–373
anthropology, mother-child separation and, 166–176
anxious attachment style, infant-mother, 157–165
apportioned grandparenting, 353
approach-avoidance tendency, children's, parenting styles and, 184–195
artificial insemination, 177
attachment, maternal, 157–165, 166–176
authoritarian parenting style, 184–195
authoritative parenting style, 184–195
aversive stimulation, 53
Avery, Arthur W., on cohabitation, 81–89
avoidant attachment style, infant-mother, 157–165

balance, adaptive coping and, 300–301
bargaining, as stage of dying, 373–374
Baumrind, Diana, on effects of parenting style on preschoolers' behavior, 184–195
behavior, adaptive coping and, 299
Benedict, Ruth, 180
Bermann, Eric A., 102, 103, 105
"best interests of the child," custody issues and, 320
*Beyond the Best Interests of the Child* (Goldstein, Freud, and Solnit), 320
birth control, 8, 10, 14
birth order, effect of, on children of divorce, 316

Black, Dean, 37
blacks. *See* African Americans
Blood, Robert O., Jr., on marital roles and decision making, 140–145
bonadaptation, family stress and, 301–302
Boulding, Elise, on family crisis situations, 279–292
boundaries, family systems theory and, 33, 39, 40, 43, 298
Bowlby, John, 28, 157, 158, 160–161, 162, 167
Broderick, Carlfred, on family systems theory, 32–41
Brubaker, Timothy H., on later-life families, 360–369
Bruch, Hilde, 171
buoyant mood, children's, parenting styles and, 184–195
Burgess, Ernest W., 227, 279, 304; on the family as a system, 13–21

Canady, Hortense, 222
capabilities and demands, and the ABCX family crisis model, 293–302
Catholic families, family values and, 226–234
centrality, grandparenting and, 353
change, demand for, family stress and, 295
Cherlin, Andrew, 306, 309, 311
child support, 309–310, 315
childless family, 14, 362
children: divorce and, 307–308, 312–326, 327–336; domestic violence and, 256–269; family crisis situations and, 283–285, 288–289; moral development of, 206–211; sex education and, 232–233. *See also* infants; grandparents; parents
circumplex model, of marriage and family systems, 42–51
cognitive development, children's, parenting styles and, 185
cohabitation, 73–80, 81–89, 308; in later life, 368
coherence, adaptive coping and, 301
cohesion, role of, in the circumplex model of family systems theory, 42–51, 54
Cohn, Ellen, 197
colonial America, courtship in, 7
commitment, domestic violence and, 257
communication, parent-child, parenting styles and, 189
community to family fit, adaptive coping and, 300–301
companionate marriage, 78, 304
companionship, as family function, 106, 146, 218, 274, 280–282
comparative ethnology, 170

*381*

complementary power struggles, in family systems theory, 36
conflict-habituated relationships, marital roles and, 149
conjugal family, order/disorder in, 272–273
contractual marriage, 304
control, parenting styles and, 189, 194
control hierarchies, in family systems theory, 35–38
convenience, cohabitation and, 84–85
conventional stage, of children's moral development, 206–211
conversion, in family systems therapy, 38
cooperative play, of children of divorce, 330
coping strategies, family stress and, 295, 297
corporal punishment, 196–205
costs, exchange theory and, 52–61, 216
courtship, 7, 39–40, 65–72, 340. *See also* mate selection
Cox, Martha, on effects of divorce on parents and children, 327–336
Cox, Roger, on effects of divorce on parents and children, 327–336
crisis situation: family, stress and, 279–292; parenthood as, 177–183
Crusades, 7
Cuber, John F., on marital roles, 146–154
culture: divorce and, 304–305; family systems and, 23–27; gender roles and, 11; moral development and, 210–211
custodial parents, 327
custody, child, divorce and, 308–309, 319–320, 327
cybernetic control, in family systems theory, 36, 39

dating, 39, 65–72, 113. *See also* mate selection
Davis, Keith E., 102, on mate selection, 90–97
death, 370–377
decision making, marital roles and, 140–145
demands and capabilities, and the ABCX family crisis model, 293–302
demographics, working mothers and, 235–236
denial, as stage of dying, 370–372
depression, 314, 319, 322; as stage of dying, 374–376
DeRoy, Helen, 279
desires, financial, working mothers and, 238
developmental issues, grandparenting and, 354–355
deviation amplifying/dampening feedback loops, in family systems theory, 36
devitalized relationships, marital roles and, 150
discipline, corporal punishment and, 196–205
disengagement, role of, in family systems theory, 43
disorganization, domestic violence and, 270–278
disoriented attachment style, infant-mother, 157–165

distress, family stress and, 295
distributive justice, exchange theory and, 58–59
diversity, grandparenting and, 353–354
divorce, 12, 25, 34, 75, 146, 177, 218, 222, 223, 228, 258, 260, 264, 270, 281, 297, 303–311, 359; children and, 312–326, 327–336; elderly people and, 361, 366–367; marital adjustment and, 130–139
domestic violence, 256–269, 270–278
dominance-submissiveness, as complementary needs, 104
Double ABCX model of family stress, 293–302
Driver, Harold E., 24
dysphoric mood, children's, parenting styles and, 184–195

economic cooperation, as function of family, 22–30, 74, 78, 117, 218, 273, 304
economic issues: divorce and, 309–311; working mothers and, 237–239. *See also* work
education: and children of divorce, 320–321, 329–336; domestic violence and, 256–269; marital adjustment and, 130–139
Edwards, Allen, 100
efficient family, 271
egalitarian family, 15, 281, 305
elderly: happy marriages of, 339–348; later-life families and, 360–369
emancipated family, 15
emancipation, cohabitation and, 84, 87
emotional gratifier, as marital role, 105
emotional survival, as function of family, 11–12, 304
empty nest syndrome, 363
endogamy, 90
enmeshment, in family systems theory, 43, 46
entrapment, domestic violence and, 257
*Essai sur le don* (Mauss), 52
ethnology, comparative, 170
ethological-evolutionary attachment theory, 158
exchange theory, family systems theory and, 52–61, 216, 258
exploitative relationships, dating and, 66–67
extended family, 22, 24, 106

family, definitions of, 3–12, 13–21, 22–31
fantasy play, of children of divorce, 331
Farber, Bernard, 92, 95, 96
fathers: divorce and, 311; husbands' role as, 280–282
feedback hierarchies, in family systems theory, 35–38, 45, 49
feminism, 217
fertility rites, 5–6
filtering processes, mate selection and, 90–97
finances, family crisis situations and, 282–283
fit, adaptive coping and, 300–301
free-play behaviors, of children of divorce, 330–332
Freud, Sigmund, 173

functional family, 271
functional play, of children of divorce, 330
Furstenberg, Frank F., Jr., on divorce, 303–311

Gelles, Richard J., on domestic violence, 256–269
gender differences: and effect of divorce on children, 316, 330, 334; grandparents and, 355–357; time shortage and, 251
generation gap, 352
generational stake, 352
Gerard, H. B., 56
Glick, Paul, 364
going steady, 69, 70–71
gold-digging, 67, 69
good boy/good girl orientation, and conventional stage of moral development, 208
Gough, Kathleen, 23
grandparents, 285–286, 349–359
Green, Arnold, 180
group marriage, 23
Groves, Ernest R., 16–17

handyman, husband as, 280–282
happy marriages, in later life, 339–348
hardships, crisis situations and, 279–292, 294, 295, 296
harmless, spanking as, 199–200
Harroff, Peggy B., on marital roles, 146–154
heterogamy, 90
Hetherington, E. Mavis, on effects of divorce on parents and children, 327–336
hierarchies of rules, in family systems theory, 35–38
Hill ABCX family crisis model, 293–302
Hill, Reuben, on family crisis situations, 279–292
Hill, Robert, 216
historical perspective, on origins of marriage and the family, 3–12
Hoffman, Lois Wladis, on working mothers, 235–244
Homans, George C., on exchange theory, 52–61
home management, family crisis situations and, 287–288
homogamy, 90, 94, 98, 261, 273, 274
homosexuality, 220
housewife role, working mothers and, 240–243
housing inadequacies, family crisis situations and, 286–287
Hughston, George A., on marriage in later life, 339–348
human capital resources, stress and, 246, 249, 253
human life, value of, moral development and, 209
hypergamy, 273, 275
hypogamy, 273, 275, 276

illness, family crisis situations and, 287–288
immortality through clan, grandparenting and, 353
imprinting, 171, 173
incest taboo, 5
income inadequacy, work and, 252–253
incomplete institutionalization, Cherlin's theory of, 306
India, Nayar people of, family structure of, 23–27
individual marriage, 73–80
individualized grandparenting, 353
individuation, marital roles and, 153
indulgence, grandparenting and, 353
Industrial Revolution, influence of, on family structure, 9–10
infants, maternal attachment and, 157–165, 166–176
influence, exchange theory and, 54–55
in-laws, 285–286, 297
isolation, as stage of dying, 370–372
Israel, family systems in kibbutzes of, 24, 25, 26, 27, 28, 29
interacting persons, family as union of, 13–21
internal releasing mechanisms, 173
intervention, in cases of domestic violence, 256–269

Jackson, Don D., on the origins of marriage and the family, 3–12
Jewish families, family values and, 226–234
joint custody, of children, 308–309, 320
justice, distributive, exchange theory and, 58–59

Kelly, Joan B., on children of divorce, 312–326
Kelly, Robert F., on work and family, 245–255
Kerckhoff, Alan C., 102; on mate selection, 90–97
kibbutzes, Israeli, family systems of, 24, 25, 26, 27, 28, 29
Kinsey, Alfred, 8, 220
kinship, 14
Kohlberg, Lawrence, on the moral development of children, 206–211
Kübler-Ross, Elisabeth, on death and dying, 370–377

Landis, Judson T., on religion and family relationships, 226–234
last resort, spanking as, 199
later-life families, 360–369; happy marriages in, 339–348
learning theory, 53, 173
Lederer, William J., on the origins of marriage and the family, 3–12
LeMasters, E. E., on parenthood as a crisis event, 177–183
Levinger, George, 101
Levy, David, 173

life cycle approach, family, 362–363
life overlaps, grandparents and, 351
life, value of human, moral development of, 209
life-cycle characteristics, time shortage and, 251
Lindsey, Ben, 78
Linton, Ralph, 23
"Linus Blanket," as type of cohabitation, 83, 87
Locke, Harvey J., on marital-adjustment tests, 122–129
logical hierarchies of rules, in family systems theory, 35–36
love: happy marriages and, 343; origins of, 6–7
lover's quarrels, 71
loyalty, divided, in children of divorce, 316

maladaptation, family stress and, 301–302
Malinowski, Bronislaw, 24
marital adjustment, 271; and happy marriages, 339–348; predictors of, 130–139; tests of, 122–129
marital role satisfaction, 140–145, 146–154
marital status, mate selection and, 94, 98–107
marriage: African Americans and, 216, 217, 221; cohabitation and, 73–80, 81–89; happy later-life, 339–348; origins of, 3–12; and transition to parenthood, 177–183; as two-step process, 73–80
mate selection, 261; among African Americans, 218–221; theories of, 90–97, 98–107. *See also* courtship; dating
maternal attachment, 157–165, 166–176
matriarchy, 281, 285
matricentric family, 15
maturity demands, parenting styles and, 189
Mauss, Marcel, 52
McCubbin, Hamilton I., on family stress, 293–302
Mead, Margaret: on mother-child separation, 166–176; on two-step marriage, 73–80
mediation, divorce proceedings and, 323
member to family fit, adaptive coping and, 300
men, courtship and, 117–118
mental health, marital adjustment and, 130–139
mental illness, divorce and, 314
Merton, Robert, 25
Metraux, Rhoda, on two-step marriage, 73–80
Middle Ages, romantic love and, 6–7
Mirsky, Arthur, 173
money, as motivation for working mothers, 237–239
monogamy, 13–14, 148, 171, 222
mood, children's subjective, parenting styles and, 184–195
moonlighting, 252
Moore, Barrington, 29
moral development, of children, 206–211
morphogenesis, family systems theory and, 35, 38, 45
mothers, working, 235–244. *See also* maternal attachment; parents

multigenerational residences, 354
Murdock, George Peter, 22, 23–27, 30, 276–277
Murray, Henry, 100
Murstein, Bernard I., on mate selection, 108–121

Nayar people, of India, family structure of, 23–27
necking, 68
need complementarity, mate selection and, 90–97, 98–107
neediness, in children of divorce, 317, 322
negative feedback loop, in family systems theory, 36, 45
neuroticism, mate selection and, 115, 116, 117
never-married people, 218; elderly, 366
noblesse oblige, exchange theory and, 59
noncustodial parents, 327
normative transitions, family stress and, 296–297
norm-senders, 104
nuclear family, 24, 29, 106, 216, 271, 273
nurturance, parenting styles and, 189, 194
nurturance-receptivity, as complementary needs, 104

occupational status, domestic violence and, 256–269
Olson, David H., on the circumplex model of family systems theory, 42–51
operant conditioning, 53
order/disorder of a social system, domestic violence and, 271, 272–273
out-of-wedlock births, 307

parallel play, in children of divorce, 330
*Parent Power* (Rosemond), 203
parental marriage, 73–80
parents: crisis of, 177–183; and moral development of children, 206–214; spanking and, 196–205; styles of, 184–195. *See also* fathers; grandparents; mothers
Parsons, Talcott, 27
passive-congenial relationships, marital roles and, 150–151
patriarchy, 15, 17–20, 25, 144, 286, 287, 288, 290
*Patterns of Child Rearing* (Sears, Maccoby, and Levin), 202
Patterson, Joan M., on family stress, 293–302
peer relationships: of children of divorce, 332–336; parenting styles and, 184–195
perceptions, adaptive coping and, 299
perceptual congruency, courtship progress and, 114–115
permissive parenting style, 184, 195
person, definition of, 16
personality adequacy, mate selection and, 115–116
Peterman, Dan J., on cohabitation, 81–89
physical development, children's, parenting styles and, 185

physical survival, as function of family, 11
Piaget, Jean, 206, 207
pile-up, family stress and, 296–297
play, patterns of, in children of divorce, 329–332
*Polish Peasant* (Thomas and Znaniecki), 280
polyandry, 5
polygamy, 5, 22
position conferrer, as marital role, 105
positive feedback loop, in family systems theory, 36, 37, 39, 45
postconventional stage, of children's moral development, 206–211
postparental families: grandparents and, 349–359; happy marriages of, 339–348
poverty, divorce and, 310–311, 315
power, balance of, marital roles and, 140–145
power struggles, in family systems theory, 36
preconventional stage, of children's moral development, 206–211
pregnancy, premarital, marital adjustment and, 130–139
premarital relationships. *See* courtship: dating
preoccupation, marital roles and, 152
profits, exchange theory and, 52–61
progenitor, as marital role, 105
promiscuity, sexual, 8
protector, husband as, 280–282
Protestant families, family values and, 226–234
psychological resources, stress and, 246
psychological survival, as function of family, 11–12
punishment: corporal, 196–205; and preconventional stage of moral development, 208

racial issues: divorce and, 307; mate selection and, 94, 98–107
rating and dating complex, 65–72
reification, marital roles and, 152
reinforcement patterns, exchange theory and, 216
reinvolvement with personal past, grandparenting and, 353
Reiss, Ira L., on the universality of the family, 22–31
religion: family relationships and, 226–234; marriage and, 8–9, 130–139, 343; mate selection and, 94, 98–107
remarriage, 34, 177, 297, 306, 315; in later life, 367–368
remote grandparenting, 353
reorientation, in family systems therapy, 38
reproduction, as function of family, 22–30
requisite variety, family systems theory and, 34–35
resources, adaptive coping and, 299
retirement, 363
rewards, exchange theory and, 52–61, 216
Ridley, Carl A., on cohabitation, 81–89
ripple effect, of divorce, 359

role, mate selection and, 108–121
role satisfaction, marital, 140–145, 146–154
romantic complex, parenthood as, 180
romantic love, 6–7
Rosemond, John, 203
Rosow, Irving, 101
rule obedience, moral development and, 209
Russell, Candyce S., on the circumplex model of family systems theory, 42–51
Russia, family systems in, 25

same-gender couples, 177
satiation, 53
satisfaction characteristics, work environment and, 249–250, 252
Scanzoni, John, on domestic violence, 270–278
secure attachment style, infant-mother, 157–165
self, conception of: family religiousness and, 229–230; mate selection and, 110–111
self-acceptance, mate selection and, 115
self-control, children's parenting styles and, 184–195
self-esteem, domestic violence and, 273–274, 275, 276
self-reliance, in children, parenting styles and, 184–195
separation, infant-mother attachment and, 157–165, 166–176
sex education, children and, 232–233
sexual partner, as marital role, 105
sexual relations, as function of family, 22–30
sexuality, 7–8, 13, 116, 232
Shutz, William, 92, 101, 102
single-parent families, 177, 217–218, 221–222, 253, 307, 308, 314, 327
Skinner, B. F., 53
Smith, James, on family systems theory, 32–41
sociability, marital adjustment and, 130–139
social behaviors, of children of divorce, 332–333
social class: marital adjustment and, 130–139; mate selection and, 94, 98–107
social development, children's, parenting styles and, 185
social institution, family as, 15
social life, lack of, family crisis situations and, 290
social psychological reinforcement, in husband-wife interaction, 274
social resources, stress and, 246
*Social Structure* (Murdock), 22
social values, and family religiousness, 230–231
social-contract orientation, in postconventional stage of moral development, 208
socialization, as function of family, 22–30, 290
solitary play, of children of divorce, 330
spanking, 196–205
speech, origins of, 6
Spiro, Melford, 24, 26
spoiling, of children, spanking and, 202–203

Sporakowski, Michael J., on marriage in later life, 339–348
spousal abuse. *See* domestic violence
Sprenkle, Douglas H., on the circumplex model of family systems theory, 42–51
Staples, Robert, on changes in black family structure, 215–225
status, exchange theory and, 59
stepfamilies, 306, 307, 327
Stephens, William, on predictors of marital adjustment, 130–139
stimulus, mate selection and, 108–121
strange-situation studies, maternal attachment and, 157–165
Straus, Murray A., 258; on corporal punishment, 196–205
stress: crisis situations and, 279–302; divorce and, 331; family, 293–302; work and, 246, 248, 251
structural consensus, in husband-wife interaction, 274
subculture: family, African Americans and, 215–223; theory of, violence and, 261
suicide, 314, 317
supportive parenting, grandparents and, 350
surrogate parenting, grandparents and, 350
symbolic grandparenting, 353
symmetrical power struggles, in family systems theory, 36
systems theory, family and, 32–41, 42–51, 52–61; grandparents and, 357–358

taboo, incest, 5
taxi dancers, 69
teenagers: pregnancy and, 351, 354; spanking of, 203–204
temporal hierarchies of rules, in family systems theory, 35–36, 40
testing, cohabitation and, 85–87
thrill-seeking relationships, dating and, 66–67, 69
Timasheff, Nicholas, 25
time shortage, work and, 251–252
total relationships, marital roles and, 151
transformation, rules of, in family systems theory, 34, 35, 37
Trobriand Islanders, family systems of, 24–25
Troll, Lillian E., on grandparents, 349–359
troubadours, 7

unemployment benefits, 249
universalism, marital roles and, 153

value, mate selection and, 108–121
value consensus, mate selection and, 90–97
valued elder, grandparent as, 353
verbal abuse, 203
violence, domestic, 256–269, 270–278
virginity, 8, 66, 232
vital relationships, marital roles and, 151
Voydanoff, Patricia, on work and family, 245–255

Wallace, Karl M., on marital-adjustment tests, 122–129
Waller, Willard, 280; on dating and courtship, 65–72
Wallerstein, Judith S., on children of divorce, 312–326
welfare, 222
widows/widowers, 218, 361, 367–368
Winch, Robert F., 91, 92; on mate selection, 98–107
Wolfe, Donald M., on marital roles and decision making, 140–145
women, domestic violence and, 256–259
work, and the family, 245–255
working mothers, family crisis situations and, 289–290
World War II, family crisis situations during, 279–292

Yarrow, Leon J., 28